CREATIVE SPIRITS

CREATIVE SPIRITS
OF THE
NINETEENTH CENTURY

BY

GEORG BRANDES

TRANSLATED BY

RASMUS B. ANDERSON

FORMERLY UNITED STATES MINISTER TO DENMARK;
AUTHOR OF "NORSE MYTHOLOGY," "VIKING
TALES OF THE NORTH," ETC.

NEW YORK
THOMAS Y. CROWELL COMPANY
PUBLISHERS

COPYRIGHT, 1923,
BY THOMAS Y. CROWELL COMPANY

PRINTED IN THE UNITED STATES OF AMERICA

AUTHOR'S PREFACE

TAINE looked upon criticism as applied science. But no methodical research can give us the key to a composite human spirit. Where a successful attempt has been made to understand such a spirit (that is to say, an attempt of which the correctness cannot be doubted, since it carries with it its quotations, so that the reader himself can apply the test) it is not to be supposed that we have before us the result of a purely scientific investigation.

Criticism is an art, though it is not usually mentioned as one of the fine arts. Even though the critic, after intense study, has long called himself the master of his material, he does not attempt the real work, that is, the committing of his results to writing, before he has gotten so far that he feels the person he is about to present actually living within himself, and he frequently must wait for months for this to take place. But if he is able to understand and present from its very inception a whole personality, then he occasionally produces a work which poetical writing never equals. For, however much a poet's description of human life may surpass the critic's in freshness and charm, wit and eloquence, in the portrayal of life, still the poets rarely or never bring forth such great and original creations as those with whose presentation the critic is occupied.

The art of poetry presents personalities in action, not the inner life of theoretically or productive gifted natures; most rarely, and with the greatest difficulty, the life of geniuses. Gifted and profound spirits that have acquired an independent and systematic view of existence, and who live in a philosophical or political system wholly their own, or in their own poetical world, are not found in the novels and dramas of our time.

We become sad when we gather the results of many hours of work at different times, and realize how little they all, collected, weigh on the scales of time. In the guise of descriptions and studies of other people, they are glimpses of our own nature, leaves torn out of our own book of life, fragments of our own existence. While we are presenting other people, it is our own work, our admiration, our interests, our friendships, our youth; a little remnant of all, which, for a moment, attracts attention on the sea of time before it sinks to the bottom—the shadow of a dream.

This kind of book has its weakness in its want of real continuity of contents; its strength in variety, which makes it probable that among readers of different tastes, each one will be able to find some fact that he desires to use, or some subject that is of special interest to him.

GEORG BRANDES.

November, 1922.

TRANSLATOR'S NOTE

This volume is published by special arrangement with the author. Three of the essays are new to readers of English. The first nine were included in a volume, now out of print, entitled "Eminent Authors of the Nineteenth Century." Dr. Brandes described them in the preface to the earlier book as follows:

The nine essays of which this book consists, and of which even those that have already appeared in periodicals, have been thoroughly revised, are not to be regarded as "Chips from the Workshop" of a critic; they are carefully treated literary portraits, united by a spiritual tie. Men have sat for them, with whom the author, with one exception (Esaias Tegnér), has been personally acquainted, or of whom he has at least had a close view. . . .

The mode of treatment in these essays is greatly diversified. In some of them the individuality of the author portrayed is represented as exhaustively as possible; in others, an attempt has simply been made to present the man in actual person before the eyes of the reader; some are purely psychological; others offer a fragment of æsthetics; others, again, are eminently biographical and historical. In all of them the characteristics of the individual are so chosen as to bring out the most important features of the author's life and words.

Even the personalities described are of a very heterogeneous nature. They belong to not less than six nationalities. Common to all of them, however, there is a something which is more easily felt than defined; they are modern authors. By this I do not mean that they all, without exception, with full consciousness, and with their whole hearts, have paid homage to the "modern" in art and in thought, but merely that they, even though in a very unequal degree—which heightens the charm to the observer—represent the modern style of mind.

To Auber Forestier, who kindly aided me in translating the stories of Björnstjerne Björnson, and to Albert O. Barton who rendered valuable assistance in preparing the last three chapters, I have to express my cordial thanks.

RASMUS B. ANDERSON.

January, 1923.

CONTENTS

CHAPTER		PAGE
I.	Hans Christian Andersen (1869)	1
II.	Paul Heyse (1875)	54
III.	Esaias Tegnér (1878)	106
IV.	John Stuart Mill (1879)	184
V.	Ernest Renan (1880)	205
VI.	Gustave Flaubert (1881)	223
VII.	Frederick Paludan-Müller (1881)	267
VIII.	Björnstjerne Björnson (1882)	306
IX.	Henrik Ibsen (1883)	349
X.	Algernon Charles Swinburne (1909)	397
XI.	Guiseppe Garibaldi (1914)	420
XII.	Napoleon Bonaparte (1915)	447

CREATIVE SPIRITS

I

HANS CHRISTIAN ANDERSEN

1869

HE who possesses talent should also possess courage. He must dare trust his inspiration, he must be convinced that the fancy which flashes through his brain is a healthy one, that the form which comes natural to him, even if it be a new one, has a right to assert its claims; he must have gained the hardihood to expose himself to the charge of being affected, or on the wrong path, before he can yield to his instinct and follow it wherever it may imperiously lead. When Armand Carrel, a young journalist at the time, was censured by the editor of the paper for which he wrote, who, pointing to a passage in the young man's article, remarked, "That is not the way people write," he replied, "I do not write as people write, but as I myself write," and this is the universal formula of a gifted nature. It countenances neither fugitive rubbish, nor arbitrary invention, but with entire self-consciousness it expresses the right of talent when neither traditional form nor existing material suffices to meet the peculiar requirements of its nature, to choose new material, to create new forms, until it finds a soil of a quality to give nurture to all of its forces and gently and freely develop them. Such a soil the poet Hans Christian Andersen found in the nursery story.

I

In his stories we meet with beginnings like this: "Any one might have supposed that something very extraordinary had happened in the duck-pond, there was such a commotion. All the ducks—some swimming, some standing in the pond with their heads downward—suddenly jumped on land, leaving the traces of their feet in the wet clay, and sending forth a loud, startled cry,"[1] or like the following: "Now, then, let us begin. When we are at the end of the story, we shall know more than we know now: but to begin. Once upon a time there was a wicked sprite, indeed, he was the most mischievous of all sprites!" The construction, the position of the words in individual sentences, the entire arrangement, is at variance with the simplest rules of syntax. "This is not the way people write." That is true; but it is the way they speak. To grown people? No, but to children; and why should it not be proper to commit the words to writing in the same order in which they are spoken to children? In such a case the usual form is simply exchanged for another; not the rules of abstract written language, but the power of comprehension of the child is here the determining factor; there is method in this disorder, as there is method in the grammatical blunder of the child when it makes use of a regular imperfect for an irregular verb. To replace the accepted written language with the free, unrestrained language of familiar conversation, to exchange the more rigid form of expression of grown people for such as a child uses and understands, becomes the true goal of the author as soon as he embraces the resolution to tell nursery stories for children. He has the bold intention to employ oral speech in a printed work, he will not write but speak, and he will gladly write as a school-child writes, if he can thus avoid speaking as a book speaks. The written word is poor and insufficient, the oral has a host of allies in the expression of the mouth that imitates the object to which the discourse relates, in the movement of the hand that describes it, in the length or shortness of the tone of the voice, in its sharp or gentle, grave or droll character, in the entire play of the features, and in the whole bearing. The nearer to a state of nature the being addressed, the greater aids

[1] The quotations are from Houghton, Mifflin & Co.'s edition of Andersen's works.

to comprehension are these auxiliaries. Whoever tells a story to a child, involuntarily accompanies the narrative with many gestures and grimaces, for the child sees the story quite as much as it hears it, paying heed, almost in the same way as the dog, rather to the tender or irritated intonation, than to whether the words express friendliness or wrath. Whoever, therefore, addresses himself in writing to a child must have at his command the changeful cadence, the sudden pauses, the descriptive gesticulations, the awe-inspiring mien, the smile which betrays the happy turn of affairs, the jest, the caress, and the appeal to rouse the flagging attention—all these he must endeavor to weave into his diction, and as he cannot directly sing, paint, or dance the occurrences to the child, he must imprison within his prose the song, the picture, and the pantomimic movements, that they may lie there like forces in bonds, and rise up in their might as soon as the book is opened. In the first place, no circumlocution; everything must be spoken fresh from the lips of the narrator, aye, more than spoken, growled, buzzed, and blown as from a trumpet: "There came a soldier marching along the high-road—*one, two! one, two!*" "And the carved trumpeters blew, 'Trateratra! there is the little boy! Trateratra!'" "—"Listen how it is drumming on the burdock-leaves, 'rum-dum-dum! rum-dum-dum!' said the Father Snail." At one time he begins, as in "The Daisy," with a "Now you shall hear!" which at once arrests the attention; and again he jests after the fashion of a child: "So the soldier cut the witch's head off. There she lay!" We can hear the laughter of the child that follows this brief, not very sympathetic, yet extremely clear presentation of the destruction of an imposter. Often he breaks into a sentimental tone, as for instance: "The sun shone on the Flax, and the rainclouds moistened it, and this was just as good for it as it is for little children when they are washed, and afterward get a kiss from their mother; they became much prettier, and so did the Flax." That at this passage a pause should be made in the narrative, in order to give the child the kiss mentioned in the text, is something to which every mother will agree, and which seems to be a matter of course; the kiss is really given in the book. This regard for the young reader may be carried still farther, inasmuch as the poet, by virtue of his ready sympathy, so wholly identifies himself with the child and enters so fully into the sphere of its conceptions, into its mode of contemplation, indeed, into the range of its purely bodily vision, that a sentence like the following may readily flow from his pen: "The biggest leaf here in the country is certainly the burdock-leaf. Put one in front of your waist, and it is just like an apron, and if you lay it upon your head, it is almost as good as an umbrella, for it is quite remarkably large." These are words which a child, and every child, can understand.

Happy, indeed, is Andersen! What author has such a public as he? What is, in comparison, the success of a man of science, especially of one who writes within a limited territory for a public that neither reads nor values him, and who is read by four or five—rivals and opponents! A poet is, generally speaking, more favorably situated; but although it is a piece of good fortune to be read by men, and although it is an enviable lot to know that the leaves of our books are turned by dainty fingers which have employed silken threads as book-marks, nevertheless no one can boast of so fresh and eager a circle of readers as Andersen is sure of finding. His stories are numbered among the books which we have deciphered syllable by syllable, and which we still read to-day. There are some among them whose letters even now, seem to us larger, whose words appear to have more value than all others, because we first made their acquaintance letter by letter and word by word. And what a delight it must have been for Andersen to see in his dreams this swarm of children's faces by the thousands about his lamp, this throng of blooming, rosy-cheeked little curly-pates, as in the clouds of a Catholic altar-piece, flaxen-haired Danish boys, tender English babies, black-eyed Hindoo maidens,—rich and poor, spelling, reading, listening, in all lands, in all tongues, now healthy and merry, weary from sport, now sickly, pale, with transparent skin, after one of the numberless illnessess with which the children of this earth are visited,—and to see them eagerly stretch forth this confusion of white and swarthy little hands after each new leaf that is ready! Such devout believers, such an attentive, such an indefatigable public, none other has. None other either has such a reverend one, for even old age is not so reverend and sacred as childhood. In considering this public we can conjure up a whole series of peaceful and idyllic scenes: yonder some one is reading aloud while the children are listening devoutly, or a little one is sitting absorbed in its reading, with both elbows resting on the table, while its mother, in passing by, pauses that she too may read over the child's shoulder. Does it not bring its own reward to write for such a circle of auditors? Is there, indeed, one that has a more unspotted and ready fancy?

There is none, and it is only needful to study the imagination of the audience, in order to become acquainted with that of the author. The starting-point for this art is the child's play that makes everything out of everything; in conformity with this, the sportive mood of the artist transforms playthings into natural creations, into supernatural beings, into heroes, and, *vice versa,* uses everything natural and everything supernatural—heroes, sprites, and fairies —for playthings, that is to say, for artistic means which through each artistic combination are remodelled and freshly stamped. The nerve and sinew of the art is the imagination of the child, which invests everything with a soul, and endows everything with personality; thus, a piece of household furniture is as readily animated with life as a plant, a flower as well as a bird or a cat, and the animal in the same manner as the doll, the portrait, the cloud, the sunbeam, the wind, and the seasons. Even the leap-frog, made of the breastbone of a goose, becomes thus for the child a living whole, a thinking being endowed with a will. The prototype of such poesy is the dream of a child, in which the childish conceptions shift more rapidly and with still bolder transformations than in play; therefore, the poet (as in "Little Ida's Flowers," "Ole Shut Eye," "Little Tuk," "The Elder-Tree Mother") likes to seek refuge in dreams as in an arsenal; therefore, it is, when he busies his fancy with childish dreams, such as fill and trouble the mind of childhood, there often come to his his wittiest inspirations, as, for instance, when little Hjalmar hears in his dream the lamentation of the crooked letters that had tumbled down in his copy-book: " 'See, this is how you should hold yourselves,' said the Copy. 'Look, sloping in this way, with a powerful swing!' 'Oh, we should be very glad to do that,' replied Hjalmar's letters, 'but we cannot; we are too weakly.' 'Then you must take medicine,' said Ole Shut Eye. 'Oh no,' cried they; and they immediately stood up so gracefully that it was beautiful to behold.'' This is the way a child dreams, and this is the way a poet depicts to us the dream of a child. The soul of this poetry, however, is neither the dream nor the play; it is a peculiar, ever-childlike, yet at the same time a more than childlike faculty, not only for putting one thing in the place of another (thus, for making constant exchange, or for causing one thing to live in another, thus for animating all things), but also a faculty for being swiftly and readily reminded by one thing of another, for regaining one thing in another, for generalizing, for moulding an image into a symbol, for exalting a dream into a myth, and through an artistic process, for transforming single fictitious traits into a focus for the whole of life. Such a fancy does not penetrate far into the innermost recesses of things; it occupies itself with trifles; it sees ugly faults, not great ones; it strikes, but not deeply; it wounds, but not dangerously; it flutters around like a winged butterfly from spot to spot, lingering about the most dissimilar places, and, like a wise insect, it spins its delicate web from many starting-points, until it is united in one complete whole. What it produces is neither a picture of the soul nor a direct human representation; but it is a work that with all its artistic perfection was already indicated by the unlovely and confusing arabesques in "The Foot Journey to Amager." Now while the nursery story, through its contents, reminds us of the ancient myths ("The Elder-Tree Mother," "The Snow Queen"), of the folk-lore tale, on whose foundation

it constructs itself at times, of proverbs and fables of
antiquity, indeed, sometimes of the parables of the New Testament (the buckwheat is punished as well as the fig-tree);
while it is continually united by an idea, it may, so far as
its form is concerned, be compared with the fantastic Pompeian decorative paintings, in which peculiarly conventional
plants, animated flowers, doves, peacocks, and human forms
are entwined together and blend into one another. A form
that for any one else would be a circuitous route to the
goal, a hindrance and a disguise, becomes for Andersen a
mask behind which alone he feels truly free, truly happy
and secure. His child-like genius, like the well-known
child forms of antiquity, plays with the mask, elicits
laughter, awakens delight and terror. Thus the nursery
story's mode of expression, which with all its frankness
is masked, becomes the natural, indeed, the classic cadence
of his voice, that but very rarely becomes overstrained or
out of tune. The only disturbing occurrence is that now
and then a draught of whey is obtained instead of the
pure milk of the nursery story, that the tone occasionally
becomes too sentimental and sickly sweet ("Poor John,"
"The Poor Bird," "Poor Thumbling"), which, however,
is rarely the case in materials taken from folk-lore tales,
as "The Tinder-Box," "Little Claus and Big Claus," etc.,
where the naïve joviality, freshness, and roughness of the
narrative, which announces crimes and murders without
the slightest sympathetic or tearful phrase, stand Andersen
in good stead, and invest his figures with increased sturdiness. Less classic, on the other hand, is the tone of the lyric
effusions interwoven with some of the nursery stories, in
which the poet, in a stirring, pathetic prose gives a bird's-
eye view of some great period of history ("The Thorny
Path of Honor," "The Swan's Nest"). In these stories
there seems to me to be a certain wild flight of fancy, a
certain forced inspiration in the prevailing tone, wholly
disproportionate to the not very significant thought of the
contents; for thought and diction are like a pair of lovers.
Thought may be somewhat larger, somewhat loftier, than
diction, even as the man is taller than the woman; in the

opposite case there is something unlovely in the relation.
With the few exceptions just indicated, the narrative style
of Andersen's nursery stories is a model of its kind.

Let us, in order to know them thoroughly, watch the poet
at his work. Let us, by studying his manner of procedure,
gain a deeper comprehension of the result. There is one
instance wherein his method may be clearly followed, and
that is when he remodels anything. We do not need, in
such a case, merely to observe and to praise in vague
generalities, by making comparison with a different mode
of narrative; we can sharply and definitely declare, point
for point, what he has omitted, what he has rendered prominent, and thus see his individual production grow up under
our eyes. One day, in turning over the leaves of Don
Manuel's "Count Lucanor," Andersen became charmed by
the homely wisdom, of the old Spanish story, with the delicate flavor of the Middle Ages pervading it, and he lingered
over Chapter VII., which treats of how a king was served
by three rogues.

Count Lucanor spoke one day with Patronio, his counsellor,
and said to him, There is a man who has come to me and
addressed me on a very important subject. He gives me to
understand that it would conduce in the highest degree to my
advantage. But he says that no man in the world, however
highly I may esteem him, must be allowed to know anything
about it, and he so earnestly enjoins upon me to keep the
secret that he even assures me all my possessions and my life
itself will be imperilled if I reveal it to any one. And as I
know that nothing can come to your knowledge that you cannot
determine whether it be meant for a blessing or with deceitful
intent, I beg of you to tell me how this matter strikes you.
Sir Count, replied Patronio, in order that you may be able to
comprehend what should, in my opinion, be done in this matter,
I beg of you to hearken unto how a king was served by three
rogues, who sought his presence. The count asked what it
was that took place.

This introduction resembles a programme; we first learn
the bold question to which the story following is to be the
answer, and we feel that the story owes its existence solely
to the question. We are not permitted to draw for our-

selves from the narrative the moral that it seems to us to contain; it must be directed with a violent effort to the question concerning the amount of confidence that is due people who are shrouded in mystery. Such a method of telling a story is the practical, not the poetic one; it places undue limits on the pleasure the reader takes in discovering the hidden moral for himself. True, the fancy is gratified to find its work made easy, for it does not really desire to exert itself; but neither does it like to have its easy activity anticipated; like old people who are permitted to keep up a semblance of work, it does not wish to be reminded that its work is mere play. Nature pleases when it resembles art, says Kant; art, when it resembles nature. Why? Because the veiled purpose gives pleasure. But no matter, let us read further in the book.

Sir Count, said Patronio, there once came three rogues to a king and stated that they were most superior masters in the manufacture of cloth, and that they especially understood how to weave a certain stuff which was visible to everyone who was actually the son of the father whom all the world supposed to be his, but which was invisible to him who was not the son of his supposed father. This pleased the king greatly, for he thought that with the aid of this fabric he could learn which men in his kingdom were the sons of those who were legally accredited to be their fathers, and which were not, and that in this way he could adjust many things in his kingdom; for the Moors do not inherit from their fathers if they be not truly their children. So he gave orders to have the men conducted to his palace in which they could work.

The beginning is delightful, there is humor in the story; but Andersen thinks if it is to be rendered available for Denmark, another pretext must be chosen, one better adapted to children, and to the well-known northern innocence. And, besides, this king in the story is merely like a figure on the chess-board. Why was it that the rogues came to him? What sort of character does he possess? Is he fond of show? Is he vain? He does not stand out distinctly before the reader's eye. It would be better if he were an absolute fool of a king. He ought in some way to be characterized, to be stamped by a word, a phrase.

"And they told him that, in order to be sure they were not deceiving him, he might lock them up in the palace until the fabric was finished, and this pleased the king vastly!" They now receive gifts of gold, silver, and silk, spread abroad the tidings that the weaving has begun, and through their bold indication of pattern and colors cause the king's messengers to declare the fabric admirable, and thus succeed in obtaining a visit from the king, who, as he sees nothing, "is overcome by a deathly terror, for he believes that he cannot be the son of the king whom he has considered his father." He therefore praises the fabric beyond measure, and every one follows his example, until one day on the occasion of a great festival he puts on the invisible garment; he rides through the city, "and it was well for him that it was summer." No one could see the fabric, although every one feared to confess his inability to do so, lest he should be ruined and dishonored. "Thus this secret was preserved, and no one dared reveal it, until a negro who tended the king's horse, and had nothing to lose, went to the king" and affirmed the truth.

> Who bids you keep a secret from a faithful friend,
> Will cheat you too as surely as he has a chance.

The moral to this neat little story is most ludicrous and at the same time but poorly indicated. Andersen forgets the moral, puts aside, with a sparing hand, the clumsy precept which causes the story to deviate from the point which is its true centre, and then tells, with a dramatic vivacity, in the form of a dialogue, his admirable story about the vain emperor, of whom it was said in the city, "The Emperor is in the wardrobe." He brings the narrative quite home to us. There is nothing whose existence people are afraid to deny for fear of passing for a bastard, but there is much concerning which people dare not speak the truth, through cowardice, through fear of acting otherwise than "all the world," through anxiety lest they should appear stupid. And this story is eternally new and it never ends. It has its grave side, but just because of its endlessness it has also its humorous side. " 'But he has nothing on!' said the whole people at length. That touched the Emperor, for it seemed to him that they were right; but he thought within himself, 'I must go through with the procession.' *And so he held himself a little higher,* and the chamberlains held on tighter than ever, and carried the train which did not exist at all.'' It was Andersen who made the narrative comic.

But we can enter still more closely into relation with Andersen's method of story-telling; we have seen him place before us in a new form a foreign tale; we can now also see how he remodels his own attempts. In the year 1830 Andersen published in a volume of poetry, ''The Dead Man, a Folk-lore Tale from Fünen,'' the same which he remoulded later under the title of ''The Travelling Companion.'' The narrative, in its original form, is aristocratic and dignified; it begins in the following way: ''About a mile from Bogense may be found, on the field in the vicinity of Elvedgaard, a hawthorn so remarkable for its size that it can even be seen from the coast of Jutland.'' Here there are pretty rural descriptions of nature, here may be detected the masterly hand of a skilful author. ''The first night he *quartered* on a haystack in the field, and slept there like a *Persian* prince in his resplendent chamber.'' A Persian prince! This is an idea quite foreign to little children. Suppose we put in its place: ''The first night he slept on a haystack, out in the fields, for there was no other bed for him; but it seemed to him so nice and comfortable that even a king need not wish for a better.'' This is intelligible. ''The moon hung, like an *Argantine* lamp, from the vaulted ceiling, and burned with a perpetual flame.'' Is not the tone a more familiar one when we say: ''The moon, like a large lamp, hung high up in the blue ceiling, and he had no fear of its setting fire to his curtains.'' The story of the doll's comedy is rewritten; it is sufficient when we know that the piece treats of a king and a queen: Ahasuerus, Esther, Mordecai, who were named in the original, are too learned names for children. If we hit upon a life-like stroke, we hold fast to it. ''The queen threw herself on her knees, took off her beautiful crown, and, holding it in her hand, cried: 'Take this from me, but do rub (with healing ointment) my husband and his courtiers.'" Such a passage is one of those in which the nursery story tone penetrates the polished form; one of those in which the style that says "thou" to the reader thrusts aside the one that says "you." In illustration, a whole swarm of comparisons throng upon us. "From the host our travellers learned that they were in the realm of the King or Hearts, an excellent ruler, and nearly related to the King of Diamonds, Silvio, who is sufficiently well known through Carlo Gozzi's dramatic folk-lore tale, 'The Three Pomegranates.'" The princess is compared with Turandot, and of John it is said: "It would seem as though he had recently read Werther and Siegwart; he could only love and die." A shrill discord for the nursery tale style. The words are not those of the child's treasury of language; the tone is elegant, and the illustrations are abstract. "John spake, but he knew not himself what he was saying, for the princess bestowed on him so blessed a smile, and graciously extended her white hand for him to kiss; his lips burned, an *electric* current ran through him; he could enjoy nothing of the *refreshments* the pages offered him, he saw only the beautiful vision of his dreams." Let us once hearken to this in the style so familiar to us all: "She looked wonderfully fair and lovely when she offered her hand to John, and he loved her more than ever. How could she be a wicked witch, as all the people asserted? He accompanied her into the hall, and the little pages offered them gingerbread nuts and sweetmeats; but the old king was so unhappy, he could eat nothing, and, besides, gingerbread nuts were too hard for him."

In his youth, Andersen, who then took Musæus for his model, had not advanced far enough to understand how to mingle jest and earnest in his diction; they were always at variance; scarcely was utterance given to a sentiment beforce the disturbing parody made its appearance. John says a few words, in which he expresses his love, and the author adds: "O, it was so touching to hear! The poor young man, who was at other times so natural, so amiable, now spoke quite like one of Clauren's books; but then, what will not love do?" On this point, with this pedantic frivolity, Andersen still persisted in 1830; but five years later the transformation process is at an end; his talent has shed its skin; his courage has grown; he dares speak his own language.

The determining element in this mode of speech was from the outset the childlike. In order to be understood by such youthful readers as those to whom he addressed himself, he was obliged to use the simplest possible words, to return to the simplest possible conceptions, to avoid everything abstract, to supply the place of indirect with direct language; but in thus seeking simplicity, he finds poetic beauty, and in attaining the childlike he proves that this childlike spirit is essential to true poetry; for that form of expression which is naïve and adapted to the general comprehension is more poetic than that which reminds the reader of industry, of history, of literature; the concrete fact is at once more life-like and more transparent than that which is presented as proof of a proposition, and the language which proceeds directly from the lips is more characteristic than the pale paraphrase with a "that."[2]

To linger over this language, to become absorbed in its word-treasury, its syntax, its intonation, is no proof of a petty spirit, and does not take place merely through love of the vocables or the idiom. True, language is but the surface of a work of poetic fancy; but if the finger be placed upon the skin, we may feel the throbbing pulse which indicates the heart-beats of the inner being. Genius is like a clock; the visible index is guided by the invisible spring. Genius is like a tangled skein, inextricable and knotted, as it may seem, it is nevertheless inseparably one in its inner

[2] Compare such passages as the following: "It was just as though some one were sitting there practising a tune which he could not get hold of, always the same tune. 'I will get it, though,' he says, no doubt; but nevertheless, he does not get it, let him play as long as he will." "The great white snails, which the grand people in old times used to have made into fricassees; and when they had eaten them, they would say, 'H'm, how good that is!' for they had the idea that it tasted delicious. These snails lived on burdock-leaves."

coherence. If we but get hold of the outer end of the thread, we may slowly and cautiously endeavor to unravel even the most tangled skein from its coil. It is not harmed by the effort.

II

If we hold fast to the clue, we shall comprehend how the childlike in diction and sphere of conception, the true-hearted manner with which the most improbable things are announced, is just what invests the nursery story with its poetic worth. For what renders a literary production significant, what gives it circulation in space and lasting value in time, is the force with which it is able to present that which is propagated through space and which endures through time. It preserves itself by means of the vigor with which, in a clear and polished way, it renders perceptible the constant. Those writings which support tendencies or emotions whose horizon is limited in time or space, those which revolve about purely local circumstances, or are the result of a prevailing taste, whose nourishment and whose image are found in these circumstances, will vanish with the fashion that has called them forth. A street song, a newspaper article, a festival oration, reflect a prevailing mood which for perhaps a week has superficially occupied the population of the city, and therefore have themselves a duration of about equal length. Or, to mount to a higher level, suppose there suddenly arises in a country some subordinate proclivity, as, for instance, the fancy for playing private comedies, which became an epidemic in Germany in the time of "Wilhelm Meister," or in Denmark between 1820 and 1830. Such a tendency in itself is not wholly devoid of significance, but psychologically considered it is thoroughly superficial and does not affect the deeper life of the soul. If it be made an object of satire, as it was in Denmark, by Rosenkilde's "The Dramatic Tailor," or in "Sir Burchardt and his Family," by Henrik Hertz, those works which, without representing the epidemic from a higher point of view, merely imitate and render it laughable, will be just as short-lived as it was. Let us now take a step higher, let us turn to the works which mirror the psychological condition of an entire race, an entire period. The good-natured drinking-song poetry of the past century, and the poetry written for political occasions, are such literary productions. They are historic documents, but their life and their poetic value are in direct ratio to the depth at which they approach universal humanity, the constant in the current of history. With greater and more marked significance in this gradual ascent stand forth those works, in which a people has seen itself portrayed for a half or for a whole century, or during an entire historic period, and has recognized the likeness. Such works must of necessity depict a spiritual condition of considerable duration, which, just because it is so enduring, must have its geologic seat in the deeper strata of the soul, as otherwise it would much sooner be washed away by the waves of time. These works incorporate the ideal personality of an epoch; that is to say, the personality which floats before the people of that time as its reflection and model. It is this personality which artists and poets chisel, paint, and describe, and for which musicians and poets create. In Grecian antiquity it was the supple athlete and the eagerly-questioning youth who was athirst for knowledge; during the Middle Ages it was the knight and the monk; under Louis XIV the courtier; in the beginning of the nineteenth century it was Faust. The works which represent such forms give expression to the intellectual condition of an entire epoch, but the most important of them express still more; they mirror and embody at the same time the character of an entire people, of an entire race, an entire civilization, inasmuch as they reach the most profound, most elementary stratum of the individual human soul and of society, which concentrates and represents them in its little world. In this way, with the aid of a few names, the history of an entire literature could be written, by simply writing the history of its ideal personalities. Danish literature, during the first half of the nineteenth century, is placed, for instance, between the two types,

Oehlenschläger's Aladdin and Frater Taciturnus in Kierkegaard's "Stages in the Path of Life." The former is its starting-point, the latter its perfection and conclusion. Now since the worth of these personalities, as before stated, depends upon how deeply they have their growth in the character of the people, or in human nature, it will readily be recognized that such a personality, for instance, as that of Aladdin, in order that it may be comprehended in its peculiar beauty, must be compared with the ideal personality which from the beginning of the period beamed upon us from the fancy of the Danish people. We find this personality by bringing together a large number of the oldest mythic and heroic characterizations of the people. If I were to cite a single name, I would choose that of Uffe the Gentle.[3] In virtues as well as in faults he is a colossus

---

[3] Uffe the Gentle, according to tradition, is the son of a Danish king. His father had been a powerful warrior in his day, but has become old and feeble. The son causes the father the most profound solicitude. No one has ever heard him speak; he has never been willing to learn the use of weapons, and he moves through life in phlegmatic indifference, taking no interest in anything about him. But when the kings of Saxony refuse to pay the old father the accustomed tribute, mock at him, and challenge him to single combat, and the father wrings his hands in despair and cries, "Would that I had a son!" Uffe, for the first time, finds voice, and summons both kings to a holmgang (duel) with him. Great haste is now made to bring weapons to him, but no harness is large enough for his broad breast. If he did but make the slightest movement, whichever one is tried on him is rent asunder. Finally he is forced to content himself with a harness that bears the marks of many blows. It is the same with every sword that is placed in his hand. They all snap like glass whenever he makes trial of them on a tree. Then the king has the ancient sword Skräpp, once wielded by his father, brought forth from the giant warrior's grave, and bids Uffe lay hold of it, but not to test it before the fight. Thus armed, Uffe presents himself before the two foreign kings, on an island in the Eider. The blind old king sits on the river-bank and with throbbing heart anxiously hearkens to the clashing of the swords. If his son fall, he will plunge into the waves and die. Suddenly Uffe aimed a blow with his sword at one of the Saxon kings, and cut him in two right across the body. "That tone I know," said the king; "that was Skräpp's ring!" And Uffe gave another blow, and cut the other king through lengthwise, so that he fell in two halves to the ground. "That was Skräpp's ring again," cried the blind king. And when the old king died, Uffe ascended the throne and became a powerful and much feared ruler.

of a Danish hero. It can readily be perceived how great a degree of resemblance all of Oehlenschläger's best characters, his calm Thor, his nonchalent Helge, his indolent Aladdin, bear to this hero, and it will be seen during the contemplation how deeply Aladdin is rooted in the character of the people, while at the same time he is the expression of the ideal of an epoch whose duration was about fifty years. It could just as easily be rendered perceptible how Frater Taciturnus is one variety of the Faust type. Sometimes, therefore, it is possible to show how ideal personalities extend through the most divers countries and peoples, over an entire continent, leaving behind them their indelible stamp in a whole group of literary works which resemble one another as impressions of one and the same intellectual form, impressions of one and the same gigantic seal, with wafers of the most varied colors. Thus the personality that becomes most prominent in Danish literature, as "Johann, the Betrayer" (in Kirkegaard's "Either Or") is derived from Byron's heroes, from Jean Paul's Roquairol, from Chateaubriand's René, from Goethe's Werther, and is at the same time represented in Lermontow's Petschorin ("The Hero of our Time"). The usual billows and storms of time will not suffice to overthrow such a personality; it was the Revolution of 1848 that first succeeded in setting it aside.

Extremes meet. For the same reason that a universal spiritual malady which exercises a powerful influence over humanity will spread simultaneously through the whole of Europe, and, because of its profundity, will cause the works that were first created as its portraits to live as its monuments; for the same reason, too, those works attain general European fame and become long-lived that reflect that which is most *elementary* in human nature—childlike fancy and childlike emotion, and consequently summon up facts which every one has experienced (all children lock up kingdoms with a key). They depict the life which existed in the first period of the human soul, and thus reach that intellectual stratum which lies the deepest with all peoples and in all lands. This is the simple explanation of the fact that Andersen alone of all the Danish writers has attained a European, indeed, more than a European, circulation. No other explanation has reached my ears, unless it be the one that would have his renown due to his having journeyed about and provided for his own fame. Ah, if journeys would accomplish such results, the travelling stipends for artists of all kinds that *must* of necessity be awarded each year would in the course of time provide Denmark with a rich bloom of European celebrities, as they have already furnished poet after poet. To be sure, the poets correspond with the way in which they are made. But even the remaining, less malicious explanations that may be brought forward, as, for instance, that Andersen alone among the greater Danish authors has written in prose, and is therefore the only one whose works can be translated without effort into other languages, or that his genre is so popular, or that he is so great a genius, state either too little or too much. There is more than *one* genius in Danish literature who is greater than Andersen; there are many who with respect to their endowments are by no means inferior to him; but there is none whose creations are so elementary. Heiberg, as well as Andersen, possessed the courage to remodel a form of art (the vaudeville) in accordance with his own peculiarities, but he did not have the good fortune to find any one art form in which he could reveal his entire talent, combine all his gifts, as Andersen was able to do in the nursery story, nor to find materials in which interests of time and locality are of such enduring importance. His best vaudeville "The Inseparable Ones" (De Uadskillelige) would only be understood where there exists, as in Scandinavian countries, a "Temperance Society of Happiness" (Ibsen's expression for long betrothals), at which this vaudeville aims its shafts. But as the possessor of talent should also possess courage, so the possessor of genius should also possess good fortune, and Andersen has lacked neither good fortune nor courage.

The elementary quality in Andersen's poetry insured him a circle of readers among the cultivated people of all lands. It was still more effectual in securing him one among the uncultivated people. That which is childlike is in its very essence of a popular nature, and a wide circulation corresponds with an extension downward. Because of the deep and grievous but most natural division of society into grades of culture, the influence of good literature is confined almost exclusively to one class. If in Denmark a series of literary productions like Ingemann's romances make an exception, it is chiefly because of qualities which remove them from the cultivated classes through lack of truth to nature in the character delineations and in the historic coloring. With Ingemann's romances it is the same as with Grundtvig's theories: if one would defend them, it could not be done by proving their truth, but by practically laying stress on their outward usefulness, the advantage they have been to the Danish cause, to the interests of enlightenment and piety, etc. Ingemann's romances stand, moreover, in noteworthy relation to Andersen's nursery stories. The latter are read by the younger, the former by the older children. The nursery story harmonizes with the luxuriant imagination and the warm sympathy of the child, and the somewhat older maiden; the romance, with the fantastic desire for action of the child and especially of the somewhat older boy, with his growing taste for deeds of chivalry, with his conceit, his love of pleasing and daring. Romances are written for grown people; but the healthy mind of the nation has slowly dropped them until they have found their natural public in the age between ten and twelve years. Truth is something relative. At twelve years of age these books seem just as full of truth, as at twenty they seem full of innocent lies. But they must be read before the twelfth year be gone, for at twelve and a half it is already too late for those who are a trifle advanced in intellectual development. With the nursery story the reverse is the case. Written in the beginning for children and constantly read by them, they speedily rose to the notice of grown people and were by them declared to be true children of genius.

It was a lucky stroke that made Andersen the poet of children. After long fumbling, after unsuccessful efforts, which must necessarily throw a false and ironic light on the self-consciousness of a poet whose pride based its justification mainly on the expectancy of a future which he felt slumbering within his soul, after wandering about for long years, Andersen, a genuine offspring of Oehlenschläger, strayed into Oehlenschläger's footsteps, and one evening found himself in front of a little insignificant yet mysterious door, the door of the nursery story. He touched it, it yielded, and he saw, burning in the obscurity within, the little "Tinder-Box" that became his Aladdin's lamp. He struck fire with it, and the spirits of the lamp—the dogs with eyes as large as teacups, as mill-wheels, as the round tower in Copenhagen—stood before him and brought him the three giant chests, containing all the copper, silver, and gold treasure stores of the nursery story. The first story had sprung into existence, and the "Tinder-Box" drew all the others onward in its train. Happy is he who has found his "tinder-box."

Now in what sense is the child Andersen's ideal form? There comes to every land a certain epoch in which its literature seems suddenly to discover what has long remained unobserved in society. Thus in literature are discovered by degrees the burgher (in Denmark by Holberg), the student, the peasant, etc. In the time of Plato, woman was not yet discovered, one might almost say not yet invented. The child was discovered at different periods in the literatures of different countries; in England, for instance, much earlier than in France. Andersen is the discoverer of the child in Denmark. Yet here, as everywhere else, the discovery does not take place without pre-suppositions and stipulations, and here, as everywhere in Danish literature, it is Oehlenschläger to whom thanks are due for the first impetus, the fundamental discovery which prepares the way for that of almost every later poet. The installation of the child in its natural poetic rights is only one of the many phenomena of the ascension to the throne of naïveté, whose originator in Danish literature is Oehlenschläger. The eighteenth century, whose strength lies in its critical understanding, whose enemy is its imagination, in which it sees but the ally and bondman of antiquated tradition, whose queen is its logic, whose king is Voltaire, the object of whose poetry and science in the abstract is the enlightened and social human being, sends the child, which is neither abstract, nor social, nor enlightened, from the parlor into exile in the remote nursery, where it may listen to nursery tales, traditions, and robber stories, to its heart's content, provided it take good care to have forgotten all this worthless trash when it becomes a grown person. In the society of the nineteenth century (I do not draw the boundary line sharply on the frontiers) the reaction takes place. The individual, personal human being takes the place of the social human being. Consciousness alone had previously been valued, now the unconscious is worshipped. Schelling's philosophy of nature breaks the spell of Fichte's *Ego* system; war is carried on against the unfruitful intellectual reflection, the folk-lore tale and the nursery story are restored to their rights, the nursery and its occupants are brought into honorable esteem once more, at times even into too great favor. In all lands the folk-lore is collected, and in most countries poets begin to remould it. The sentimental German authors of the transition period (Kotzebue and Iffland) bring children on the stage, in view of touching the audience, even Oehlenschläger introduces children into his works and is, therefore, obliged to endure the censure of Heiberg. So far as society is concerned, silence has been enforced by Rousseau with his pedagogic declamations and theories, such attention as was never known before, is bestowed on the child and above all on the childlike *nature,* and the enthusiasm for the education of children (Campe) is gradually supplanted by the enthusiasm for the child's "state of nature" (see Rousseau's tendency, as displayed even in Götz von Berlichingen's conversation with his little son).

There is but a step from the child to the animal. The animal is a child that will never be anything else than a child. The same tendency to make life a social life, which thrust aside the child, also banished the animal. The same thirst for simplicity, for nature, for all that is innocent and *unconscious* which led poetry to the child, led it also to the animal, and from the animal to all nature. Rousseau who champions the cause of the child, champions at the same time the cause of the animal; and first and foremost, as his Alpha and Omega, his "præterea censeo," the cause of nature. He studies botany, writes to Linné, expresses to him his admiration and affection. The scientific contemplation of nature determines the social, which in its turn determines the poetic. Bernadin de Saint-Pierre, through his exquisite story "Paul and Virginia," introduces descriptions of nature into French prose, and, what is particularly noteworthy, simultaneously with his discovery of the landscape he introduces, as his hero and heroine, two children. Alexander von Humboldt takes "Paul and Virginia" with him on his journey to the tropical regions, admiringly reads the book aloud to his travelling companions in the midst of the nature which it describes, and refers with gratitude to what he owes to Saint-Pierre. Humboldt influences Oersted who in his turn profoundly influences Andersen. The sympathetic contemplation of nature operates on the scientific, which in its turn operates on the poetic. Chateaubriand, in his highly-colored brilliant manner, depicts a nature closely related to the one which Saint-Pierre has received in his peaceful, nature-worshipping soul. Steffens, in his celebrated lectures, first introduces to Denmark the natural system of nature. About the year 1831, at the period, therefore, when Andersen's nursery stories originated, there is founded in England (the land which took the lead in bringing forward the child in literature) the first society for the prevention of cruelty to animals. Branches are established in France and Germany, where societies spring up in Munich, Dresden, Berlin and Leipsic. Kierkegaard in his "Enten— Eller" (Either—Or) turns the establishment of these societies into ridicule; he sees in it but a phenomenon of the tendency to form associations, which in his eyes is a proof of the lamentable condition of individual personality. If we return now to Denmark, we will observe that the national landscape painting, with its literal imitation of nature, takes its decisive upward soaring flight at precisely the time when nursery stories are devised. Skovgaard paints the lake in which "the ugly duckling" went splashing about, and at the same time—as by a miracle—the large city becomes too small for the citizen of Copenhagen. He finds it wearisome to gaze the whole summer long on its paving-stones, its many houses and roofs, he longs to see a larger bit of the sky, he repairs to the country, lays out gardens, learns to distinguish barley from rye, becomes a rustic for the summer months. One and the same idea, the recovered idea of nature, extends its influence through all the spheres of life, just as the water of an upland stream flowing downward is distributed through a series of different basins. Could an idea produce a more singular effect, or a more suggestive one for contemplation? During the past century there has been nothing similar. We may, as has been wittily remarked, rummage through Voltaire's "Henriade," without finding a single blade of grass; there is no fodder for the horses in it. We may turn over the leaves of Baggesen's poems, without stumbling on a single description of nature, used even as an accessory. What a leap from this poetry to such poetry as that of Christian Winther, in which the human figures are merely used as accessories and the landscape is almost universally the main point of interest, and how far removed was the world, even in his day, from so much as dreaming of a poetry like that of Andersen, in which animals and plants fill the place of man, indeed, almost make man superfluous![4]

Now what is there in plants, in animals, in the child, so attractive to Andersen? He loves the child because his affectionate heart draws him to the little ones, the weak and helpless ones to whom it is allowable to speak with compassion, with tender sympathy, and because when he devotes such sentiments to a hero,— as in "Only a Fiddler," —he is derided for it (compare with Kierkegaard's criticism).[5] but when he dedicates them to a child, he finds the

[4] The fables of the past century (for instance, Lessing's fables) are merely ethic.
[5] G. Brandes. S. Kierkegaards. Ein literarisches Charakterlied. Leipsic, 1879.

natural resting-place for his mood. It is owing to his
genuine democratic feeling for the lowly and neglected that
Andersen, himself a child of the people, continually introduces into his nursery stories (as Dickens, in his novels),
forms from the poorer classes of society, "simple folk,"
yet endowed with the true nobility of the soul. As examples of this may be mentioned the washerwoman in "Little
Tuk" and in "Good-for-Nothing," the old maid in "From
a Window in Vartou," the watchman and his wife in "The
Old Street-Lamp," the poor apprentice boy in "Under the
Willow-Tree," and the poor tutor in "Everything in its
Right Place." The poor are as defenseless as the child.
Furthermore, Andersen loves the child, because he is able
to portray it, not so much in the direct psychologic way of
the romance,—he is by no means a direct psychologist,—
as indirectly, by transporting himself with a bound into
the child's world, and he acts as though no other course
were possible. Rarely, therefore, has charge been more
unjust than that of Kierkegaard when he accused Andersen
of being unable to depict children; but when Kierkegaard,
who, moreover, as a literary critic combines extraordinary
merits with great lacks (especially in point of historic
survey), takes occasion, in making this criticism, to remark
that in Andersen's romances the child is always described
"through another," what he says is true. It is no longer
true, however, the moment Andersen, in the nursery story,
puts himself in the place of the child and ceases to recognize "another." He seldom introduces the child into his
nursery stories as taking part in the action and conversation. He does it most frequently in the charming little collection "A Picture-Book without Pictures," where more
than anywhere else he permits the child to speak with the
entire simplicity of its nature. In such brief, naïve child-
utterances as those cited in it there is much pleasure and
entertainment. Every one can recall anecdotes of a similar
character. I remember once taking a little girl to a place
of amusement, in order to hear the Tyrolese Alpine singers.
She listened very attentively to their songs. Afterward,
when we were walking in the garden in front of the pavil-

ion, we met some of the singers in their costumes. The little maiden clung timidly to me, and asked in astonishment: "Are they allowed to go about free?" Andersen has no equal in the narration of anecdotes of this kind.[6] In his nursery stories we find sundry illustrations of the fact, as in the charming words of the child in "The Old House," when it gives the man the pewter soldiers that he might not be "so very, very lonely," and a few kind answers in "Little Ida's Flowers." Yet his child forms are comparatively rare. The most noteworthy ones are little Hjalmar, little Tuk, Kay and Gerda, the unhappy, vain Karen in "The Red Shoes," a dismal but well-written story, the little girl with the matches and the little girl in "A Great Sorrow," finally Ib and Christine, the children in "Under the Willow-Thee." Besides these real children there are some ideal ones, the little fairy-like Thumbling and the little wild robber-maiden, undoubtedly Andersen's freshest child creation, the masterly portrayal of whose wild nature forms a most felicitous contrast to the many good, fair-haired and tame children of fiction. We see her before us as she really is, fantastic and true, her and her reindeer, whose neck she "tickles every evening with her sharp knife."

We have seen how sympathy with child-nature led to sympathy with the animal which is doubly a child, and to sympathy with the plants, the clouds, the winds, which are doubly nature. What attracts Andersen to the impersonal being is the impersonal element in his own nature, what leads him to the wholly unconscious is merely the direct

[6] The following composition was recently written in Copenhagen by a little maiden of ten years on the theme, "An Unexpected Joy." "There dwelt in Copenhagen a man and his wife who were very happy. All went well with them, and they were extremely fond of each other; but they felt very sorry because they had no children. They waited a long time, still they got none. At last the husband went away on a long journey and was gone ten years. When the time was at an end, he returned home, entered his house, and was happy indeed to find five little children in the nursery, some playing, some in the cradle. *This was an unexpected joy!*" This composition, however, is an example of the kind of naïveté which Andersen never uses. The point would attract a French story-teller, but, like everything else that alludes to sex, it leaves Andersen perfectly cold.

consequence of his sympathy. The child, young though it may be, is born old; each child is a whole generation older than its father, a civilization of ages has stamped its inherited impress on the little four-year-old child of the metropolis. How many conflicts, how many endeavors, how many sorrows have refined the countenance of such a child, making the features sensitive and precocious! It is different with animals. Look at the swan, the hen, the cat! They eat, sleep, live, and dream undisturbed, as in ages gone by. The child already begins to display evil instincts. We, who are seeking what is unconscious, what is naïve, are glad to descend the ladder that leads to the regions where there is no more guilt, no more crime, where responsibility, repentance, restless striving and passion cease, where nothing of an evil nature exists except through a substitution of which we are but partially conscious, and which therefore, robs our sympathy of half its sting. An author like Andersen, who has so great a repugnance to beholding what is cruel and coarse in its nakedness, who is so deeply impressed by anything of the kind that he dare not relate it, but recoils a hundred times in his works from some wanton or outrageous deed with the maidenly expression, "We cannot bear to think of it!" Such an author feels content and at home in a world where everything that appears like egotism, violence, coarseness, vileness, and persecution, can only be called so in a figurative way. It is highly characteristic that almost all the animals which appear in Andersen's nursery stories are tame animals, domestic animals. This is, in the first place, a sympton of the same gentle and idyllic tendency which results in making almost all Andersen's children so well-behaved. It is, furthermore, a proof of his fidelity to nature, in consequence of which he is so reluctant to describe anything, with which he is not thoroughly familiar. It is finally an interesting phenomenon with reference to the use he makes of the animals, for domestic animals are no longer the pure product of nature; they remind us, through ideal association, of much that is human; and, moreover, through long intercourse with humanity and long education they have acquired something human, which in a high degree supports and furthers the effort to personify them. These cats and hens, these ducks and turkeys, these storks and swans, these mice and that unmentionable insect "with maiden's blood in its body," offer many props to the nursery story. They hold direct intercourse with human beings; all that they lack is articulate speech, and there are human beings with articulate speech who are unworthy of it, and do not deserve their speech. Let us, therefore, give the animals the power of speech, and harbor them in our midst.

On the almost exclusive limitation to the domestic animal, a double characteristic of this nursery story depends. First of all, the significant result that Andersen's animals, whatever else they may be, are never beastly, never brutal. Their sole faults are that they are stupid, shallow, and old-fogyish. Andersen does not depict the animal in the human being, but the human in the animal. In the second place, there is a certain freshness of tone about them, a certain fulness of feeling, certain strong and bold, enthusiastic, and vigorous outbursts which are never found in the quarters of the domestic animal. Many beautiful, many humorous and entertaining things are spoken of in these stories, but a companion piece to the fable of the wolf and the dog —the wolf who observed the traces of the chain on the neck of the dog and preferred his own freedom to the protection afforded the house dog—will not be found in them. The wild nightingale, in whom poetry is personified, is a tame and loyal bird. "I have seen tears in the Emperor's eyes; that is the real treasure to me," it says. "An emperor's tears have a peculiar power!" Take even the swan, that noble, royal bird in the masterly story, "The Ugly Duckling," which for the sake of its cat and its hen alone cannot be sufficiently admired,—how does it end? Alas! as a domestic animal. This is one of the points where it becomes difficult to pardon the great author. O poet! we feel tempted to exclaim, since it was in your power to grasp such a thought, to conceive and execute such a poem, how could you, with your inspiration, your pride, have the heart to permit the swan to end thus! Let him die if needs must be! That would be tragic and great. Let him spread his wings and impetuously soar through the air, rejoicing in his beauty and his strength! let him sink down on the bosom of some solitary and beautiful forest lake! That is free and delightful. Anything would be better than this conclusion: "Into the garden came little children, who threw bread and corn into the water. And they ran to their father and mother, and bread and cake were thrown into the water; and they all said, 'The new one is the most beautiful of all! so young and handsome!' and the old swans bowed their heads before him." Let them bow, but let us not forget that there is something which is worth more than the recognition of all the old swans and geese and ducks, worth more than receiving bread-crumbs and cake as a garden bird,—the power of silently gliding over the waters, and free flight!

Andersen prefers the bird to the four-footed animal. More birds than mammals find place with him; for the bird is gentler than the four-footed beast, is nearer to the plant. The nightingale is his emblem, the swan his ideal, the stork his declared favorite. It is natural that the stork, that remarkable bird which brings children into the world,—the stork, that droll, long-legged, wandering, beloved, yearningly expected and joyfully greeted bird, should become his idolized symbol and frontispiece.

Yet plants are preferred by him to birds. Of all organic beings, plants are those which appear most frequently in the nursery story. For in the vegetable world alone are peace and harmony found to reign. Plants, too, resemble a child, but a child who is perpetually asleep. There is no unrest in this domain, no action, no sorrow, and no care. Here life is a calm, regular growth, and death but a painless fading away. Here the easily excited, lively poetic sympathy suffers less than anywhere else. Here there is nothing to jar and assail the delicate nerves of the poet. Here he is at home; here he paints his Arabian Nights' Entertainments beneath a burdock leaf. Every grade of emotion may be experienced in the realm of plants,— melancholy at the sight of the felled trunk, fulness of strength at the sight of the swelling buds, anxiety at the fragrance of the strong jasmine. Many thoughts may flit through our brain as we follow the history of the development of the flax, or the brief honor of the fir-tree on Christmas evening; but we feel as absolutely free as though we were dealing with comedy, for the image is so fleeting that it vanishes the moment we attempt to render it permanent. Sympathy and agitation gently touch our minds, but they do not ruffle us, they neither rouse nor oppress us. A poem about a plant sets free twofold the sympathy to which it lays claim; once because we know that the poem is pure fiction, and again because we know the plant to be merely a symbol. Nowhere has the poet with greater delicacy invested plants with speech than in "The Fir-Tree," "Little Ida's Flowers," and in "The Snow Queen." In the last named story, every flower tells its own tale. Let us listen to what the Tiger-lily says: "Hearest thou not the drum? Bum! bum! those are the only two tones. Always bum! bum! Hark to the plaintive song of the old woman! to the call of the priests! The Hindoo woman in her long robe stands upon the funeral pile; the flames rise around her and her dead husband, but the Hindoo woman thinks on the living one in the surrounding circle; on him whose eyes burn hotter than the flames; on him, the fire of whose eyes pierces her heart more than the flames which soon will burn her body to ashes. Can the heart's flame die in the flame of the funeral pile?"—"I do not understand that at all," said little Gerda.—"That is my story," said the Tiger-lily.

Yet a step farther, and the fancy of the poet appropriates all inanimate objects, colonizes and annexes everything, large and small, an old house and an old clothes-press ("The Shepherdess and the Chimney Sweep"), the top and the ball, the darning needle and the false collar, and the great dough men with bitter almonds for their hearts. After it has grasped the physiognomy of the inanimate, his fancy identifies itself with the formless all, sails with the moon across the sky, whistles and tells stories like the wind, looks on the snow, on sleep, night, death, and the dream as persons.

The determining element in this poetic mind was, then, sympathy with all that is childlike, and, through the representation of such deep-seated, elementary, and constant spiritual conditions as those of the child, the productions of this imagination are raised above the waves of time, spread beyond the boundaries of their native land and become the common property of the divers classes of society. The time when genius was looked upon as a meteor fallen from the skies, has long since passed away; now it is known that genius, as all else that comes from nature, has its antecedents and its conditions, that it holds relations of general dependence with its epoch, is an organ for the ideas of the age. Sympathy for the child is only a phenomenon of the sympathy of the nineteenth century for whatever is naïve. Love of the unconscious is a phenomenon of the love of nature. In society, in science, in poetry and in art, nature and the child had become objects of veneration; in the realms of poetry, art, science, and society, there takes place a reciprocal action. If there arise, therefore, a poet whose affections are attracted to the child, whose fancy is allured by the animal, by plants, and by nature, he dares follow his impulses, he gains courage to give utterance to his talent, because a hundred thousand mute voices about him strengthen him in his calling, because the tide he believes himself to be stemming, rocks him gently as it bears him onward to his goal.

Thus it will be seen we can study the poet's art by studying the ideas which are his inspiration. To contemplate these in their origin and their ramifications, in their abstract essence and their concrete power, is, therefore, no superfluous act, when it becomes our task to make a study of individual poetic fancies. For the bare idea cannot make poetry; but neither can the poet make poetry without the idea and without the surroundings which give it its impetus. About the fortunate poet there gathers a multitude who, in a less felicitous way, are working in his own vein; and about this multitude the people swarm as mute but interested fellow-laborers. For genius is like a burning reflector, which collects and unites the scattered rays of light. It never stands alone. It is merely the noblest tree in the forest, the highest ear in the sheaf, and it is first recognized in its real significance and in its true attitude when it is seen in its rightful place.

III

It does not suffice to indicate the quarter of the globe in which a genius dwells; we cannot travel through Denmark with a map of Europe for our guide. In the first place, it is necessary to see the locality more accurately described, and, even then, we no more know a genius because we happen to be familiar with his relations and surroundings than we know a city because we have walked around its walls. For though a genius may be partially, he cannot be exhaustively, explained by the period in which he lives. What is transmitted to him he combines under a new law; a product himself, he brings forth products which he alone of the whole world is able to bring forth. We need only exert our powers of observation a little, or hearken perhaps to the opinion of a foreigner, to feel how much there is that is national, local, and individual in Andersen's nursery stories. I was once talking with a young Frenchman about Denmark. "I am very well acquainted with your country," said he. "I know that your king is named Christian, that your greatest author is an unrecognized genius whose name is Hr. Schmidt, that Hr. Ploug is your fatherland's most valiant warrior, whom no battle-field ever saw retreat, and that Hr. Bille is the Gambetta of Denmark. I know that you have a body of learned men who are distinguished for their scientific independence and free investigations, and I know Hr. Holst, whom you call the "Tyrtäus of Danebrog." Seeing that he had oriented himself pretty well, I interrupted him with the question, "Have you read Andersen's nursery stories?" "Have I read them?" cried he, in reply. "Why, I have read no other Danish book. "What do you think of them?" asked I. *"Un peu trop enfantin,"* was the answer, and I am convinced that if Andersen's nursery stories were submitted to a French child five years old, he, too, would find them *"un peu trop enfantin."*

I have stated that the childlike element in Andersen is universally intelligible. This is true, but it is not the whole truth. This childlike tone has a decidedly Teutonic impress; it is best understood in England and in Germany, less well in any of the Latin nations, least of all by the French. In fact, Andersen is very little known and read in France. England is the only land in which romances and semi-romances are devoted to the portrayal of the spiritual life of little children (Dickens's "Paul Domby" and "David Copperfield," Miss Wetherell's "The Wide, Wide World," George Eliot's "The Mill on the Floss"), and English child nature is unique of its kind. It is only needful to open the first illustrated French book for children that comes to hand to observe the difference. The English child and the French child are as dissimilar as the acorn and the beechnut. Moreover, Andersen could never gain firm foothold in France for the reason that the field is already occupied, having been taken possession of long since by La Fontaine.

There are two kinds of naïveté. One is that of the heart, the other that of the understanding; the former is frank, free, simple, and touching, the latter has a distorted appearance, is jocose, full of ready wit, and subtile. The one evokes tears, the other a smile; the former has its beauty, the latter its charm; the former characterizes the good child, the latter the *enfant terrible;* and Andersen is the poet of the former, La Fontaine of the latter naïveté. The latter form of naïveté is that expression of precocity which utters the appropriate word without exactly knowing what it says, and which has, therefore, the appearance of a cloak; the other naïveté is that of innocence which takes it for granted that its Garden of Eden is the whole world, and consequently puts the whole world to shame without being aware that it is doing so, and at the same time with so appropriate a choice of words that it assumes the appearance of a mask.

If we compare Andersen's nursery stories with the fables of La Fontaine, we shall find a fundamental difference in the contemplation of life exhibited and thus become acquainted with the limits of the Northern mode of viewing life, for every attempt at definition is in itself a limitation.

One of the most marked traits in La Fontaine's and the Gallic mode of contemplating life is the war against illusion. The humorous play in La Fontaine's naïveté is dependent on the fact that, harmless as this naïveté is, good-natured and gentle as it always shows itself to be, it now and then gives undoubted evidence that it is not altogether foolish, that it will not allow itself to be duped, that it knows very well how to estimate and value all the stupidity and hypocrisy, all the preaching and all the empty phrases with which humanity permits itself, as by common consent, to be led by the nose or by the heart. With a smile it passes by all the earnestness at whose core is corruption and hollowness, all the greatness which at bottom is but audacity, all the respectability whose essence is a lie. Thus it puts "Everything in its Right Place," which is the title of one of Andersen's most popular tales. The key-note of its earnestness is poetic enthusiasm, and its keen wit has a sting which is carefully concealed. French satire is a rapier with a provisional button. In "Tartuffe," "Candide," and "Figaro," it effected a revolution before the revolution. Laughter is the oldest Marseillaise of France.

The most marked trait in Andersen's mode of viewing life, is that which gives the ascendency to the heart, and this trait is genuinely Danish. Full of feeling itself, this method of contemplation takes every opportunity to exalt the beauty and significance of the emotions. It overleaps the will (the whole destiny of the Flax, in the story of its life, comes from without), does combat with the critique of the pure reason as with something pernicious, the work of the Devil, the witch's mirror, replaces pedantic science with the most admirable and witty side-thrusts ("The Bell," "A Leaf From the Sky"), describes the senses as a tempter, or passes them over as unmentionable things, pursues and denounces hardheartedness, glorifies and commends goodness of heart, violently dethrones coarseness and narrowness, exalts innocence and decorum, and thus "puts everything in its right place." The key-note of its earnestness is the ethic-religious feeling coupled with the hatred felt by geniality for narrowness, and its humorous satire is capricious, calm, in thorough harmony with the idyllic spirit of the poet. Its satire has only the sting of a gnat, but it stings in the tenderest places. Which of the modes of contemplation is the best? Such a question is not worthy of an answer. I love the beech, but I love the birch as well. Only because they please me, not in view of casting the balance in favor of either of these modes, I quote the following lines of George Herwegh:—

> My eyes with tears have often been bedewed,
> When hearts I've seen all bruised and maltreated,
> By hounds of understanding, too, pursued.
>
> Within the breast one little word is seated,
> Yet wisely is its utterance subdued,
> For hearts that beat too high will be defeated.

As different as these modes of contemplating life are the poetic endowments of the two authors. La Fontaine writes clear, elegant, highly melodious verse, whose poetry is a light enthusiasm and a gentle melancholy. Andersen writes a grotesque, irregular prose, full of harmless mannerisms, and whose poetry is a luxuriant, gushing, rapturous conceit. It is this fantastic element which makes Andersen so foreign to the French people whose rather gray poetry wholly lacks the bright-hued floral splendor found among the Northern people and attaining its highest beauty in Shakespeare's "Midsummer Night's Dream," a splendor which may be detected throughout Andersen's nursery stories, and which imparts to them their finest perfume. And as the fantastic caprice of this element is Norse-Danish, its idyllic key-note is purely Danish. No wonder that the earliest and most original of these nursery stories were written during the reign of Frederich VI. and bear the stamp of his day. We recognize this monarch in all the fatherly, patriarchal old kings represented in them; we find the spirit of the age in the complete lack of social, to say nothing of political satire, that we detect in them. No wonder, too, that Thorwaldsen could never weary of hearing these stories read aloud as he counted his numbers in the game of Lotto, for his Danish temperament was naïve, and his art, with all its greatness, was as idyllic as the art which produced these poetic creations.

A genius, born in an age whose every influence opposes his development, is either hopelessly crushed or goes to ruin like any inferior talent. An Andersen born in Denmark in 1705, instead of 1805, would have been a most unfortunate and thoroughly insignificant individual, perhaps even a maniac. A genius born at a period when everything unites to come to its aid, produces classic, genial creations. Now, this first harmony between a poet and his era (in a measure also, his country) corresponds to a second one between the individual faculties of genius, and to a third one between genius and its peculiar type of art. The nature of genius is an organically connected whole; its weakness in one direction is the condition of its strength in another; the development of this faculty causes that one to be checked in its growth, and it is impossible to alter any single particular without disturbing the entire machinery. We may wish that one quality or another was different than it is, but we can readily comprehend that any decided change is out of the question. We may wish our poet had stronger personality, a more manly temperament, and more mental equilibrium; but we have no difficulty in understanding that the lack of defined personality, and the incompleteness of the character whose acquaintance we make in "The Story of my Life," stand in the most intimate relationship with the nature of his endowments. A less receptive mind would not be so susceptible to poetic impressions, a harder one would not unite so much flexibility with its more rigid attitude, one more susceptible to criticism and philosophy would not be so naïve.

Since, then, the moral attributes are requisite to the intellectual, so, too, they are mutually contingent one upon the other. An overflowing lyric sentiment, an exalted sensibility, cannot exist with the experience and method of a man of the world, for experience chills and hardens. A lightly vaulting fancy that hops and soars like a bird, does not admit of being united with the logically measured crescendo and decrescendo of dramatic action. An observation by no means inclined to be cold-blooded cannot possibly penetrate psychologically to the heart of things; a childlike, easily quivering hand cannot dissect a villian. If, therefore, we place genius of this kind face to face with sundry defined and well-known types of art, we can determine beforehand precisely what its relations with each of them will be.

The romance is a species of poetic creation which demands of the mind that would accomplish anything remarkable in it, not only imagination and sentiment, but the keen understanding, and the cool, calm power of observation of the man of the world; that is the reason why it is not altogether suited to Andersen, although it is not wholly remote from his talent. In the entire scenery, the background of nature, the picturesque effect of the costumes, he is successful; but where psychological insight is concerned, traces of his weakness may be detected. He will take part for and against his characters; his men are not manly enough, his women not sufficiently feminine. I know no poet whose mind is more devoid of sexual distinctions, whose talent is less of a nature to betray a defined sex, than Andersen's. Therefore his strength lies in portraying children, in whom the conscious sense of sex is not yet prominent. The whole secret lies in the fact that he is exclusively what he is,— not a man of learning, not a thinker, not a standard-bearer, not a champion, as many of our great writers have been, but simply a poet. A poet is a man who is at the same time a woman. Andersen sees most forcibly in man and in woman that which is elementary, that which is common to humanity, rather than that which is peculiar and interesting. I have not forgotten how well he has described the deep feeling of a mother in "The Story of a Mother," or how tenderly he has told the story of the spiritual life of a woman in "The Little Sea-Maid." I simply recognize the fact that what he has represented is not the complicated spiritual conditions of life and of romance, but the element of life; he rings changes on single, pure tones, which amid the confused harmonies and disharmonies of life, appear neither so pure nor so distinct as in his books. Upon entering into the service of the nursery story all sentiments undergo a process of simplification, purification, and transformation. The character of man is farthest removed from the comprehension of the poet of childhood, and I can only recall a single passage in his stories in which a delicate psychological characteristic of a feminine soul may be encountered, and even this appears so innocently that we feel inclined to ask if it did not write itself. It occurs in the story of the new porcelain figures, "The Shepherdess and the Chimney-Sweep."

'Have you really courage to go forth with me into the wide world?' asked the chimney-sweep, tenderly. 'Have you considered how large it is, and that we can never come back here again?' 'I have,' said she. And the chimney-sweep gazed fixedly upon her, and then he said: 'My way lies up the chimney. Have you really courage to go with me through the stove, and to creep through all the flues?' . . . [And he led her towards the door of the stove.] 'It looks quite black,' said she, but still she went with him and on through all the intricacies of the interior, and through the flues, where a pitchy darkness reigned. [After long, long troublesome ascent they reached the top of the chimney and seated themselves on its edge.] The heaven and all its stars were above them, and all the roofs of the town below them; they could see far around, far away into the world. The poor shepherdess had never pictured it to herself thus; she leaned her little head on her sweep, and wept so bitterly that all the gilding of her girdle came off. 'O this is too much!' said she; 'I cannot bear it. This world is too large. O were I but again on the little table under the looking-glass! I shall never be happy till I am there again. I have followed you into the wide world; now, if you really love me, you may follow me home again.'

A more profound, more mercilessly true, more self-evident analysis of a certain kind of feminine enthusiasm and its energy when it undertakes to act boldly without regard to consequences, and without looking backwards,

can be found, I think, in the works of no other Danish
writer. What delicacy of presentation: the momentary
resolute enthusiasm, the heroic conquering of the first horror, the endurance, bravery, firmness, until the moment
which requires courage, when the firmness is shattered, and
the yearning for the little table under the looking-glass is
awakened. Many a voluminous romance would have been
exalted by such a page, and we find in it a compensation
for the fact that Andersen is no master in the province of
the romance.

The drama is a species of poetic production that requires
the faculty for differentiating an idea and distributing it
among many characters; it requires an understanding of
conscious action, a logic power to guide this, an eye to the
situation, a passion for becoming absorbed and overwhelmed
in the inexhaustible study of individual, many-sided characters. Therefore it is that the drama is still farther removed from the genius of Andersen than the romance, and
that his lack of capacity for the dramatic style increases
with mathematical exactness in the same ratio as each
variety of dramatic art is removed from the nursery story,
and consequently from his gifts. He naturally succeeds
best with the nursery-story comedy; although, to be sure, it
possesses little more of comedy than the name. It is a
mixed species, and if it were put to the test of the Spanish
story, it would be recognized as a bastard. In the comedy
of special situations he is happy with respect to the poetic
execution of single scenes ("The King's Dream"), but
singularly unfortunate in the execution of the idea as a
whole ("The Pearl of Good Fortune"). The comedy
proper is not poorly suited to his gifts. Certain of his
nursery stories are, indeed, veritable Holberg comedies;
"The Happy Family" is a Holberg character-comedy, and
"It is Quite True" possesses a decided Holberg plot. In
stories of this kind character delineation comes easier to
him than in the grave drama, for in them he walks directly
in the footsteps of Holberg, so strikingly does his talent
accord in a single direction with that of this early Northern
dramatist. Andersen is, as I have already remarked, no

direct psychologist; he is rather a biologist than an especially well-informed student of human nature. His predilection is for describing man through animals or plants, and seeing him develop from the rudiments of his nature. All art contains an answer to the question, What is man? Inquire of Andersen how he defines man, and he will reply, Man is a swan hatched in the "duck-yard" of Nature.

To a person who takes an interest in psychological investigations, who, without being able to grasp a complex character, possesses a refined development of observation for single qualities, for characteristic peculiarities, animals, especially those with which we are familiar, afford great relief. We are usually accustomed to credit each animal with an individual attribute, or at all events, with a limited group of attributes. The snail is slow, the nightingale is the unpretending singer with the glorious voice, the butterfly is the fair inconstant one. There is nothing then to prevent the poet who possesses the gifts needed to represent these striking little traits, from following in the footsteps of Holberg, the man who wrote "Den Vægelsindede" (The Fickle One), as Andersen did in "The New Lying-In Room." He betrays here, moreover, one of his many points of similarity with Dickens, whose comic characterizations are frequently limited to a few traits repeated *ad infinitum*.

In the epopee, which belongs in our day to the impossible forms of poetry and which demands all the qualities that Andersen lacks, he can merely find play for certain petty fancies, as for instance, when he characterizes the spirit of China, in his "Ahasuerus," in a droll lyric episode, or when he permits the twittering swallows (exactly as in a nursery story) to describe the festal hall of Attila.

In his descriptions of travel very naturally a large number of his best qualities come to light. Like his favorite, the migratory bird, he is in his element when he travels. He observes with the eye of a painter, and he describes like an enthusiast. Yet even here two faults are apparent: one is that his lyric tendency at times runs away with him, so that he chants a hymn of praise instead of giving a description, or exaggerates instead of painting (see, for instance, the gushing and untrue description of Ragatz and Pfäffers); the other, that the underlying, personal, egotistical element of his nature, giving evidence that his innermost personality lacks reserve, occasionally obtrudes itself in a most disturbing manner.

The latter tendency characterizes with especially marked force the style of his autobiography. The criticism that can with justice be made on his "Story of My Life" is not so much that the author is throughout occupied with his own private affairs (for that is quite natural in such a work); it is that his personality is scarcely ever occupied with anything greater than itself, is never absorbed in an idea, is never entirely free from the ego. The revolution of 1848 in this book affects us as though we heard some one sneeze; we are astonished to be reminded by the sound that there is a world outside of the author.

In lyric poetry Andersen has met with foreign success— even Chamisso has translated some of his songs; yet I am always loathe to see him lay aside his bright colored, realistic prose dress, that is so true to nature, in order to veil himself in the more uniform mantle of verse. His prose has fancy, unrestrained sentiment, rhythm, and melody. Why, then, cross the brook to find water? His poems, too, are frequently distinguished by a peaceful and childlike spirit, a warm and gentle sentiment. We see that the result of his attempts in the different regions of poetry proceeds quite directly, like the unknown x in mathematics, from the nature of his talents on one side, and the nature of the kind of poetic creation he has chosen on the other.

Thus the nursery story remains his sole individual creation, and for it he requires no patent, since no one is likely to rob him of it. In Andersen's day it was a common thing to attempt to classify all kinds of poetic creations with their varieties in an æsthetic system, according to the method of Hegel; and Hegel's Danish disciple, Heiberg, projected a complicated system in which the rank of the comedy, the tragedy, the romance, the nursery story, etc., was definitely fixed, while to Heiberg's own art-form an especially high rank was accorded. It is, however, in a certain measure pedantic to speak of general classes of art. Every creative artist thoroughly individualizes his own species of art. The form which he has used, no other has it in his power to use. So it is with the nursery story, whose theory Andersen made no attempt to describe, whose place in the system there has been no effort to establish, and which I, for one, should take good care not to define. There is, indeed, something very curious about æsthetic systematic classification; it impresses one very much in the same way as division of rank in the State: the more one broods over it, the more heretical one becomes. Perhaps this arises from the fact that to think is in the main synonymous with becoming a heretic. Yet like every natural type, Andersen's nursery story has its individual character, and his theories are comprised in the law it obeys, whose boundaries it may not overstep without bringing to light a monster. Everything in the world has its law, even that species of poetry which transcends the laws of nature.

Andersen somewhere remarks, that he has made attempts in pretty much every radiation of the nursery story. This remark is striking and good. His nursery stories form a complete whole, a web with manifold radiations, that seems to address the beholder in the words of the spider's web in "Aladdin," "See how the threads can become entwined in the delicate net!" If it will not seem too much like bringing the dust of the schoolroom into the parlor, I should like to call the reader's attention to a celebrated scientific work in Adolf Zeising's "Æsthetic Investigations," in which can be found a complete series of æsthetic contrasts, in all their different phases (the beautiful, the comic, the tragic, the humorous, the touching, etc.), arranged in one great star, just as Andersen has planned in respect to his nursery stories.

The form of fancy and the method of narration in the nursery story admit the treatment of the most heterogeneous materials in the most varied tones. Within its province may be found sublime narratives, as "The Bell"; profound and wise stories, as "The Shadow"; fantastically bizarre, as "The Elfin Mound"; merry, almost wanton ones, as

"The Swineherd," or "The Leap Frog"; humorous ones, as "The Princess on the Pea," "Good Humor," "The False Collar," "The Lovers"; also stories with a tinge of melancholy, as "The Constant Tin Soldier"; deeply pathetic poetic creations, as "The Story of a Mother"; oppressively dismal, as "The Red Shoes"; touching fancies, as "The Little Sea-Maid"; and those of mingled dignity and playfulness, as "The Snow Queen." Here we encounter an anecdote like "A Great Sorrow," which resembles a smile through tears, and an inspiration like "The Muse of the Coming Age," in which we feel the pinion strokes of history, the heart-throbs and pulse-beats of the active, stirring life of the present, as violent as in a fever, and yet as healthy as in a happy moment of enthusiastic inspiration.[7] In short, we find everything that lies between the epigram and the hymn.

Is there, then, a boundary line which limits the nursery story, a law which binds it? If so, where does it lie? The law of the nursery story lies in the nature of the nursery story, and its nature is dependent on that of poetry. If, at the first moment, it would seem that nothing is prohibited a species of poetic creation which can permit a princess to feel a pea through twenty mattresses and twenty eiderdown beds, it is but a semblance. The nursery story, which unites unbridled freedom of invention with the restraint its central idea impresses upon it, must steer between two rocks: between the luxuriance of style that lacks ideas, and dry allegory; it must strike the medium course between too great fulness and too great meagreness. This, Andersen most frequently succeeds in doing, and yet not always. Those of his stories that are based on materials derived from

[7] There is not a single Danish poet, who, to such a degree as Andersen, has scorned to produce effect through the romance of the past; even in the nursery story, which from the beginning has been handled by the romantic school of Germany in a manner that can be compared with the style of the Middle Ages, he is always solely and entirely in the *present*. He, as well as Oersted, dares to sacrifice the interesting element in his enthusiasm for King John and his time, and he heartily joins with Ovid in exclaiming,—

Prisca juvent alios! ego me nunc denique natum
Gratulor. Haec aetas moribus apta meis.—ARS. AMAT. III. 121.

folk-lore, as "The Flying Trunk," or those that may be classed with the fairy-tale proper, as "Thumbling," do not attract grown people as they do children, because the story in such instances conceals no thought. In his "Garden of Paradise" everything preceding the entrance to the garden is masterly, but the Fairy of Paradise herself seems to me to be invested with little, if any, beauty or charm. The opposite extreme is when we see the barren intention, the dry precept, through the web of poetic creation; this fault, as might be expected in our reflecting and conscious age, is one of more frequent occurrence. We feel it keenly because the nursery story is the realm of the unconscious. Not only are unconscious beings and objects the leaders of speech in it, but what triumphs and is glorified in the nursery story is this very element of unconsciousness. And the nursery story is right; for the unconscious element is our capital and the source of our strength. The reason why the travelling companion could receive aid from the dead man, was because he had entirely forgotten that he had formerly helped this same dead man, and even simple Hans gains the princess and half the kingdom, because with all his folly he is so exceedingly naïve. Even stupidity has its genial side and its good luck; with the poor intermediate beings, the Nureddin natures alone, the nursery story knows not what to do.

Let us consider some instances of sins against the unconscious. In the beautiful story of "The Snow Queen" a most disturbing influence is exercised by the scene where the Snow Queen requests little Kay to make figures with the ice puzzle for the understanding, and he is unable to represent the word "Eternity." There is also clumsy and unpoetic bluntness in "The Neighboring Families" whenever the sparrow's family mention the rose by the abstract, and for a sparrow rather unnatural, term, "the beautiful." It would have been understood, without this hint, that the roses were the representatives of the beautiful in the narrative, and in encountering this abstract word in the nursery story we recoil as though we had come into contact with a slimy frog.

This tendency to allegory in narratives for children appears most frequently, as might be expected, in the form of instruction and moralizing; in some of the nursery stories, as in "The Buckwheat," the pedagogic element plays an exaggerated rôle. In others, as "The Flax," we feel too strongly at the conclusion—as in Jean Paul—the tendency to exhibit, in season and out of season, the doctrine of immortality. Toward the end of the latter story a few little, somewhat "insipid beings" are created who announce that the song is never done. In some cases finally the tendency is more personal. A whole series of stories ("The Duckling," "The Nightingale," "The Neighboring Families," "The Daisy," "The Snail and The Rose-Tree," "Pen and Inkstand," "The Old Street Lamp") allude to the poet's life and the poet's lot, and in single cases we see traces—a rare exception with Andersen—of invention being dragged in forcibly in order to bring out the tendency. What sense and what conformity to nature is there, for instance, in the fact that the street lamp can only let others see the beautiful and symbolic sights that had been interwoven with its experience when it is provided with a wax candle, and that its faculties are useless when provided with an ordinary light? It is quite incomprehensible until we conceive it to be an allegory on a poet's supposed need of prosperity in order to accomplish anything. "And so genius must run after cupboard lore!" wrote Kierkegaard on the occasion of the appearance of "Only a Fiddler." Still more infelicitous is the scene where the street lamp, in its melted-down condition, in its other life, finds its way to a poet and thus fulfils its destiny. So strongly as this the tendency has rarely shown itself.

The first duty of the nursery story is to be poetic, its second to preserve the marvellous element. Therefore, it is first of all necessary that the order of the legendary world be sacred to it. What in the language of legendary lore is regarded as a fixed rule, must be respected by the nursery story, however unimportant it may be in relation to the laws and rules of the real world. Thus it is quite inappropriate for the nursery story, as in Andersen's "The

Dryad," to part its heroine from her tree, to let her make a symbolic journey to Paris, to go to the "bal Mabille," etc., for it is not more impossible for all the kings of the earth to place the smallest leaf on a nettle than it is for legendary lore to tear a dryad away from its tree. But in the second place, it lies in the nature of the nursery story form that its outline can frame nothing that, in order to obtain its poetic rights, requires a profound psychological description, an earnest development, such as would be adapted either to the nature of the drama or the romance. A woman like Marie Grubbe, a sketch of whose interesting life Andersen gives us in the story of "Chicken-Grethe," is too much of a character for it to be possible for the author of the nursery story to describe or interpret; when he attempts to do so, we feel a disproportion between the object and the form.[8] There is less occasion, however, to marvel at these few blemishes than at the fact that they so very rarely occur. I have only called attention to them because it is interesting to become acquainted with the boundary lines by observing how they have been overstepped, and because it seemed to me more important to ascertain how the Pegasus of the nursery story, notwithstanding all its freedom to race and fly through the circle, has its firm tether in the centre.

Its beauty, its strength, its power of flight, and its grace, we do not see by observing its limits, but by following its many and bold movements within its circle. Upon this fact we will in conclusion cast a glance. The nursery story field lies before us like a large, rich flowery plain. Let us freely stroll about this, let us cross it in all directions, now plucking a flower here, now there, rejoicing in its coloring, its beauty, its *tout-ensemble*. These brief little poetic creations stand in the same relation to the poetry of greater compass as little flowers to the trees of the forest. Whoever on a beautiful day in spring takes a walk in a forest by the seaside in order to view the beeches in their youthful splendor, with their brown velvety buds encased in light green silk,

[8] Her life was used later as the historic foundation for the brilliant romance "Fru Marie Grubbe," by J. P. Jacobsen.

and after gazing aloft for awhile bends his eyes downward to the earth, will find that the carpet of the forest is as beautiful as its ceiling of tree-tops. Here grow in lowly state many colored anemones, white and dark red mayflowers, yellow stars of Bethlehem, and saxifrage, starwort, buttercups and dandelions. Near together are the buds, the full-blown flowers, and those which already bear seed, the virgin and the fecundated plants, the flowers without fragrance and those with pleasant perfume, the poisonous, and the useful, the healing weed. Frequently the plant which takes the humblest place in the system, as the flowerless fern, is the most beautiful to the eye. Flowers which seem to be complex prove on closer scrutiny to consist of very few leaves, and plants whose bloom seems to be one flower, bear on their top a wealth of blossoms only united by the stalk. So, too, it is with the nursery stories. Those which in respect to their worth seem the most insignificant, as "The Leap-Frog," often contain a whole life philosophy in a nutshell, and those which appear to be a single whole, as "The Galoshes of Fortune," are often composed of a loosely united cluster of blossoms. Some are in the bud, as "The Drop of Water"; others are about bursting the seeds, as "The Jewish Girl," or "The Stone of the Wise Men." Some consist of but a single point, as "The Princess on the Pea"; others have grand, noble form, as "The Story of a Mother," a tale that is a special favorite in India, and that resembles that tropical flower, the calla, which in its sublime simplicity consists of but a single leaf.

I open the book at random, and my eye falls on "The Elfin Mound." What life and what humor! "In the kitchen there was a great quantity of frogs among the dishes; adders' skins, with little children's fingers inside; salad of mushroom-seed; wet mice's snouts and hemlock, . . . rusty nails and church-window glass were among the delicacies and kickshaws." Does any one think that the children are forgotten here? By no means. "The old Elfin King had his golden crown polished with powdered slate-pencil. It was the pencil of the head scholar; and to obtain this one is very difficut for the Elfin King." Does

any one think there is nothing here for grown people? A
still greater mistake! "O how I long to see the old Northern
Elf! His sons, people say, are coarse, blustering fellows
..." They "went with open throats, for they disdained
the cold." What a banquet! The skeleton horse is
among the invited guests. Does any one think that Andersen
would forget the character of the guests at a festal
gathering? "The Elfin maidens were now to dance, simple
as well as stamping dances ... Confound it! their legs
grew so long, one did not know which was the beginning
nor which was the end, one could not distinguish legs from
arms; all was twirling about in the air like sawdust; and
they went whizzing round to such a degree that the Skeleton
Horse grew quite sick, and was obliged to leave the table."
Andersen is acquainted with the nervous system of the
skeleton horse, and is mindful of his weak stomach.

He has the genuine gift for creating supernatural beings,
in modern times so rare. How deeply symbolical and how
natural it is, for instance, that the little sea-maid, when
her fish-tail shrivelled up and became "the prettiest pair of
white feet a little girl could have," should feel as though
she were treading on pointed needles and sharp knives at
every step she took! How many poor women tread on
sharp knives at every step they take, in order to be near
him whom they love, and are yet far from being the most
unhappy of women!

What a splendidly drawn band is that multitude of
sprites in "The Snow Queen," what a superb symbol the
witches' mirror, and how thoroughly the author has comprehended
this queen herself, who, sitting in the midst of
the desert snow field, had imbibed all its cold beauty!
This woman is to a certain degree related to Night, one of
Andersen's peculiarly characteristic creations. It is not
Thorwaldsen's mild, sleep-bringing night, not Carstens'
venerable, motherly night; it is black, gloomy, sleepless,
and awful night. "Out in the snow sat a woman in long
black garments, and she said, 'Death has been with you in
your room; I saw him hasten away with your child; he
strides faster than the wind, and never brings back what

he has taken away.' 'Only tell me which way he has gone,' said the mother. 'Tell me the way, and I will find him.' 'I know him,' said the woman in the black garments; 'but before I tell you, you must sing me all the songs that you have sung to your child. I love those songs; I have heard them before. I am Night, and I saw your tears when you sang them.' 'I will sing them all, all!' said the mother. 'But do not detain me, that I may overtake him, and find my child.' But Night sat dumb and still. Then the mother wrung her hands, and sang, and wept. And there were many songs, but yet more tears." Then the mother journeys onward, weeps out her eyes in order that for this price she may be borne to the opposite shore, and in the great hot-house of Death gives her long black hair to an old gray-haired woman in exchange for the old woman's white hair.

We meet with a countless multitude of fanciful creations, little elf-like divinities, such as Ole Shut-Eye (the sandman), or the goblins with the red caps, and the northern dryad, the Elder-Tree Mother. We feel Andersen's strength when we compare it with the weakness of the contemporary Danish poets in this respect. What pale forms are not Heilberg's Pomona, Astræa, or Fata Morgana! Andersen invests even a shadow with a body. What says the shadow? What does it say to its master? "I, as you know well, have from a child followed in your footsteps." This is true. "We have grown up together from childhood." This is not less true, and when after his call he takes his leave, he says, "Farewell! here is my card; I live on the sunny side of the street, and am always at home in rainy weather."[9] Andersen is familiar with the shadow's pangs of yearning, its customs, and its delights. "I ran about the streets in the moonlight; I made myself long

---

[9] Here, as everywhere, the poet has his faithful allies in language, in the play of words, which dance forward under his pen as soon as he places it on paper. We see, for instance, what a swarm there is in "The Old Street Lamp" or "The Snow Man." We see how he avails himself of the sound-language of animals, for instance. "'Quack!' said the little toad, and that means the same as when men say 'Alack!'"

up the walls—it tickles the back so delightfully!" The story of the shadow, which by no means reminds us of Chamisso, is a little world in itself. I do not hesitate to pronounce it one of the greatest master novels in Danish literature. It is the epopee of all shadows, of all people who are feeble imitations, of all those characters that lack originality and individuality, all those who imagine that through mere emancipation from their prototypes they can attain independence, personality, and true, genuine, human existence. It is also one of the few stories in which the poet, in spite of his tender-hearted optimism, has ventured to allow a hideous truth to stand forth in its entire nakedness. The shadow resolves, in order to insure himself against all revelations concerning his past, to take the man's life. " 'Poor Shadow!' (that is the man) said the Princess; 'he is very unfortunate; it would be a real work of charity to deliver him from the little life he has; and when I think properly over the matter, I am of opinion that it will be necessary to do away with him in all stillness!' 'It is certainly hard!' said the Shadow, 'for he was a faithful servant!' and then he gave a sort of a sigh. 'You are a noble character!' said the Princess." This story is one of those in which the transition from the natural to the supernatural can most readily be observed. The shadow worked its way up "so as to become its own master," until it seems quite natural that it should at last make itself free.

We close the book, and open it again at another place. Here we meet with "The Leap-Frog." A brief and comprehensive treatise on life. The main characters are a Flea, a Grasshopper and a Leap-Frog, made of the breastbone of a goose; the king's daughter is the prize for the highest jumper. "Pay heed, all of you," says the muse of the nursery story. "Spring with understanding. It is of no use to jump so high that no one can see you; for then the rabble will insist that it would have been as well not to have jumped at all. Only look at all the greatest minds, thinkers, poets, and men of science. For the multitude it is the same as though they had not jumped at all; they reap

no harvest of reward, a body is needed for that. Neither is
it of any use to spring high and well, for those who spring
right into the face of the Powers that be. In this way, forsooth, a person would never make a career. No; take the
Leap-Frog for a model. He is almost apoplectic; first of
all he has the appearance of one that cannot jump at all,
and many motions he certainly cannot make either; nevertheless, he makes—with the instinct of stupidity, with the
dexterity of indolence—a little side-jump, into the lap of
the princess. Take example from this; he has shown that
he has understanding." What a pearl of a nursery story!
and what a faculty for making psychological use of animals! It cannot be denied that the reader is at times inclined to cherish a doubt as to what this fancy of permitting
animals to speak can signify. It is one thing whether we
readers feel that it strikes home to us, and then whether
the character of the animal is really hit, the animal that
has not one human quality. Meanwhile, we can readily
comprehend that it is impossible to speak of animals, even
in a purely scientific way, without attributing to them
qualities with which we are familiar through our own
nature. How, for instance, could we avoid painting the
wolf as cruel? Andersen's skill only consists in producing a poetic, a striking seeming conformity between the
animal and its human attributes. How true it is when the
cat says to little Rudy: "Come out upon the roof with me,
little Rudy. It is all nonsense to fancy one must fall down;
you won't fall unless you are afraid; come, set one of your
paws here, the other there, and take care of yourself with
the rest of your paws! Keep a sharp lookout, and be active
in your limbs. If there be a hole, spring over it, and keep
a firm footing as I do." How natural it is when the old
snail says: "You need not be in a hurry—but you always
hurry so, and the little one is beginning just the same way.
Has he not been creeping up that stalk these three days?
My head quite aches when I look up at him." What finer
description of a lying-in room than the story of the hatch-
ing of the young duckling? What more probable than that

the sparrows, when they want to abuse their neighbors, should call them "those thick-headed roses."[10]

One story I have reserved until the end; I will now search for it, for it is, as it were, the crown of Andersen's work. It is the story of "The Bell," in which the poet of naïveté and nature has reached the pinnacle of his poetic muse. We have seen his talent for describing in a natural way that which is superhuman, and that which is below the human. In this story he stands face to face with nature herself. It treats of the invisible bell which the children, who had just been confirmed, went out into the wood to seek—young people in whose breasts yearning for the invisible, alluring, and wondrous voices of nature was still fresh. The king of the country had "vowed that he who could discover whence the sounds proceeded should have the title of 'Universal Bell-ringer,' even if it were not really a bell. Many persons now went to the wood, for the sake of getting the place, but one only returned with a sort of explanation; for nobody went far enough; that one not farther than the others. However, he said that the sound proceeded from a very large owl, in a hollow tree; a sort of learned owl, that continually knocked its head against the branches. . . . So now he got the place of 'Universal Bell-ringer,' and wrote yearly a short treatise 'on the Owl'; but everybody was just as wise as before." The children who had been confirmed go out this year also, and "they hold each other by the hand; for, as yet, they had none of them any high office." But soon they begin to grow weary, one by one, and some of them return to town, one for one reason, another on another pretext. An entire class of them linger by a small bell in an idyllic little house, without considering, as the few constant ones, that so small a bell could not possibly cause so enticing a play of tones, but that it must give "very different tones from

[10] Compare, for the sake of antithesis, the method and form of the speech of the glove, the neckerchief, the flask, in Heiberg's "Christmas Pastimes and New Year's Farces"; furthermore Alfred de Musset's "Le merle blanc," and Taine's "Vie et opinions philosophiques d'un chat," in his work, "Voyage aux Pyréneés."

those that could move a human breast in such a manner"; and with the small hope, their small yearning, they betake themselves to rest near their small discovery, the small bell, the small idyllic joy. I fancy the reader must have met some of these children after they were grown up. Finally but two remain, a king's son and a poor little boy in wooden shoes, and "with so short a jacket that one could see what long wrists he had." On the way they parted; for one wished to seek the bell on the right, the other on the left. The king's son sought the bell in the road that lay "on the side where the heart is placed"; the poor boy sought it in the opposite direction. We follow the king's son, and we read admiringly of the mystic splendor with which the poet has invested the region, in altering and exchanging the natural coloring of the flowers. "But on he went, without being disheartened, deeper and deeper into the wood, where the most wonderful flowers were growing. There stood white lilies with blood-red stamens; sky-blue tulips, which shone as they moved in the winds; and the apple-trees, the apples of which looked exactly like large soap-bubbles: so only think how the trees must have sparkled in the sunshine!" The sun goes down; the king's son begins to fear that he will be surprised by night; he climbs upon a rock in order to see the sun once more before it disappears in the horizon. Listen to the poet's song of praise:——

And he seized hold of the creeping-plants, and the roots of trees,—climbed up the moist stones where the water-snakes were writhing, and the toads were croaking,—and he gained the summit before the sun had quite gone down. How magnificent was the night from this height! The sea—the great, the glorious sea, that dashed its long waves against the coast —was stretched out before him. And yonder, where sea and sky meet, stood the sun, like a large, shining altar, all melted together in the most glowing colors. And the wood and the sea sang a song of rejoicing, and his heart sang with the rest: all nature was a vast, holy church, in which the trees and buoyant clouds were the pillars; flowers and grass the velvet carpeting; and heaven itself the large cupola. The red colors above faded away as the sun vanished, but a million stars were lighted, a million diamond lamps shone; and the king's son

spread out his arms toward heaven, and wood, and sea; when
at the same moment, coming by a path to the right, appeared,
in his wooden shoes, and short-sleeved jacket, the poor boy who
had been confirmed with him. He had followed his own path,
and had reached the spot just as soon as the son of the king
had done. They ran toward each other, and stood together,
hand in hand, in the vast church of nature and of poetry, while
over them sounded the invisible, holy bell; blessed spirits floated
around them, and lifted up their voices in a rejoicing hallelujah.

Genius is the wealthy king's son, its attentive follower
the poor boy; but art and science, although they may have
parted on their way, meet in their enthusiasm, and their
devotion to the divine, universal soul of nature.

II

PAUL HEYSE

1875

"How does it happen," I asked recently of a distinguished portrait-painter, "that you, who formerly have made successful efforts in several other branches of art, have at last confined yourself wholly to portrait-painting?"

"I think it is because it has given me the most pleasure," replied he, "to study and to perpetuate an object which has never existed before, and will never appear again."

With these words he seemed to me strikingly to designate the interest which attracts a person to distinct individuality, that of the inner as well as that of the outer being. To the critic, too, the individual is an especially alluring object; to him, too, the execution of a portrait is a singularly fascinating occupation. Unfortunately, his means of communication are deplorably far behind those of the painter. What can be more difficult and more fruitless than the attempt to express in words that which is purely individual—that which in accordance with its very nature must mock at every effort of reproduction? Is not personality, in its uninterrupted flow, the true *perpetuum mobile*, which does not admit of being constructed?

And yet these insolvable problems ever charm and attract anew. After we have gradually become familiar with an author, have come to feel ourselves perfectly at home in his writings, to perceive dimly that certain of their characteristics dominate others, and then happen to be by nature of a critical turn of mind, we can find no peace until we have rendered ourselves an account of our impressions, and made clear the indistinct image of the character of another *ego* that has arisen within our own soul. We hear or read criticisms on an author and find them absurd. Why are they absurd? Other statements seem to us but half true. What is lacking to make them wholly true? A new work of importance from his pen appears. How far have the earlier works been a preparation for it? We almost become curious to learn how we ourselves would characterize his talent—and we satisfy our curiosity.

I

Whoever casts a glance on the long row of closely printed volumes which form Paul Heyse's complete works, and remembers that the author was born in the year 1830, will first of all be apt to exclaim, "What industry!" Involuntarily he will trace back this astonishing productiveness to a will power of rare endurance. None the less, however, does it owe its origin to a singularly fortunate nature. This nature possessed within itself so luxuriant a fruitfulness that it has yielded its harvest without the least effort of the will, without any undue exertion; it has yielded a harvest of such variety that we might believe it to be fostered according to a defined plan and with a painstaking will; nevertheless, it has obviously been permitted to act with thorough independence. To allow nature to rule, to follow one's own pleasure or bent (sich gehen zu lassen[1]), has been from the outset, as we soon come to feel, Heyse's motto, and so it happens that with qualities which usually lead to a wandering scanty, fragmentary productiveness, he has completed and perfected each undertaking, having written lyric and epic poems, one grand epos (Thekla), a dozen dramas, more than fifty "novellen," and two large romances. He began early; while yet a student, he entered on his literary career. Free from care as a pedestrian tourist who gayly whistles as he strolls along, never hurrying, pausing to drink at every spring, lingering before the bushes by the wayside, and plucking flowers as well as

[1] One's movements, step by step to measure,
 Mars all one's chances.
Who dares not follow one's own pleasure (sich gehen zu lassen)
 Not far advances.—*P. H.*

berries, resting in the shade, and wandering along in the shade, he has gradually trodden a pathway of such extent that we could only expect to see it traversed by one who maintained a breathless march, with eyes fixed unwaveringly on the goal.

The voice followed by Heyse as an author is unquestionably the voice of instinct. North German though he is, nothing is farther removed from him than cool deliberation and premeditation. Born in Berlin, he nevertheless takes root in Munich, and finds in the ardent South German race and in the throbbing South German life the surroundings most congenial to his temperament; at home in South Germany, he yet feels constantly drawn to Italy, as the land where the human plant has attained a more beautiful and luxuriant growth than elsewhere, one that is less disturbed by reflex action, and where the voice of the blood speaks most distinctly, most powerfully. This voice is the siren voice which allures Heyse. Nature! Nature! keeps ringing in his ear. Germany has authors who appear almost wholly devoid of inspiration, and who have only been made what they are by a vigorous North German will (as Karl Gutzkow, for instance); others (as Fanny Lewald) whose works bear the impress of an active North German intellect. Neither through volition nor deliberation does Heyse create and fashion his works, but simply by heeding the inner impulse.

Many an author is tempted to impart to his reader an idea of himself differing somewhat from the correct one. He takes pleasure in representing himself as that which he *would like* to be,—in former times, as being endowed either with keener sensibilities or deeper melancholy than he ever possessed, in our day as being now more experienced, now colder or harsher, than he really is. More than one distinguished author, as Mérimée, or Leconte de Lisle, has so shrunk from manifesting his emotions that he has succeeded, on the other hand, in exhibiting an appearance of lack of feeling by no means natural to him. Such people make it a point of honor not to breathe freely and easily until they have crossed the snow-line where the human element in our natures ends, and their contempt for those who lay claim to the sympathy of the multitude on the plane below leads them to yield to the temptation to force their way up to a height whither pride, not instinct, bids them ascend. For Heyse this temptation does not exist. He has never for a moment been able or willing to write himself into either greater warmth or coldness than he actually felt. He has never professed to be writing with his heart's blood when he was fashioning calmly as an artist, and he has patiently submitted when the critics censured him for lack of warmth. On the other hand, he has never been able to report, as so many of the most eminent French authors have done, a horrible or revolting occurrence with the same stoic tranquillity, and in the same tone that would be suitable in stating where a man of the world purchases his cigars, or where the best champagne could be obtained. He aims neither at the ardent style of passionate temperaments, nor at the self-control of the worldling. In comparison with Swinburne he seems rather cold, and in comparison with Flaubert naïve. But the narrow path in which he wanders is precisely that which is pointed out to him by the instinct of his innermost being, by the purely individual and yet so complicated being which is the result of his nature.

II

The power which an individual obeys as an artist, necessarily becomes the power which in his works is exalted to the place of honor. That is the reason why Heyse as an author glorifies nature. Not what a human being thinks or desires, but what he is by nature interests Heyse in him. The highest duty in his eyes is to honor nature and heed her voice. Sin against nature is the true sin. Give her free scope, and let her act her own pleasure.

There are, therefore, not many authors who are such marked fatalists as Heyse. In free will, according to the traditional sense of the word, he does not believe, and is evidently quite as sceptically opposed to Kant's categorical imperative as his Edwin or his Felix.[2] But if he does not believe in innate ideas, he does believe in innate instinct, and this instinct is sacred to him. In his "novellen" he has described how unhappy the soul feels when this instinct is either disturbed or rendered uncertain. In his "Kenne Dich Selbst" (Know Thyself) it is intelligence, in his "Reise nach dem Glück" (Journey after Happiness) it is morality that is the disturber of the peace.

In the first of these "novellen" Heyse has represented the anguish which proceeds from a too early or a premeditated invasion on the instinctive life of the soul. "That beautiful stupor of youth, that dreamy, unconscious plenitude of the powers, the pure faculty of enjoyment of the yet unexhausted sense, was lost to young Franz through his premature struggle for self-consciousness."[3] He here portrays the sleeplessness of the mind, which is as dangerous for the health of the soul as actual sleeplessness is for the welfare of the body, and shows how one in whom the reflex faculty is maimed "loses that mysterious, obscure substance which is the very pith and marrow of our personality."

In "Die Reise nach dem Glück" it is conventional morality, which by supplanting instinct has shattered the soul. A young girl, having conquered her own natural impulses from motives of inculcated morality, has banished her lover from her presence late at night, and thereby become the innocent cause of his death. The remembrance of this misfortune haunts her constantly. "If one's own heart does not point out the way, one is sure to go astray. Once before in my life I was made wretched because I refused to hearken to my heart, let it cry as loudly as it would. Now I will pay heed if it but whispers to me, and I will have ear for nothing else."[4]

In instinct the entire nature is present. Now if the inner devastation which results where instinct has lost its guiding power, be in Heyse's eyes the most profound of all misfortunes, to the characters he delights most in delineating, the

[2] Kinder der Welt, ii. 17. Im Paradiese, i. 31.
[3] Gesammelte Werke, iv. 135.
[4] Ibid., v. 199.

consciousness of life present the exact opposite; that is, the most profound sense of happiness in the enjoyment of the totality and harmony of their natures. Heyse, as a matter of course, is far removed from considering self-introspection as a principle inimical to the healthy sense of life. His own views appear to be about the same as those expressed by the invalid in "Kenne Dich Selbst" in the words: just as agreeable as it may be for him to awaken in the night, to consider and to know that he is able to sleep still longer, just so glorious it appears to him to arouse from his dreamy state of happiness, to collect his thoughts, to reflect, and then, as it were, to turn over on the other side and indulge in further enjoyment. At all events, in his romance "Kinder der Welt" (Children of the World), he has permitted Balder, the most ideally fashioned character in the book, to carry out this last thought in a still more significant way. Melancholy views have just been expressed, speculations regarding the sun which shines indifferently on the just and on the unjust, and looks down upon more wretchedness than happiness, and about the infinite, ever-recurring miseries of life, and more to like effect. Franzel, the young socialist printer, has been expatiating upon the opinion that one who had truly considered the lot of humanity, could never find rest or peace, and in his distress has called life a lie when Balder attempts to show him that a life in which repose was possible, would no longer deserve the name. And then Balder explains to Franzel in what the enjoyment of life for him consists; namely, in "experiencing past and future in one." With the utmost originality he declares that he could have no enjoyment if his experiences were incomplete, and that in his silent moments of contemplation all the scattered elements of his being were united in one harmonious whole. "Whenever I have wished to do so, that is to say, as often as I have desired to make for myself a genuine holiday of life and to enjoy to the utmost my little existence, I have, as it were, conjured up all the periods of my life at once: my laughing, sportive childhood, when I was yet strong and well, then the first glow of thought and feeling, the first pangs of youth, the foreboding of what a full, healthy, mature life must be, and at the same time the renunciation which usually becomes a habit only to very old people." To such a conception of life, human existence is not divided into moments, which vanish, leaving us to bemoan their disappearance, nor is it broken into fragments in the service of reciprocally contending impulses and thoughts; to one who possesses the faculty of casting out an anchor at any moment, of realizing the totality and reality of one's own being, life cannot lacerate like a bad dream. "Do you not think," says Balder, "that he who can generate within himself at any moment, if he but choose, such a fulness of the sense of existence, must consider it empty talk when people say, it were better never to have been born?"[5] It must be remembered that it is a cripple whose days are numbered, who utters these words; and a cripple, moreover, whom the poet has evidently modelled after the image of the so differently thinking Leopardi. The peculiar kind of epicurean philosophy expressed by them, and which, through a synthetic reflection, gathers together all time in the eternal present, is in reality the poet's conclusive conception of life. It is the hearkening of harmoniously planned nature to her own harmonies. The infinite gods make all their gifts to their favorites complete, all the infinite joys and all the infinite sorrows. This life-philosophy admits into its inner harmony even the discord of infinite pain, and succeeds in finding for it a satisfactory solution. Here is the point wherein Heyse most sharply differs from Turgenief and the other great modern pessimists of poetry. He makes bold to impute to his favorite characters even the most unlovely and shocking errors, in order that he may restore to them, after divers trials and afflictions, their inner peace. The young baron in the romance, "Im Paradiese" (In Paradise), is an instance of this. A sin against his better self weighs upon his conscience. He has lost that inner harmony with his own emotional nature, "on which everything depends." It becomes manifest in the course of the book that through this failing, he has, besides,

[5] Kinder der Welt, ii. 162.

transgressed against his best friend. Nevertheless, through all the mistakes and misfortunes, which are the inevitable result, he finds himself again. The harmony of nature was but temporarily set aside; not, as he had feared, hopelessly destroyed.

Instinct is directly the voice of the blood. Hence it comes that Heyse's characters are deeply rooted in family and race. Like the law of Moses, they seem to teach that the soul is in the blood. They follow the voice of the blood, and to it they appeal. The undeveloped ones among them are the vigorous expression of the type of a race; the developed ones know their own nature and respect it; they accept it as it is with the feeling that it cannot be altered; they are so thoroughly guided by the instinct of their natures as are the characters of Balzac by selfishness. In order to render clear my meaning, let me quote a few passages from the "Kinder der Welt." When Edwin falls passionately in love with Toinette, his brother Balder, unknown to him, goes to her to implore her not to reject his brother, through caprice or frivolity, and throw herself away on a stranger. Her answer to his appeal is that she has but just learned and comprehended wherefore it is that in her whole life she has never been able to gain happiness. She has been informed of the secret of her origin, namely, that her unhappy mother had been betrayed into her father's power through force, and from this fact she draws the certainty that it is impossible for her to love. "My friend," says she, "I feel sure you mean well by me, you and your brother, but it would be criminal in me to persuade myself that you could help me now that everything is so clear to me, and that I am convinced that my destiny irrevocably *lies in the blood.*" (The words are emphasized in the text.) This is in her eyes the last irrefutable argument. In all the characters of the book this respect for nature, almost bordering on superstition, is prominent. As it is with Toinette, so it is in the case of her opposite pole Lea. They are contrasts in every point; in this one particular alone they accord. After Lea, who has become the wife of Edwin, has learned how much power the memory of Toinette still exercises over his heart and is overpowered with grief at the discovery, she is one day reading a book by Edwin, and for a time consoling herself by considering how much she understands of his writings that would be above the comprehension of another woman, when suddenly she flings away the book, for the thought rushes through her brain "how powerless is all comprehension of *minds* in comparison with the blind, irrational elemental attraction of *natures* which enslaves all freedom and infatuates the wisest." She is a woman apparently of a purely intellectual mould. A lively, ardent desire for knowledge and for clearness of mental vision has led her to Edwin; he gave her instructions in—philosophy. One would therefore suppose that she, on her part, would at this crisis have attempted to combat the magic power of the blood by an appeal to the intellectual forces which have for so long united her with Edwin. On the contrary. Far from being characterized as all mind and soul, she is beyond all else a *nature*. She has always loved Edwin passionately, but she has feared that his love, less ardent than her own, would be made to recoil by outbursts of her passion, and yet she—the philosopher—has said to herself, in her loneliness: "Love is folly—blissful madness—laughter and weeping without sense or meaning. Thus I have always loved him until reason was lost and forgotten." Now that the happiness of her wedded life is at stake, she breaks out into the words: "If he perceives that the blood of my mother flows in my veins,—hot Old Testament blood, —perhaps he will discover that he made a grievous mistake when he thought that he could form with a such a being 'a marriage of reason.' Perhaps the day may come when I dare tell him everything, because he himself is no longer satisfied with a modest life-happiness, because he has come to demand something prouder, more unrestrained, more overwhelmingly profuse—and then I can say to him, 'You need not seek far; still waters are deep.' "[6] Everything is here characteristic, the tracing back to origin and race, as well as the protest of this ardent, passionate nature

[6] Kinder der Welt, iii. 210, 242, 256.

against the disguise of spontaneous passion as a reasonable sacrifice. Only those who are familiar with this fundamental trait of Heyse will have true comprehension of and interest in one of his dramas which might otherwise be considered his weakest, and which in many respects appears to me not wholly worthy of him; I mean "Die Göttin der Vernunft" (The Goddess of Reason). Is it not extremely singular that Heyse, with the whole gigantic French Revolution to choose from, should single out this theme of all others and treat it in precisely the way he has done? Many a poet in the selection of such a subject would have in view an organ for the pathos of the revolution, or would allow the purely ideal inspiration of the goddess of reason in the historic crisis to ennoble a past which, though frivolous and undignified, has nevertheless tragically avenged itself. Such a poet as Hamerling could no doubt make something appropriate out of the theme. Heyse, true to his temperament, paused awestruck before this apparition; a woman, a bit of nature, with feminine instincts and feminine passion, is proclaimed to be reason, the goddess of reason, that is to say, the dry, rigid, dead, rationalistic reason of the eighteenth century! Thereupon Heyse creates a fictitious woman who by virtue of the depth of her nature (upon the whole, far in advance of her time) is overpowered by the feeling that vast, all-embracing life does not admit of being traced back to any scholastic formula, a woman who loves and fears, suffers and hopes, who trembles for the life of her father and that of her lover, who in her anguish lest her lover should misunderstand her, falls into a state of despondency, who as a genuine child of her author has said: "To me the highest aim is to do nothing which causes me to be at variance with myself," and then permits this woman—her every fibre quivering with passion, in a frenzy of personal despair, without a thought of the universal and the abstract, of the Republic or of intellectual freedom, and while her father is being murdered before the church door—to be driven to proclaim from the altar the new gospel of reason, which she herself has once mockingly designated the world's law that two times two make four. This drama appears to me of far greater value as a contribution to the psychology of its author than from a poetic point of view.

Nevertheless, it would be an injustice to Heyse to infer from what has hitherto been made prominent, that he recognizes nothing higher than elemental nature and its impulses. By the word instinct is meant something wholly different from *isolated* impulses. Instinct is the inner need of being true to one's self. Therefore, it is that Heyse can consistently permit an independent sympathy to triumph over the ties of blood, and even over the closest bonds of relationship. In the novel "Der verlorene Sohn" (The Lost Son), a mother conceals, and tends unawares the innocent murderer of her son, and after he, through his amiability, has won the heart of the mother as well as that of the daughter, the poet makes him lead home the daughter as his bride. "The lost son" had been killed in honorable self-defence in the midst of great peril, and his opponent did not even know his name. Even when the mother learns the particulars concerning the death of her son, she places no hindrances on account of them in the way of the marriage, but bears alone, and without confiding her secret to a living mortal, the misfortune that has befallen her. Here, then, with the full accord of her character, a purely spiritual tie enters into the place of the ties of blood; the mother adopts as a son him through whose hand her own son has fallen; but in so doing she acts in harmony with the depths of her nature, and preserves her soul intact. It is the same in all cases where Heyse allows the personality, through considerations of duty, to repress a genuine passion, a deep love. Wherever this takes place (as in the drama "Marie Moroni," in the novelette "Die Pfadfinderin"—The Path-finder—or in the romance "Die Kinder der Welt") it is in order to maintain loyalty to self, in order not to forfeit the unity and healthfulness of the individual being, and duty may be seen to flow freely forth from the well-springs of one's own nature, inasmuch as the command not to be at variance with self is esteemed the highest law of duty. So far is Heyse removed from conceiving nature to be inimical to spirituality and duty.

In his eyes nature is all-embracing; everything that lies within the range of our possibilities, all that we perform or achieve, so far as it be of any value, bears infallibly her stamp, and over all which is not within our power, over our entire hereditary destiny, she rules directly, immediately, all-powerfully, and absolutely. Even the most unfortunate character which Heyse has portrayed, however badly fate may have dealt with him, finds consolation in the fact that he is a child of nature; that is to say, that he has not been shorn of his birthright. "If the elements of my being, which exclude me from happiness, have met and become intermingled through a great blind dispensation of the universe, and if I be doomed to ruin because of this combination, it is an unpleasant, but by no means an unendurable thought. On the other hand, a Heavenly Father, who *de cœur léger,* or perchance through pedagogic wisdom, would permit me, poor creature, to drift about so sorrowfully between heaven and earth, in order to accord me later a recompense throughout eternity, for my wasted time—no, dear friend, all the royal or unroyal theology in the world cannot make that seem plausible to me."[7]

Thus with Heyse, even he whose life has been the most aggravating failure, takes his refuge in the conception of nature as the last consoling thought; and thus he himself, in the most painful moments of his life, takes refuge therein, and to this the marvellous poems "Marianne" and "Ernst," the most profound and most touching of all his writings, have remained as witnesses. Nature is his starting-point and his final goal, the source of his poetry and its last word his one and all, his consolation, his creed.

III

What he honors, worships, and represents, expressed in a general way, is, therefore, nature. Now as he follows his own nature, it is his own nature which he represents,

[7] Kinder der Welt, iii. 109.

and its fundamental trait is to be elementally harmonious. Such a designation is very broad and vague. In its indefiniteness it may make Heyse seem, at first, like a follower of Goethe, and would be equally appropriate for the great master himself. This harmony, more closely defined, is not a world-embracing one, however; it is one that is comparatively narrow, it is an aristocratic harmony. There is much which it excludes, much which it fails to conciliate, does not, indeed, come into contact with. Not as a naturalist, but as a worshipper of beauty does Heyse contemplate the motley doings of life. It is plainly manifest that he fails to comprehend how an artist can take pleasure in depicting forms that in real life he would close his doors upon; in fact, he has himself, with great frankness, declared that he has never been able to draw a figure devoid of some lovable trait, or a female character, in whom he was not, to a certain degree, in love.[8] That is the reason why his entire gallery of human forms, with but few exceptions (such as Lorinser or Jansen's wife), consists of homogeneous characters. They have not only lineage, but noble lineage, that is, innate nobility. The quality they have in common is what Heyse himself calls *nobility* (*vornehmheit*). How does he understand this word? Nobility in all his characters is the inherent incapacity to commit any low or base deed; in the child of nature this is regulated by the simple goodness and healthfulness of the soul; in the person of culture, by the conscious sense of his human worth, mingled with the conviction of the privileges of a full, vigorous, human life, which bears within itself its norm and its tribunal, and rather dreads incompleteness than error. Heyse himself once defined his favorite terminus. In Salamander we read:[9]—

> I never yet of virtue or of failing
> Have been ashamed, nor proudly did adorn
> Myself with one, nor thought my sins of veiling.

[8] Kinder der Welt, i. III; Gesammelte Werke, vi. 206.
[9] Gesammelte Werke, iii. 300.

> Beyond all else betwixt the nobly born
> And vulgar herd, this marks the separation,—
> The cowards whose hypocrisy we scorn.
>
> Him call I noble, who, with moderation,
> Carves his own honor, and but little heeds
> His neighbors' slander or their approbation.

And in almost similar words Toinette, once so blinded by aristocratic display, expresses the following fundamental thought: "There is but *one* genuine nobility: to remain true to one's self. Ordinary mortals are guided by what people say, and beg others for information regarding how they themselves should be. He who bears within himself the true rank, lives and dies through his own grace, and is, therefore, sovereign."[10] Genuine nobility is the stamp borne by the entire race of beings that has sprung from this poet's brain. They all possess it from the peasant to the philosopher, and from the fisher-maiden to the countess. The simple bar-maid in "Der Reise nach dem Glück" expresses a conception of life fully coinciding with what has just been stated;[11] and any one who will take the pains to turn over the leaves of Heyse's works will discover that the little word "vornehm" (noble), or an equivalent, is always one of the first the author brings forward as soon as he makes any attempt to characterize or to extol. It is sufficient to examine a single volume of his "novellen" to see how the word "vornehm" is applied to the external appearance, look and bearing: in "Mutter und Kind" (Mother and Child); in "Am todten See" (On the Dead Lake); in "Ein Abenteuer" (An Adventure.)[12] Or in order to be convinced of the thrilling significance of this characteristic, it is only needful to glance through Heyse's two romances. In his "Kinder der Welt" all the personages that appeal to the sympathies of the reader, respectively call each other noble spirits: Fran-

[10] Kinder der Welt, ii. 47.
[11] Gesammelte Werke, v. 201. On page 175 the word "vornehm" is used by her.
[12] Gesammelte Werke, viii. 44, 246, 321.

zelius styles Edwin and Balder "the true aristocrats of humanity"; Edwin in his most extravagant transports of passion can find no more exalted praise for Toinette and Lea than that they bear the impress of nobility, and when Toinette, after her interview with Lea, acknowledges the latter to be the worthy wife of Edwin, it is the same expression which as a matter of course presents itself to her; in her letter, she designates Lea "Edwin's *noble,* wise, and most charming life companion."[13] And in the romance "Im Paradiese," the first draught of which we doubtless possess in the versified fragment "Schlechte Gesellschaft" (Bad Society), the so-called "bad" coterie of artists is represented throughout as the truly good and noble, in contrast with the so-called aristocratic society.[14] Not one of the artists is an aristocrat, in the ordinary acceptation of the word. Their origin, like that of the heroes in "Kinder der Welt," is extremely insignificant. But their nobility lies in the blood; they belong to the chosen ones of the earth, who act wisely and rightly, not from a sense of duty, or through the wearisome conquering of evil propensities, but because of their natures. What Toinette somewhere calls "the honest intention to put humanity to no shame," is represented, too, in the romance "Im Paradiese" as the natural nobility, in contradistinction to that *noblesse* which is based upon artificial principles.

Few poets, therefore, have portrayed such a series of characters without guile and without vulgarity as Heyse. No one has had more perfect faith in humanity. The most substantial proof of how urgent is his need of rendering prominent upon every occasion the genuine metal in human nature, is afforded by the fact that whenever a change in the character of any of his *dramatis personæ* does prepare a surprise for the reader or the spectator, it it always in the way of exceeding the expectations and showing the personality to be far better and more admirable,

[13] Kinder der Welt, ii. 355. "That you are the best, deepest, purest, noblest of women"—"Poor, brave, free-born breast—how well it has preserved its patent of nobility." Kinder der Welt, iii. 309.
[14] Im Paradiese, iii. 6.

far more noble-minded, than any one had supposed. In almost all other poets the disappointment is of an opposite character. In Heyse's "novellen," as, for instance, in "Barbarossa" or "Die Pfadfinderin" (The Female Pathfinder), the reconciliation is effected by permitting the bad character to repent, and since the germ of the nature of the person in question was originally good, and although possessing many irritable and evil qualities, he yet had no really vicious blood in his composition, there comes about a sort of treaty of peace between him and the reader to the astonishment of the latter. Far more significantly, however, than in his "novellen" this characteristic optimism comes out in Heyse's dramas. They unquestionably owe to it their best and most effective, perhaps their most decidedly dramatic, scenes. Let me cite a few examples. In "Charlotte Elizabeth" the Chevalier de Lorraine has availed himself of all manner of unworthy means in his efforts to undo the heroine and banish from France the chief male character of the piece, the German ambassador, Count Wied. Challenged by the count, the chevalier is severely wounded; and when the count, caught in the meshes of political intrigue, is sent to the Bastille, the chevalier appears in the fifth act in the audience chamber of the king. What can he want? To present still more damaging charges against the count? To continue his dishonorable conduct which has already been productive of so much misfortune to his opponent, and of a wound to himself? Will he have revenge? Does he mean to avail himself to the utmost of the position? No; he comes to make the solemn declaration that the count has acted like a true nobleman, and that he himself is to blame for the duel. He even desires to be himself sent to the Bastille in order that his opponent may not think that he, wholly losing sight of honor, has reported a false cause of the duel; in other words: even in this corrupt courtier there lives a sense of honor as the residue of the ancient French spirit of chivalry, taking the place, to a certain degree, of conscience, and compelling him, at the decisive moment, to rise from his couch of pain in order to interpose in behalf of the enemy whom he has pursued with savage thirst for revenge and without any regard of consequences.

In the beautiful and national play "Hans Lange," there is a scene which, when performed on the stage, holds the spectator in breathless suspense, and whose close always elicits tears from many eyes; it is the scene where the life of the young squire is at stake. He is lost if the horsemen surmise that it is he who, disguised as the son of the Jew, is lying on the bench. Then the head servant Henning is ushered in by a party of horsemen, who have heard him muttering in the stable that he knew very well how to solve the difficulty for them. Henning has been supplanted by the young squire; before the latter came to Lanzke, Henning was like a child of the house; now he has become less than a stepchild, and he has always owed a grudge to the man who has been thus preferred before him. With the most artistic skill, the scene is now so conducted that Henning, in spite of the entreaties and curses of those who are initiated into the secret, gives the surrounding group clearly to understand that he means to be revenged on the young squire, that he knows where he is, and that no power in the world will restrain him from betraying his enemy,— until he has heaped coals of fire on the head of the other; and then, contenting himself with the fright he has caused, finally speaks out plainly, in order to put the pursuers, who by this time, of course, blindly trust him, on the wrong scent.

And, finally, of precisely the same nature is the decisive and most beautiful scene in the patriotic drama "Colberg." A council of war is being held, and even the burghers are called upon to take part in it, for the importance of the crisis makes it desirable that every voice should be heard. All hope for the beleagured city seems to be gone. The French general has issued a proclamation, summoning Gneisenau to honorable capitulation. The entire corps of officers resolve forthwith that there can be no question of a surrender of the citadel, and Gneisenau thereupon lays before the citizens the proposal to entreat the enemy to grant them a truce in order that the burghers, their wives, and children, may leave the city, which is exposed to all possible horrors. Then the pedantic old pedagogue Zipfel, a genuine, old-fashioned German philologist, rises to act as spokesman for the burghers. With many circumlocutions, with Latin form of speech, he spins out his remarks, amid the impatience of all. He is interrupted; he is given to understand how very well known it is that he is only aiming at leaving the dangerous defence of the city to the commandant and the troops. Finally, he succeeds in making clear the object he had in view in his long narration about the great Persian war, and Leonidas with Spartans; it was to give force to the opinion that it behooved them one and all to remain and die at their posts. This scene Heyse has written *con amore*. It embraces, so to say, his entire system. For nowhere does his good faith in humanity so triumph as in cases where, in the old fogy, he can reveal the hero, and, in the poor pedant, show the man of inflexible will, which no other has discovered him to be than the poet who so well knows that every one of his creations bears within the depths of its soul an indelible stamp of nobility.

IV

Those authors who, as Spielhagen, for instance, most frequently linger over the conflicts of consciousness and of the will, and are fondest of depicting great social and political conflicts, will as a matter of course have better success in portraying men than women. Such a male character as Leo, in the romance "In Reih und Glied" (In Rank and File), would seek in vain for its equal, but a female character of the same excellence Spielhagen has not drawn. Any one, on the other hand, whose spirit seeks the nobility and grace of the absolutely natural, of visible and spiritual beauty, will as a matter of course give the preference to women, and draw them better than men. Herein Heyse resembles his master, Goethe. In almost all of his productions the female characters are placed in the foreground, and the male forms serve mainly to render them prominent, or to develop them. -As woman's nature unfolds its secret being, and shoots forth its fairest bloom in love, since in love, nature as nature, through a thousand illusions, becomes ennobled and spiritualized, so Heyse glorifies in an eminent way the love of woman. He renders homage to love, and he renders homage to woman; nevertheless, it is his greatest delight to represent these two great powers in conflict one with the other. For when love gains the victory, when it appears as the power to whose mandates the feminine heart may not bid defiance, it sparkles with radiance, vanquishing resistance, as though possessed of omnipotent might, and producing the effect that every woman under its influence, in defiance against it, in conflict with it, animated by it, rouses in all the pride of her sex, and is invested by love with that aristocratic beauty, which no one represents better than Heyse.

Inherent maidenly pride is to Heyse the most beautiful thing in nature. An entire group of his "novellen" might bear the tile "Mädchenstolz" (Maidenly Pride) Kierkegaard somewhere calls the essence of woman "a surrender, whose form is resistance." This is an utterance as from Heyse's own heart, and it is this resistance which, as a token of the noble-born nature, interests and charms him. It is that eternally impenetrable stronghold in the feminine disposition which captivates him, the sphinx-like element of her nature, whose riddle he feels ever impelled to solve. The sweet kernel is doubly sweet in its hard shell, the fiery champagne doubly flaming in its surroundings of ice. The feminine natures which Heyse depicts (from L'Arrabbiata to Julie and Irene in his "Im Paradiese") are enveloped in a coat of ice-mail, which conceals, repels, misleads, breaks, and melts away. Woman asserts her nobility by refusing, as long as possible, to give her *ego* out of her own keeping,—by guarding and cherishing the treasure of her love. She maintains her nobility by placing her *ego* exclusively in the hands of one single person, and offering resistance to all the rest of the world. She is subject to no blind force. But once let her maidenly pride be broken, and conquered, she finds herself again on the opposite side of the gulf, and yields freely, I might almost say as freely as nature. A seduction never occurs among Heyse's creations; if such a thing be alluded to a single time, as a past event, as in "Mutter und Kind" (Mother and Child), it only serves to place in the sharpest possible light proud self-assertion and equally proud conscious self-surrender.

This self-assertion, this power of resistance (Rabbia), is portrayed by Heyse with manifold variations; Atalanta, in the drama "Meleager," possesses the entire untamed wildness of the Amazon type; she prefers life and sport amid the freedom of nature—the race, feats of skill with the lance, and the occupation of the wildwood—to effeminate luxury and flattering caresses; she would rather wear the crown of victory than the bridal wreath. In Syritha we see the first coyness, which, roused by marriage, flees; in "L'Arrabbiata," maidenly pride, which feels how close to the timid request, in the soul of man, lies coarse desire; in the maiden of Treppi, we have the instinctive refusal of maidenhood; in Marianne ("Mutter und Kind"), womanly pride which increases twofold in the so-called fallen woman, under her sense of unmerited shame; in Madeleine ("Die Reise nach dem Glück"), the sense of duty opposed to the conceptions of morality inculcated from childhood; in Lore ("Lorenz und Lore"), the feeling of shame of a young girl, from whose lips a confession of her love has escaped in the presence of death; in Lottka, the melancholy reserve caused by a sense of inherited degradation; in fair Kätchen, the indignant despair of a young girl at finding herself attractive to every one, which makes her wish all her admirers and her own beauty far away; in Lea, the aversion of a highly developed and reserved woman to allowing any one to have a suspicion of her weakness; in Toinette, the abhorrence of an ice-bound heart to feigning a passion it does not yet feel; in Irene, the strict conventionality of a little princess; in Julie, the coldness of a Cordelia nature—until the supreme moment arrives when all these bonds are burst, when all these hearts are kindled, when the man-hatred of the Amazon, and the coyness of the young maiden, and the modesty of dawning womanhood, and the pride of the wife, and the sense of duty of those who have been strictly brought up, and the melancholy of those who have been humbled, and the mantle of the snow-queen, all, all flame up, like wood on one mighty funeral pyre, and ascend in sweet incense on the altar of the god of love.

For not in resistance, which is only the form and the cloak, but in self-surrender, does Heyse see the essence of womanhood and woman's true nature; and adorer of nature as he is, he does honor to Eros as the irresistible one who breaks through all barriers. Woman never regrets having subjected herself to his power, but she may repent her defiance. Bettina, somewhere in her letters, makes about the following remark, "The strawberries I plucked I have forgotten; but those I left untouched are still branded on my soul." Heyse has made more than one variation on this theme; after the maiden of Treppi has repented her youthful coyness during seven long years, chance brings the object of her affections once more to her native village, and she overcomes, by virtue of an enthusiastic and superstitious conviction of the power and justice of her love, all external and internal obstacles, even the indifference and coldness of the returned wanderer himself. Madeleine, in the "Reise nach dem Glück," as before mentioned, has driven her lover at night from her door, and having been compelled to ride away in the dark, he had a fall from his horse which killed him on the spot. Remorse for this defiance of love gives her no rest. "Of what avail was my virtue?" said she; "it was sound and whole, and by no means threadbare; and yet it chilled me to the innermost recesses of my heart."[15] It is not enough, though, that she regrets having followed the dictates of conventional morality: the image of the deceased haunts her year after year; it seems to be jealously watching over her each time in her life that she thinks it possible to forget the past, and find happiness anew; she hears the finger of the dead man knocking at the door, as he knocked that night she drove him for her. Severe are the punishments of Eros for those who do not sacrifice on his altar. And Heyse in others of

[15] Gesammelte Werke, v. 197.

his creations still further amplifies this idea. Here the repulsed lover meets his death, simply as an accidental result of the rigor shown him by the being for whose presence he yearned so ardently. Let us suppose the case to be one where, instead of an humble petitioner, one who threatens violence approaches, and that the resistance of the proud woman be not based on a sense of duty that conquers temptation, but is merely self-defence at the time of a dreaded invasion, how then? Even then Eros bestows chastisement, as a zealous god. The drama "Die Sabinerinnen" (The Sabine Women) was evidently written by Heyse for the sake of one single character. How, otherwise, could it have occurred to him to choose for tragic treatment this purely burlesque material, so little adapted to tragedy. This character is Tullia, the Sabine king's daughter. Carried off by a Roman warrior, held captive in his house, she kills him, when, on the bridal night, he dares approach her. If a tragic woe should now befall the rash woman in order that the Roman might be avenged, no one would be surprised; but the psychological point is in harmony with Heyse's entire erotic system; for through the murder of her husband she endeavored to kill the awakening impulse of her own heart, and thus sacrilegiously rebelled against Eros.

>   And stooping,
> He bowed his face until it reached my brow;
> His flutt'ring breath went rippling over me,
> And stealthily, like streams of poison, ran
> His low-toned voice through all my veins.

Now left alone with her shattered soul, she recoils with horror at a deed which is so genuinely feminine, and in which she is so entirely justified. The apparition of the dead man haunts her wherever she goes, but still more than the aspect of his dead body, the remembrance of his caresses. "Only a day and a night have passed since that deed was accomplished," says she, "and yet it lies behind me as a thousand years and a thousand deaths. One thing alone is, and ever will be, present with me: his kiss upon my eyelids, his hand within my own." Toward the end she expresses to her sister the fundamental idea in these words:—

> From Love, oh, do not flee!
> She will o'ertake you if you do. Go humbly
> And kneel before her shrine. For deadly anger
> She heaps on those who dare defy her will,
> And sucks their blood. And is not every maiden
> In bondage stern to this grim god? O sister,
> I only must atone for free resistance.[16]

Even the man that has approached her through violence, cannot be hated by the young virgin. He broke the peace; but what else does Love? He outwitted her; but is not Love crafty? He mocked; but does not Love scoff even at the most powerful and most free? In other words: is not Eros himself a worker of violence, without shyness or shame, a criminal who overleaps all customary bounds.

All? That is saying too much. Heyse has indeed sometimes, as in the instances cited, shown a tendency, reminding one of Kleist, for all purely pathological erotic problems; but his nature is entirely too harmonious, too mature, and by far too typically German, to admit of his describing passion as bursting all the law and order of society. He is developed enough to see clearly that the laws of passion and the laws of society are two wholly dissimilar things, which have very little in common; yet he pays the latter the respect it deserves, that is, a conditional one. From his earliest youth it has interested and pleased him to show how relative is the truth, and how limited the worth of these laws; to bring forward in his poetic creations instances where their boundaries are overstepped in such a way that the exceptions to the rule seem right, and even the most hardened and narrow-minded person would hesitate to condemn them. In his anxiety to do full, incontestible justice to the exceptional cases, Heyse has sometimes—as in his first drama, "Francesca von Rimini," which is not included in his "Gesammelte Werke"—sought out extremely quaint exceptions; but it is his universal endeavor so to enclose the case with palisades, that no assault on usual morality can

---

[16] Gesammelte Werke, ix. 73.

cause the downfall of the barricade. When Goethe brings together Egmont and Clärchen, he does not present the case as though it required an apology; the beauty of the relationship is its defence. Heyse, the less grand poet, whose caution is quite equal to his daring, has always fixed an eye on conventional morality, and has continually endeavored to conciliate it, either by ceding the point to it, so to say, in all other cases but just this one where its infringement was unavoidable, or by so atoning for the offence that the individual who is guilty of it is allowed to purchase the forbidden happiness, with his eyes fully open, and of his own free will, at so high a price that it appears too costly to be alluring to any Philistine.

In "Francesca von Rimini" the circumstances are as follows: Lanciotto is ugly, coarse, and corrupt; his brother, Paolo, noble and handsome. Lanciotto is inflamed with passion for Francesca. Misguided by brotherly love for the thoroughly unworthy Lanciotto, Paolo has allowed himself to be deluded not only into playing the part of suitor, but even disguised as bridegroom on the wedding day, to take the place of his brother, who feared that with his hideous person he could never obtain the maiden's consent. Not until shrouded by the darkness of the bridal chamber, does Lanciotto dare approach his bride. Now Paolo also loves Francesca, as she loves him in return. Therefore, it is no wonder that the young wife, upon discovering this gross deception, the victim of which she has become, feels dishonored by the caresses of her husband, and far from viewing her love for Paolo as a sin, she regards it as justified and sacred.

> The kiss thou gavest me the holy wafer was
> Which my dishonored lips did purify from taint.

In order to make his intrenchment as solid as possible, it will thus be seen that the poet, in this naïve work of his youth, has constructed the most improbable, most far-fetched, case in the world; for what can be more preposterous than for Paolo out of pure, simple-hearted kindliness to a despicable brother, to expose the woman he loves to the basest deception, which, moreover, annihilates his own life-happiness. But in this exaggerated example will, nevertheless, be found the type according to which, in Heyse's numerous later "novellen," with their plentiful tact and exquisite delicacy, the moral collision is constructed. Let me single out at random several examples. In "Beatrice" it is legal marriage which breaks up the love romance, a forced marriage, as unholy as the marriage of Francesca, although stronger reasons are given for it. In "Cleopatra" the young German resists the love of the fair Egyptian, as stubbornly as Kleist's Count Wetter von Strahl resists the passion of Kätchen von Heilbronn. Not until her yearning for him brings Cleopatra to the brink of the grave, is the liaison between them formed. The proud Gabrielle in the work "Im Grafenschlosse" does not allow herself to be persuaded into the "conscience marriage" with the Count, until he has jeopardized his life for her sake. The young wife in "Rafael" purchases a few hours of companionship with her lover through a lifelong incarceration in the cloister; the self-surrender of Garcinde and Lottka is ennobled by the fact that the outwardly fettered but inwardly free *ego* was unable to conceive of a self-surrrender, forbidden by circumstances, under any other conditions than those whose consequences are death. The right to the happiness of a fleeting moment is purchased by suicide.

The goblet of bliss, drained by these personages, has seasoned their destiny with poison. Heyse, therefore, affirms for these *heroic* souls the right to solve the problem of a conflict of duties in a different way than is customary for "the timid Philistine whose half-way measures are circumscribed by petty customs and considerations," and in the introduction to his "Beatrice"[17] he himself formulates his ethic heresy in the following words: "Genial, self-dependent natures can do much toward extending the boundary lines of the moral sphere, by permitting the measure of their inner power and magnitude to shine forth

[17] Gesammelte Werke, viii. 168.

as an example, through their actions, just as genial artists can burst through those barriers of their art that have been handed down to them by tradition."

No less than through this intimately allied association with ruin and death does Heyse ennoble love, legitimate or illegitimate, as indicated above, through the nature of the self-surrender. It is always conscious. These women whom he characterizes never allow themselves to be carried away by their emotions; they give themselves up as a free gift—when they yield at all. Thus it is in works dating from Heyse's earliest youth, as "Der Kreisrichter"[18] (The Circuit Judge), thus in "Rafael," in "Lottka," and in so many of the "novellen" in prose and in verse. Everywhere the self-sufficiency and the right of spontaneity of the individual is preserved. The woman gives herself as a free gift to her lover, she goes freely forth to meet her own destruction, or with her own hand inflicts death upon herself; and where the bliss of love is not ennobled by the price it costs, it is at least exalted by the pride with which it is bestowed and received. By virtue of this pride the personality, itself governed by the strongest power of nature, feels independent and regal in the assertion of its sovereign dignity. In the romance "Im Paradiese" Heyse has for the first time treated as a main problem the freedom of love in antithesis to the laws of society, and maintained its justice. The fundamental idea of this romance is none other than that the morality and dignity of love between man and woman is independent of the outward ratification of the marriage tie. According to his wont, Heyse has provided the case here given with the most forcible motives. Jansen cannot, without putting his friend to shame, become free from his despicable wife, and without Julie all his hopes as an artist and a man would perish. Yet when Julie in the presence of the assembled friends, adorned with the myrtle-wreath, freely weds Jansen, a decided attack is aimed at the purely exterior morality of society,

[18] Gesammelte Werke, vi. 71: "I have been sold once in my life. How mankind will now blame me if I give myself as a free-will offering in order to suppress the anguish of that disgrace!"

although the incident is not brought forward as an example for imitation. The poet who in the "Kinder der Welt" urgently impresses it upon the consciences of his contemporaries, that the morality of the individual is not dependent on his metaphysical convictions, in his "Im Paradiese," strives to teach that the purity and dignity of a union of love must not be judged by the laws of outward morality, but that love both without and within the marriage relation may be true and false, moral and immoral. Everything depends, according to Heyse's views, upon the true nobility of the heart.

V

I have already said that Heyse as a poet is originally a pupil of Eichendorf. Like the hero in his "Ein Abenteuer" (An Adventure), he appears to have chosen for the companion of his first journeyman-years the romantic "Taugenichts" (Good-for-nothing). Where, in one of his "novellen" (Lottka), he introduces himself as a youth, he sings in Eichendorf's own key, and we recognize that very early in life he has been in the habit of whistling, with rare skill, the melodies of romance. Musje Morgenroth, in the collection of romantic folk-lore tales for children, which as a student he published under the title "Der Jungbrunnen" (The Fountain of Youth), is a genuine brother of the celebrated Eichendorf hero. The book is the work of a boy, and yet it is not without a certain interest, as it marks the first standpoint of our poet. It shows also with what talents he was equipped from the outset: the boyish, yet never inelegant prose flows smoothly, and the verse, which is of a vastly higher character, with all its echoes, is unaffected, fresh, and regular in form. His song is not original, but it is pure; it is in the usual key of romance, but it is sung with youthful freshness and grace. The fact of producing naïvely during the years of boyhood is in itself a phenomenon, and the unusual amount of innate command of language secures the student author from exaggeration or mannerism. The gift of language, inherited evidently from his father, the well-known philologist, develops in the son into a fluency, a facility for handling words and rhythm, which even in his earliest youth was not far removed from vituosoship. This almost Rückert-like flow of language, as a fundamental element in Heyse's natural endowments, influenced all the other peculiarities which he gradually developed. From the very beginning he sang not because he had more in his heart than the rest of mankind, but because it was far easier and more natural for him than for others to express that of which his heart was full. Since no mighty inward revolutions or startling outward occurrences were necessary to unseal his lips, as are usually required to rouse the creative fancy of those for whom it is difficult to find form of expression, and who succeed only in moments of passion in bringing forth to the light of day the treasures of their inner being, he turned his gaze not within but without, pondered but little on his *ego*, his calling, and his capabilities; but fully conscious that he bore within his own soul a clear mirror, which reflected everything within his immediate surroundings that interested him, he allowed his gaze, with the keen susceptibility and true creative impulse of a plastic artist, to wander in all directions.

Of a plastic artist, I said; for he did not long continue to carol forth the music of romance. He himself has said,—

> Fair is romantic poesie,
> Yet what we call *beauté de nuit*.

True men, Heyse thinks, understand how to grasp their ideas in the light of day, and he is too thoroughly a child of the sun to be able to linger in the twilight of romance. A lyric poet he is not in the main, and the strength of romance, conformably to its nature and of necessity, lies in lyric poetry. Nor did the surroundings of nature imbue him with an independent poetic interest; such a freshness of the sea and of the landscape as is breathed for instance by the Danish novels of Blicher will not be found in his works; he is not a landscape-painter, and has always availed himself of the landscape merely as a background. What first and earliest met his gaze, as soon as he was developed enough to see with his own eyes, was man; and let it be observed, not man as an intelligence served by organs, or as a will walking on a pair of legs, or as a psychological curiosity, but man as a plastic form. Like the sculptor or the figure-painter it is his wont, according to my opinion, on closing his eyes, to see his horizon first and foremost populated with outlines and profiles. Beautiful external forms and movements, the poise of a graceful head, a charming peculiarity of carriage or walk, have occupied him in precisely the same way as they engross the attention of the plastic artist, and are reproduced by him with the same partiality, indeed, at times with technical exactness of expression. And not only the narrator, but the personages that appear on the scene, often form the same kind of conceptions. Thus, for instance, the main character in "Der Kreisrichter" (The Circuit Judge) says: "The young people here are healthy, and health constitutes half of the beauty of youth. There is also race development. *Notice the refined form of their heads, and the delicate moulding of their temples, and the natural grace of their bearing in walking, dancing, and sitting down.*"[19] A striking example of the poet's method of contemplation may be found in "Die Einsamen" (The Solitary Ones), where his dissatisfaction at being able to paint so imperfectly with the means which his art affords, breaks forth in the following words: "Only the mere outlines!" he raved to himself. "Only a few dozen lines! How she went trotting about on her little donkey, one leg thrown across the back of the animal, resting firmly and securely, the other almost grazing the ground with the tip of her foot, and her right elbow supported on the knee that was in repose, her hand playing gently with the chain about her neck, her face turned toward the sea. What a mass of black tresses on the neck! Something red lends a radiance thereto. A coral necklace? No; fresh pomegranate blossoms. The wind plays with the loosely knotted kerchief; how dark is the glow of the cheeks, and how much darker the eye!"[20]

[19] Gesammelte Werke, vi. 40.   [20] Gesammelte Werke, vi. 5.

Such are the pictures of plastic figures, simple, picturesque situations, with which Heyse's imagination has had to operate upon from the beginning, and which serve to form for it a starting-point. And though it may be felt ever so keenly how much more sensible it is to describe a poet than to praise him, still it were scarcely possible to restrain an outburst of admiration upon considering how exceedingly well Heyse, in every instance, has succeeded in presenting his characters, especially, however, his female characters, to the reader's eye. He does not belong to the descriptive school; he does not characterize in detail, as either Balzac or Turgenief; he describes with a few delicate strokes: yet his creations remain fixed in our memories, from the simple reason that they all have defined style. A peasant maiden from Naples or Tyrol, a servant girl, or a young fräulein from Germany, all obtain, when depicted by his hand, a higher, more visionary, and yet ever-memorable life, because they are all ennobled by strictly ideal methods and the art of representation. They are as perfect in form as statues; they have the carriage of queens. With the exception of the painter Leopold Robert, of whom some of Heyse's Italian works are reminders, no one, to my knowledge, has displayed so grand a style in the delineation of peasants and fishing people as Heyse. And as the forms of the outer person, so those of the inner being are of an exquisitely finished style. Did not the expression seem almost too daring, I should say that Heyse's descriptions of love are plastic. The romantic school always conceived love to be of a lyric nature. If Heyse's love stories be compared with the love stories of the romantic school, it will be found that while the romantic writers give their strength in analyzing their romantic transports as such, and forming a nomenclature for the rarest moods which it has usually been thought impossible to name, in Heyse's writings every psychological force is mirrored in a look or in a gesture; everything becomes with him contemplation and visible life.

VI

I remarked that the faculty of preserving and idealizing forms constituted *one* of the starting-points of this poet's imagination. It has, however, another. Quite as inherent as his capacity for delineating character is his fondness for experiencing and inventing "adventures." By adventures, I understand events of a peculiar and unusual nature, which —as is scarcely ever the case in real adventures—have a sure outline, and so clearly defined a beginning, middle, and end, that they appear to the imagination like a work of art enclosed in a frame. From any chance, outward or inward, observation—the fragment of a dream, an encounter on the street, the sight of a tower dating from the Middle Ages, in some ancient city, in the glow of the setting sun—there springs up for him, through the most rapid association of ideas, a history, a chain of events; and as he is by nature an artist, this series of events ever assumes a rhythmic form. Like the beings he creates, it has clear, firm outlines, and inner equilibrium. It has its skeleton, its filling up of flesh; above all, its well-defined and slender shape. The faculty of relating a story in brief, concise form, of imparting to it, so to say, a harmonious rhythm, has its origin directly in Heyse's thoroughly harmonious nature. The "novellen" form, as he has carved it out and engraved it, is an entirely original and independent creation, his actual property. Therefore he has become especially popular through his prose "novelle."[21] The "novelle" with him always has extremely few and simple factors, the number of the personages introduced is small, the action is concise and may be surveyed with a single glance. But his fiction does not exist for the sake of the personages alone, as in the modern French novels, which only satisfy a psychological or a physiological interest; it has its own peculiar mode of development and its independent interest. A novel like Christian Winter's "Aftenscene" (Evening Scene), whose quaint, old-fashioned grace of style renders it so fascinating, possesses the fault of having no incident. With Heyse

[21] Heyse und Kurz, Novellenschatz des Auslandes, Bd. VIII.

the "novelle" is not a picture of the times, or a *genre* painting; something always *does happen* with him, and it is always something unexpected. The plot, as a rule, is so arranged that at a certain point an unforeseen change takes place; a surprise which, when the reader looks back, always proves to have had a firm and carefully prepared foundation in what went before. At this point the action sharpens; here the threads unite to form a knot from which they are spun around in an opposite direction. The enjoyment of the reader is based upon the art with which the purpose of the action is gradually more and more veiled and hidden from view, until suddenly the covering falls. His surprise is caused by the skill with which Heyse apparently strays farther and farther away from the goal which rose beyond the starting-point, until he finally discovers that he has been led through a winding path and finds himself exactly above the point where the story began.

Heyse himself, in this introduction to his "Deutscher Novellenschatz," has expressed his views on the principle to which he does homage in his "novellen" compositions. Here, as in the introduction to the "Stickerin von Treviso" (The Embroidery Woman of Treviso), he calls the attention of those who would place the entire importance on style and diction, to the fact that the narrative as a narrative, what children call the story, is unquestionably the essential foundation of the "novelle" and possesses its own peculiar beauty. He lays stress on the statement that according to his æsthetic taste, he would give the preference to *that* "novelle" whose main motive is most distinctly finished, and—with more or less intrinsic worth—betrays something peculiar, specific, in the original design. "*A strong silhouette,*" he continues, "should not be lacking in what is called a 'novelle' in the proper sense of the word."[22] By the term "silhouette" Heyse means the outlines of the story, as shown by a brief summary of the contents; and he illustrates his idea with a striking example and a striking description. He gives the synopsis of one of the novels of Boccaccio, as follows:—

[22] Heyse und Kurz, Deutscher Novellenschatz, Bd. I. s. xix.

"Frederigo degli Alberighi loves, without meeting with any return; roving in knightly fashion, he squanders all his substance, and has nothing left but one single falcon; this, when the lady whom he loves is led by chance to his house, and he has nothing else with which to prepare a meal for her, he places on the table before her. She learns what he has done, suddenly changes her resolution, and rewards his love by making him the lord of her hand and her fortune."

Heyse calls attention to the fact that in these few lines lie all the elements of a touching and delightful "novelle," in which the fate of two human beings is accomplished in the most charming manner, through an accidental turn of affairs, which however, serves to give deeper development to the characters; and he therefore invites modern storytellers, even when engaged on the most touching and rich materials, to ask themselves where "the falcon" is, the specific object that distinguishes this story from a thousand others.

In the demand he makes on the "novelle," he has especially characterized the task he has imposed on himself and faithfully fulfilled. He prefers eccentric to typical everyday instances. As a rule, we are quite as sure of finding "the falcon" in his prose narratives, as a certain judge was of finding a woman at the bottom of every crime. In "L' Arrabbiata," the biting of a hand is "the falcon"; in the "Bild der Mutter" (The Mother's Portrait) it is the elopement; in "Vetter [Cousin] Gabriel," it is the letter copied from the "lover's letter-writer." If the reader will himself search for the aforesaid wild bird, he will gain an insight into the poet's method of composition. It is not always so easily captured as in the cases just cited. With a power of investigation, a nimble grace, which is rare in a man who is not of Roman race, Heyse has understood how to tie the knots of events and disentangle them again, to present and solve the psychologic problem which he has *isolated* in the "novelle." He has the faculty of singling out exceptional, unusual cases from the general state of culture, and the condition of the society of which he is a member, and presenting them purely and sharply in the form of a "novelle," without permitting the action to play into the unreal and fabulous, as is the wont of romantic novelists, and without ever allowing it to run into a merely epigrammatic point. His "novellen" are neither brief romances nor long anecdotes. They have at the same time fulness and strictly-defined form. And circumscribed as this form may be, it has yet proved itself sufficiently flexible to be able to embrace within its limits the most diverse materials. The "novellen" of Heyse play on many strings; most abundantly on the tender and the *spirituelle*, but also on the comic (as in the amusing tale, "Die Wittwe von Pisa"—The Widow of Pisa), the fantastic (as in the Hoffman-like "Cleopatra"); indeed, in a single instance, the awful (in the painful nocturne, "Der Kinder Sünde der Väter Fluch"—The Sins of the Children the Curse of the Fathers). The "novelle" as it is treated by Heyse borders on the provinces of Alfred de Musset, Mérimée, Hoffman and Tieck; but has, however, its own special domain, as well as its very individual profile.

VII

Meanwhile, ready as I am to recognize the significance of this sharp profile as the individual characteristic of the Heyse "novelle," and its significance for the novel in general as a work of art, it is equally hard for me to allow this to pass as the decisive norm for the estimation of individual stories.

The novel is, indeed, as every work of art, an organism in which beautiful proportions, relatively independent of one another and of a totally dissimilar character, contribute to produce a combined impression. We have been dwelling upon the characterizations, and the action; style is the third element. According to my convictions, these three elements are not subordinate one to the other, but co-ordinate; and each one of them, when developed in a masterly way, affords the reader an equally perfect enjoyment.

It is very certain, as Heyse makes evident, that a one-sided development of diction leads to clever capriciousness without any scheme; whoever places too great importance on "the plot" is in danger, on the other hand, of retrograding into mere sensational literature.

"Spring Floods," by Turgenief, is a novel whose action moves on in an unsatisfactory manner,—of the style, in the stricter sense of the word, I cannot judge, as I have never read the story in the original,—but is this lack of much importance in such a masterwork of individual characterization? Does not the description of the Italian family, in and by itself, outweigh every imperfection in the plan of occurrences? What matters it if the reader would rather have had the end somewhat different, and cannot read it a second time, even though he may read three-quarters of the novel over and over again with unchanged enjoyment?

Blicher's "Diary of a Village Sexton" is a novel in which the action is of but little moment, and most of the characters are absolutely repellant, on account of their coarseness; but it is, nevertheless, a work of the highest artistic worth; its main strength lies in its style, in the masterly execution of the honest sexton's language, which belongs to a period of almost two hundred years past. This language is a guarantee for the cutting truth of the narrative, a truth which is not reached by the path of idealism, and which, therefore, is neither sought nor found by Heyse; I mean that truth which by the French is designated "la verité vraie."

And cannot Heyse be attacked with his own weapons? I think he can. By the stress he lays on what the novel within the novel is, he seems to oppose alike the overestimation of style, and of ideal purport. But of all his "novellen" in verse "Der Salamander" (The Salamander) appears to me to stand the highest; of his prose works "Der letzte Centaur" (The Last Centaur) is one of my favorites. The first of these seems to me to bear off the palm on account of the diction; the last, on account of the idea.

There is no need of taking pains to seek for a "falcon" in Salamander; there is no plot in it, the characters have no development worth mentioning, and yet every reader of any susceptibility will experience such lively enjoyment under the influence of the magic of these terzettos, that it will seem to him as if this poem, in addition to its own merits, possessed also all those which it lacks. Of the epic repose, of the objective style, which is Heyse's precise ideal in the domain of the "novelle," not much will here be found. This epic repose is perhaps less adapted on the whole to the restless spirit of our time. The realization on this ideal of Heyse's has, properly speaking, only perfectly succeeded in the few prose "novellen," which do not touch upon the civilization of modern society, as in those genial pasticcios of the olden time: "Die Stickerin von Treviso" and "Geoffroy und Garcinde," where the noble, simple style of the old Italian or provençal form of narrative is idealized, or when the materials are taken from the life of the people in Italy or Tyrol; for the people in those lands are themselves a simple piece of the Middle Ages cast in *a form*. Such a story as that little jewel "L' Arrabbiata," which was the foundation of Heyse's fame, actually attains its rights through its plain, rigid setting; adorned with the decorations of style, or with psychologically polished facets, it would lose its entire beauty, if not become impossible. In the same way "Die Stickerin von Treviso," which probably, next to the work just named, has reaped the greatest harvest of applause, in its touching simplicity and grandeur, is so thoroughly one with its chronicle form, that it cannot be conceived of without this. But in instances where scenes from purely modern civilization are described, the style cannot be too individual and nervous. Heyse himself cannot avoid making his aim in this respect proportionate to his materials; how feverish is the recital in the pretty invalid story in letters "Unheilbar!" (Incurable.) However, it is apparently with the utmost reluctance, and without the free exercise of his will, that he permits himself to be carried away into such a passionately surging and trembling style as in "Salamander." This creation is pure style, its beauty depends wholly and entirely on the captivating charm of its metric

diction, and yet throughout not a word will be found that
it not to the purpose. The entire work teems with active
life, every change in style is deeply felt and transparent;
the struggling soul of the writer lies like an open book
before the reader. The situations are insignificant and
commonplace; no Bengal illumination, not even a final
tableau. But these remarkable, incredibly beautiful, un-
naturally easy, nervously passionate terzettos, which question and answer, jest, sing and lament, invest the theatrical,
the enamored yet thoroughly composed blasé coquette, the
heroine, and the passion she inspires, with such a charm
that no exciting story, with crisis and pole, could be more
captivating. Toward the close of the poem the glorious
terzettos, which throughout have been transformed into
quite a new species of metre, ring out in a manner as
surprising as it is genial and bold, in the chords of a triple
ritornelle, invested with all the freshness of nature. Such
a poem as this will maintain its place in spite of all theories.

Upon the whole, however, it seems to me that Heyse has
formed an incorrect conception of the significance of poetic
style. Theoretically, he fears its independent development,
and cannot tolerate any works which are "mere diction
and style." Nevertheless, in such poems as "Das Feen-
kind" (The Fairy Child), and still more in such poems
as "Frauenemancipation" (Female Emancipation), he has
himself furnished productions of this kind. The first of
these poems is refined and graceful, but the raillery in it
is of too ample length—we do not care to eat an undue
amount of whipped cream; the other, whose tendency,
however, is the best, suffers from a loquacity without any
salt. But a distinctly marked style is by no means the same
thing as the formal virtusoship of diction. That an artist
of language like Heyse, the translator of Guisti, of the
troubadours, of Italian and Spanish folk-songs, must possess this in the fullest degree, is understood as a matter of
course. And yet the truly artistic style is not that formal
grace which spreads uniformly over everything. Style,
in the highest sense of the word, is fulfilment, a form completed from every point of view. Where the coloring of

language, the phraseology, diction, and personal accent, still possess a certain abstract homogeneousness, where the author has failed to mirror the character at every essential point in all the outer forms, the drapery of language, or however light a texture it may consist, will hang stiff and dead about the personality of the speaker. The perfect modern style, on the contrary, envelops it as the flowing robe envelops the form of the Grecian orator, serving to relieve the attitude of the body and every movement. The diction of the mere virtuoso, even when "brilliant," may be traditional and trivial; genuine style is never so. With the mode of narration of Heyse's "novellen," I have not much fault to find; his dramatic diction, on the contrary, does not please me so well.

There are no doubt many who think that if Heyse's historic dramas have not gained the recognition accorded his "novellen," it is because they are invested with too little action, and too much style. If the word style, however, be understood as I have here defined it, it should certainly rather be asserted that the iambic form used was worn threadbare, and that these works have not style enough. The diction in "Elizabeth Charlotte," for example, neither sufficiently bears the coloring of the period in which the scenes are laid, nor of the persons who speak. Only compare it with the dry posthumous memoirs of the princess. The poet who, with his fabulous facility for orienting himself in every poetic form, can produce a drama as easily as he can tell a story, has taken his task almost too easily. The little tragedy "Maria Moroni," a drama which may be ranked next to his "novellen," through its plan as well as through its characterization, might worthily stand side by side with the Italian dramas, of Alfred de Musset, of which it reminds us, were not its language-coloring by far too dull and cold. The dialogues of Musset not only sparkle with wit, but glow with ardor and with life. In his dramas Heyse is not personally present with his whole soul at every point. And yet this "at every point" is the style.

Inasmuch, therefore, as I have placed the highest estimate on "Salamander," of all the versified "novellen," on ac-

count of its excellence of diction, so for the sake of its
idea I would give a high place to the prose narrative, "Der
letzte Centaur" (The Last Centaur), although the latter is,
at the same time, farthest removed from the requirements
of the definition. It does not treat of an occurrence or a
conflict in a defined sphere of life, nor of any especial
psychologic instance, but of life itself; it permits the entire
modern life to be mirrored at once within a narrow frame.
A shot at the central point is so refreshing; why deny it?
The peripheric character of some others of Heyse's works
is to blame for their not being of greater interest. After
reading through a long series of "novellen" one cannot
help longing for an art form which is capable of embracing
the more significant, universally current ideas and problems in poetic form.

VIII

Heyse's dramas are in the highest degree heterogeneous:
civil tragedies, mythological, historic, patriotic plays of the
most dissimilar artistic nature. His talent is so pliant that
he feels at liberty to enter upon any theme. A strong impulse for the historical, Heyse has never had; his historical
dramas have all sprung from a patriotic sentiment, and
are effective chiefly through this sentiment. The one of his
groups of dramas for which the poet is most noted is that
which deals with antique subjects. At a time when modern
political action was everywhere demanded of the higher
drama, this employment of old Grecian and Roman materials was lamented over and derided in Germany, with
an utter lack of comprehension. People asked what in all
the world there was in such a subject as the rape of the
Sabine women, or Meleager, or Hadrian, that could possibly
interest the poet or any one else. To those who read critically it is very evident what must have attracted Heyse to
these themes. They incorporate for him his favorite ideas
concerning woman's love and woman's destiny, and his
own being is mirrored in them. Any one who will compare
the warm-blooded drama "Meleager" with Swinburne's
"Atalanta in Kalydon," which handles the same material,

will find occasion for many interesting observations, concerning the peculiarity of the two poets. "Hadria" has perhaps perplexed the critic the most. What could attract the poet to a relation so wholly foreign to us as that between Hadrian and Antinous, one, too, that is so decidedly a reminder of the shady side of antique life, seems almost incomprehensible. I, for my part, rank "Hadrian" highest of all of Heyse's dramas. I have never been able to read this tragedy of the handsome young Egyptian who, passionately loved by the ruler of the world, surrounded by all the pomp and splendor of the court, free in every respect, and bound alone to his imperial admirer, languishes for freedom,—I have never been able to read this tragedy, I say, without thinking of a certain young poet who, already in his earliest youth summoned to a South German court, soon became an object of envy as the favorite of an amiable and intelligent monarch, as the darling of fortune, while in many a secret moment he wished himself far from court, and in many a fettered moment felt how little even the favor of the best master weighed in the balance against the freedom of one who was entirely unprotected but entirely independent.

In this drama, by way of exception, all that is scenic is of the highest effect. The actual reason why Heyse, with all his great ability for the stage, still failed to meet with decided success in his dramas, is unquestionably because he does not possess the German pathos proper, that of Schiller. Not until the pathos is broken, not until it has become half pathological, is he able to treat it with entire originality. Genuine dramatic pathos from the depths of the heart, with him easily becomes inartistically national, patriotic, and somewhat commonplace. This is the reason why the representation of manly action proper is not his province. To however high a degree he may have command in his poetry over the passive qualities of manhood, such as dignity, earnestness, repose, dauntless courage, he nevertheless, like Goethe, wholly lacks the active momentum. A vigorous, effective plan of action that follows a defined goal is as little the essential part of his dramas as of his novels and romances. If there now and then appear an energetic action, it is occasioned by despair; the individual is forced into a dilemma in which the only apparent means of escape may be gained through the utmost daring alone. (Compare the action of the young forester in "Mutter und Kind," when he kidnaps the son of his sweetheart, or the elopement in "Das Bild der Mutter"—The Mother's Portrait.) In the romance "Im Paradiese" a good example of this will be found in the scene where Jansen in exasperation at all the incompleteness amid which his life has been passed, dashes to pieces the models of his saints. It was an unmanly thing in Jansen to carry on a saint factory,—the whole idea is amusing as a passing jest, but does not admit of being made permanent without disfiguring the character, course of action, when he pours out the vials of his wrath against the dead plaster images. Although from the reason already cited the genuine dramatic nerve and sinew are almost always lacking in Heyse's works, the hindrances which are placed in the way of the poet's decided success on the stage are not of such importance that he may not overcome them with time and celebrate a scenic triumph. By way of preliminary, a few years ago he made his début, to the astonishment of every one, in a species of poetic composition which seemed to be wholly remote from his province, but in which, in a very short time, he won the greatest success.

It is still fresh in the public memory what an excitement the "Kinder der Welt" created when it first appeared in Spener's "Zeitung." For a whole month this feuilleton was the universal theme of conversation. The guileless novelist, who was so completely an alien to worldly life, had suddenly unveiled himself as a purely modern thinker, who ended a philosophic romance with the words of Hölderlin:—

> Cease not to guard with heav'nly buckler
> Fair innocence; thou guardian of the bold,
> Forsake her not!

It had been apparently overlooked previous to this that through Heyse's insinuating poetry there ran a vehement demand for freedom, a complete independence of dogmas and conventional fetters. At his new departure, therefore, people were more astonished than they had any reason to be. Heyse is of a mixed origin: from his Teutonic father he has inherited the positive side of his character, the fulness and beauty of his disposition; from his mother, who was a Jewess, a critical vein. For the first time both sides of his nature were revealed to the great public. It must have produced a marked impression on the minds about him that this Fabius Cunctator who had so long held aloof from the problems of the day, now felt that the moment had come for him to take his position in their ranks, and fight the fight of the times. The romance is a dignified and noble protest against those who would fetter freedom of thought and instruction in our day. It has to back it all polemics against dogmas. All its main personages, with a clear consciousness of their position, are made to live in that atmosphere of freer ideas, which is the vital air of modern times. It is one of those works which possess the intensity of a long-repressed, late-matured personal experience, and therefore has a vitality to which no awkwardness of form, no lack of form, can be prejudicial. The book, as a first attempt, is wanting in many of the elements of the genuine romance; the hero, as might have been expected, lacks much in resolution, in active manly vigor; it does not concentrate itself in a single, absolutely dominating interest; the all-engulfing erotic element does not permit the idea to stand forth clear and central, as is was conceived by the poet. The decisive turning-point of the work seems to be impending where Franzelius, after the burial of Balder, is thrown into prison on the denunciation of Lorinser. Here Edwin says expressly:[23] "You desire *open* war, you yourself demand it, and there shall be no peace until it has been honestly fought out." But the *open* war does not take place; the entire little band of heroes of the book content themselves with the defensive, and when Edwin has finally completed his epoch-making work, the romance ends. Closely associated with

[23] Kinder der Welt, ii. 265.

this lack is the undue softness of feeling in those parts which treat of Balder. The absence of that strict observance of proportion and limits which distinguish Heyse's "novellen," is plainly felt in this romance. But how would it be possible that great merits in a work of such extent should not be purchased with some lacks. Not only have the ideal female characters here the same points of excellence as in the "novellen"; but the poet has also enlarged his sphere in a high degree; even the least ideal figures, Christiane. Mohr, Marquard, are incomparable. And what a flood of genuine humanity streams through this romance! What a fund of true, versatile culture it contains! It is not only a courageous book, it is also an edifying one.

On certain foul attacks which it drew down upon its author, I will not linger. The denunciations of a couple of insignificant German sheets alone interest me because one of these abusive articles, which so stated the purport of the book that it was represented as dealing solely with the coarsest sensuality, was brought out in Norway by the Norwegian translator of Goethe's "Faust," with an introduction in which all Norwegian fathers of families were warned against allowing the book to cross their thresholds.[24]

[24] Did not a critic of this sort take it upon himself to get up a "warning" in the same style, against Goethe's "Faust"? "The purport of this immoral work," he wrote, "is the following: A physician (Dr. Med.), already pretty well advanced in years, is weary of study, and hankers after carnal pleasures. Finally he signs a bond with the devil. The latter leads him through divers low diversions (which, for instance, consist in making half-drunk students still more drunk) to a burgher's daughter, a young maiden, whom Faust (the doctor) at once attempts to seduce. A couple of rendez-vous at the house of an old procuress prepare the way for this. As the seduction, however, cannot be brought about speedily enough, the devil gives Faust a jewel-case to present to the young maiden. Wholly powerless to resist this gift, that is to say, not even seduced, simply purchased, Gretchen yields to Faust; and in order to be all the more undisturbed with her lover she doses her old mother with a narcotic, which kills the old woman. Then after being the cause of her brother's death, she destroys her child, the fruit of her shame. In prison she employs herself in singing obscene songs. That her lover left her in the lurch we cannot wonder when we consider his religious principles. He is, as the scene in which his donna questions him about his faith clearly proves, no Christian; indeed, he does not even seem to believe in a

For a sharp thrust from France, Heyse had every reason to be prepared. It came not unmerited; for the remarks concerning the literature and intellectual tendency of that country occurring in his romance are quite in the style of the general German sentiment; but the cut might have been given in a more chivalrous and skilful manner than the very ignoble and narrow-minded article by Albert Réville in the "Revue des Deux Mondes," which was dictated by national hatred and a love of self-amusement.

Freedom of thought was the fundamental idea of the "Kinder der Welt"; freedom of moral action is the fundamental idea of the romance "Im Paradiese," yet not in such a way that this work must be considered an attempt at justification; for if the freedom of thought Heyse advocates may be designated as absolute, the freedom of moral action is only relative. Moreover, "Im Paradiese" is a work of quite a different character than the first romance. Even the fact that the scenes of the early romance are laid in keen, critical Berlin, the second one in merry, pleasure-loving Munich, indicates the difference. While the "Kinder der Welt" may be called a philosophic romance, "Im Paradiese" is a sort of *roman comique,* light, graceful, and full of a raillery blended with earnestness. Its greatest value is in being the psychology of an entire city of importance, and the portrait of the social and art circles of this city. All Munich is embraced in this book, and as a matter of course, the artist life of this city of artists occupies the main place. The conversations and reflections on art have not the useless and abstract character in the pages of this book that they assume in the ordinary art-romance; we feel that it is no theorist but a connoisseur who speaks, and a genuine studio atmosphere is diffused throughout all

God, although he endeavors to grasp at all sorts of empty subterfuges to conceal his absolute unbelief.

"As this wicked book, notwithstanding all this, finds, as we hear to our astonishment, many readers, indeed, even lady readers, and is in constant demand at the circulating libraries in our city, we beg of all fathers of families to watch over the spiritual welfare of those belonging to them, to whom such profligate reading is all the more dangerous because its immoral teachings are veiled in a polished, insinuating form."

portions of the book. The entire æsthetics of the author may be condensed into Ingre's old definition, *"l'art c'est le nu."*

So far as the entanglements and composition of the plot are concerned, "Im Paradiese" denotes an undoubted progress. The interest is sustained throughout, and what is more, it continually increases; a commendation that cannot be bestowed on "Kinder der Welt." Now and then, however, the means used to forward the plot are applied in rather an unskilful manner. For instance, the entire rôle play by the dog Homo as *deus ex machina* is especially marked in its exaggerations. He reminds us, with his superhuman penetration, of those lions of the sculpture of the "Zopf" period, with human and majestic countenances, framed in masses which too strongly resemble the big wigs of real life. Yet in German romances not the plot, but the delineation of character is the main thing, and in almost all its subordinate figures this book reveals a new side of Heyse's talent. Such forms as Angelica. Rosenbusch, Kohl, Schnetz, have sportive, manifold life that formerly had been almost entirely excluded from Heyse's style. In a word, Heyse's mind has gained humor, the humor of mature manhood, one might almost say, of forty years of age; but a delicate sagacious, quiet humor which renders complete the gift of the poet and invests its coloring with the true blending.

IX

We have run through the circle of ideas and forms in which this poetic soul has found its expression. We have seen how Heyse, at last, in the romance accommodated himself to the thought agitating modern times, and to which the "novellen" form was not able to give adequate space. Moreover, I pointed out one "novelle" which was not less distinguished by its fundamental thought than "Der Salamander" was by its style.

Each time that Heyse has attempted to gain a modern interest for ancient myths, he has been fortunate. The charming little youthful poem, "Die Furie" (The Fury), is among the best that he has written. In a little drama, "Perseus" (not included in his collected works), he has given a new intepretation of the Medusa myth; he has felt pity for poor, beautiful Medusa, to whom was allotted the cruel fate of turning every one into stone, and he informs us that the envy of the goddesses who were jealous of her love for Perseus is alone to blame for this. Her head falls by the hand of her own lover, while she, in order not to harm him through her pernicious gaze, buries her face in the sand. Heyse has transformed the ancient myth into an original and sorrowful Mährchen. The story of the "Centaur" is bright, and full of profound thought. We are not astonished when "Im Paradiese" informs us the this story inspired the favorite fresco of the painter Kohle. The pilgrimage "unserer lieben Frau von Milo," which as a picture we almost think we see before our eyes, so vividly in the fresco described, is intimately related as a poem to "Der letzte Centaur" (The last Centaur)! That sounds almost like the last of the Mohikans! What does Heyse know of the last Centaur? How could he possibly introduce him into a regular "novelle"? It is done with consummate art, and yet in the most natural way in the world. He first, so to speak, brings together two circles, then a third circle, and in the latter he conjures up the Centaur. The first circle is the world of the living, the second the world of the dead, the third easily and naturally comprises the world of the supernatural. The story begins, contrary to Heyse's custom, in a purely autobiographical way, therefore, with the strongest possible elements of reality. The author, late one evening, approaches a wine-house, where, in his youth, he was in the habit of meeting every week his dearest friends and comrades, all of whom are now dead, and lets them pass in review before his mind's eye. Finally he enters the wine-house, feels weary, and suddenly it seems to him as though he were summoned to join the old circle, and as the door is opened, lo! his friends all sit together. But not one of them extends a hand to him who is entering, and their faces wear an expression of formality, seriousness, and sorrow. Every now and then they drink long draughts from their wineglasses, while their pale cheeks and dim eyes sparkle and glow for a moment, but directly afterward they sit rigid and silent once more, staring into their glasses. One of them alone is not bowed down by the destiny that has overtaken them, and of which, from a mute agreement, not a word is spoken in the society. It is Genelli, the distinguished painter, whose "Centaur" in the "Shackschen Sammlung" at Munich is the admiration of all travellers. One of the company remarks that such a Genelli creation looks so life-like that one is almost inclined to believe that the artist himself was a participator in the scene. And as the master calmly replies "And so he was," we glide imperceptibly from the realm of the dead to the world of fiction. He has seen the Centaur with his own eyes, one beautiful summer afternoon, as it came trotting, without thought of evil, into a little Tyrolese village, where Genelli sat over his wineglass. In olden times, the Centaur was a country physician by profession, had grown weary during a professional tour across the mountains, had laid himself down to sleep in a glacier-cave, was then frozen in and now, after the lapse of centuries, the ice had melted about him, and he could freely gaze on the changed world with his wondering eyes. It is Sunday, and just church time, when, with his mighty body,—a Farnese Hercules above, a superb, heroic battle-charger below,— with floating mane and long trailing horse tail, with a spray of roses behind one ear in his thick hair, he trots through the empty streets, only now and then terrifying some old woman, who flees, with shrieks of alarm, from the strange apparition. He sees the church door open, the building full of people, and a marvellously beautiful woman with a child on her arm, painted over the altar. Filled with curiosity, meaning no harm, he trots through the portal, over the stone flags, and approaches the altar. It can easily be comprehended what a hubub is caused by this monster, newly arisen from hell. The parson shrieks aloud, waves toward the beast whatever consecrated thing he may happen to hold in his hand, and cries "Apage! apage!" (which the Centaur understands because it is Greek). The congregation makes the sign of the cross over and over again; and filled with astonishment, this beast of ancient story then trots out of the door again, and accompanied by all the old women and all the children of the village, who are naturally very much shocked to see "the lofty traveller so lightly clad," presses onward to the village inn, where Genelli is sitting on the balcony. The master then informs the Centaur that he has awakened to life either a couple of hundred years too late or too early. At the time of the Renaissance he would doubtless have been well received. "But at the present day, among this narrow-chested, broad-browed, enervated, unmanned, worn-out race that is called the modern world!" Genelli could not venture to make out a very cheering horoscope for him. "Wherever you may show yourself, in cities or in villages, the street-urchins will run after you and pelt you with rotten apples, the old women will cry murder, and the priest will report you to be the foul fiend himself, etc." And it comes to pass as Genelli has prophesied. While the worthy Centaur, with the good nature that belongs to the strong, allows the public to stare at him, to feel his soft, velvety hide, while he, in genial mood, drains glass after glass of wine, and hands back his empty glass over the railing of the arbor to the pretty bar-maid, to whom he at once gave his rose, hatred and envy are lying in ambush to work his destruction. A complete conspiracy has been formed against him. "At the head stood, of course, the reverend clergy, who deemed it detrimental to the spiritual welfare of their parishioners to come into closer contact with a certainly unchristian, wholly naked, and no doubt, very immoral beast-man." Equally incensed was an Italian who had been exhibiting on the market-place a stuffed calf with two heads and five legs. The horse-man could be seen gratis, he was alive and drank and talked, and who knew whether he might not even be moved to treat the by-standers to some skilful feats of horsemanship. The calf, on the other hand, was a peaceful genius, and gave no signs of any such extravagant undertakings. The Italian cannot enter into competition.

"There is a difference," he explains to the parson, "between a legalized, natural sport, that is carried on with the full approval of the police, and a monster that is wholly beyond the limits of probability, such a one as has never been known to exist before, who, travelling without passport or license, makes the country unsafe and steals the bread from the mouths of honest five-legged calves." But the most passionate opponent of the Centaur is the little bow-legged village tailor, the bridegroom elect of the pretty bar-maid. The tailor, too, discloses his mind to the parson, and expresses his anxiety lest the new fashion introduced by the unknown should ruin the whole tailor's trade, and, moreover, overthrow all conceptions of decency and good morals. So, while the Centaur, in his cheerful mood is just engaged in carrying the fair Nanni on his back round the court-yard of the inn, and, at the same time, entertaining the by-standers with an exceedingly graceful and peculiar dance, all the conspirators appear with a company of mounted gens-d'armes to capture him. Without honoring them with the slightest attention, he continues his dance, and softly pressing the maiden's hands on his breast, he makes a magnificent leap over the heads of the peasants and away he goes. Pistol-balls follow him, with sharp reports, without hitting him, and soon he stands free on the next mountain slope. There moved by the piteous entreaties of the maiden, he allows her to glide gently down to the ground. "Greatly as she had been flattered by the chivalrous homage of the stranger, and pitiful as was the figure her own sweetheart displayed beside him, she could not expect a solid support from this mounted foreigner." Her practical nature triumphs, and like a hunted chamois she springs from stone to stone into her tailor's arms. An expression of divine scorn glides over the countenance of the Centaur; he is seen to move away, and shortly afterward he has vanished from the eager gaze of those who are staring after him.

Here Genelli's voice is hushed, the little circle breaks up, and the poet awakens in the ante-room of the inn.

All the qualities which make a poetic work an enjoyment

to the reader are combined in this "Märchen"; an exalted humor, which casts a gentle glow over all the details, the tenderest semi-tone and the finest clare-obscure, that permits the action of the piece to glide gently from the light of day into a dream of a circle of the dead, and then again allows the twilight of the shadow-world to be illumined by a sunbeam from old Hellas. Add to this a profound thought, which is entirely original to its poet. For this sportive tale is in reality a hymn to freedom in art as well as in life, and to freedom as Heyse has conceived it. In his eyes freedom does not consist in a struggle for freedom (as, for instance, in the case of the Norwegian author Henrik Ibsen), but it is the protest of nature against dogmas in the religious sphere, of nature against conventionality in the social and moral sphere. Through nature to freedom! that is his path and that his watchword. Thus the Centaur as half human being, half divinity, is to his fancy a beloved symbol. How beautiful is the Centaur in his proud strength gained from the remnant of old Grecian blood he has preserved in his veins! What must he not have suffered, the poor Centaur, for the remnant of heathenism, that has arisen in him, and that, after having been frozen in a few thousand years, has ventured out into the light of day in our age when all the glaciers are beginning to melt away! How much more instructive, how much more sedate and moral, does the whole civilized world about him find his interesting rival, the stuffed calf, with two tongues and five legs, which are by no means intended for progress, but are conservative legs that with all due propriety keep the place ascribed to them. Such curiosities never exceed the limits of any civil custom, never exhibit themselves without permission from the public authorities and the clergy, and are therefore none the less unusual. They will always remain rivals of the Centaur, considered by some as his equal and by others as far outshining him.

And is not the poet himself, on his Pegasus in this petty modern social world of ours, the living representative of "the last Centaur"?

X

I have noted down some expressions of opinion concerning Heyse, favorable and unfavorable all mixed together.

"Heyse," says one, "is the woman's doctor, the German woman's doctor, who has thoroughly understood Goethe's saying,—

> 'Es ist ihr ewig Weh und Ach
> So tausendfach u. s. w.'

That he is no poet for men, Prince Bismarck has rightly felt."

"On the contrary," says another, "Paul Heyse is very masculine. He is pronounced weak by some because he is pleasing, because a finished grace has lent its impress to his creations. People do not realize how much strength is requisite in order to have this exquisite charm!"

"What is Heyse?" says a third. "The denizen of a small town, who has so long played hide and seek with Berlin, with the social life of the world, with politics, that he has estranged himself from our present, and only feels at home among the troubadours in Provence. I always scent out something of the Provençale and of the provincialist in his writings."

"This Heyse," remarks a fourth, "in spite of his fifty years and the maturity of his authorship, has the weakness to wish to persuade us throughout that he is an immoral, lascivious poet. But no man believes him. That is his punishment."

"I have never in my life been so greatly envied," once said a lady, an old friend of Heyse's youth, in my presence, "as I was to-day, in one of our higher schools for young ladies, which I was visiting, when the rumor was circulated that I was about to pass the evening in a circle where I would meet him. The little damsels (Backfische) unanimously commissioned me to carry to him their enthusiastic greetings. How gladly would they one and all have thrown themselves into his arms! He is and always will be the idolized author of young maidens."

"One can define Paul Heyse," said a critic, "as the Mendelssohn-Bartholdy of German poetry. He appears like Mendelssohn when compared to the great masters. His nature, like that of Mendelssohn, is a German lyric, sensitive temperament, permeated with the most refined Southern culture. Both men lack the grand pathos, the energetic power, the storm of the dramatic element; but both have natural dignity in earnestness, charming amiability and pleasing grace in jest, they are thoroughly cultured in regard to form, they are virtuosos in execution."

III

ESAIAS TEGNÉR

1878

LITERARY fame in the Scandinavian countries is for the most part a matter of mere local importance. Works written in languages which are spoken by a few million people only, and which in no portion of the world are studied or read as polite languages, are likely to have every chance of European and American renown against them. As a general thing, but few poetic productions are translated into other tongues; and, indeed, to a work that appeals to the sense of beauty, above all to a metrical work, the outer form of language is what the enamel is to the teeth: it invests it at the same time with durability and brilliancy.

Nevertheless, it is a well-known fact that certain northern authors have succeeded in finding more recognition in foreign countries than at home; they represent, as it were, to the entire reading-world the poetic life of their fatherland, and their names are blended in the public consciousness with the name of their native land. Such fame has been attained by but one of the poets of Sweden,—Easais Tegnér.

He is not the greatest among those who have contributed to the poetry of the Swedish language; before him and after him another greater poet produced in this tongue creations superior to his in clearness of style and fidelity to life. With Bellman and Runeberg, however, he must be classed; and, while inferior to them in poetic fancy, he may be said to surpass both in intellectual vigor.

Three times in the course of history, the Swedish people has succeeded in combining the classic and the popular in its poetry. The first time was when Bellman, during the reign of Gustavus III., selected his types from life among the people and in the inns of Stockholm, and sang "The Songs of Fredman" to a zither accompaniment, with a mimic display of masterly skill. The second time was when Tegnér, fifty years later, turned back to the heroic life of the ancient North, found in an old saga materials for a romance cycle, and gave Sweden a picture of Viking life and Viking love in the North, as his contemporaries conceived it. Finally this combination of the classic and the popular occurred about a generation ago, when—forty years after Finland had been torn from her old mother country—the greatest of Finland's sons, inspired by recollections of his childhood, depicted the honorable struggle of his fatherland against Russian supremacy, and thereby the national characteristics of the Finnish people, in a more realistic style than any one else had yet ventured to employ. Runeberg, in his soul-stirring bivouac poetry, has compressed into the smallest limits war idyls and tragedies of the battlefield.

Neither in a drama nor in an epic poem, therefore, has one of these three Swedish poets found the possibility of presenting to the world the best fruits of his genius. All three, however widely they may otherwise differ, have triumphed in the same species of art, one that is lyric in form, and whose contents compose an epic cycle of short poems. The first of these poets has produced burlesque dithyrambs; the second, old Norse heroic lays; the third, anecdotes of modern warfare; but each one has arranged his choicest poems in a connected series, and these three groups of songs alone invest Swedish poetry with cosmopolitan rank.

The most celebrated of these three cycles is the "Fridthjof's Saga," and when Tegnér is mentioned outside of Sweden, it is exclusively as its author. This work has become the national poem of the Swedish people, and translations into all European tongues—among others, eighteen different German, and twenty-two different English translations—have spread it broadcast over the earth. Sweden has not been lacking in gratitude to the man to whom she owes so much. Such noble and eloquent words have been spoken, written, and sung throughout Sweden, in honor of Tegnér, that no one could bestow on him greater praise than has already been accorded him by the children of his native land. Sweden has exalted the glorified form of the poet, in supernatural size, upon a mighty pedestal, proved by closer scrutiny to be a miniature mountain of massive eulogies, biographies, and festal songs, while at the base incense without stint has been burned. What then remains for the critic? Nothing, unless perchance to cleanse from the beautiful face, with tender hand, the blinding fumes of the incense, in order that the delicate features may stand out clearly, and seem more human, more lifelike. Perchance, too, it may devolve on him to compare the statue carefully with the original, and draw a pen-and-ink sketch of the latter, in which it is plainly indicated where the statue lacks precision or has a too abstract conception. The writer of these pages, at all events, enters on his task with the innate sympathy of the Scandinavian, the impartiality of one who is not a Swede, and the honest purpose of the critic, to represent the form in the sharp sunlight of truth.

I

The ancestors of Esaias Tegnér, both on his father's and on his mother's side, were Swedish peasants. As in so many other instances of the prominent talent of the north, his descent may be traced from the peasant class through the ranks of the priesthood. This generally comes to pass in the following way: the grandfather plows his fields with his own hand, the son displays a thirst for knowledge, and through many sacrifices on the part of his parents, and the support of kindly disposed people, progresses far enough in his studies to enter on a theological course; for during many centuries the priest was the absolute representative among the peasants of the learned class. In this son, the vigorous untutored peasant-nature becomes subjected to its first rude polish; the preacher no longer plows his own fields, although he may supervise their cultivation; the preacher begins to think, although the final result of his studies is not the consequence of his thought. In the grandson, or great grandson, the original fundamental nature finally becomes so refined, that it produces scientific, technical, or poetic talent. Thus is was in the case before us. The father of Tegnér was a priest, the mother a priest's daughter, and these clerical progenitors were the children of peasants. The aristocratic sounding name was formed when the father Esaias Lucasson, from the little village Tegna (Tegnaby), was entered in the Latin register of the gymnasium as Esaias Tegnerus.

The parsonage was early blessed with sons and daughters, and at Kyrkerud, on the 13th of November, 1782, was born the fifth son of the house, the eventually so celebrated Esaias. He was only nine years old when the home was broken up by the death of his father. The latter left his family without means of support, and his widow, whose heart was filled with anxiety for the future of her six fatherless children, joyfully seized the opportunity offered her to place her youngest son as clerk with a highly esteemed state official living in the vicinity. In the office of Assessor Branting, through tasks in penmanship and keeping accounts, the boy acquired habits of industry which lasted through life; and of even greater value to the little clerk was the opportunity afforded him, at the early age when all impressions are the most profound, of making the acquaintance, from the travelling carriage, of the picturesque, natural beauties of the home region, during the extensive trips he was permitted to share with his worthy chief, whose duties as assessor compelled him to traverse every portion of Wermland. Although active and industrious when at work, young Esaias was inclined to be forgetful and absent-minded at times, to become wholly absorbed in his book, or waking dreams, and he would often be found wandering along some solitary road soliloquizing in a low tone. He read poetry, works of history, above all else northern sagas; and in a collection of the latter, Björner's "Kämpadater," he discovered "The Saga of Fridthjof the Bold," which lingered twenty-five years in his fancy before it began to germinate.

These two impressions, that of Sweden's nature and of the old Norse myths and sagas, were inseparable; they mingled together, gliding softly one into the other in the young soul. Often, when perched on the back seat of Branting's carriage, the future poet was driven between forest-decked mountains, through deep ravines, along the banks of those mighty waters that stream through the land, it seemed to him as though Nature were vying with him in freaks of fancy. Romantic indeed were the landscapes presented to his view in the long summer days, when twilight and dawn flowed gently together, and the roseate glow never vanished from the horizon, while an old northern landscape charmed him in winter, when the snow was piled in high banks, when the brooks hung in long icicles from the rocks, and the youth felt as though he actually saw, in the moonlight playing on the snow, winter personified, in the colossal form of a god, with a snow-storm in his beard, and a wreath of fir upon his head.

Swedish poetry, [says Tegnér somewhere,] is, and ever will be, a poetry of nature in the strictest sense of the word; for it centres in our glorious natural scenery, in our lakes, rocks, and waterfalls; [and when, shortly after the completion of "Fridthjof," he wishes to explain the origin of the poem, he himself mentions, in addition to his early, familiar acquaintance with the old Norse sagas, the fact that he was born and brought up in a remote mountain parish] where Nature herself makes poetry in weird and gigantic forms, and where the ancient gods still wander about in the flesh, of winter nights. In such surroundings, [he continues,] left wholly to myself, it was not singular that I acquired a certain predilection for the untamed and the colossal that has never left me.

And not only the contents, but also the fundamental form of his own as well as of all other Swedish poetry, Tegnér, in his riper years strove to trace to impressions of the peculiar nature of Sweden. He is astonished at the exclusive preference of his people for the lyric, at the tendency of this people to crowd the entire world of poetry into a few strophes, and he inquires into the reason of this characteristic. "Does it not lie for the most part in the nature itself which surrounds us? Are not the mountains, with their valleys and torrents, the lyric of Nature, while the gentler plains, with their calm rivers, are Nature's epos? Many of our mountain regions are true dithyrambs of nature, and man delights in making poetry in the same key as that of the nature about him." And then boldly endeavoring to draw the utmost inference of his thought, he bursts into the query, "Does not a lyric vein permeate all Swedish poetry? Are not the most prominent representatives of our national traits in ancient as well as in modern times, rather lyric than epic characters?" He was evidently thinking of such minds as Sweden's greatest kings and greatest generals, and perhaps not least of all of himself.

It is an undoubted fact that the nature about him attracted him, as a poet, far more through its fanciful than through its utilitarian element. I say designedly "as a poet," for as a man he cherished a healthy, practical interest in the means of subsistence and sources of industry of his people. He has, however, never depicted this people in its struggles with material nature. There cannot be found in his works a single scene representing the great mining operations through which Swedish iron is brought to the light of day; he has never presented a picture of the hardy miner or the sturdy smith; never vouchsafed a view of the blazing, steaming, glowing furnace in the midst of the snow. These realistic impressions rebounded from his romantic fancy, inclined as it was to view everything in the abstract, to symbolize. Sweden did not present herself to his mind's eye as the workshop of the nation; his Svea was a shield-bearing maiden, and her dower of iron was in his eyes less the source of the natural wealth of the land than the broad girdle about her waist and the once so mighty sword within her hand.

II

Very early it was discovered that the gifted boy possessed talents which made it seem desirable to furnish him with higher opportunites for education than those afforded in the office of Assessor Branting. A conversation that took place one evening, during a long country drive, when young Esse, as the boy was called, replied to the religious reflections of his pious chief, concerning the signs of God's omnipotence in the bright starry firmament, with an exposition of the laws governing the heavenly bodies, that he had derived from a popular work on philosophy, gave the first impetus to the step of entering Esaias on a learned career. An instinct, to which the future bishop ever remained true, led him to grasp with both hands the rational explanation of the workings of the universe, and to cast aside the theological in all cases where the latter seemed to him superfluous.

Under the guidance of his elder brother, he was now initiated into the study of Latin, Greek, and French, and he taught himself sufficient English to be able to read the poems of Ossian, at that time in the height of their glory. Like a foal trotting at its mother's side, he accompanied his brother to the various homes where the latter officiated at tutor; and in the last family in which his brother taught, Esaias, when but fourteen years of age, found in the youngest daughter of the house his future wife. Like so many other precocious youths, he avoided the boisterous sports of his comrades; his greatest delight was to sit alone in his chamber, absorbed in Homer; and he had to be dragged by main force to sleighing parties and skating matches, although he was by no means an unskilful skater. In the year 1799 he entered the university of Lund, devoted himself to the ancient languages, philosophy, and æsthetics; and in 1802, according to the pathetic custom of the land, was crowned with laurels as master (magister) of philosophy. From 1802 to 1810 he lived in Lund as a young instructor (docent) of good renown; from 1810 to 1825 he gave lectures on Grecian literature that were very popular and well attended. In the year 1812, in accordance with a very poor Swedish custom, he was at the same time presented with a professor's chair, and appointed pastor of several parishes in the vicinity of Lund; in 1826, finally, he left the little university town in order to retire as a bishop to the rural solitude of Vexiö.

Let us bestow a glance upon the young magister of Lund. He is pleasing to behold,—blue-eyed, rosy-cheeked, with yellow, curly hair, vigorously built, and with a tendency to corpulency. As long as he remained a bachelor he was a retired dreamer, who brooded over his own fancies in solitude; but so soon as he had placed foot beneath his own table, his intellectual powers unfolded, and he proved himself to possess a light-hearted nature that was social in the highest degree, and bubbling over with merriment. A child of the world, who knew how to do honor to a good table and noble wine; an easily inflamed and by no means seraphic Apollino; an adorer of all female beauty; a genius that emitted brilliant flashes of well-considered and sparkling wit, rather than the glowing flames of a deep-seated fire; an individual who was tolerably unconcerned about his conventional dignity, but who was none the less thoroughly well prepared to maintain the proud sovereignty of his own personality; such is the phase of character Tegnér presented to the outside world. Beneath this exterior are concealed his deeper traits. These are partly of a poetic, partly of an oratorical, nature; a lyric inspiration and a glowing style that are peculiarly his own.

III

The lyric inspiration of Tegnér early reveals itself as an innate tendency to enthusiasm for everything that stands out in bold relief from the gray and prosaic background of every-day life. All deeds of heroic valor; all brilliant honors, let them be gained as they may, attract him by their radiance, and he revels even in their tinsel. A strong respect for the great names of history, a decided disinclination to apply discriminating criticism to fame once established, form one of the deepest and most unchangeable traits of his character. It is the unusual climax attained by this fundamental tendency which impels him to write poetry. Indeed, it is this which makes him a poet. In order, however, the better to understand this tendency, we must go back to the sources of his inspiration, investigate what ideal he seeks, discovers, or creates, see in what sort of inner images he objectizes the natural peculiarities or intellectual attributes which correspond to the best of his native powers. He does not dream of Oehlenschläger's Aladdin form; he is neither unsophisticated enough nor bold enough to do so. Just as little is he inclined to mirror himself in a Hamlet or a Faust. The heroes of scepticism and of thought are far too abstract for his vigorous, boyish imagination; it dreams of sturdier ideals. Still less do his conceptions concentrate about a Manfred type. Guilt does not allure him, and the mysterious has for his frank nature no charm. Brought up and developed amid idyllic conditions, and surrounded by universal good-will in the little town which he himself named "an academic village," he could not possibly give way to the cosmopolitan prose pathos of the long repressed Schiller. The ideal which slowly shapes itself in his mind is a national and northern romantic ideal.

It is a luminous image of stormily progressive and remodelling power, partly of a warlike, partly of a civilizing nature. All of the forms which Tegnér, in the course of years, has shown marked preference for delineating, have been invested with it. In one of his university addresses, for instance, he undertook to give a characterization of Luther. In order to accomplish this he places his hero in the point of view from which it is his wont to consider men of action. First he emphatically declares that every word and action of Luther bore the stamp of "overwhelming vigor."

There was something chivalrous, in fact, I might almost say, romantic, in his character, his every undertaking. . . . His action was like a battle completed, his word like one just begun. He was one of those mighty souls who, like certain trees, flourish only amid storms. His grand, adventurous life always seemed to me like a heroic poem, with its struggles and its final victory.

We are all the more strongly impressed with the character of the orator from this very one-sided treatment of a many-sided theme when we note that Tegnér has therein presented determining qualities which, with slightly altered attributes, he can apply a few years later, almost word for word, to King Gustavus III. of Sweden, whose personality differs as widely as possible from that of Luther. Scarcely any proof is needed to show that between the sturdy Saxon reformer and the theatrical, Gallicized, and sceptical monarch there was no other bond of union than that which Tegnér's admiration created for both. Tegnér said of Gustavus, "In his nature there was not only something grand, but at the same time something chivalrous; lofty heroic power was displayed in him, not with shield and sword, but with the lightest drapery of grace. He was a grand, romantic, heroic poem, with all its adventures and fascinations, but at the same time with the tenderest effusions of the heart and the most wanton gambols of joy."

Grandeur, strength, and adventurous romance, then, are the common fundamental qualities for both Luther and Gustavus; both are knights of chivalry, and the lives of both appear to Tegnér like a romantic epic poem. What else and what more could he say about Fridthjof? What else, in truth, has he said, when in his own characterization he called attention to the fresh life, the bold defiance, and the haughtiness of this hero and this heroic poem!

In this tendency we have the deepest, firmest foundation on which his conceptions of heroic ideals gradually came to rest.

There are some youthful, innocent odes dating from the period of Tegnér's sixteenth year, written on the occasion of the rumor of Bonaparte's death in Egypt. In them the poet glorifies Bonaparte as the hero of freedom, whose honor is not purchased through blood and tears, yet who will bring enlightenment and joy to the whole world. It is an echo from the refrain of the humanitarian period which rings from these childish lips. They hail Napoleon with a categorical "Live for humanity or perish!" The mature man views the subject differently. In the great religious, political and literary reaction against the period of enlightenment, the anti-Gallican current which won Sir Walter Scott and Oehlenschläger, was wholly obnoxious to Tegnér. The reaction, however, struck an æsthetic chord which harmonized with his temperament. This was its contempt for utility as a measure for the worth of a deed. The fact was, ultra-utilitarianism, and the species of philanthropy interlinked with it, had opposed itself to the conception of the chivalrous and the romantic.

The old chivalrous dream, [says Tegnér,] of the honor of nations, was either declared point-blank to be a freak of the imagination, or else to be synonymous with their domestic welfare. Everything in history was estimated, as in a counting-house, according to its practical results; and no higher estimate placed on a house of correction, or a threshing-machine, than on Alexander's adventurous expedition to India, or the fruitless victory of Charles XII.

He does not exaggerate; poor Alexander the Great was ranked in Sweden, by an inspired enlightener of the people, as far inferior to that benefactor of mankind who invented the cheap and nutritious Brunswick mum.[1] Tegnér's youthful conceptions of virtuous, useful heroes now become modified by the prevailing controversies, and are brought into harmony with the protest of the entire romantic bent of his mind against the narrow-minded care for the welfare of humanity as a main essential. Moral considerations give way before the romantic-metaphysical adoration of the hero of fate.

> Wherefore scorn me thus forever,
> Legions frail and transitory,
> Shorn of will, devoid of might?
> Catch the butterfly, but never
> Stay the eagle, crown'd with glory,
> As it seeks its mountain height.
>
> * * * * *
>
> Ask the storm, amid its wailing,
> Ask the sky's majestic thunder,

[1] A strong kind of beer, first brewed by Chr. Mumme, of Brunswick, Germany, in 1492. Pope says: "The clamorous crowd is hushed with mugs of mum."—Tr.

When earth quails 'neath its alarms,
If the lily 'tis assailing;
Tho, the grove be thrilled with wonder,
If a loving pair it harms.

Thus he expresses himself in the poem entitled "Hjelten" (The Hero), 1813. These sentiments, to be sure, are far from being Tegnér's final views. Accustomed as he was to gaze upward to individual personality as the highest form of existence, he was only likely to be moved on some special occasion and in a half defiant way to give vent to such pantheistic notions as those in this poem. And, as a consciously reflecting spirit, he was much rather inclined not to believe in the unconscious than to overestimate it, making, for instance, a large number of polemic attacks on the doctrine of a blind poetic inspiration; yet his preference for the warlike stormy march of progress was so deeply rooted in his heart that he did not recoil from giving such bold expression to it as in the poem just cited.

Still more strongly than in the various lays to the honor of Napoleon, does he express his contempt for material gain as the result of deeds of heroism in his poem, "Alexander on the Hydaspes." The poet has chosen the moment when the exhausted and dispirited troops implore the great Alexander not to conduct them farther into Asia, but to lead his army homeward. The king replies scornfully: "Do you think that I, as a youth, came down from the Macedonian mountains to furnish you with gold and purple raiment? I seek honor; honor alone and nothing else!" —a reply which, in point of sharpness and precision, leaves nothing to be desired. The disregard of human life and human happiness evinced by the highly endowed and intrepid despot is represented as unconditionally justifiable.

It is therefore very easy to understand how Charles XII., whom the Swedish people, with justice, have never ceased to admire, could become a hero without reproach to Tegnér. He scarcely even deems it a stain upon Charles that, with all his brilliant qualities, he plunged Sweden into such depths that it has never since been able to regain its place among the great powers of Europe. It was no mere chance that it was Tegnér, among all the poets of Sweden, who wrote the glorious poem on this king, which, although composed merely as a poem for a special occasion, became the national song of Sweden. An impractical rushing into danger always fired his imagination: the stubbornness that, with gaze fixed upon a self-written code of honor, despised prudent actions, was in his eyes scarcely a fault, and consequently an indifference as to whether a deed would lead to victory or destruction, if it were only brilliant and noisy, was, in his estimation, a virtue.

> Northland's strength defies and never
> Death can conquest from us sever,
> For e'en should we fall at last,
> Life in battle's sport was past,[2]

are the words his "Gerda," in the epos of the same name, addresses to Bishop Absalom.

The circumspection of the statesman and the lawgiver had no power to rouse his enthusiasm; but he loved the royal youth "before whose word the meshes of the statesman's wiles are rent asunder" (Tegnér's "Charles XII."). The long-considered plans of the military commander did not seem to him the true evidence of warlike genius; but he admired beyond measure instantaneous inspiration on the battle-field, and the courageous impetuosity which followed it.

This is apparent when Tegnér describes a hero so different from, and so vastly superior to, Charles XII., as the Deliverer of Protestantism, Gustavus Adolphus. What he commends in him is not so much his merits as a political leader and warlike commander-in-chief, as it is the qualities which place him, as much as possible, on a parallel with a soldier-general like Charles XII. He lingers with enthusiasm over the "sudden, lightning flashes of thought on the battle-field," which characterized him, as "every other warrior-like genius." He extols Gustavus because he loved danger for danger's sake, and delighted in toying

[2] R. B. Anderson's Viking Tales, p. 143.

with death. In short, he holds fast to the narrow old Norse measure of manliness, and endeavors to apply it even in cases where it is far surpassed by genuine greatness. For instance, he considers it almost ignominious in Wallenstein to have (for good reasons) declined the battle that Gustavus, "his chivalrous opponent," offered him at Nuremberg.

What gives this ideal of Tegnér its final *retouche* is the candor he demands of his heroes. His own honest and sturdy nature mirrors itself therein. Of Wallenstein he says that he might have been called a great man "had he been noble and candid." Magnanimity will not suffice; candor is equally essential. The old Norse berserkers, in their martial fervor, flung their shields on their backs, and this mode of action found so much favor in Tegnér's eyes that he would gladly have seen it transported to the intellectual battle-field. Indeed, frankness seemed to him even a sort of guaranty for nobility of thought, and he regards the former with more warmth than the latter; for in his derogatory characterization of Wallenstein, he lays especial stress on his gloomy, reserved nature, without charging him with a single really ignoble trait. With him he contrasts Gustavus Adolphus, as the luminous, frank nature, endowed with a candor which was less doubtful in Tegnér himself than in the king who was, as a rule, retiring and little accessible.

Thus every form with which Tegnér's muse is occupied, receives a gentle pressure which moulds it into the form of the ideal hero, ever hovering before the poet's own mind.

IV

Closely allied to the lyric inspiration with Tegnér is the supplemental faculty which makes him witty in social intercourse, happy in epigram and impromptu, prominent as a professor, remarkable as a letter writer, orator and preacher, and beyond all else great in his metrical flow of poetically constructed language; a faculty which cannot be called outright a talent for rhetoric, but which provisionally, although perhaps rather vaguely, might be designated, in his case, as the intellectual faculty. His intellect was not the French *esprit*. The latter, in its most characteristic form, as with Voltaire, is pure understanding unadorned by imagery. The *esprit* of Tegnér, on the contrary, ran continually into imagery. He thought in figures, consequently he spoke in figures. The gift of abstract thought was lacking in him, indeed he was so wholly devoid of it that he did not even believe in its results in others: metaphysics was to him an abomination as a phantom of the brain, woven of threads which he could not discern; dogmatics were his terror, as a tissue of absurdities, to which his understanding could find no outlet. And he had a good, healthy, self-reliant understanding which instinctively abhorred all obscurity to thought and of speech. He had so lively an impulse to render perceptible all that he thought and felt, that figure after figure crowded upon him. It was this that gave his language those electric flashes of sparkling light which so captivated his contemporaries; it was this that rendered his epistolary style so entertaining, and caused exasperated critics to compare his poetry to gorgeous-colored empty soap-bubbles; it was this finally that made him witty, for there is a certain kind of wit that depends on the surprising succession of swiftly-dissolving images. This intellectuality might be called the fruitfulness of form. The mood into which he was transported by intellectual productiveness sprouted and blossomed incessantly; it was only by way of exception that it could project grand, wholly-completed images, or simple figures, formed of a few main outlines, but it produced a continuous flow of miniature figures which stood antithetically or contrastingly opposed to one another, which glided one over the other, were united and transmitted onward. His mind was loaded, revolver-like, with fancies, and they followed one another in swift succession, shot after shot, all aimed at the same point, striking surely, but each thrusting aside the one that had preceded it. Idea and figure were not separated in his mind, nor were their relations far-fetched, as Tegnér's opponents believed and asserted; and yet they were not purely one and the same.

In his imagination, thought and figure were related in about the same degree as the initial letters in the old monastic manuscripts were related to the miniature paintings with which they were interwoven and illuminated. If we call up before our mind's eye a manuscript in which the overwhelming majority of characters, not single ones alone, are thus illuminated, we can form a certain conception of the series of harmonious associations of ideas and figures which Tegnér's brain incessantly produced. Or if we recall one of those marble designs from the early days of the Italian Renaissance, in which the artist has executed at his pleasure small images on the larger statue, where he has chiselled, for instance, on the helm fallen from the head of Goliath, and lying at David's feet, a little bas-relief of a quadriga in full gallop, which forms, it is true, a part of the whole, but which, owing to its loose connection with it, as well as to its independent claims to consideration, dissipates the interest. If we think of a poetic mind calculated to conceive such bas-reliefs, and of a diction inclined to color these, we can form an approximately correct idea of Tegnér's manner of treating his poetic motive. His style is a sort of chromatic architecture and sculpture, and possesses the attractive and the repellent qualities of both. Colored sculpture is generally looked upon in our day as a species of barbarism; and yet the Greeks have employed it, nor was it ever wholly discarded by them. It cannot be called un-Grecian, and yet to most people in our day, it appears tasteless and antiquated. Those poems and speeches in which Tegnér's most characteristic manner stands forth with its utmost strength and distinctness, may be compared to those Grecian and Roman statues that produce quite as much effect through their exterior splendor as through their ideal beauty. The goddesses had golden chains about their necks, wore beautiful long veils, and ear-rings; they possessed a complete wardrobe, and an entire casket of jewels. Precisely in the same way have the jeweller and the artist worked together in Tegnér. In many instances the result has been a successful and attractive whole, which could be rejected by a pedant or a doctrinist alone. Not rarely, however, the result has been an excessive exaggeration. A pamphleteer of Tegnér's time (the witty Palmär), once censured this tendency in words which suit the comparison just used. "Greet your muse," said he, "and beg it not to overburden itself with metaphors, as is its wont. These jewels, even when they are genuine, must be worn with moderation. Let these trinkets be placed about the neck, in the ears, and on the fingers, if you will, but—on the toes—fie, for shame!"

I can more accurately explain my meaning through examples. Mary, in "Axel," resolves to follow the Russian army as a soldier.

> Beneath a soldier's cap
> She hides away her ringlets, dark as night;
> In a buff vest her slender form is laced;
> Alas, for such fair form in such array!
> O'er shoulder, known by Grecian poet's song,
> Death's spy-glass, the dread carabine, is hung.[3]

The expression, "death's spy-glass," for the dread carabine, is picturesque, and so far not bad; but none the less must it be said that the figure is not altogether appropriate. Not only has it nothing whatever to do with Mary's form, but it answers only to a gun in general, not to the particular weapon on her shoulder; for this would scarcely kill a Swede. Upon me this figure produces the same effect as if I were to see on the margin of the text, a carefully executed miniature of the dismal skeleton, with the scythe in one hand, and holding the carabine to its eye with the other, in order to take aim.

In the "Children of the Lord's Supper," the old priest beseeches the children he is about to confirm, to choose prayer and innocence as the guides of their lives. Both are personified with a few strokes, and then the figure is

[3] Translated by J. S.

engraved in a small biblical relief, of the kind that is seen in Italy on the bronze doors of churches and baptisteries.

Innocence, child beloved, is a guest from the world of the blessed:
Beautiful, and in her hand a lily; on life's roaring billows
Swings she in safety; she heedeth them not, in the ship she is sleeping.[4]

Or an example may be taken from Tegnér's epistolary style. He waxes eloquent (1817) against the European reaction. "Gaze at the signs of the times from the North and from the South! Do you know any vulgarity, any barbarism, any insane prejudice their regeneration does not promise? The serpent of time often sheds its skin; but more perverse than at this precise moment, it has never been, as far as history extends, even though it hissed nothing but hymns, and though its back were as completely covered with biblical texts as a tombstone." Is there not in this energetic but thoroughly unaffected effort at clear perception, something that reminds us of chromatic sculpture. Do we not see before us, in due form, the serpent of time, with its red outlines; and does not its back, all covered with peculiar ciphers, look like the image of a god, in the shape of a beast, covered with hieroglpyhics, or tile inscriptions, on some ancient Assyrian or Egyptian wall? And when finally the similitudes are read with which Tegnér, in "Fridthjof," endeavors to paint female beauty, can it not readily be comprehended why attention should be called to the hard metallic glow of the coloring of an antique idol?

> The bards praise Gerda's fair cheeks too high,
> Fresh snows which playful north-lights dye!
> I cheeks have seen whose daylights clear,
> Two dawnings blushing in one sphere.[5]

It would be unjust to cite this last stanza as an adequate specimen of Tegnér's picturesque method; nevertheless

[4] Longfellow's translation.
[5] R. B. Anderson's Viking Tales, p. 159.

there is something typical in it. Most of the similitudes produced by the fancy of Tegnér, so far exceed the brilliancy of nature, that to me they appear very much the same as the image he makes his Ingeborg weave of Fridthjof's falcon:—

> Here on his hand,
> Work I thy form on the cloth's broad band;
> Pinions of silver, and glowing
> gold talons sewing.[6]

With a predilection of this kind, something conventional and stiff can scarcely be avoided. The inclination to transform every idea into a figure beguiles Tegnér, in uninspired moments, into a common-place use of once applied similes, which keep recurring in an almost stereotyped way. Thus he has (merely to keep to the birds) a few bird forms which he never wearies of dragging in eagle, nightingale, and dove. They stand as equivalents for strength, poetry, and piety. The eagle used for this purpose by Tegnér retains no more of the nature of the real eagle than may be seen in the eagles that adorn royal escutcheons; Tegnér's eagle is purely heraldic. In his poetry may be found lines like these: "Alas! poor Psyche, fly as she will, on earth she is but an eagle with butterfly's pinions"; or similes like the following: "Within her throat a nightingale she carried, and a snow-white dove by night and by day did linger in her bosom." An eagle with butterfly pinions is a creature totally contrary to nature, and when a nightingale is firmly fixed in a female throat, it does not exactly contribute to the perspicuity of the thought.

In his address on entering the Swedish Academy, he defends himself in figurative language. He emphatically pronounces it to be the aim of poetry to offer images, not ideas, to the imagination, and considers it the character of language to be a gallery of faded pictures which the poet must of necessity revive. In this he is far from wrong, although he would have done well to take to heart the truly Hellenic remark once made by the Grecian poetess Corinne to Pin-

[6] R. B. Anderson's Viking Tales, p. 240.

dar, that "seeds should be sown with the hand, not with the sack." Fortunately for him the main lack of his poetic endowment, the peculiar mingling of poverty and prodigality, was so popular in its nature that, in his country and at his time, it tended to smooth the path to fame rather than to obstruct it.

V

Tegnér was born about the middle of the reign of Gustavus III. The assassination took place when he was ten years old; consequently he, who in later years was so fond of styling himself a Gustavian, had childish reminiscences alone of that period, and no other personal impressions of the character of Gustavus than those gained as second hand from a legend, embellished or idealized by tender hands. Even this was scarcely needed to make the period seem like one of rare brilliancy, in comparison with the leaden epoch which followed. Gustavus III. was a man of great energy, endowed with remarkable talents, unusual virtues, and dazzling vices; he was a vain despot, yet had an enlightened mind; he was one of the many crowned followers of Voltaire that were the product of the eighteenth century; he was full of superstition and yet a free-thinker, frivolous yet intellectual, in matters of trifling import displaying a petty spirit, but having traits of true greatness; he was brave, magnanimous, a hero of the stage, with genuine courage in his breast. During his whole life he attracted about him, through the magic of his mental powers, all the gifted literary men of his land, especially the poets, who saw in him a colleague; not one of them could boast so distinctly marked a dramatic talent as his. Thus it was that for a long time he imprinted upon the manners, the forms of speech, the literature of Sweden, the stamp of an exquisitely refined, light, frivolous culture; and it is the conversational tone of his day that invested Tegnér's letters, even in the reign of Charles John (Bernadotte), with their grace and their soaring flights of fancy. His was a form that had remained fixed in history, like one of Bernini's admirable statues; full of mannerism, coquettish, affected, if you will, with airily rustling drapery, but presenting an attitude that was bold and unflinching, and producing an impression of the most profound significance. Nor could this be denied, however little satisfaction might be taken in the figure. And what had come after him? First, the regency of the brother of Gustavus, the duke of Södermanland, which embraces the period from Tegnér's tenth to his fourteenth year. The regent, a wretched imbecile, who had grown prematurely gray in the service of Venus, and who was well adapted to be the prey of every Phryne and every Cagliostro, was wholly governed by his favorite Reuterholm, who represented the type of brutal and incompetent passion for rule. Not from love of freedom, but simply as an indirect way of censuring the murdered king, these empty-pated men introduced freedom of the press into Sweden, and, without any preparation or gradual transition, all the inflammatory writings of the French Revolution now flooded the land. The long-continued ignorance concerning what was transpiring in France and throughout Europe was followed by a tumultuous and immature enthusiasm for freedom. During the reign of Gustavus the word republican was still synonymous with the word philosopher; so that in the year 1789 a courtier like Rosenstein could commend his nephew to the king by stating that the young man, although somewhat infected with republican views, had kept these so well within bounds that they "only served to increase his love for his *king*, his fatherland, and honor." Later, as contrasted with the pitiful wreck on the throne, the word became invested with a more accurate significance. With eager suspense the people followed the defensive war of the French Republic; its victory was decisive for public opinion; the peaceful citizens of the small towns of Sweden spoke in the same tone as the extreme left of the French convention.

No sooner had that misfortune occurred than the freedom of the press, established half a year earlier with so much false pathos, was abolished, and throughout Sweden the persecution of Jacobinism became rife; even the loyal Swedish Academy, because it voted against admitting to its membership the totally uncultured favorite of the regent, was treated as a Jacobin club, and closed.

An act of baseness of the worst sort caused contempt to reach its climax. The conspiracy of Armfelt, the Swedish Alcibiades, was discovered, and the duke-regent endeavored to avail himself of this opportunity to make the fair young Mlle. Rudenskjöld, one of the ornaments of the court, cruelly atone for the obstinacy with which she had dejected the gallant propositions of the aged married libertine. Intercepted letters furnishing proofs that Armfelt had been her lover, she was arrested, and accused of being a participator in his crime; but when the duke, through his chancellor, judicially ordered her to be whipped on the public market-place for her immorality, the exasperated populace branded him with so deep a stigma that it could neither be effaced by time, nor covered with the white hairs of old age; not even the deportment of Bernadotte toward Charles XIII., with its wily assumption of simplicity, could bury it in oblivion.

While all these events were taking place, Tegnér was still too young to be able to enter into or understand them; but the after effects on his mind were profound and strong. No remote corner of the land was too far distant to be reached by the sparks from the crater of the revolution; no youth, whose intelligence had once been aroused, was so absorbed in his studies that he escaped hearing outbursts of contempt for royalty and government, which he at once applied to his own land. Persecuted "Enlightenment" became a magic, a beloved word to every youth. The Swedish Academy, which under other circumstances might readily have become an object of his displeasure, simply as an academy, as an official and antiquated institution for the gilding of mediocrity, very early appeared to Tegnér as a knightguard of the light, the worth of which had been fully tested. The prevailing revolutionary spirit had no power over his harmonious soul, and only led him to the conditional royalism which is revealed throughout his writings.

He was in favor of royalty when the king was worthy of his throne, not otherwise.

In the year 1796 the regency came to an end, and from that time until 1809 (that is, from Tegnér's fourteenth to his twenty-seventh year), Gustavus (IV.) Adolphus reigned as king. Pedantically honorable, rigidly grave, rigorously frugal as this monarch was, he could not but produce, when he first appeared upon the stage, a pleasing contrast to his uncle. It soon became apparent, however, that this youthful form was wholly unnational. The physiognomy proved to be rather Spanish than Swedish. Gustavus IV. bears a striking resemblance to the type of regents of the Spanish decadence, with character modelled after the great, lamentable shadow of Philip II., who held sway in Madrid so long after his death. The same petty adherence to etiquette, the same haughty gloom, the same awkward formality, the same melancholy piety, combined with fanatic faith in royalty by the grace of God. The court which, ten years earlier, had presented the appearance of a festal painting by Watteau, was now as quiet and as ceremonious as the Spanish court under Charles II., and even the great Philip could not have punished the crime of lese-majesty with more severity than Gustavus, the fault of neglecting to raise the hat in the street to him. In Rosenstein he had had a noble tutor, with a thoroughly independent mind. Gustavus III. had permitted this most honorable instructor to have full sway. "Rosenstein has my full consent to educate my son as a philosopher," said he; "the boy will be a royalist as soon as he ascends the throne." This father, as a matter of course, was in nowise responsible for that inflexible faith in revealed religion which allowed his son to read in the Apocalypse prophecies concerning his own destiny. The fact was, the reaction with which, amid the fitful changes of the century, the air was everywhere freighted, had stolen through secret by-paths into the mind of the crown prince, and had completely overpowered it. The frivolity of the father, to be sure, had served as a warning, and had given the first backward impulse; the murder of the father gave the second. Soon Gustavus IV. had gone farther in his ever-present consciousness of majesty than any Bourbon. He forbade the daily papers to use the pronoun "we" in such applications as, "We are waiting with impatience for news," "We have had a severe winter," because this seemed to him equivalent to an encroachment on that royal prerogative which is known as *Pluralis majestatis*. All the publications that appeared in the land were subjected by his orders to the strictest supervision; and personally he cherished so great a horror of books that he burst into loud utterances of delight whenever he heard that a printing-house had failed. He himself never read anything except his Bible and the regulation work on military tactics.

And this was the king, who, in the foolish war against Napoleon, never rested until he had lost Stralsund and Rügen, and whose insane war against Russia led to the definite conquest of all Finland by a Russian army. Runeberg in his poem "The King" in "Fänrik (Ensign) Staal," has erected for Gustavus IV. the monument he deserved. In the year 1809 a couple of courageous officers compelled him to abdicate the throne. The duke of Södermanland followed him as Charles XIII., and it was shortly afterward, when the adopted son of the latter died, that the French party in Sweden, through a mistaken idea of pleasing Napoleon and the illusory hope of thus winning back Finland, had Bernadotte chosen crown prince. His form emerged in a brilliant light from the gloomy background of the shadows of his predecessors. During a period of thirty-three years, the celebrated commander-in-chief guided the politics of Sweden; and this king whose reign is contemporaneous with Tegnér's most vigorous years, shares with Tegnér the honor of having given the name to the generation he ruled over. The period from 1810 to 1840 belongs to Charles John, and to Tegnér.

Such are the pictures of the rulers who at that time, one after another, imprinted their physiognomies on Sweden, and whose profiles are stamped on the coins that passed through the fingers of Tegnér when he was a child, a clerk, a student, and a *magister*.

VI

Tegnér is instructor (docent) at the University of Lund; he is twenty-two years old, and is passing his summer vacation on the Rämen estate in the Myhrmann family, with whose youngest daughter, Anna, he is betrothed.

Here one day in September there appears, on a visit, the afterward so celebrated historian and poet, Erik Gustav Geijer, a young man of Tegnér's own age, who is freighted with the latest wisdom of the day, and bubbling over with a youthful impulse to impart and discuss his ideas. He makes attempt after attempt to approach Tegnér, but fails to find common ground on which they can meet. The slender son-in-law elect of the house is variable and full of moods, an enamored dreamer, a laughing mocker. There is a glitter of merriment in his eyes, his words are flashes of lightning. It is no more possible to follow the channel of his thoughts than the course of the sunbeam through the foliage. The two young people are taking a walk together and have entered into a discussion on the way. Let us listen to what they are saying. The leader of the conversation is Geijer, who asks,—

"What Tegnér really thinks of the civilization of this locality? If he does not believe that all the so-called popular enlightenment is an evil? He, Geijer, looks on the sound reason of the masses as the most unfortunate delusion that it could ever occur to any one to venerate. Only the chosen ones of humanity had the higher sense which enabled them to grasp science in its full truth. Was not that the opinion also of the *Herr Docent?*"

"No, not by any means; he would call that mysticism."

"Mysticism! What did Tegnér understand by mysticism?"

"Well, to lie flat on one's back, to take a little nap and allow one's self to be shadowed by the power of the Most High."

"Seriously speaking, did Tegnér admit of no intellectual intuition?"

"No, he cared nothing for the Teutonic mania—but he

cared all the more for blueberries;" and just here there were growing some most excellent ones in the enjoyment of which he became profoundly absorbed: "Moreover, he did not doubt that Geijer understood the matter better than he did; he (Tegnér) had always heard Geijer called a genius, and such people only could meddle with philosophy. He, for his part, who knew of himself that no more reason than was absolutely necessary to carry him through the world had fallen to his lot, was not very fond of playing blindman's-buff, except with pretty young girls, and enjoyed least of all to do it with such learned gentlemen as Kant and Schelling."

"But without mysteries and without mysticism there was no religion."

"Did Geijer recognize the faculty in Lund, or not? This honorable body of pedants had accorded to him, Tegnér, the well-merited testimony that he led a quiet, God-fearing life, something that in these latter days was rare enough. On the other hand, so far as the dogma deemed so highly essential to salvation, the doctrine of the Trinity, was concerned, it was wholly beyond his intellectual horizon."

"Nevertheless, it could very easily be explained. There was no contradiction in the idea of the Trinity; for the antithesis already presupposed unity. God as the absolute being was not created, but had been from all eternity, and yet, must be conceived as an existing Being, for He is the creator of all things, and is in all things. The simple solution of this seeming contradiction was, that the parts which mutually presupposed one another were in reality one; the Redeemer and the Father, speculatively comprehended, were one, although not a unit. . . . Was not that clear to every nobly born mind?"

Tegnér, who was quite lost in the contemplation of the gambols of a wagtail, replied absently, "That he did not recognize the privileges of nobility."

"In what sense not? Geijer, in the highest degree, advocated hereditary aristocracy."

"And I," replied his opponent, his mouth full of blueberries, "I was always, from childhood up, a bit of a Jacobin."

This word had, as already indicated, a less terror-inspiring significance in Sweden than in France, apart from the fact that from Tegnér's lips it came half as a jest. But in the jest there lay the earnest verity that he belonged to the honest friends of freedom in civil life and in thought, who had not been intimidated by the bloody deeds of the Revolution. With genuine horror he had perceived, in the beginning of the century, the approach from the South of the religio-political reaction in Sweden, and it was as yet an unenrolled soldier in the army of the civilization of enlightenment that here ran against one of the first and farthest removed outposts of romantic feudalism.

Tegnér, in common with all the prominent men whose youth fell at the close of the eighteenth century, came into the world early enough to steer out into life with sails inflated by the great cosmopolitan wind of freedom, then sweeping over the earth. His earliest reading was the Gustavian classics of Sweden, which were based on Locke, so far as their philosophy was concerned, and on Voltaire in regard to their literary tendencies. Both Kellgren and Leopold were disciples of Voltaire, and both were political liberals, who did not even attempt to conceal their convictions at court. They were careful not to wound the religious sentiments of the multitude by scoffing; but they cherished all the traditions of the century, and fought in their behalf a brilliant fight. Kellgren's satiric poem, "The Enemies of Light," was a banner. In the same direction as the poetry of these men, only fraught with even more poetic fruitfulness, Schiller's influence guided young Tegnér. On the boundary line of youth, like Schiller, he celebrates enlightenment in a poem on Rousseau, and he writes reflective verses, in the spirit of the times, on such themes as religion, culture, and tolerance.

Neither family tradition nor the force of education led the priest's son to opposition to Christian dogmas. Together with all the rest of his intellectually awakened contemporaries he had received, when yet a boy, the cold douche of Voltaire. When sixteen years old he wrote: "I am now reading Voltaire; but I do not see how I can get through even the most important and most essential parts. It is all admirable, and it is difficult to choose among so many beauties." Most of the young men of his day who had entertained similar presumptions, were quickly borne by the altered spirit of the times to religious conservatism. For this Tegnér was too honest and too great. What insured him from losing his independence in religious matters was that vigorous element of his being, called by himself the pagan element, that was the natural result of the solid structure and the genuine steadfastness of his character. Two classes of men about him were swept onward in the reaction against the eighteenth century, with such force that they were borne by it to orthodoxy, and to feudalism. One class was composed of authors whose natures were inclined to run through the whole scale of the emotions of the Middle Ages,, that is,—rather in fancy than in reality,— to give way to contrition and self-contempt in order to be uplifted by the supernatural aid of grace to everlasting bliss, and whose poetry was distinguished by an excess of nervous excitability of all forms,—by mystic Platonic devotion, sighing, melancholy, intensely sensual erotic tenderness, alarming arrogance. This class formed the romantic phalanx proper, called in Sweden the Phosphorists. The characteristics mentioned are apparent in an unequal degree in Atterbom, Stagnelius, Hammerskjöld, etc., but are found in all. The second class of men had broader shoulders and healthier spirits; they were historic enthusiasts who had been blinded by the national sentiment, by the love of the faith and the institutions of the past, to all that was just and great in the criticism of the preceding century; such men as Geijer, and the Gothic union of Upsala, whose centre he was, and to whose national efforts Tegnér lent his aid without entering into either the religious or the political sympathies and doctrines of the society.

The pagan element that Tegnér discovered in his own nature, derived its nourishment from two sources in his earliest studies; first from his relations to northern antiquities, and second from his devotion to Greek poetry. In a letter of 1825, he wrote: "A certain spiritual kinship with our barbaric ancestors, which no culture can wipe out, always impelled me to turn back to their grotesque but magnificent forms." What he especially had in mind when he referred to this spiritual kinship was that wilfulness of the ancient Norseman which betrayed itself in his case in a challenging manner, and in that tendency to melancholy which had been one of the characteristics of the ancients. In Tegnér it was not revealed by romantic lamentations, but by a grave and sometimes gloomy temperament, which, after his fortieth year found such abundant food that it degenerated into weariness of life and contempt for humanity. The poetic symbol for this Titanic element in his composition, for gigantic strength of nature, for inner unrest beneath the weight of a mighty pressure, he sought now among the Scandinavians, now among the Grecians; and thus the old Norse and the old Greek mythology became blended in his fancy. The old Norse giant speaks to him in the same way as Goethe's Prometheus:—

> I hate the radiant Asas
> And Ask's fair children,
> Who bow before the Gods
> That I despise.

And his lament, "The Age of the Asas" (Asatiden), is so nearly allied to Schiller's "Gods of Greece" that the poet must unquestionably have derived his ideas from this poem.

Ye lofty mem'ries, engraved on historic page,
  Like empty harness that no one can wear, all lonely;
With shrinking awe ye're viewed by this trifling age,
  For hero life in the North is a saga only.

Sleep calmly, thou Past! In vain would Idun to-day
  Drag forth thy deeds from their graves as some rusty token;
Here strangers only to unknown gods now pray,
  The sinews of song and the blade of action lie broken.

Here, too, Norse and Greek paganism are blended in the author's memory.

In fact, the pagan element in Tegnér's composition first attained its higher consecration when he became acquainted with old Hellenic literature. In it he found a pre-Christian culture, which gained its climax in propitiatory beauty, not in defiant personal struggles. He saw in it human nature rounded and polished in a manner that was at once poetic and religious. Viewed from the standpoint of this world of beauty, that supernatural element which had waged such passionate warfare against the past century, no longer rose offensively before the mind, but rather fell away as superfluous. Tegnér's deism overshadowed his polemic tendency, and assumed the form of a Hellenic adoration of reason and beauty. The purely human element, which had been the source of beauty in Grecian poetry, soon became in his eyes the essential poetic element, and this is the reason why throughout his life he refused to recognize devotional poetry as true poesy. This was made manifest on sundry occasions, as, for instance, in reference to the poetic writings of Franzén. In 1823, he writes to Brinkman of Franzén: "But the beautiful rests finally on the rational, precisely as the dome, no matter how high it may arch, has its invisible points of support in the temple walls. But the temple walls of our dear Franzén are a trifle too well adorned with crucifixes which obscure the impression." Of the "Columbus" of the same poet, he writes nine years later, after he is bishop, therefore: "How much nearer to the heart would be a fresher and more vigorous romantic tone, without legends, without attempts at conversion, and without missionaries. I hate, God forgive me! the pious tone in life as well as in poetry," and with a significance closely allied to this, he expresses himself in his last years (1840) in regard to a little volume of poetry: "Such excess of piety always appears to me, poor heathen, a trifle sickly and dull." For this reason, also, quite contrary to the custom of the priesthood, he passionately protested to Adlersparre against allowing the unchristian traits in the great modern heroes of genius, such as Goethe or Byron, to be effaced. His open, thoroughly honest nature was immediately on its guard against pious frauds.

Poetry in and for itself seemed to him a power of a religious nature; or more accurately speaking, he called poesy the highest, purest, most human expression of humanity, and all else that we are in the habit of revering as high and noble, he pronounced mere modifications of poetry. Religion itself is to him "a practical poesy, a branch of the great parent stem of poetry, engrafted on the tree of life." In other words, religion is a poesy which is believed; its dogmatic part, therefore, forms a metaphysical poem, whose value depends on the worth of the practical teachings that can be evolved from it,—an inference which Tegnér, it is true, never draws without a proviso, but which can always be read between the lines in his writings.

With all the more freedom from reserve he has given voice to his unprejudiced humanism in expressions of sympathy for purely human greatness, and for those pagan virtues which are condemned by the church fathers as vices. To Geijer who, to be sure, was not strictly orthodox, but who was an unconditional believer in divine revelation, he wrote in the year 1821: "As concerns your opinion that a special revelation, Christianity, for instance, is theoretically necessary to the human mind, I must say a doubt may be entertained. It were difficult to explain why the highest human development, the actual years of jubilee of our race, should have occurred in the south, as well as in the north, before the name of Christianity was ever heard. Let us thank God for our purer faith, but do not let us forget that the records of the nobility of the human race are full of pagan names." Whenever Tegnér desires to glorify a character, he does not rest until he has shown a side from which it appears truly Grecian or Roman. In order to place this unconscious, purely instinctive effort in the sharpest light, I choose two examples where he has depicted heroes of the Christian faith as champions of the days of antiquity, and later arrives at the conclusion that, owing to preconceived sympathies, he has erred. In his reformation speech, he had incorporated in the person of Luther everything that the champions of classic culture of that day, an Ulrich von Hutten or a Franz von Sickingen, had fought for and gained. Seven years later, when forced by his official position to more emphatic historic-theological studies, he writes in deep dejection: "The lofty conceptions which I cherished in former times, regarding Luther and the reformation, are greatly modified. How many Luthers are not yet needed?" In his Festival speech of 1832, he had said of Gustavus Adolphus that his was "a heroic nature of the great and purely human stamp of which Greece and Rome had presented so many prototypes," and these words, as a whole series of epistolary passages testify, were chosen with a polemic design, because he knew that the other orators would represent the king essentially as a theologian in armor, and a "martyr of the concordance book." Five years later he himself writes concerning Gustavus Adolphus: "To the height of the now current cosmopolitan ideas, he was, to be sure, wholly incapable of soaring; as a forerunner of a new epoch he can scarcely be considered. The freedom of thought for which he did combat was nothing else than freedom of conscience, and it is very doubtful if Protestantism ever presented itself to him from any point of view but the purely theological." More profound investigation had in this instance, too, brought the honest poet to renounce the position he had once assumed. But this repeated withdrawal from an audacious, yet passionately maintained attempt to find the purely human, the colossal pagan element, in all heroes,—as though they were every one cast in a perfect mould,—even in those about whose brow orthodoxy had so firmly laid its iron ring, that no room remained for Tegnér's free Grecian laurel wreath, conclusively manifests how vigorously a free classic humanitarianism had penetrated through every pore into the poet's soul.

He had begun by intense admiration for all that was knightly, adventurous, or defiant, for honor, as such alone, with all its tinsel. In this enthusiasm, which he never lost, his feelings were those of a child of nature and a child of his people. "For," declares Tegnér's poem to Charles

John (Karl Johann), "beyond all else in the Swedish mind stands honor, true or false, it matters not; it still lives in the memory." Tegnér is not only a child of nature, however; he is also a child of history, and history places him between the enlightenment period of the eighteenth, and the religious reaction of the beginning of the nineteenth century. He follows neither. With vigorous individuality he makes his choice among the elements of culture that are offered to him, until an independent mode of contemplation of human life, especially the relations between religion and poetry, is formed in his mind; and we see him, with his warm poetic temperament, rousing himself to involuntary, and often fruitless, efforts to bring reality into harmony with the great humanist ideal in which his method of contemplation finds its outlet. What injustice Runeberg did Tegnér when, in the year 1832, he wrote: "In him scarcely the glimmer of an ideal can be seen, indeed, not so much as an inner struggle that allows us to detect any traces of a dim foreboding that there is such a thing." Forty-four years later, the great Finnish rival of Tegnér indicated in a footnote that this assertion now seemed to him almost too presumptuous, but this was not enough; it would have been a simple act of justice had he contradicted his former statement.

VII

From Tegnér's humanistic contemplation of the world followed, with inner consistency, the political standpoint he took during the first fifty years of his life, and from his combined religious and political views followed, of a necessity, his literary party-standpoint.

He was not, like the majority of the poetic minds in Germany and Denmark of that day (a Tieck, an A. W. Schlegel, an Oehlenschläger, a Heiberg), indifferent to politics. While, for instance, a phenomenon like the holy alliance scarcely embittered an hour of the lives of the poets just named, the letters of Tegnér overflow with an indignation and a scorn at this confederation of rulers, which can only be distinguished from similar emotions of Byron by the fact that the proud and independent Englishman gave public expression to his wrath in great works of poetry, whose plain language lashed the despots of Europe with scorpions, while the civil officer and professor at Lund was obliged to confine himself chiefly to private outbursts of indignation: yet not altogether. Throughout his entire youth, his political sentiments find voice in fugitive poems, and even though they do not occupy much space in his poetry, their significance can scarcely be estimated highly enough; for it was the seething, fermenting element in his soul that gave breadth to it, and prevented Tegnér from being made petty by the petty circumstances amid which fate had cast his lot. Had not the politics of Sweden and of Europe thrown his mind into a continual state of oscillation between indignation and enthusiasm, his poems would never have attained the grandeur of style which occasioned their transmission beyond the borders of their native land.

His first political poems owed their origin to Sweden's debasement under Gustavus IV. So it is with that "Svea," in which he writes:—

O Finland, home of truth! O Ehrnsvärd's[7] monument!
So lately like a bloody shield from Sweden's bosom rent!
A monarch rules our fens, whose name is scarcely known,
And where our herds once grazed stands now the stranger's throne!

Yet very early the poet's gaze turned from the special concerns of his fatherland to the world's politics. The fanatic hatred of Gustavus IV. for Napoleon had evoked in the youthful soul of Tegnér only admiration for the hated emperor; the alliance of Bernadotte with the armies in league against Napoleon had no power to break the sympathy of the poet; and while the romantic school, as early as 1813, allowed itself to be transported to such outbursts of joy over the deeds of the crown prince as: "In Charles John's footsteps walks Sweden's angel," or the following

[7] Referring to Sveaborg, Finland, built according to the plans of Field-Marshal Count Augustus Ehrensvärd, whose name is hewn in gigantic characters on the granite rock from which the great ship-basin is constructed.

absurd panegyric concerning the French-speaking Gascon:
"At the head of the army flashes Thor, with his mighty,
luminous hammer, and Charles John the god of thunder
is called," Tegnér devoted a series of poems to the defence
of the revolutionary element in the mission of Napoleon.
At the final downfall of the latter he wrote that bitter and
severe poem, inspired by despair at the triumph of the
reaction, "The New Year, 1816." Hearken to its energetic
finale:—

> Huzzah! religion is Jesuit hight
> And Jacobin every human claim;
>
> The world is free and the raven is white;
> Long life to the Pope and him we'll not name!
> I'll go to Germany, famed in story,
> There sonnets I'll write to our age's glory.
>
> Thou'rt welcome, New Year, with thy lies and deceit
> Thy mysteries, murders, and dubious worth!
> A ball from thy arquebus now would be sweet,
> I trust thou wilt fire on our earth.
> Her brain is aglow, she is restless and dreary,
> One shot, and she need no longer be weary.

This public expression of opinion strictly corresponds to
Tegnér's private letters of the same period. In 1813 he
writes:—"Whoever fancies that Europe can be free helped
by Russians and their consorts, or that the success of the
Cossacks is of advantage to Sweden, may be right, but his
views and mine widely differ. I was born and I grew up in
hatred of the barbarians, and I hope, too, to die in the same
frame of mind, untainted by modern sophistry." In 1814
he gives vent to still greater dejection, as follows: "Who
can believe in the restoration of European equilibrium; or
rejoice at the victory of absolute worthlessness over power
and genius?" In 1817, finally, with marvellous accuracy,
he characterizes the spiritual reaction, in the following
words: "Politics is the main essential; the inner revolution of the tendency of thought is on the whole political;
the religious and scientific transformations we are experiencing, are both more or less chance results and reactionary

processes, and are, therefore, without significance or permanence. When the masonry of a house is completed, the scaffolding falls away. It is true that these results at the first glance appear serious enough; but does not their exaggerated and caricature-like nature, the hair-splitting tendency of science, and the monastic flavor of religion, betray conclusively that they are merely a reaction against the former practical and free-thinking spirit? Does it not seem now as though people were both profound and pious out of spite, and because twenty years ago it was deemed boorish to be either? . . . The most important thing of all would doubtless be a change of base in religious dogmas, for religious movements when genuine, are also practical; but what reason have we to conclude that such a change exists among the majority, except as a fashion and a grimace, and with many perhaps from still worse motives?"

Meanwhile, this reaction had most emphatically made its appearance on Sweden's own soil. In opposition to the old Franco-Swedish tendency in literature, represented by the Swedish Academy, the "Phosphorists" proclaimed, in all essentials, the principles of the German romantic school; metaphysical proofs were furnished of the mysteries of Christianity, the period of enlightenment was derided, the academy was treated as an assembly of old powdered periwig blocks, and the advocates of Alexandrines were pursued with sonnets. As for the rest, there was the Madonna and the Calderon worship, incense was burned at the altars of Schlegel and Tieck, contempt for Schiller and enthusiasm for the kingdom by the grace of God, were the fashion.

When Charles John assumed the reins of government, he, "the Republican on the throne," as he was at first called, the marshal of Napoleon, with all the traditions of the Revolution behind him, could not possibly feel warranted in entering into closer relations with the men of the new school. They manifested *trop de zèle;* they did not recognize the sovereignty of the people, by which both himself and his dynasty must be supported; they had their friends abroad in the camp, where endeavors were made for the restoration of the old legitimist royal family to the

European throne. The adherents to the romantic school naturally desired nothing more ardently than to convince the king that his doubts of their loyalty were wholly groundless. Count Fleming, in order to prove the harmlessness of the young school, translated into French for the king, an essay by Geijer. The king declared that he did not understand it. "What is the true meaning of this new school?" he asked. A courtier replied: "Nothing in the world, your majesty, but this: when you ask any one in the old school, what is two and two, he will answer, four; but if you ask a person in the new school, his answer will be, it is the square root of sixteen, or a tenth of forty, or something else that requires a little reflection." "That is precisely what I thought," said Charles John. Atterbom was appointed instructor in German literature to Prince Oscar; Geijer filled precisely the same place to Charles John that Chateaubriand at one time held toward Napoleon I. Ere long the unhappy influence of the conservative youth of the *doctrinaire* party became apparent. The reactionary elements of society made use of the doctrines of this party, and soon there arose in Sweden a bold and powerful reaction, which, the moment it became apparent at court, frightened Charles John from further attempts at reform, and drove him into paths which were in disharmony with the previous course of his life. He was, for instance, most unfavorably inclined at first to hereditary nobility, all the more so because the earliest parliamentary opposition to his government had proceeded from the nobility, but after his alliance with Geijer and his comrades, he even wished to force a hereditary nobility on Norway, where all aristocracy had long been abolished.

Under these circumstances, Tegnér felt himself, as it were, a member of the great European opposition. He pronounces the holy "Mohammedan" alliance to be a stillborn embryo, "whose burial on the gallows-hill he had every hopes of living to see;" he calls the politics of the period "infernal"; he writes to Franzén: "Concerning European politics of the present day, no honest man, not even a German, can express himself without a sense of shame and horror. In poetry it can be at best but the object of a Juvenal satire. To name the truly diabolical tendency of the obscurantism of the day, whenever there is a question of anything noble or great, whether it be in verse or in prose, may be designated a bitter irony." In the politics of the interior, he demands ministerial responsibility, equality before the law, the right of voting supplies, parliamentary representation,—in short, the usual programme of the opposition in liberal Europe. Such were the views to which he gave publicity in his great speech at the marriage of Prince Oscar, in 1823,—a noble wine served in polished crystal. In modern times, according to his conception of affairs, two powers were confronting each other, —personal merit, which had no other support than itself, and inherited rank; a plebeian and a patrician principle. This contrast had appeared in its sharpest form during the struggle between the despotism that arose from the Revolution, and that which came from the legitimists. Tegnér calls attention to the fact that the prince's young bride, who had but shortly before landed in Sweden, combined through her birth the two contending elements, and thus, as it were, united the past with the present. For her father (the son of the Empress Josephine, Eugène Beauharnais), "like so many other distinguished men, was a son of his own deeds, whose pedigree was an outgrowth of his sword," and on the maternal side she was descended from one of the oldest princely families of Europe (the mother of the bride was Amalie of Bavaria, of the house of Wittelsbach).

It does not occur to me to see in this attempt to symbolize the origin of the august lady anything more or less than a well-planned, well-expressed compliment. But from the lips of Tegnér it is interesting; for to him this marriage between the son of the general of the Revolution and the daughter of ancient royalty had a profound significance. At the time when he made this speech, he was engaged in writing a poem designed to end with a similar reconciliatory union, in the long-delayed marriage between the son of a peasant, Fridthjof—who, through his deeds of valor, had fought his way up to equal rank with the most renowned of heroes— and the king's daughter, Ingeborg, who traced her origin to the gods of Valhal, and whose brothers, in their princely arrogance, had denied Fridthjof her hand. In "Fridthjof's Saga," the same two principles—that of personal merit and that of the nobility of birth—form the two poles through which passes the axis of the poem. Even in the second canto of this poem, where the friendship between King Bele and Thorstein, Viking's son, is described, the ancient yeoman says:—

> Obey the king. With force and skill
> Shall one the sceptre sway.[8]

and the aged king on the other hand tells of that

> Warrior-might which always more
> Was prized than royal birth.[9]

In the last canto the aged priest of Balder exclaims:—

'Thou hatest Bele's sons! but wherefore hate them?
Forsooth, because that to a yeoman's child
They would not give their sister,—she, descended
From Seming's blood, th' illustrious Odin's offspring!
Yes, sprung from Valhal's throne is Bele's race,—
Bright genealogy, just source of pride!
But birth is chance, is fortune, thou observest,
And cannot be a merit. Know, my son,
That man still boasts of fortune, not of merit.
Say! is't not gen'rous gods who were the givers,
Should any noble quality adorn us?
With haughty pride thou art thyself inflamed
At all thy hero exploits, all thy fierce-nerv'd
Resistless strength; but did'st thou give thyself
This force?[10]

The speech on Oscar's wedding-day, and the final chord in "Fridthjof's Saga," mark an epoch in the career of the poet, when his political views of life had found repose in a

[8] R. B. Anderson's Viking Tales, p. 171.
[9] Ibid., p. 175.
[10] Ibid., pp. 356-7.

fitful harmony, for which he had struggled with unwearied persistence. A few years earlier and the Revolutionary fermentation was seething with passionate impatience within his breast; a few years later and his displeasure at the early stages of Swedish liberalism drove him to the opposite extreme; but on the dividing line that separated these two currents, there was vouchsafed to him a bright and inspired moment, with a free poetic horizon on either side.

VIII

"Man is the flower of the metallic race of the earth, and his language is the magnetic fluid of this race, which, by the force of his will, is shed upon the world. If all speech is at bottom music (the ear of nature is of metal, and what the spirit of the world whispers into it is music), we need to seek a long time before we can discover the kind of kinship that transforms it into material substance for the poetic fancy."

This hard piece of eloquence is given here as a sample of the style of which Atterbom, the leader of the romantic school, made use in his youth. It contains so decided a challenge to parody that it is no wonder Tegnér yielded to the temptation to aim some mocking darts at it.

The religious and political views of Tegnér, combined with his literary standpoint, gave him a lofty watchtower, situated far above the two contending parties of the old and the new school, but from which he almost exclusively aimed his shafts at the latter. He who had entered the new century in early youth, and who was but twenty years old when he had experienced, in Lund, Sweden's upward soaring flight of poetic fancy, could not possibly feel his poetic needs satisfied by the insipid didactic and comic poems of the Gustavians. There was nothing, however, that incited him to combat against them, and they passed away all too soon, one after the other, until Leopold alone remained as the last surviving representative of the ancient *régime*. When Tegnér was in the full vigor of his manhood, Leopold was blind, and even had he otherwise been inclined to attack the old man, it was now impossible for him to do so. On the other hand, the first appearance of the "Phosphorists" upon the scene had provoked his displeasure in the highest degree. They discoursed in a philosophic idiom, which was intelligible neither to himself nor to any other uninitiated person. They opposed the academy as foreign, —that is to say, French,—and were themselves German to the core. Moreover, to Tegnér the French traditions were much dearer than the German. Not even his predilection for Grecian lore had estranged him from the classic French rules of taste. In his eyes Grecian characteristics very early became synonymous with self-control in art, and French poetry was in every respect well governed. It was no mere chance, therefore, that led him to the remark that the French national spirit "in many instances is more nearly allied to the Grecian than the Germans and their apes, since Lessing's time, have been willing to admit." His admiring attitude toward the old academicians during the sharp controversy against the "Phosphorists" recalls vividly, indeed, strikingly, Byron's contemporaneous enthusiasm for Pope and contempt for the lake school. The causes were in part akin: fidelity to childhood's impressions, delight in contradiction, partiality to intelligent lucidity and Latin rhetoric; but this attitude had still deeper ground in the relation to the Grecian peculiarities, and to the French studies of the antique,—a relation which is not found in Byron, but which characterizes Tegnér. Byron's art was employed in giving an organ to passion: Tegnér, like the ancients, desired that passion might be clad in strict decorum, in order to avoid a pathological effect. He had never liked reality, and had as little fancy for metaphysics; but the ideal form he loved. The inner schisms which he conceived to be the problem for art to solve were not deep; at heart he did not wish to see more violent struggles between body and soul, condition and desire, duty and happiness, etc., represented in poetry than could be reconciled with the harmony of healthfulness. It was rather the pure, polished form that fascinated him than the natural freshness of the Greeks, consequently the quality which the

French classic style had in common with the Grecian. All these instincts brought him very near to the old school, and removed him from the new.

His chief warfare against the latter was waged by the young instructor (magister) in his great metrical speech delivered at Lund in 1820, the celebrated "Epilog," in which he demanded of the young academicians the banner-oath to the banner of light. The popularity of this poem was so great that during the summer following its delivery no two young students could talk together ten minutes without devoting at least five of them to quoting and interpreting the "Epilog." Certain lines of this speech have an almost proverbial force and truth.

> Heed not, tho' indolence to you may whisper,
> That far too mighty is the strife for powers like yours,
> That 'twill be fought as well without your aid.
> Alone a general never wins a battle;
> 'Tis won for him by solid ranks of soldiers.

He ends by placing the Temple of Truth, as the ancients conceived it, face to face with the Tower of Babel, erected by the adherents to the romantic school, the heavy, barbaric structure, "whose obscurity peeps through the narrow windows." If we pay strict heed, however, to the architecture of the Pantheon, which he describes as that of the ancients, we shall observe that its style, with its singular mingling of Roman and Gothic, far from being antique, is an involuntary reproduction of Tegnér's own personal art ideal, which is the fruit of so many classic and romantic combinations.

> The ancients built to Truth a lofty temple,
> A fair rotunda, glowing as the firmament.
> The open dome let in from ev'ry quarter
> A flood of light, while through the pillard forest
> The winds of heaven with tender music frolicked,
> But now our people build a Tower of Babel.

A rotunda whose light is obtained from every quarter, not from above alone, and which does not rest on simple

masonry, but is combined with pillared forests, is rather a
reminder of St. Peter's church with its complex style than
of any structure built by the ancients. It was, in truth,
rather a temple for all mankind, like this church, than the
simple Roman house of gods, that floated before Tegnér's
eye as the symbol of truth. What he wished to extol was
simply transparency and lucidity in the realm of poetry,
as in that of thought. The adoration of the hidden roots
of life, of the obscurity of night, the mother of all things,
and of the shadows, the source of color, as preached in
Germany by Novalis, in Denmark by Hauch, in Sweden
by Atterbom, seemed to him suspicious, indeed odious; he
viewed it in the same spirit with which an ancient Apollo
worshipper might have attended a Moloch service, and
protested against it in the name of the light.

In the name of the light, and above all else in the name
of poetic art, of whose psychologic origin he had early
formed an original conception. By the romantic schools
of all lands poesy was comprehended as the dearly purchased product of suffering and sorrow, as the pearl which
is the result of diseased secretions. To Goethe it was the
ideal confession of the soul, the noblest means of salvation
from impressions and memories, that laid siege to the
healthfulness of the character. Kierkegaard compared the
poet to the unhappy being who is tortured by a slow fire
in the brazen steer of Phalaris, and whose cries resound
like music in the ears of the tyrant. Heiberg has the poet
sing that if he had been good he would have produced poor
poetry; but since he is bad he has written good poetry, for
that touches him the most deeply which is denied himself.
All these views accord in the one idea that poetry has its
origin in yearning, in regret, in pain; in short, in something negative.

Tegnér traces its origin to healthfulness. Over and over
again he attacks in his letters what he calls the hysteric
cramps of the romantic school. "Nothing is so repulsive
to me as this eternal litany over the torments of life, which
belongs to reality and not to poetry. Is not poetry the

healthfulness of life? Is not song the jubilee of humanity, bravely streaming forth from fresh lungs?" And this application is not the expression of a momentary mood with Tegnér; it keeps recurring again and again as a stereotyped definition. He does not comprehend how poetry, "which is nothing else than the healthfulness of life, nothing but a leap of joy from the borders of everyday life, can color the fresh round cheek with a hectic flush."

The definition assumed poetic proportions and melodious form in the sportive poem "The Song," called forth by a romantic elegy of the same name. It contains the programme of Tegnér's poetry, as follows: "The poet has no cause for lament, he has never been driven from the Garden of Eden. With heavenly delight he embraces life, as a bride,

> 'For song is not eternal longing,
> 'Tis one glad shout of victory.'

Disharmony that has no solution is unknown to him.

> 'My golden harp shall never borrow
>   Sad tones that I have brought to light;
> The poet was not made for sorrow,
>   The sky of song is ever bright.'"

It was a hard and bitter Nemesis that condemned him, who, in the year 1819 possessed sufficient vital strength and flow of spirits to write these lines, to become, only six or seven years later, wellnigh mute as a poet, after he had produced one of the most despairing poems of all literature; yet both before and after his "Ode to Melancholy" (Mjeltsjukan) was written, the doctrine of the inner equilibrium of the poet and of poetry's consciousness of victory was still realized in the writings of Tegnér. As his soul passed through crisis after crisis, as disappointment and sorrow undermined his cheerful and sanguine temperament, he preferred silence rather than to permit the depressed state of his soul to have a depressing influence

on his art; and if he still intoned an occasional song, it was
in order to reveal himself in poetic composition as the
mobile, youthful nature he no longer was in actual life.

The muse of Tegnér never had that melancholy fundamental quality that is common to the folk poetry of all
northern lands. It has, indeed, nothing corresponding to
the folk-song, nothing of its naïveté, nothing of its simple
minor chords. Tegnér admired popular poetry; he did not
believe his songs superior to it, as the artistic poets of the
preceding century had felt; but he considered it, and
justly, an unattainable model. The artistic type of his
lyric muse, therefore, is not the folk-song,—neither that
of the Finns, as in the case of Franzén, nor that of the
Servians, as with Runeberg, nor that of the Swedes, as with
Atterbom,—but the cantata, now in the style of the heroic
song, and now in the style of the bravour-aria. The last
word is not used in the sense of a vocal selection calculated
to shine through its embellishments alone, but is meant to
represent the abundantly ornamented and full outburst of
an overflowing vital courage. All the art forms of which
Tegnér avails himself,—the hymn, the ballad, the love-song,
—receive under his treatment a character which I know
not how to characterize more sharply than with the word,
bravour.

IX

We find the poet in the humble white house at the corner
of Franciskan and Kloster streets in Lund, pacing the floor
of his spacious two-windowed study, murmuring and hum-
ming his verses to himself, and now and then pausing
before an open cabinet that serves him for a desk, to write
down his strophes as he completes them. In the room two
canary birds are warbling; accompanied by their song he is
composing his "Fridthjof." He is at this time about forty
years old; neither passion nor disease have as yet imprinted
their traces on his visage. The furies are lurking on his
threshold; but it almost seems as if they purposed to await
the completion of the main work of his life before they

crossed it, and seized upon him for their prey. His brow is clear and arched; his gaze bright and free.

> Both earnest and profoundly true
> Is every feature of his noble face,

as he says of his Axel.

He has chosen his theme, or more correctly speaking, his theme has emerged from the memories of his childhood and presented itself so alluringly before him that he has designed the outlines of its treatment, and commenced his work within them. He wishes to furnish a picture of life in the ancient north. With full conviction he had formerly joined the "Gothic" union; for he saw in the national historic and poetic tendency of this society the true medium course between the cosmopolitan rationalistic culture and the exaggerated Teutonic enthusiasm of the "Phosphorists." He soon experienced the grief, however, of seeing how his worthy and ardent ally, Pehr Henrik Ling, who had taken a position in the intellectual life of Sweden similar to that of Arndt and Jahn in Germany, drove the Swedish public in alarm from the poetry of northern antiquity by his boasting language and his colossal disregard of form. His awkward touch on harp strings made of northern bear sinews destroyed the superb material which, in the hands of Oehlenschläger, had won all hearts in Denmark. Tegnér concluded to take one single saga as a central point about which to gather all the most characteristic images of the ancient north: viking life and brotherhood in arms, the wisdom of the Hávamál and the vows made on Frey's boar at Yuletide, the heroic song and the election of kings at the Thing, the self infliction of wounds with the point of the sword and the runic stone, the poesy of life and of death in ancient times. There must be a good, pure atmosphere in the poem; a sharp, fresh breeze must blow through it; Scandinavians should feel at home in it; but beyond all else there must be none of the icy temperature of the old Norse poems of the worthy Ling! This saga was, of course, a love story, and with the yearnings and sorrows of love the hard web of his material must be permeated.

The material was Norse, but the treatment must be Swedish; Norway and Sweden which not long before had been divided, must now be blended together in song. There was a rustling in his mind's ear as of the clash of shields and the whizzing of a shower of arrows, the rattling of quivers and the clinking of foaming beakers, the stamping of fiery coursers and the restless flight of hooded falcons, blows on the sword and strokes with the sword, and through it all the long, languishing, cooing, dreamy nightingale note and the still more thrilling call of the quail in the stillness of the summer night. As regards the scenery he truly had no need to transplant himself in fancy into its midst; he had become too thoroughly familiar with it in his childhood and youth in the country to require any such effort. He knew them well, these trees with white trunks and drooping crowns; one of them bore two characters in its birch trunk: were these the letters, "E" and "A," or was it an "F" and an "I" in runes? He knew, between fir-overgrown coasts, this smooth icy path over which the steel-footed warrior sped, while behind him came rushing the sledge in which sat that fair young queen who would soon pass over her own name on the ice.

> And many a rune, too, on the ice he engraves;
> Fair Ing'borg drives o'er her own name on the waves.[11]

And when the springtime came, when the billows beckoned enticingly, when the sea spoke aloud of deeds of valor, while the boats along the coast seemed most urgent in their invitations to come on board and seek a knowledge of the world, he was well aware what a viking must have felt at such a moment.

> Ellide, too, now has no sport on the sea;
> Now ceaseless her cable she jerks to get free.[12]

But it was not possible to journey forth into the world. At the foster-father's house, at Hilding's,—at Myhrman's, on the Ramen estate,—dwelt the fairest of the fair, the beloved

[11] R. B. Anderson's Viking Tales, p. 308.
[12] Ibid., p. 196.

one whom it was impossible to forsake. And all the memories of youth, sweet and childlike, overpower him at this thought. He remembers how it was his wont to carry to Anna the first anemone that blossomed and the first strawberry,

> The first pale flow'r that spring had shed,
> The strawberry sweet that first grew red.[13]

And he dreams of so many good times when he and she (or was it Fridthjof and Ingeborg?) paused in their wanderings by the rustling waters of the forest streamlet, and there was no other way for Ingeborg to cross than to let him bear her over in his arms, and smiling he wrote,

> So pleasant feels, when foam-rush 'larms,
> The gentle cling of small white arms! [14]

And unconsciously there blends with these memories another erotic enthusiasm of a more recent date, another form, that of the fully matured Ingeborg—not Anna Myhrman, whose footsteps are heard in the adjoining room. The footsteps of the excellent housewife who is now in the meridian of life do not reach his ear; no, it is a younger, more attractive face, a slenderer form, another, more musical voice; he dare not love this woman, it were contrary to divine and human law; she is married to King Ring, to Fridthjof's friend, whose confidence in him is unbounded. Fridthjof must away, far out to sea, to deaden his yearning with deeds of valor and victories. But one day—late though it may be, one day will come the hour of atonement, and the stormy heart of Fridthjof will find repose.

The old Norse Fridthjof's Saga is a narrative written in Iceland about the year 1300; it is assumed that the historic portions of the incidents took place about the year 800. Fridthjof, the son of a bonde, who has brought up with the king's daughter Ingeborg, sues for her hand and is rejected. In order to be revenged on her brothers, he refuses to give them his powerful aid in the war against King Ring, and avails himself of their absence to enter into a betrothal with

[13] R. B. Anderson's Viking Tales, p. 157.
[14] Ibid., p. 157.

Ingeborg, who has been shut up by her brothers in Baldershage, a place consecrated to Balder, where it was forbidden man to embrace a woman, for it was supposed that Fridthjof would not dare seek a rendezvous in that sacred spot. But Fridthjof defies the gods, visits Ingeborg, and violates the temple. Meanwhile peace is concluded with Ring on condition that the brothers give the aged king their sister to wife. Of Fridthjof they demand that he go forth on their errand to collect tribute from Angantyr, in the Orkney Islands. During his absence they set fire to the home of his fathers. Fridthjof returns, finds the king sacrificing in Baldershage, and casts the purse of silver he has brought with him into Helge's face with such force that Helge falls down in a swoon. Through an accident Balder's image is cast into the fire, and the whole house becomes wreathed in flames. Fridthjof flees, returns, visits King Ring, saves the life of the old king, and, when finally the latter dies, marries Ingeborg.

In this plot Tegnér's poetic eye detects the main features of an object of universal human interest, and susceptible of generalizing symbolism. Fridthjof struggles for his love with reckless defiance; in spite of all the powers that be, he is determined to conquer his happiness amid storm.

> His good sword pointing to the norn's fair bosom,
> 'Thou shalt,' saith he, 'thou shalt give way!'[15]

He refuses to obey a royal mandate. In the prime of his manhood he becomes, first a violator of the temple, then a temple burner, then the outlawed, proscribed "Wolf in the Sanctuary" (*varg i veum*). He flees and does penance, renounces and is purified, and receives at last the hand of the beloved object of his affections as a reward, not for his struggle, but for his persistent fidelity. Not the maiden but the widow, not happiness itself but the pale reflection of happiness, he embraces as his bride. Was not this in itself a symbol of human life?

One step more and the symbol stands completed in all its radiance. There was a central point to the saga which,

[15] R. B. Anderson's Viking Tales, p. 237.

beneath the poet's gaze, must necessarily become transformed to a fruitful germ. This was the sanctuary of Balder. About a Balder's temple everything revolves; here Ingeborg is imprisoned; here Ingeborg and Fridthjof meet; here the kings offer sacrifice. The temple was honored; it was violated; it was burned to the ground.

Balder was a peculiar god; in him paganism, as the contemporaries imagined it, was brought into contact with the Christianity many would gladly have adapted to it. Balder represented paganism without fierceness, Christianity without dogmatism. The Jesus in whom Tegnér believed, like him whom Oehlenschläger acknowledged, had more of the nature of a Balder than of a Christ. And it was the temple of Balder that Fridthjof, in his youthful arrogance, had burned. This burning of the temple must necessarily be made the main catastrophe of the saga; it determined, with overwhelming force, a highly spiritual conclusion. Fridthjof must necessarily end by rebuilding the temple which he had burned to ashes.

For is not youthful vigor in its uncurbed impetuosity always a violator of the temple, and do we not all end in our years of maturity with an honest effort to atone for the profanation committed in the heat of youthful passion? Do we not all, to the best of our ability, build the temple larger, stronger, more beautiful than we found it? As it was with that emperor who found a metropolis of wood and left behind him one of marble, so it will be at all times with energetic and earnest natures who discover their surroundings to be swayed by a hallowed temple of poor wood; they will burn it to ashes, and leave behind them another Balder's temple, and the strongest among them one like that of Fridthjof.

> Of granite blocks enormous, joined with curious care
> And daring art, the massy pile was built, and there
> (A giant work intended
> To last till time was ended)
> It rose like Upsal's temple, where the North
> Saw Valhal's halls fair imag'd here on earth.[16]

[16] R. B. Anderson's Viking Tales, p. 341.

Thus conceived, the poem grouped itself about a grand, simple, fundamental thought, and with this before his eyes Tegnér proceeded, first of all, to plan the final romance.

Of course, every feature of the old narrative could not be used. But of the changes he undertakes, only those have psychologic interest in which his poetic character is to be recognized.

First of all, he removes everything that from an erotic point of view could give offence to a reader, above all, to a lady reader of his day. For this reason all family bookcases were thrown open to his poem. According to Tegnér's own confession, he gained the idea for his "Fridthjof" from Oehlenschläger's "Helge," and in Denmark people have never been quite able to comprehend how it was that the imitation attained so much greater fame than the vigorous original; but how was it possible that a poem which, like that of Oehlenschläger, from beginning to end treated of a northern Vendetta, of fratricide, arson, drunkenness, rape, tarring, and incest, could ever vie for public favor with a poetic work like "Fridthjof's Saga," which was made, as it were, for a birthday or a Christmas present, and which, in fact, for more than twenty years, has been a standing confirmation gift for young girls in Germany? To be sure, Tegnér keeps up an incessant play (with a relish, too, that to me personally is very distasteful) on words and expressions, with which, according to accepted literary standards, the idea of something sensual is connected; he compares Ingeborg's bosom to "budding roses" and other protuberances, which a female bosom is as wholly unlike as it is possible to be; but in this harmless dalliance of the poet is exhausted all tendency to sensuality in the poem. His Scandinavians of old love like a well-bred couple of affianced lovers in modern Sweden. Yet, while they do not for one instant forget themselves, the poet is less strict, and we sometimes feel his eye fixed on Ingeborg's white neck. It would certainly have been better had the poet's eye been more chaste and had Fridthjof been more human. From the way in which the sexual element of this love story is treated, we are strongly reminded that the poet is not only invested with an academician but with a priestly office, and is about to mount to a still higher one. Plainly enough Tegnér has wished to make the poem conform thoroughly to modern views of heroic virtue and female chastity. Therefore, although he allows Fridthjof to pass the night with Ingeborg in Baldershage, it is done in all propriety and honor, and he has Fridthjof, when accused in the Thing, solemnly declare that he had not broken Balder's peace. Thus Tegnér does not hesitate to rob his poem of its actual ideal centre of gravity, the conscious and defiantly executed desecration, if by so doing he succeeds in preserving the decorum of his narrative. Fridthjof declares that his love belongs rather to heaven than to earth; at his rendezvous with Ingeborg he wishes that he were dead, and, with the pale maid in his arms, could wander to Valhal—certainly a most unnatural thought for an impassioned lover in the hour of his bliss.

> To that far heaven my love belongeth,
> More than this earth,—receive it then;
> In heav'n 'twas nurtured, and it longeth
> To reach its starry home again.[17]

Strange words from the lips of a poet who, moreover, was never weary of pursuing Platonic love with mockery, and with pretty sharp mockery too. His own was a fiery, passionate temperament. Notwithstanding his marriage, his years, and his office, he was an ardent and, as rumor declared, frequently a successful adorer of the fair sex. His conversational tone with ladies was often so loose as to scandalize people; and in letters, aphorisms, and poems published after his death, he made no concealment of his realistic conception of love. He does not even pay homage to the spiritualistic presentation of the relation of the sexes in poetry. He writes, for instance:—

Aeneadum genitrix, hominum divumque voluptas is not only poetized by the ancients, but deified as well. Our sentimental, nervous contemplation of love is by no means the only one,

[17] R. B. Anderson's Viking Tales, p. 213.

still less the most vigorous. How pale and weak, even from a purely poetic point of view, are most of the modern erotics with their water-colored tintings when compared to the eternal fresco paintings of the ancients!

And yet I should hesitate to believe that Tegnér would allow himself to be guided in this point exclusively by conventional motives. He was educated in far too idealistic doctrines ever to draw, with full consciousness, from a model, nor has he had a defined model for Ingeborg, as can plainly be detected in the poem itself, which on that account lost in individual realistic life what it gained in typical grandeur. Yet wholly without a model no artist can paint, and entirely without remodelling the dispositions and impressions of real life no poet can compose, least of all so subjective a poet as Tegnér. In the beginning of the poem he was inspired by the memories of his intercourse with his betrothed bride on the country estate of her parents; the idyllic element of Fridthjof's love undoubtedly arises from these memories, but not its dreamily enthusiastic pathos. Numerous indications point to the fact that Tegnér, who, like most poets, was always half in love, was thoroughly enamored during the years when he was writing his "Fridthjof's Saga."

At the time when the canto in which Fridthjof's love attains its highest lyric expression was written (1824), Tegnér's affections may perchance have still been in a state of ecstatic, half-unconscious frenzy, now intersected with budding desire, now with that languishing for death, which sometimes accompanies even prosperous love, when an excess of passionate yearning, filling and torturing the soul, calls forth the wish that the heart might break:—

> How bless'd were he already yonder!
> How bless'd who now with thee could die,—
> And, conqu'ring, 'mong the gods could wander,
> Embracing his pale maid on high.[18]

Perhaps he was simply not in a condition to carry into poetic practice his own poetics of love. As there are, un-

[18] R. B. Anderson's Viking Tales, p. 213.

doubtedly, poets who, with full justice, can take for their motto the line,—

"*Vita verecunda est, Musa jocosa mihi,*"

so, too, there are poets who, especially at the time when romantic idealism governed poetry, have felt themselves constrained by an inner impulse to realize the formula of the opposing ranks.

The second modification of his materials—in which Tegnér's literary individuality vigorously betrayed itself—is the removal of all that might strike us as burlesque in the ancient narrative. The burlesque features appeared to the idealistic poet simply disturbing and odious. I choose a prominent example.

The ninth chapter of the old saga, in which Fridthjof brings the tribute to the sacrifice-offering kings, represents Balder-worship in the following vivid manner:

Then Fridthjof went in and saw that there were but a few people in the hall of the dises; the kings were there at the time sacrificing, and sat drinking. Fire was burning on the floor, and the wives of the kings sat at the fires and warmed the gods, whereas other women were anointing the gods and wiping them with napkins. Fridthjof went before King Helge, and said, 'Here you have the tribute,' Herewith he swung the purse wherein was the silver, and threw it at his nose so violently that two teeth were broken out of his mouth, and he fell into a swoon in his high seat; but Halfdan caught him, so that he did not fall into the fire. . . . But as Fridthjof walked over the floor toward the door, he saw that goodly ring (which he had given Ingeborg) on the hand of Helge's wife while she was warming Balder at the fire. Fridthjof took after the ring, but it stuck fast to her hand, and so he dragged her along the floor toward the door, and then Balder fell into the fire. But when Halfdan's wife caught after him quickly, the god that she had been warming also fell into the fire. The flame now blazed up around both the gods, as they had previously been anointed, and thence it ran up into the roof, so that the whole house was wrapped in flames. Fridthjof got hold of the ring before he went out.[19]

The objections that may be raised to the historic reliability of this presentation are not unknown to me. But

[19] R. B. Anderson's Viking Tales, pp. 97, 98.

what a superb piece of prose from an ethnographic and picturesque point of view! How plainly the narrative brings the whole naïvely burlesque scene before the mind's eye!

Whoever has beheld in the Berlin museum the little clay image of an old Norse goddess, can form a vivid conception of these odious little idols which the pious women hold on their laps, anointing them and warming them by the fire. Everything is admirable here; the old northern piety which leads the people to see a Balder in the puppet, with the same burning faith that in our day leads men and women of the people in the South to see the Queen of Heaven in another puppet, and the surrounding scenery with the smoking wood-pile in the centre and the drinking knights in the adjoining hall. A more modern poet with a lively appreciation of the coloring of time and locality would not have had the heart to alter the slightest trifle in such a scene; he would have viewed it as a treasure-trove. I do not speak of the realists; realists do not write romance cycles; I have in mind the great stylists among the poets of the present day. It is a scene which might have been introduced into Victor Hugo's "*La légende des siècles*" (The Legend of the Centuries); but still better adapted would it have been for so rigid an artist as Lecomte de Lisle, who might have interwoven it in his "Poèmes barbares." To Tegnér, however, this scenery only seemed rude, odious, wholly unavailable for poetic art. The sharp contrasts between barbaric and Hellenic poetry did not exist for him; he strove to the best of his endeavors to Hellenize his barbaric material. From principle he refrained from mingling the wild burlesque element with a pathetic or beautiful whole. Instead, he painted—and with profound art—a night in which the midnight sun stands high in the heavens; in which Balder's pyre, the symbol of the sun, burns on the consecrated stone, while pale priests, with silvery white beards, stand with flint-knives in their hands around the temple wall. The statue of Balder towers up on a pedestal, with Fridthjof's ring entwined about its arm, and the king, with his crown on his head, is busied about the altar. This scenery is far more beautiful than that of the saga, but it is abstract and much less individual.

Besides the scandalous and burlesque elements in his material, there is a third thing which Tegnér recoils from and avoids. It is guilt.

It belongs to Tegnér's poetic system to shun all sharply pronounced guilt, no less than all that is decidedly odious or quaint. His hero is too benignly good to be carried to extremes of passing rage, revenge, or fierceness. He makes an assault and controls himself at once. He does not take revenge, as in the saga, for the mortification and grief the kings have inflicted on him; he does not scuttle their ship on his return home in order to punish them for the injustice they have done him; his weapon-brothers sink the vessel later, in order to facilitate Fridthjof's flight. We saw, furthermore, that Fridthjof, in his relations to Ingeborg, according to Tegnér's treatment, was guilty of no actual profanation of the temple. But most strikingly does the poet's solicitude to avoid profound guilt reveal itself where Fridthjof's relation to the burning of the temple is described. In the saga Fridthjof always displays a haughty spirit towards Balder. He declares that he rates the favor of Ingeborg of more account than that of Balder. When the return of the kings compels him to give up his nightly visits in Baldershage, he speaks with a certain irony concerning Balder to Ingeborg, saying, "Well and handsomely have you treated us, nor has the bonde Balder been angry with us." [20] And finally, when through his heedlessness fire has arisen in Balder's temple, in his destructive rage he flings a flaming firebrand at the roof. Tegnér gives the scene quite differently. The state of mind of his Fridthjof toward Balder is most pious; he kneels before him at Ingeborg's side, and commends to his protection their mutual love; he makes energetic efforts to extinguish the fire in the temple, and when these fail, he moves away weeping and full of anguish.

Thus transformed, the character as a whole is more

[20] R. B. Anderson's Viking Tales, p. 82.

human and more noble, although undeniably less primitive, but the idealizing and modernizing process rendered it impossible to avoid a certain conflict between the character as it was represented by the poet, and several of the energetic traits that were attributed to it by the saga, and that passed unaltered into the poem. During the completion of the work, the poet must many times have queried within himself, whether it were after all worth while to treat ancient materials, when the antiquarian and the poetic elements could not be harmonized without incessant and useless compromises. His letters are full of evidences of this doubt; when the work was at length finished, after a struggle with the materials that lasted fully five years, they criticise "Fridthjof" most severely; they remind the admirers of the poem that poetry must be a "growing and not a preserved fruit"; they ring continued changes on the theme that "Fridthjof" is too much of an ancient saga to be a modern poem, and is in too high a degree modern poetry to be an old Norse saga; they declare that all poetry must be modern, "in the same sense that flowers are so in the springtime," and they condemn all that is archæological in the poem, as newly built ruins. Nevertheless, the universal critical mood has not erred when it rather took umbrage at the too modern than at the too antique element of the poem. A rigid stylist would not have had Fridthjof forbid the presence of women on board ship in his "Viking Code," with such a sentimental play of words as the following:—

> For the dimple deceives on her cheek, and her tresses
> Would net-like entrap thee above.[21]

Tegnér himself draws a parallel between his work and such studies as Goethe's "Iphigenia" and Walter Scott's "The Lady of the Lake." The last parallel has more truth than the first, although Tegnér himself says, "the Scotch particularism in Scott, like the Judaical tone in the Old Testament, limits and suppresses what might otherwise have freer and higher flight." Tegnér finds himself

[21] R. B. Anderson's Viking Tales, p. 292.

in a literary-historic station, which is half-way between the two extremes, Walter Scott and Byron. Half a century of his life falls within the lifetime of Goethe, and he witnessed the whole of Byron's life. From Goethe, whom it was difficult for him to understand, he learned but little; he showed himself most susceptible to his influence when it approached him through Oehlenschläger; for the Byronic impression his temperament was more open, yet he held himself bravely above all contamination, and the effort to do so was facilitated in a higher degree by the romantic idealistic vaccine with which he had early been inoculated. As a poet he was too filled with his own *ego* to comprehend the impersonal element in the creative powers of Goethe; on the other hand, his egotism was not sufficiently profound to enable him to follow Byron on his voyages of discovery within subjectivity. Like Scott and Oehlenschläger he is national, closely bound to his country, his people and its heroic past; but there is in his nature a tendency against distinctly marked personality: he approaches the Byronic type at a certain remoteness.

As soon as the sixteenth to the nineteenth cantos of "Fridthjof" appeared in the year 1820, a universal cry of admiration rang through Sweden. Even the members of the romantic school, deeply moved, extended their hands for reconciliation. Before the entire work was completed (1825) Tegnér's fame had spread to the neighboring countries, especially to Germany, where Tegnér's first translator, Frau Amalia von Helwig, so well known as the friend of Goethe, made the aged poet acquainted with fragments of "Fridthjof," and won for it his favor. He called the attention of the German public to the poem, and although what he wrote about Tegnér in the vigorless style of his old age scarcely amounts to a dozen lines, it can readily be understood what an event a recognition on the part of Goethe grew to be in a small country like Sweden. Goethe's words read as follows: "We need not enter into any detailed statement to prove to those readers already friendly to the North, how admirable these cantos are. May the author as speedily as possible complete the entire

work, and may the excellent translator continue to take
pleasure in her labors that we may possess this sea-epic
complete in the same purport and tone as what has already
appeared! We would only add the brief remark that the
vigorous, gigantic, barbaric style of antique poetry, approaches us, in a manner nearly incomprehensible to ourselves, with a new, musingly tender, yet undisfigured and
highly agreeable form." To this day the Swedes never
weary of referring to these words of praise. The admiration for Tegnér in his fatherland increased with the growing popularity of the poem; indeed, after his death it
became so strong that it drowned almost all criticism, and
finally reached its climax in such exaggerations as that of
Mellin, who proclaimed Tegnér to be the "greatest poet
of the Teutonic race." That homage to the man, however,
which is and will always remain the best, is that which is
at the same time homage to the truth.

X

On life's exalted summit, where the waters
  Of living streams are parted, once I stood,
And watched the current seeking divers quarters;
  Around me all was bright and fair and good.
    *   *   *   *   *   *   *
A melancholy demon then did waken,
  Who suddenly my heart's warm blood did taste;
And lo! the scene grew gloomy and forsaken,
  The sun and moon extinguished were in haste,
My glowing landscape autumn hues had taken,
  Each flow'r was withered, ev'ry grove a waste;
All vigor from my frozen senses vanished,
All courage, all rejoicing now was banished.

While Tegnér was still occupied in putting the last
touches to his "Fridthjof," the furies that had been lurking on his threshold shook their snaky locks before his eyes
and stretched forth their long, lank arms to embrace him.
They were the furies of disease, of passion, of life-weari-
ness, and of dawning insanity, and they joined hands and
danced round him in a circle.

The year 1825, the same in which "Fridthjof" appeared

and proclaimed his fame to every quarter of the globe, was the year that marked the great crisis of his life. Physical as well as mental was the crisis. It has, to be sure, a purely bodily side; yet apart from the fact that this must be obscure even to a physician, it is only the mental and emotional side that the critic can study, and in it seems undoubtedly to have been the prime cause of the disorder. The mental and emotional catastrophe, however, is almost as obscure as the physical. It has hitherto remained unnoticed, chiefly because the editions of Tegnér's poems have been made, *in usum delphini*, by his surviving relatives. Their division into periods is thoroughly confusing; the poems are sparingly dated; indeed, as I have discovered, most of the love poems are pre-dated twenty-five years, in order to make the reader believe they were intended for Tegnér's wife when she was his betrothed bride. "The Ode to Melancholy" (Mjeltsjukan), the poem of which a strophe and a half have just been given, is inserted in the last edition, not dated between a poem of 1812 and another one of 1813. Tegnér's letters prove that it dates from 1825.

This year begins for Tegnér with violent illness; even on New Year's day of the year he is so ill that he believes death to be nigh at hand. In March he writes that his mind becomes every day more and more clouded. "God preserve me from melancholy and misanthropy," he says. In July he writes: "Blindness seems to me one of the most horrible of earthly misfortunes—next to one which I myself have experienced." Everything that formerly gave him pleasure is now distasteful to him. His disease continues as an inner restlessness, yet without any actual bodily pain. "My fancy, which was very excitable at the outset, is now like a whirlpool, that casts into swift rotation and soon destroys everything it can draw into its vortex."

The physicians think his liver is affected. "The fools! the soul is affected, and for it there is no medicine but that which is obtained in the great universal drug-shop beyond the grave." He declares that he cannot impart to his friends the cause of his sufferings. In November the violence of his malady seems to yield to a certain repose. He makes, so he says, fine daily progress in indifference, in which the happiness and wisdom of life consists. The destiny of the wise man, he thinks, is to become ever more and more of a tortoise. As long as he has a single exposed nerve, his whole being is a prey to torture. He feels "how thoroughly the dregs of contempt for the biped race are lodged in the depths of his soul." "Ah!" he exclaims, "genuine inner grief that attacks the strong soul nourishes itself, just as it does with war when it is rightly organized, or a wild beast when it has attained its full growth." On his birthday, Nov. 13, he sinks into the deepest melancholy; he thinks it would be better to celebrate, as do the Egyptians, the day of death. What puts him especially out of tune is the fact that this birthday is the last one that he will pass in Lund, where he has made his home for twenty-six years; having been appointed bishop he will be compelled to hold intercourse with strangers who will not understand him; as bishop he will come into possession of a disorganized diocese, and will be decried as a despot. In former times this would have been a matter of total indifference to him, nor would he have concerned himself in the least about the mob; but now he is nervous, hypochondriac, and out of tune, and he begins to comprehend the meaning of fear of man. "And yet this is not my only, not even my greatest, sorrow. Night, however, keeps silence, and the grave is mute; it behooves her sister, Sorrow, equally well to hold her peace." When finally, on the last day of the year, he draws the balance of what he has learned and gained in it, he writes:

Ah, the old year! what I have suffered in it no one knows, unless it be the Great Recorder above yonder clouds. Nevertheless, I am indebted to the year. It has been more gloomy, but also more earnest, than all the others combined. I have learned at my own expense how much a human heart can endure without breaking, and what power God has deposited beneath the left side of a man's breast. As I said before, I am indebted to the year, for it has made me rich in what is the standing capital of human wisdom and independence: a vigorous, deeply rooted contempt for the human race." The excitability of his nervous system permits him to have a rest by day or by night. My mind is in an unchristian state, for it has no Sabbath.... I cannot drink mineral water in the coming summer. But is there not a mineral water that is called 'Lethe'?

What has happened? That bodily pain and disease exist here in a high degree is undoubted. Esaias Tegnér had had an elder brother, Johann, whose brain was diseased, and who, at thirty-nine years of age, died of insanity; the younger brother was continually brooding over the thought that insanity was a family inheritance. Thomander, later a bishop, who visited Tegnér in March, 1825, writes of him: "He has now more gloomy hours than formerly; many a one, but no one more than himself, fears for his reason; it is a fixed idea of his that he will become insane, because his brother and other relatives have been so." No one, however, can doubt that the melancholy which so suddenly warped the cheerful and fresh disposition of Tegnér had other causes than bodily disease; too many utterances point to a defined, concrete fact,—a fact, to be sure that Tegnér himself will not communicate, but the nature of which is, nevertheless, plainly indicated. It is "the heart" that is affected. It is contempt for humanity that has overpowered him. It is contempt for "the character" of another person that is the first cause of his weariness of life, and this person "is or has been dear" to him. We need not have studied Tegnér very profoundly to conclude that there is a woman behind all this, and that every one of these outbursts may be traced back to an unhappy or an unsatisfied erotic passion.

Among the letters of Bishop Thomander there is one dated 1827, in which it is mentioned that Tegnér, while he was still in Lund, cherished warm sentiments of affection for the beautiful wife of one of his friends. From her piano he never moved when she was singing. "Lovely Rose,"[22] by Atterbom, was his favorite song. Thomander

[22] "Lovely Rose" is a passionate love-song, whose interest centres in the anguish of a butterfly at being removed from the rose at night, and only being permitted to caress her during the day.

writes that in a house where he met Tegnér, he warned the elder daughter not to sing "Lovely Rose," because he knew that if she did "the evil spirit would come over Saul"; but owing to a misunderstanding the forbidden song was sung, and Tegnér's good humor was banished for several days. In one of Tegnér's letters of May, 1826, we read in corroboration of this: "To listen to singing was something to which I had become especially accustomed during the last years of my stay in Lund, where I had daily opportunity of hearing a female voice that still echoes in my heart." To the lady here in question, Tegnér had written for his friend, in 1816, a sort of versified love-letter, in which her beauty, her goodness of heart, and her singing are extolled to the skies. He speaks in it of the danger of looking into her eyes. It appears that what was then called a danger in jest became a real danger for Tegnér several years later. His admiration for the disposition and talents of this beautiful woman seems gradually to have kindled a flaming passion, and this passion was evidently reciprocated. Local tradition has not a little to tell of his relation with her, which, moreover, could not have left his domestic happiness undisturbed. At all events, it certainly added much to his grief at parting from Lund. Still living contemporaries of Tegnér have, furthermore, communicated to me an occurrence which served as an essential motive for his contempt for humanity, especially his contempt for woman. He discovered that a very distinguished lady, with whom he was captivated, had yielded to the advances of a wholly unpolished, boorish man. Did it so greatly shock him who was himself faithless to find faithlessness everywhere, that he gave way completely to weariness of life? Did he simply tell himself that he was scorned because he was old and almost gray, and was he cast into a state of despair because the happiness of youth was at an end for him? Was he so agitated at finding animal passion where he had honored the crown of female culture and beauty, that in his morbid condition this indignation at a single individual grew to universal loathing of life? I cannot decide the question. I can only see that the bitter melancholy bored, in the once so trusty ship of his destiny, the hole through which the black waters of misanthropy and of insanity rushed in and deluged everything. During the shipwreck he wrote the melancholy lines:—

> For thee, mankind, with praise I am o'erflowing,
> God's image, thou, of true and perfect plan!
> And yet two lies betray thy record glowing,—
> The one is woman hight, the other man.
> From songs of old were truth and honor flowing,
> They best were sung when cheating erst began.
> Thou child of heav'n! One truth thou ownest now,—
> The mark of Cain, deep branded on thy brow.
> A fiery mark, by God's own finger, given,
> Why did I never heed the sign before!
> This smell of mould beneath yon starry heaven
> Doth poison vernal bloom for evermore;
> And by the grave alone the smell is given,
> Tho' wardens strict may guard the marble door.
> Alas! corruption is the soul of life,
> No pow'r can crush it; ev'rywhere 'tis rife.

The state of discord into which the soul of Tegnér sank during the latter part of the time when "Fridthjof" was in the course of progress, has left its traces even in this cheerful and harmonious poem. One of the last-written cantos is that which bears the title "Fridthjof's Return." Its contents, by way of exception, are not modeled after the old Norse poem. Fridthjof returns home, learns that Ingeborg has been persuaded to become King Ring's wife, and in the first burst of his indignation exhausts himself in a stream of wrath at the faithlessness of the beloved object of his affections. No critical reader can fail to see how nearly related the following outburst is to the just-cited strophes of "The Ode to Melancholy."

> 'O woman, woman!' cried Fridthjof, madly,
> 'When thought with Loke first sheltered gladly,
> A lie it was! and he sent it then
> In woman's shape to the world of men!
> Yes! a blue-eyed lie, who with false tears ruleth,
> Enchanteth always, and always fooleth;

A rose-cheek'd lie, with rich swelling breast,
And in spring-ice virtue and wind-faith drest.
With guileful heart she, deceitful, glances,
And perjury still on her fresh lips dances!
And yet how dear to my soul was she—
How dear was then, ah! yet is, to me!

* * * * * * *

'In human bosom all faith is spent,
Since Ing'borg's voice has to guile been lent;

* * * * * * *

'Where sword-blades scatter the barrows' seed,
O'er hill, o'er dale shall my footsteps speed;
All crown'd, perchance, I may meet a stranger,
I'd know if then I shall spare from danger!
Some youth, perchance, I may meet, all calm,
And full of love 'mid the shields' alarm,—
Some fool on honor and truth depending,
From pity I'll hew!—his poor life quick ending;
I'll save from shame; he shall glorious die;
Not guil'd, betray'd, nor despis'd—as I!'[23]

We detect here in Fridthjof's inner being the same spiritual process we have just observed in the character of Tegnér. Not content with condemning the one woman for her faithlessness to himself, he extends his condemnation to the entire sex. "Woman is a lie," says Fridthjof, as well as the author of the "Ode to Melancholy." He who builds on "fidelity and honor" is a fool, are Tegnér's words in one instance as well as in the other. One single bitter experience increases in proportions with Fridthjof, as well as with his author, until it becomes contempt for the human race, and weariness of life. No wonder, since they are more nearly akin than are father and son.

From this time forth the chapter of woman's faithlessness as woman is the standing theme with Tegnér. His letters are variations on this theme. It is impossible for him, for instance, to mention a good or a bad translation without either remarking that beautiful translations, like beautiful women, are not always the most faithful, or that fidelity and beauty are rarely good friends. He cannot

[23] R. B. Anderson's Viking Tales, pp. 269-271.

speak of a gift from a woman without calling her heart
the worst, the most dangerous, present she could make.
Woman in general he regards henceforth as a sort of
"society machine or musical box that sounds very nicely
indeed, when properly wound up." As for love, it becomes
so inclined to suicide that the moment it is no longer compelled to sigh in vain, it dies by its own hand. Of Ingeborg, he writes, "In the nature of the heart of woman,
there certainly exists reason sufficient for her faithlessness
to her lover, yet this fact must receive some sort of gilding
from a poet who desires to behave politely to the fair sex."
Indeed, so confirmed did Tegnér gradually become in this
habit of describing woman as unreliable and fickle that
many years later, when in the capacity of bishop he made
his school addresses, he was unable to refrain from edifying
the schoolboys with his theory. In an address of the year
1839 he calls the boys happy because of the wealth of
hope that belongs to their youth. Then he adds, "Hope,
in all languages known to me, is of the feminine gender,
nor does it deny its sex. True, it deceives; but believe
gladly, believe long in the fair deceiver, and clasp her to
your bosom." Tegnér must undeniably have been very
full of bitterness to give vent to it at so inopportune a
moment and to so very unsuitable a public. But not this
single passionate disharmony alone can be dated from the
crisis indicated in the life of the poet; from this period,
a more vehement, more passionate tone altogether began
to manifest itself in his letters and in his poetry. Indeed,
a truly Shakespearean tragic passion may be found in
them. The world is out of joint, and how can it ever be
set right again by Hamlet's arm. He no longer places
reliance on Ophelia; she must get her to a nunnery if she
will remain pure. For, frailty, thy name is woman! What
is life? "A brief reprieve under the gallows." And what
is the history of the world? "A dog's dance." A loathsome comedy is everything that Hamlet sees about him:
painted decorations for the stage with paper roses and
theatrical sunshine." He could easily go mad over it;
very likely it will at last make him mad; but first the lie

and pitiful wretchedness of life must be unmasked, without mercy, without forbearance.

There is a wild recklessness in Tegnér's letters of 1825, never before detected in him. He is asked, for instance, about his colleagues, the theologians. They are "Hesekiel's cherubs with the heads of oxen, yet without wings." And the bishops? "Born or manufactured imbeciles." And the Apostle Paul himself? "Grecian sophistry engrafted on Judaic crudeness." What does he say about royalty? "The power is as absurd as it is abominable when it falls into the hands of trivialty, helplessness, or stupidity,— look at the state calendars of Europe." And what about providence? "Providence is a conception without the slightest support. I know very well what Lessing and the other Germans have maintained: that the world's history is the universal doom of providence. That is a pretty poetic fancy, and I, too, could well give expression to it in verse; but I do not seriously believe it."

It seems to me as though in all these despairing words regarding human worth and female fidelity, regarding kings and bishops, Christianity and history, I heard an undercurrent of that thrilling elegy, "The Ode to Melancholy":—

Ho, watchman, tell! How late may be the hour?
Will this dark night forever find no end?
A blood-stained moon peeps forth from clouds that lower,
In tearful mood the stars their presence lend.
As though in league with old-time, youthful power,
My mocking pulses through my veins the life-blood send.
With ev'ry throb how boundless is the anguish,
Alas! my torn and bleeding heart must languish!

XI

No feature better illustrates Sweden's stage of civilization in the lifetime of Tegnér than the manner in which science and religion were connected. The relations between State and Church were so intimate, I had almost said so naïve, that a professor, simply as such, was at the same time a priest, and the natural, the looked-for advancement for a capable professor in Greek, botany, or history, was that he should be—made a bishop. It was a kind of government household arrangement that was a vivid reminder of the private housekeeping in Molière's "Harpagon." The university teacher, whose desk in Lund was exchanged on Sunday for the pulpit in the country, was a sort of Maître Jacque with his vestment above his professor's coat, and was in a position to ask the State, in the event of any perplexity, a question similar to that of the celebrated servant of the miser, who said: "If you please, is it your coachman or your cook whom you are addressing? I am both."

The original cause of Tegnér's desire for advancement was of a purely economic nature; he had debts, and the increase of income served him in very good stead. Like all the cultivated people of his day, he was accustomed to draw a line of distinction between the esoteric and the exoteric side of religion; and although in point of character he deemed himself a pagan, his frame of mind was often a most pious one. He was too thoroughly a poet not to yield to frequent and changeful impressions, and thus it was that he failed at first to consider his convictions any hindrance to his acceptance of the office of bishop. Yet scarcely did he bear the title of bishop before he began to despise, from the bottom of his soul, all the ambiguity and incompleteness in which he found himself involved, and to which his duty toward his family held him bound. And so his misanthropy and his distaste for life, which had arisen during the years of the crisis indicated, increased more and more. Energetic and loyal to duty as he was, he threw himself with all his might into the exterior affairs of his office; he became the civilizer and organizer of his bishopric, an ardent and enterprising school director, a superior and daring educator of his clergy. The purely civil standpoint he took in his conception of the Church is very similar to that assumed at the same time in England by Coleridge, who was upon the whole far less of a freethinker. "The former religious significance of the Church can, of course, never be re-established," says Tegnér, "for the system on which it depends has now slumbered during three centuries of history, and it would be of no avail whatever for one or another to act as though he believed in the somnambulist. But the Church has also a civil significance, and this can and must be supported as an integral part of the human social order. If this significance, too, be allowed to fall victim to torpidity and lethargy, I see no reason why the clergy, together with the entire religious apparatus, be not suppressed for the benefit of the state treasury." In order to comprehend how strong he must have felt the demands upon him to be, the low degree of culture and morals of the clergy in Sweden of that time must be fully realized. On him it devolved to impart to the priests under him the elements of human culture, and to remove from office the worst drunkards among them. There had been given to him an Augean stable to clean.

His dull, spiritless occupations wore on his already shattered health and spirits. "The examinations are now at hand, and I shall have to pass a whole week," he cries, "in the gymnasium. Then come the clerical examinations and the ordinations. After this there are no less than eight new churches to be consecrated during the summer. And through all this, addresses must be made,—continual addresses about nothing and for nothing. 'Words, words, words,' says Hamlet. Pity me; I am wearied to death with speeches and discontent, and yet must continue to torment myself without cessation. No one pays heed to what I say, nor do I myself take any interest in it, for that matter. That is what I call talking to the winds, and dissipating one's life in ceremonies." There came moments when everything of a priestly nature seemed an abomination to him. In such a moment he wrote jestingly to a friend, whom he was asking to purchase him a pair of horses: "Not black ones; I cannot endure the parson's color." It was a sorrowful mistake that so modern a spirit should be thus enveloped in a costume of the middle ages; the vestment had no power to transform him as it has transformed so many others; but it tormented him, slowly devouring his vitals, like some poisoned garment.

And yet the days of his brilliancy were not past. Before his sun set, a glorious rose-tinted sky was yet in store for him. The many scattered clouds that had gathered above his head and in his horizon, only served, as is so apt to be the case, to make his sunset richer and more glowing. The period of lyric enthusiasm was forever past for Tegnér; faith in the future and in progress, which is the source of life's courage, had long been exhausted. But one faculty he had yet in reserve, one talent which had hitherto been subordinated to the creative fancy and to lyric inspiration, and that was the poetic-rhetorical gift. This attained its highest bloom during the time that he officiated as bishop.

As Tegnér's talent for the production of what are by himself styled "lyric" characters, is closely allied to the lyric propensity of the whole Swedish nation, so, too, this second faculty of his harmonizes marvellously with fundamental qualities of his people. The Swedish nation has a peculiar gift for representation. The Swedes love what looks well, and understand better than the Danes and the Norwegians how to make advantageous arrangements; in customs, social life and speech, they have more form and, at the same time, a more formal manner than other Scandinavians. Their language itself is ceremonious; the word "you" is wholly lacking as a mode of polite address, so that the name or title of the person addressed must be incessantly repeated. No northern people understand as well as the Swedes how to conduct a procession, a festival, a public ceremony, a grand entrance, or a coronation, with the *tout ensemble* requisite to secure a good effect. To this national love of representation, whose nursery gardens, from readily intelligible reasons, were always the Church and the universities, corresponds a peculiar kind of national, festive eloquence. Swedish eloquence is at the same time more pathetic and more pompous than that of the other Scandinavian people. It has something of an ecclesiastical vibration, which the Church contributes, something of the professor-like stamp which the universities preserve, and finally, after the Swedish Academy was founded, it assumed an academic element of its own, which may be designated a proclivity for euphemism, an inclination to paraphrase thought and to call things by beautiful names. Of the deficiencies of this school Tegnér had but few, but he possessed all that vigor and richness of language, all the clearness and figurative splendor of diction, all the faculty to express different phases of sentiment and to bring an entire assembly into accord with them that had been developed by it. All this attained its finest bloom in Tegnér's festal addresses and poems. His most renowned festal poem was produced in the year 1829.

The students at Lund had invited Oehlenschläger to be present at their Commencement, and when Tegnér learned this he resolved to avail himself of the opportunity to crown Adam Oehlenschläger with one of the laurel wreaths destined for the *magisters* of the day. A Swedish idea, and a poetic one, too! Moreover, the idea of a noble, not vain poet! So far removed was Tegnér from every exaggerated effort to obtain recognition that it seemed to him quite natural to crown another as his master. He had finished his address and called upon the rector to confer the degrees of master of arts, when turning to Oehlenschläger, who stood by the high altar in the cathedral, he once more took up the word, and thus accosted the rector,—

Ere you begin to distribute your laurels, hand one to me;
Not for myself, but for one through whom I to all would pay honor.
The Adam of skalds is here, the king of Northern poets,
Heir to the throne in poesy's realm, for the throne is Goethe's.
Oscar, if he but knew it, would surely sanction my action;
Now not in his name, far less in my own, but in that of song immortal.
That illustrious name, resounding in Hakon and Helge,
Would I proffer this wreath; it grew where Saxo lived.
Past is the age of division,—in realms of the free-born spirit
It should never have been,—and familiar tones now ringing
Across the Sound enchant us all, and yours more than others.
Therefore, Svea offers this wreath, I speak in the name of Svea;
Take from a brother's hand this gift, and wear it this day to remember.

And amid the din of kettle-drums, trumpets, and cannon, he placed the wreath on Oehlenschläger's head. May the ceremony belong to the moment alone, and the kettle-drums, trumpets, cannon, the entire janizary music vanish on the instant! It was, nevertheless, a grand and a beautiful moment, and the remembrance of it has tended to fraternize the northern peoples as little else could have done.

XII

The year 1830, that brought the July Revolution to France, led to a change in the political temper of Sweden, and soon in the entire political situation; it was a year that gave to liberalism a new impulse, significantly modifying its aims and altering the language of its press. Before 1830, the ideal of the Swedish liberals had been freedom; now it became democracy. As a matter of course, the advance of liberalism drove the conservative groups to the opposite extreme. Upsala was the head-quarters of the reactionary party; here Geijer held sway, and the loyal students followed him so faithfully that, in a serenade to Charles John they thus designated their party: *"obéir, mourir, et se taire"* (to obey, to die, and keep silence). In retaliation the Stockholm liberal press called Upsala a foul nest of Tories, and the university professors, dried-up moles. A new style of journalism developed itself, which, owing to the prevailing absolutism, could only obtain a hearing through a personal, unrestrained tone. The style of this press was frivolous and sharp; it wounded with pin pricks and *persiflage*. Neither the court nor the person of Charles John was spared. If this tone pleased in certain circles of the metropolis, it excited lively displeasure elsewhere, especially in the provincial towns, and no one was more thoroughly annoyed by it than Tegnér, whose shattered mind was too thoroughly out of tune to permit him to see the good that might possibly arise one day from all these sins against good taste and against respect for the name of the old king. He offered a passionate protest against it, and the liberal papers attacked him like a swarm of wasps. The consequence was that he soon turned wholly against the liberal press as well as against the doctrines promulgated by it. Intellectual aristocrat as he was, the demagogic tendency was repulsive to him; an ideal conception of the people he had never attained in his best days, and now, after all faith in human purity and spiritual beauty was destroyed in him, he was less able than ever to acquire it. Amid these circumstances he was obliged to come upon the scene as a professional politician, his position as bishop compelling him to take part in parliamentary affairs at Stockholm. It cannot be wondered at that this was done in a conservative direction; indeed, Tegnér came forward as a true *enfant terrible* of conservatism, for when the old martial spirit came over him he spared neither friend nor foe. Henceforth, through all his writings, as well as through his speeches in parliament, ring bitter sallies against the new form of journalism, which seems to him a symptom of Sweden's decay. Listen to his words:

> The Swedish colors were yellow and blue,
> And strength and honor of yore in them were clad;
> But now the mire is your national hue, falsehood
> Your Epic Song, and slander is set free
> Six days each week, nor scarcely rests the seventh.
> Its eye doth pierce the life of every mortal,
> At every key-hole it doth place its ear.
> Ye men of Sweden, is this your boasted freedom?

His illness, from the first outbreak, had given him no peace. A trip to the baths at Carlsbad in the year 1833 brought him no relief, to say nothing of recovery. The most substantial value of the journey was the purely intellectual result that Tegnér became rather better acquainted with Germany than he had hitherto been. He had but little sympathy for this country, its obscure philosophy of that time being repellant to him, and he thought that it had spent its energies in the appropriation of foreign literary productions without having the ability to impart to these an individual stamp. He compares the Germans with the Caspian Sea, which is watered by a number of streams,

yet being without an outlet, evaporates in mist. On his
journey, during which great attention, both from private
sources and from orders of the king, Friedrich Wilhelm
IV. himself, was shown the poet whose fame had spread
throughout Germany, he received at least a superficial
impression of the positive qualities of the people. He
writes, among other things: "Germany, in spite of her
chaotic nebulous state, has undeniably been for a long
time the seat of learning of Europe, and Prussia is undoubtedly the present centre of intelligence of the civilized
world." He was too old, however, to begin his school-
days afresh; and doubly weary of life, now that all hopes
of improvement were at an end, he returned to his stulti-
fying calling and his vain struggle against the political
development of Sweden.

His loathing of the press, which he sought in vain to
subdue, went so far that his heart finally became estranged
from both the government and the people of Sweden. He
writes: "O my poor fatherland! At the public leaders
themselves I do not wonder; they live by their calumnies
just as the executioner lives by his heads, and the flayer
by his scourge; but what shall be said of a people, of the
body of most worthy Swedish people, that not only endures
this miserable, paltry state of affairs, but encourages,
bribes, permits, admires it? It can only be explained by
the supposition that our nation, with a few rare exceptions,
has degenerated into a vulgar mob. As far as I can see,
nothing remains for us but to bid farewell, if not to the
land of Sweden, at least to the Swedish language, and to
write Finnish, or Lappish." In another place we read:
"My dream of the honor and sound reason of the Swedish
people is long since ended and forever dissipated." And
with a turn that is interesting, because it proves how nearly
related, in Tegnér's own estimation, to his opposition to
the romantic school was his warlike attitude to the liberals,
he writes: "You can readily fancy my opinion of the royal
Swedish public. The thought—it was but a dream—that
anything great could be accomplished by such a mob, I
have long since abandoned. These people are and always

will be degraded. In whatever form folly may appear, political or literary, as Phosporism or Rabulism, the masses are always ready to fall into it. So pitiful a race is not worth wasting powder on."

These utterances all date from the year 1839 and the first month of 1840. Such a burden of hopelessness and misanthropy might cause the strongest spirit to succumb; how much more one that was already undermined by sixteen years of disease! When Tegnér was in Stockholm during the session of parliament of 1840, the catastrophe occurred. Insanity broke out. He gave vent partly to wild outbursts of sensuality in the height of delirium, partly and most frequently he occupied himself with colossal plans, gigantic financial operations, schemes of emigrations on a large scale, and magnificent conquest. His star was extinguished.

It was kindled anew, to shine with a milder, fainter light for several years longer, but its red Mars-like glow was never seen again. What must not the unhappy man of genius have suffered before insanity came to a decisive outbreak! As early as 1835 he told Adlersparre that his soul was on fire and his heart was bleeding, but that his malady to which people were wont to give the pet name of hypochondria, should be called by its real name, madness. "It is an inheritance," he added, "and it is beyond my power to free myself." On the occasion of his last visit to Wermland, he said: "I am the personification of Antisana; I stand with my feet in the snow, but my head burns and I spit fire." He prophesied that he had not long to live, but spoke with a wail of anguish of the manner in which he was doomed to die. It was: "to be devoured bit by bit by that thousand-tongued monster hypochondria." What did he not suffer? I made use of the expression that the furies had crossed his threshold. He himself saw his calamity under a similar form. "You do not know the influence of the fury to whom I have been wedded, without the aid of parson or bridesmaid; indeed, without the slightest wooing," he wrote. "She is begotten of the union of a nightmare and a vampire; and even when she is not riding on my breast or sucking my heart's blood, she gives me to understand that she is near, and meditates honoring me in a short time with a visit." Actual delirium, after such a preparatory state, must have come almost as a deliverance. The physicians ordered a journey to a hospital in Schleswig, then in high standing.

The sojourn at the insane asylum did not last long; but it is interesting to follow the poet even there, so beautiful and peculiarly individual were the ravings by which he was tormented. A person who accompanied him to the place has preserved for us the following outburst of his while the malady lasted: "The whole confusion arises from the damnable zeal of the people here about the diadem they wished to put on my head. You might otherwise think it was a superb affair: pictures in miniature, not painted, but living, truly existing miniatures of fourteen of the noblest of poets, formed a wreath. There were Homer and Pindar, Tasso and Virgil, Schiller, Petrarch, Ariosto, Goethe, etc. Between each pair there glowed a radiant star, not of tinsel, nor yet of diamonds, but of actual cosmic material. In the centre of the brow there was a diadem in the form of a lyre, which had borrowed something of the sun's own light. As long as this lyre stood still all was well; but suddenly it began a rotary motion. Swifter and swifter became its movements, until it made every nerve in my body quiver. Finally it fell to whirling round with such speed that it was transformed into a sun. Then my whole being became agitated and broken; for, you must know, the diadem was not entwined about my head, but about the brain itself. And now it swung round with a wholly incomprehensible violence, until all at once it burst. Darkness, darkness, darkness and night spread over the whole world, whichever way I might turn. I became bewildered and feeble; I who have always despised weakness in men, I wept and shed hot, scalding tears. All was over."

Is not this rather the poetry of insanity than insanity itself? And how the true nature of the poet comes out even in this singular dream,—the youthful dream of wreaths and crowns, heated red-hot in the forge of insanity!

In place of the cool laurel wreath which he had wound about Oehlenschläger's head, the norns had now placed this fiery ring about his brow. Happily, it grew cool again, and in the spring of 1841 the poet was able to return home.

In his last great poem, "The Crowned Bride" (Kronbruden), in which he has described himself, we see the aged bishop as a village patriarch surrounded by a venerating parish. The years glide by in that milder frame of mind which age brought with it; a stroke of paralysis in the year 1843 announced that death was not far distant, and Nov. 2, 1846, the weary poet breathed his last.

If we take a retrospective view of the development of this nature in whose rich soil the germs of genius and insanity lay as close together as in a double nut, we shall see the vigorous and cheerful temperament burst forth like a spark of fire from the flint-like ground of the Swedish peasantry. He draws nourishment from the natural beauties of Sweden and from the old sagas of Scandinavia. He raves about deeds of valor and combat, and expresses his enthusiasm in language of flame-gilded imagery. He makes the acquaintance of the spirit of antiquity, and the innate defiance of his character becomes softened into a Greco-religious harmony. His religious freethinking leads him to political freethinking, and his religious conciliatory spirit brings with it an attempt at the political conciliation of the opposing tendencies of the century. His spiritual standpoint determines his literary standpoint, the promulgation of the Gospel of lucidity, of light, and of song, as the expression of spiritual healthfulness. From this lofty height he completes the most important work of his life, the ideal picture of northern antiquity, as it was dreamed by its own contemporaries. In order to be just to his work, we must bear firmly in mind the period in which it arose. If we compare it with a northern master-work of our own day (with Björnson's "Bergliot," for instance), we shall find it neither Norwegian nor characteristically northern. It is only relatively northern, but its most beautiful cantos are unconditionally beautiful. This work, which was destined to afford, in the great struggle of the day, the decisive testimony of the significance of poetic healthfulness, was scarcely completed before it became apparent that the germs of disease in the poet's soul had attained such vigorous growth that some great spiritual crisis alone was needed to wither all the life-courage about which the ill-favored parasite had entwined its tendrils. The summer of life was over. The late autumn yielded yet a few beautiful fruits, and the tree was dead.

The impression I most desire to convey is that the man who gave world-wide fame to the name Esaias Tegnér, was beyond all else entirely human, in faults as well as in virtues, a thoroughly conscientious, upright soul, highly excitable, but with a radiant love of beauty and truth. His human earthly presence is so full of worth that in spite of all its weaknesses it is of profound interest even to foreigners, while the purely ideal image of Tegnér as a poet, will always stand forth in glorified outlines before the people in whose language he wrote, and upon whom he has acted like a radiant beam of the sun of the nineteenth century.

[It may be of interest to note that our American poet, H. W. Longfellow, in his younger days spent some time in Sweden, made Tegnér's acquaintance and mastered the Swedish language. On his return to America he published a complete translation of Tegnér's *The Children of the Lord's Supper* and a review and partial translation of *Fridthjof's Saga*. This was the first introduction of Tegnér to American readers.
—TRANSLATOR.]

IV

JOHN STUART MILL

1879

I

One day in July 1870, as I was pacing the floor of my room in Paris, with a book in my hand, I heard a modest knock at the door. The clock-maker, thought I, for it was the appointed time when, once each week, on the stroke of the hour, an assistant of the clock-maker was in the habit of making his appearance to wind up all the clocks of the little *hotel garni*.

I opened the door. Without there stood a tall, thin, elderly man, in a rather long black frock-coat buttoned about the waist. "Walk in!" said I, and resumed my book without bestowing further scrutiny upon him. But the man stood still, raised his hat, and questioningly mentioned my name. "That is my name," I replied, and before I could ask any question in return, I heard uttered in a subdued voice, the words, "I am Mr. Mill." Had the gentleman introduced himself as the king of Portugal, I could scarcely have been more astonished, and I do not know what he could have said that for the moment would have given me greater pleasure. My feeling was the same that a corporal of the young guards, under the first empire, might have experienced, had the great Napoleon, during one of his rounds in the camp, paid him the honor to notice his existence by giving his ear a pull.

I had attempted to make Stuart Mill known in my fatherland, and on this account he had repeatedly written to me, besides sending numerous pamphlets and newspapers, likely to be of interest to me, both to Copenhagen and to Paris; so he knew my address, and as he was passing through Paris, where, strange to relate, he did not possess a single acquaintance, he did not hesitate to traverse the long distance from the Windsor Hotel to the Rue Mazarin to honor his young correspondent with a visit.

As he mentioned his name to me, I recalled at once his portrait. It gave, however, as little idea of the expression of his countenance and the hue of his skin, as of the way in which he walked and stood. Although sixty-four years of age, his complexion was as pure and fresh as that of a child. He had the smooth, childlike skin and the rosy cheeks that are scarcely ever seen in elderly men of the continent, but that not seldom may be observed in the white-haired gentlemen who take their noonday horseback rides in Hyde Park. His eyes were bright, and of a deep, dark blue, his nose slender and curved, his brow high and arched, with a strongly marked protuberance over the left eye; he looked as though the labor of thought might have forced its organs to extend in order to make more room. The face, with its large and marked features, was full of simplicity, but was not calm; it was, indeed, continually distorted by a nervous twitching, which seeemed to betray the restless, tremulous life of the soul. In conversation, he had difficulty in finding words, and sometimes stammered at the beginning of a sentence. Seated comfortably in my room, with his fresh, superb physiognomy, and his powerful brow, he looked like a younger and more vigorour man than he really was. When I accompanied him on the street later, however, I observed that his walk, in spite of its rapidity, was rather halting, and that, notwithstanding his slender form, age had left its impress on his bearing. His dress made him seem older than he was. The old-fashioned coat he wore proved how indifferent he was to his external appearance. He was clad in black, and a crape band was wound in many irregular folds about his hat. Although she had been long dead, he still wore mourning for his wife.

No further signs of negligence were visible; a quiet nobility and a perfect self-control pervaded his presence. Even to one who had not read his works it would have been very evident that it was one of the kings of thought that had taken his seat in the red velvet arm-chair near the fireplace, whose mantel clock my unfounded suspicion led me to suppose he had come to wind up.

II

He spoke first of all of his wife, whose grave in Avignon he had just left. He had purchased a house in that city, where she had died, and always passed half of the year there. Already in his introduction to her essay on the "Enfranchisement of Women," which was the foundation of his own book on "The Subjection of Women," he had given public utterance to his enthusiastic admiration for the deceased. He had there said, the loss of the authoress was one that, even from a purely intellectual point of view, could never be repaired; he had declared that he would rather see the essay remain "unacknowledged, than that it should be read with the idea that even the faintest image could be found in it of a mind and heart which, in their union of the rarest, and what are deemed the most conflicting, excellences, were unparalleled"; indeed, he had called "the highest poetry, philosophy, oratory, or art," "trival by the side of her," and had ended with the prophecy, that if mankind continued to improve, its spiritual history for ages to come would be nothing but "the progressive working out of her thoughts and realization of her conceptions." In this tone, too, he spoke of her in my room. We may well suppose that the man who could thus express himself was no great portrait-painter, and we may doubt the objective correctness of his judgment; we cannot, however, accuse him of viewing marriage as a mere contract, a charge frequently brought against him on account of his ultra-rationalistic standpoint on the woman question. Great poets, like Dante and Petrarch, have erected over the women who were fantastically beloved by them a fantastic monument; but I do not know that ever a poet gave such true and such warm expression to his loving veneration of a female character as Mill, in the words in which his opinion of her worth and her enduring significance to him was couched. The inscription he had cast on her tombstone in Avignon is no evidence of an artistic talent for the lapidary style; it has too many and too eulogistic words. How energetic and beautiful, though, is the sentence with which it ends, "Were there even a few hearts and intellects like hers, this earth would already become the hoped-for heaven."

I asked Mill if his wife had ever written anything else than the essay edited by him. "No," he answered; "but all through my writings you will find her ideas; the best passages in my books are by her." "In your 'System of Logic' too?" I asked once more. "No," he replied, half apologetically; "my Logic was written before I was married." I could not avoid thinking that the contributions of Mrs. Mill to the inductive logic, even in the opposite case, could scarcely have been very considerable; a little thinking and reasoning would, under all circumstances, have fallen to the lot of Mill himself. The tone of reverential submissiveness apparent in his conversation was, however, peculiar to the temperament of the great thinker.

His nature was endowed with a decided inclination to serve not a cause alone, but its personal incarnation, and thus he was led to worship one after the other, two individuals, who, rare and significant though they may have been, were by no means his superiors,—his father and his wife. To his father (and to Bentham) he looked up in his early youth, to his wife all the rest of his life.

No one who has read Mill's "Autobiography" will have forgotten the gloomy description he gives of the desperate state of languor which ushered in his manhood. It was a long and painful crisis, during which his nature reacted against the excessive development of his faculties caused by his abnormal education. Instead of admiring the perfect intellectual organization which enabled him to come forth uninjured from the overfreighted and dangerous school of his father, English mediocrity was fond of pronouncing him, because of this hot-house culture, **an abnormal being who was by no means fitted to be a teacher** and an example. In the incredibly large and varied store of information imparted to him when he was a mere boy, the proof of the unnaturalness of his teachings and the "inhumanity" of Stuart Mill was found. What could be expected from a reading-machine that had studied Greek at three years of age, and at thirteen had gone through a course of political economy? The crisis which followed this overloading has been no less misinterpreted than was the encyclopedic education of the boy. Its symptoms were total indifference to all objects that previously had seemed to the young man worth desiring, and an unbroken state of joylessness, during which he asked himself whether the complete realization of all his ideas, and the achievement of the reforms for which he had been eager, would cause him genuine satisfaction, and found himself compelled to answer the question in the negative. Philosophers have discovered in this crisis nature's contradiction of Mill's utilitarian theory, inasmuch as, according to his own confession, the realization of the greatest possible happiness for the greatest possible number would have failed to make him happy. Theologians have found in it the stealthy approach of that secret melancholy, that deep-seated despair, which is always experienced by unbelievers, even when they themselves are not aware of it. Still, it is scarcely evidence against utilitarianism that morality alone is not sufficient for happiness, and it would be poor testimony, indeed; in behalf of the indispensability of dogmatic belief that a highly gifted and eminently critical youth of twenty years of age (who, moreover, both earlier and later managed to make his way cheerfully through the world without dogmatic belief) passed one whole winter in a state of profound aversion to action, overwhelmed with that sense of the misery of existence, with which every speculative mind is compelled to contend, and which almost every one is forced to conquer at least once in a lifetime. Among highly developed men there are but few who have not known this self-abandonment; with some it is of short duration, with others it becomes chronic: the exterior cause, as well as the weapons to be used against it, alone differ. Every one has his armor against discontent, one the impulse to work, another ambition, another family life, another frivolity; but through the meshes of his coat of mail weariness of life will occasionally find its way. With Stuart Mill this armor was manifestly the certainty of being in harmony with the mind of another person whom he esteemed more highly than himself. We must not overlook his own utterance that if he had, during the sorrowful crisis, "loved any one sufficiently to making confiding his griefs a necessity, he should not have been in the condition he was." Had Mill at that time been acquainted with his future wife, the crisis would certainly not have assumed such an acute character: *she* would have helped him to conquer his profound dejection more surely than dogmas and moral systems. This is very obvious from the pertinent words with which he has described his condition, "I was thus, as I said to myself, stranded at the commencement of my voyage, with a well equipped ship and a rudder, but no sail." The sail of this ship, which bore so rich and precious a freight, was and always remained his enthusiastic tendency to bow in profound submission before a chosen idol. At that period the influence of his father was markedly on the wane, that of his wife had not yet begun; consequently he stood still.

So much, at least, was made very plain in my first conversation with Mill, that the gain of this woman friend was the greatest boon of his life. Only in one of the passages that he has written about her has he succeeded in giving an exact idea of the peculiar nature of her character, and that is where he compares her to Shelley. A female Shelley—so she stood before him in his youth; later, even Shelley, who was so early snatched away, seemed to him a child in thought and intellectual maturity in comparison with what she became. He states many times, in very decided terms, what he owes to her: the perception of the region of ultimate aims, that is, the final consequences of theory; and of that of the nearest means, that is, of the immediately useful and practically attainable. The original endowment which he himself acknowledges, was now directed to the fusion of these extremes, to finding the medium course in political and moral truths.

Nevertheless, it does not seem to me probable that Mrs. Mill inspired her husband with any direct new thought. Her essential significance to him must, I think, be sought in two other points. In the first place, she strengthened his mental courage, and it is the boldness rather than the novelty of thought that gives its character to such classic works, as "On Liberty." Many times, even during our first conversation, he returned with regret to the lack of courage that everywhere withholds writers from supporting new ideas. He said, "There are writers of the first rank, such as George Sand, whose actual originality consists in courage. I leave out of consideration," he added, "her indescribably beautiful style, whose music can only be compared with the pleasing sounds of a symphony." The very confidence that a sense of harmony with the thought of another arouses, had enabled the wife of Stuart Mill to promote in him the courage he so extolled in George Sand.

In the second place, through her female universality, Mrs. Mill prevented her husband from running into any prejudice whatsoever. She confirmed in his mind a certain scepticism that led him to keep open amid the ice of doctrine one spot that would never freeze; and in thus inclining him to be sceptical, she became the cause of his progress. While the majority of so-called freethinkers have almost always purchased relative free thought in one point with double obduracy in other respects, Mill was continually on his guard against conventional prejudice; indeed, until the day of his death he carried on a sharp warfare against it, ferreting it out in its stronghold with the utmost intrepidity, in order to denounce and annihilate it.

Finally, there can be no doubt that Mrs. Mill was largely responsible for the active part her husband took in advocating the elevation of woman's social position. I felt interested to learn whether he had ever replied to his assailants on the woman question. He had given them no answer, nor did he purpose to pay any heed to them. "Why," said he, "forever keep repeating the same thing? Not one of them has produced anything of value." I touched upon the opposition of several physicians, whose objections were based on the necessities of nature to which a woman is subjected. He spoke harshly and positively against the prejudices of physicians in general. Long and tenderly he lingered, on the contrary, on the pleasure women took in performing the duties of the medical profession, and of the decided inclination they not infrequently manifested for it. He mentioned Miss Garrett, who had recently taken a medical degree in Paris, and praised her as the first woman who had had the courage to make such an attempt. In a letter to me, he had once designated the woman question as "in his eyes the most important of all political questions of the present day." At all events, it was one of those which during the last years of his life personally occupied him the most.

He did not hesitate, either in his written or in his spoken words, to use the strongest expressions in order to place in the right light his conception of the unnaturalness of women's state of dependence. Indeed, he had not been afraid to challenge universal laughter through his vehement assertion, that, as we had never seen woman in freedom, we did know nothing whatever until now of her nature; as though Raphael's Sistine Madonna, Shakespeare's young maidens, all the literature about women, in fact, had taught us nothing of the feminine character. On this point he was almost fanatical. He, who in all the relations between man and woman was refinement and delicacy itself, allowed himself to be positively insulting in his expressions when an opinion differing from his own on his favorite topic was uttered in his presence. One day I chanced to be visiting a celebrated French *savant* when the mail brought him a letter from Stuart Mill. It was an answer to a communication in which the Frenchman had expressed the opinion that the change in the social status of women, demanded in Mill's essay on "The Subjection of Women," might turn out well in England, where it would harmonize with the character of the race, but that in France, where the talents and tastes of the women were so contrary to it, there could be no possibility of success. Mill's pithy reply, which was handed to me with a smile, read as follows: "I see in your remarks that contempt for woman which is so prevalent in France. All that I can say on the subject is, that the French women pay this contempt back with interest to the men of France."

The peculiarity of Mill's standpoint in this emancipation question was, that it was based solely and entirely on a Socratic ignorance. He refused to see in the accumulated experience of ages any proof in regard to the boundaries of the so long enthralled feminine mind, and insisted that *à priori* we knew nothing at all about woman. He proceeded from no doctrinal view of especial feminine faculties, resting content with the simple proposition that man had no right to deny woman any occupation to which she felt attracted; and he declared everything like guardianship to be utterly useless as well as unjust, since free competition would of itself exclude woman from every occupation for which she was incapacitated, or in which man decidedly surpassed her. He has repelled many people by immediately deducing the final logical consequences of his theory the first time the question was brought forward, and by advocating the immediate participation of women in the affairs of government; but, as an Englishman, he had a too matter-of-fact mind not to limit the practical agitation to a single point. I remember asking him why—in utter disregard of what appeared to me the first requisite of all, economical emancipation—every effort in England and America was concentrated on political suffrage, which was so much more difficult to attain. He replied, "Because when that is gained, all the rest will follow."

III

He rose to take this leave, and having been informed that I meditated a trip to London, he asked me if I would make it with him. Fearing to intrude, I declined, and received an invitation to visit him in England. I had at that time just read Mill's masterly work on the philosophy of William Hamilton, was very full of it, and my mind was burdened with a thousand philosophic questions aroused by it. I was, therefore, greatly rejoiced that so rare an opportunity offered itself to discuss my doubts with the author himself, and a week later I rang the bell at the garden gate in front of Mill's country seat in Blackheath Park, near London, that little wicket gate before which I have never stood without a feeling of joyous expectation, and which I have never closed behind me without a sense of having been intellectually enriched.

My university education in Copenhagen had been an abstract metaphysical one; the professors of philosophy of the institution were men who, although mutually opposed to one another and supposed to be advocates of diametrically opposite standpoints, in all essentials bore the impress of the same school. They had begun their career as theologians, and had later become Hegelians, some influenced by the left flank of the Hegel school, others by the right. They had finally, together with all the rest of the world at that time, become "emancipated from Hegel," which, however, must be so interpreted as to admit of Hegel's still remaining first and last in their mental sphere. The methods of Hegel, employed now more naïvely, now in a more sophistic way, were preached from a *cathedra*, devoted to the worship of the absolute, the subjective-objective; his works were cited, his few witticisms repeated, and a wearisome, never-ending controversy against his supposed errors was carried on, from which we students gathered that they were almost all founded on his undervaluation of the real, especially in his faulty discernment of the natural sciences. We were taught, however, to consider his errors more precious than the truths of other thinkers, since truth could only be attained, as was shown by the example of our worthy professors, by creeping through the loop-hole of some error of Hegel. The University of Copenhagen, notwithstanding its otherwise by no means too friendly sentiments towards Germany, held it as an incontestable fact that modern philosophy was a German, as ancient philosophy had been a Grecian science. The existence of English empiricism and of French positivism was not recognized at the university; of English philosophy, in especial, we only heard as of a system that had long since been overthrown, and whose death-blow had been dealt to it by Kant. It had only been possible for me, by a vigorous effort of the will, to tear myself free, as best I could, from the bonds of the school prevailing in Denmark, and at the period when I met Stuart Mill I was still wavering between the speculative and the positive tendency. I made no secret to Mill of my state of uncertainty.

"So, then, you are very familiar with Hegel," said he. "Do you understand German?"

"To be sure I do; I read it almost as readily as I do my mother-tongue."

"I do not understand the German language," he said, in reply, "and have never read a line of German literature in the original. In fact, I know so little German that when I have been in Germany, I have had difficulty in finding my way at railroad stations and elsewhere."

"Have you made the acquaintance of the German philosophers through translations?"

"Kant I have read in a translation, of Hegel not a syllable either in a translation or in the original. I know him only through reviews and refutations, best of all through a concise presentation of his views by the only Hegelian in England,—Stirling."

"And what impressions have you received of Hegel?"

"That the writings in which Hegel has attempted to apply his principles may perhaps contain some good things, but that everything purely metaphysical in what he has written is sheer nonsense!"

I was startled, and suggested that I supposed this remark was to be taken *cum grano salis*.

"No; every word is meant to be understood literally," replied he. Then he dwelt on the outlines of the system, on the first preliminaries, the theory of *being* that is identified with *nothing*, and exclaimed, "What would you expect from a whole that begins with such sophistry? Have you really read Hegel?"

"Certainly; I have read most of his writings."

Mill (with a highly incredulous air), "And you have understood him?"

"I think so; at least, in all the principal features of his works."

He (with almost naïve astonishment), "But is there actually anything to understand?"

I did what I could to reply to this singular and rather diffusive question, and Mill, by no means convinced, yet as though he entered into my thought, said, "I understand very well the reverence, or the gratitude, you cherish for Hegel. We are always grateful to those who have taught us to think."

Never have I felt so keenly, as during this conversation, how thoroughly Mill was a man cast in one mould, a genuine Englishman, wilful and obstinate, equipped with a singularly iron will, and absolutely devoid of any flexible critical power of appropriation. What took the deepest hold of me, however, was the impression of the ignorance in which the most noteworthy men of different countries, even of the few lands most closely akin to their own, are of their mutual merits, and that in this second half of our nineteenth century. It seemed to me one could do much good by simply studying, confronting, and understanding these great minds that fail to understand one another.

I endeavored to bring into play against the principles of empirical philosophy the mode of contemplation I owed to my university training. To my astonishment, all the arguments I brought forward, and on whose effect upon Mill I had counted much, had long been familiar to him. "Those," said he, "are the old German arguments." He traced them all back to Kant, and had his answers to them ready.

It would not be in place in these pages to treat of the real significance of the controversy between the two modern schools, a problem which, in Germany, by almost all thinkers, is solved from the Teutonic point of view; as a matter of course, Stuart Mill would not admit that David

Hume had been refuted by Kant, an opinion which I now thoroughly share with him, and which I believe will be universally prevalent when the Kant worship begins to be somewhat on the decline. (I already find a trace of this change of conception in Germany in Fr. Paulsen's admirable work on Kant's "Theory of Knowledge.") At that time, to be sure, I had a presentiment that there must be some way of reconciling the rationalistic and the empiric theory of knowledge, but I did not yet know Herbert Spencer's simple solution of the problem. Mill spoke briefly but decidedly against all attempts at mediation, and concluded, with the mingling of modesty and decision that was peculiar to him, in the following words, which have remained fixed in my memory, "I believe that we must choose between the theories."

In the same spirit he expressed himself concerning the various modern philosophers, whose thought was nearly related to his own. He recommended me to become acquainted with Herbert Spencer, yet would not advise me, he said, to study Spencer's later works; he thought that in these Spencer had deviated from the "good method." On the other hand, he urgently commended to me Spencer's "Principles of Psychology," and the two chief works of his, in my estimation, far less intellectual contemporary Bain,—"The Senses and the Intellect" and "The Emotions and the Will." He presented me with a copy of the "Analysis of the Human Mind," by his much-revered father (the edition prepared and supplied with notes by himself and Bain), extolling the book to me as the main work of the English school in this century; and I having expressed to him my admiration of his critique of Hamilton's philosophy, he sent me the book the very next day. Almost of itself the conversation fell on Taine's recently issued volume, "De l'intelligence," in which Mill is so zealously investigated, profited by, and refuted, and in which the English tendency has perhaps placed its most enduring monument in French philosophy. Mill praised Taine, called his book one of the most profound and important works of modern France, and said about the same things to me regarding it that I found repeated later in his review of it ("Fortnightly Review," July, 1870). As a whole, he liked the book; but he had the same kind of objections to offer against the last chapters as against the later works of Herbert Spencer. We must, according to his conviction, most decidedly "choose," once for all, between the conditional knowledge of empiricism and the absolute certainty of intuition, and Taine, in the last volume of his work, had attempted to establish axioms which, not being derived from experience, had validity for the whole universe, independent of the boundaries of our experience. Mill, himself, thought, as is well known, that even the propositions of algebra and of geometry, whose empiric origin he endeavored to establish, could only be sure of a limited dominion. He extolled to me the little book "Essays by a Barrister," from which he himself quoted a few sentences. The barrister finds it quite conceivable that our multiplication-table, as well as our Euclid, may be utterly valueless in another solar system. "The question is," he says, "whether our certainty of the truth of the multiplication table arises from experience or from a transcendental conviction, excited by experience, but anterior to and formative of it." To illustrate the former of these views he presents a few striking examples:—

There is a world in which whenever two pairs of things are either placed in proximity or are contemplated together, a fifth thing is immediately created, and brought within the contemplation of the mind engaged in putting two and two together. This is surely neither inconceivable, for we can readily conceive the result by thinking of common puzzle tricks, nor can it be said to be beyond the power of Omnipotence, yet, in such a world, surely two and two may be five; that is, the result to the mind of contemplating two twos would be to count five. This shows that it is not inconceivable that two and two might make five; but, on the other hand, it is perfectly easy to see why in this world we are absolutely certain that two and two make four. There is probably not an instant in our lives, in which we are not experiencing the fact. We see it whenever we count four books, four tables or chairs, four men in the street, or the four corners of a paving stone, and we feel more sure of it than of the rising of the sun to-morrow, because our experience upon the subject is so much wider, and applies to such an infinitely greater number of cases. Nor is it true that every one who has once been brought to see it is equally sure of it. A boy who has just learned the multiplication table is pretty sure that twice two are four, but is often extremely doubtful whether or not seven times nine are sixty-three. If his teacher told him that twice two made five, his certainty would be greatly impaired.

It would be possible to put a case of a world, in which two straight lines should be universally supposed to include a space. Imagine a man, who had never had any experience of straight lines through a medium of any sense whatever, suddenly placed upon a railway, stretching out on a perfectly straight line to an indefinite distance in each direction. He would see the rails, which would be the first straight lines he ever saw, apparently meeting, or at least tending to meet, at each horizon; and he would thus infer in the absence of all other experience that they actually did enclose a space, when produced far enough. Experience alone could undeceive him. A world in which every object was round with the exception of a straight, inaccessible railway, would be a world in which every one would believe that two straight lines enclosed a space.

In his conversation, Mr. Mill expressed his adherence to these humorous sophistries, which have been so keenly criticised by Spencer, and he added, "If we possessed the sense of sight without the sense of touch, we would have no doubt that two or more bodies might exist in the same place, so completely is every so-called *a priori* axiom dependent on the character of our organs and experiences."

IV

Our conversation turned one day on the then existing circumstances in Rome. I compared the religious condition of Rome with that of France; I reminded Stuart Mill of the phenomenon observed by both of us in Paris of the *beau monde* congregating in a church, and added: "In your Dissertations and Discussions, you have written some words which you will scarcely now defend. You say: 'So far as the upper ranks are concerned, France may as properly be called a Buddhistic as a Catholic country; the latter is not more true than the former.' Would you still maintain this?" He answered: "It was at that time more true than now. In our day a new reaction has taken place, the possibility of which I could not conceive. In my youth I did not believe that man could retrograde; now I know it." A portion of the blame for this retrogression he ascribed to the French university philosophy. He spoke with a deprecation which was not to be wondered at, coming from his lips, of Cousin and his school. "But in spite of all," he concluded, "I cling to my old conviction that the history of France in modern times is the history of all Europe."

This view, which is reflected in all the works of Stuart Mill, is, in my judgment, a one-sidedness which can easily be accounted for by his ignorance of the German language and literature, and his undervaluation of the English situation, in which he, as a matter of course, was well able to detect the evils. He had visited France when he was very young; he told me he had passed his fifteenth year there, and had during that time learned all the French now at his command. As the French language was the only foreign tongue he spoke fluently and frequently (even though not without a strong English accent), and as through his whole life he had exerted himself to introduce French ideas into England, and to impart to his countrymen a love for the French national spirit, France necessarily represented to him Europe almost as though he were a native-born Frenchman.

Among all the Frenchmen whom Mill knew, Armand Carrel was, I believe, the one whom he held in the highest esteem. The essay he has written about this young French journalist is perhaps the most beautiful and the most overflowing with sentiment of anything he has written. In his great admiration for Armand Carrel, I find a partial explanation of his vehement antipathy to Sainte-Beuve. He could never forgive Sainte-Beuve for the fact that he, who had once been a collaborator of the "National," and a friend of Carrel, had become friendly to the Empire, and allowed himself to be elected senator. And yet this isolated fact was scarcely sufficient to warrant the hard words Mill dropped concerning Sainte-Beuve in my presence. Sainte-

Beuve was distasteful to him for the same reason that Carrel so greatly pleased him. He had not thoroughly studied him; his "Port Royal," for instance, he had never read; but a mind with such keenness and such firmly rooted principles as Mill's, was naturally repelled by the pliant and undulating temperament of Sainte-Beuve. Stuart Mill was a man of almost metallic character, rigid, angular, and immovable; the spirit of Sainte-Beuve, on the contrary, was like a lake, broad, tender, elastic, and of great circumference, yet moving altogether in little ripples of an undefined and varying size. Therefore Stuart Mill was, as it were, created to be an authority; his tone was that of one accustomed to command, and even when his demeanor was the boldest, he seemed, through the very conciseness and confidence with which he substantiated his results, to repulse every contradiction. Sainte-Beuve, on the contrary, never closed a subject entirely and without reservation; he was never quite catholic, nor quite romantic, nor quite imperial, nor quite a naturalist; one thing alone he was absolutely and entirely—Sainte-Beuve, in other words, the critic with feminine sympathy and ever-lurking scepticism. He was of the tiger race, yet was no tiger. He attached himself thoroughly to no one and to nothing, but he rubbed against everything, and the inevitable friction produced sparks. Mill's repugnance to him was like the antipathy of the dog for the cat. It was impossible for Sainte-Beuve to write simply; he could not pronounce a verdict without making it dependent on a whole system of subordinate conditions; he could not utter ever so brief a eulogy without spicing it with all kinds of malice. The greatest critic of France, after the death of Saint-Beuve, once said to me, "A laudatory sentence from Saint-Beuve is a veritable nest of leeches." Now, take in comparison the character of the mind and the whole style of Stuart Mill; his thoughts always on a grand scale, embracing the universal, allowing the individual to slip from notice; his diction unadorned, without artistic finish, naked as a landscape, whole sole beauty is the simplicity and power of the position of the land.

On one of the last days of my stay in London the conversation with Stuart Mill turned on the relation between literature and theatre in England and in France. He expressed the opinion, so common in our day, that the French who in the seventeenth century appropriated Spanish, in the eighteenth century English, and in the nineteenth century German ideas, in reality possess no other literary originality that that which lay in the form. Stuart Mill, whose mind was pretty much devoid of a sense of the purely æsthetic, and who cared more for the idea in art than for art itself as art, apparently did not realize that the poetic and artistic originality of the French would remain unaffected even by this undue limitation of its inventive genius; for where form and contents are inseparable, originality in form is identical with originality in general. Without permitting myself to touch on this point of view in my conversation with Mill, I merely replied, that one characteristic commonly held up as a reproach to the French, their so-called superficiality, was most highly useful to them when they imitated, for their imitation is but a semblance. With a strong tendency to be influenced by everything foreign, the French unite an almost total lack of capacity to form an objective impression of the foreign; consequently the national stamp is always plainly recognizable beneath the thin coating of foreign gloss. By way of example, I mentioned Victor Hugo, as an imitator of Shakespeare, and Alfred de Musset, as an imitator of Byron. "However," I added, "I will heartily admit the superiority of English poetry to the French if you will reward me by conceding the superiority of French dramatic art over the English." I had the previous evening attended the performance at the Adelphi Theatre, of Molière's "Le malade imaginaire," under the title of "The Robust Invalid," and having very often seen the play in Paris, I had a fine opportunity to compare the English mode of acting with the French. The invalid and the servant-girl were allowed all manner of coarse exaggerations; they bawled aloud in the roughest conceivable way, even had the audacity to end the second act with a *cancan;* and this while English prudery demanded that the scene with the syringe, and all expressions supposed to violate decency, should be omitted. "Yes," said Mill, "the theatre with us has fallen into decay. So far as the comedy is concerned, this may be accounted for by the fact that English nature is so devoid of form, and so untheatrical, and because our gestures are so stiff and so rare, while the French, even in their daily lives, always demean themselves like actors; yet in the direction of tragedy we can show some great names. Who knows, though, but that in our day reading may supplant theatre-going and compensate for it?"

He led the conversation from the theatre to English authors, and discussed with warmth two men as totally different from himself as Dickens and Carlyle. Thoroughly matter-of-fact as he was himself, he could appreciate as well as any one the poet with the great, warm heart, and the historian with the gushing, visionary imagination. Dickens was at that time just deceased; a few days previous to our conversation I had stood on the spot in Westminster Abbey where his body had but recently been laid to rest. His grave was still covered with living roses, while heavy, cold stone monuments covered the surrounding graves; it had the effect of a symbol. I communicated my impression to Mill, who expressed deep regret that he had not known Dickens personally, and had only learned through others of his amiability in private intercourse.

The last words we exchanged concerned the directly impending Franco-German War, to which Mill looked forward with gloomy misgivings. He considered it a misfortune for all humanity, for the entire European civilization.

I gazed long into his deep, blue eyes, before I could prevail upon myself to bid him a final farewell. It was my earnest desire to imprint upon my mind this so earnest and so stern, yet at the same time so bold, countenance, with all its youthful freshness. I wished to render it impossible for me to forget the peculiar greatness stamped on the man's form and on his every word. It is of considerable importance in grasping the character of an author to learn in what relation the impression of his human disposition stands to that of his disposition as an author. I have never known a great man in whom these two impressions were so thoroughly harmonious as in Mill. I have never discovered any quality in him as an author that I have not rediscovered in my personal intercourse with him, and I have found his different characteristics in both spheres exalted above and subordinated to one another in precisely the same order and manner. There are authors in whose writings some definite quality—for instance, philanthropy, or wit, or dignity—plays a more prominent rôle than in their lives; others whose writings display not a trace of those qualities, such as humor or free humanity, which render them amiable in their private lives. Most authors are far inferior to their books. In Stuart Mill no such inequality existed, for he was the very incarnation of truthfulness. There occurs in Mill's "Autobiography" a situation which affords an opportunity of measuring the degree of this truthfulness. I have in mind his position when he, the social reformer, who was so far removed from all demagogism, at a meeting of electors, comprised chiefly of the working class, was asked if he had written and made public the statement that the working classes of England were, as a rule, liars. He answered at once, and briefly, "I did." "Scarcely," he adds, "were these two words out of my mouth, when vehement applause resounded through the whole meeting. It was evident that the working people were so accustomed to expect equivocation and evasion from those who sought their suffrages, that when they found, instead of that, a direct avowal of what was likely to be disagreeable to them, instead of being affronted, they concluded at once that this was a person whom they could trust."

Mill gives the most modest interpretation of the proceeding, but the reader surmises what a halo of truthfulness must at that moment have hovered about him whose accusation of pervading falsehood was met with storms of applause from men spoiled by the flatteries of demagogues. In daily life, too, Mill bore that invisible nimbus of exalted love of truth. His whole being radiated with purity of character. It is needful to look back to the most sublime philosophic characters of antiquity, to Marcus Aurelius and his peers, if peers he has, to find a parallel to Mill. He was equally true and equally great, whether he addressed his maturely considered thought in some renowned work to a circle of readers spread over the whole globe, or whether, in his own home, without any assumption of superiority, he dropped an accidental remark to a chance visitor.

V

ERNEST RENAN

1880

It was not my intention to call on Renan during my stay in Paris from April to September, 1870, for I have always had an absolute horror of robbing celebrated men of their time under pretext of paying tribute to them. When, however, Taine—Renan's most intimate friend—repeatedly urged me to look up his "friend, the philologist," I gathered up my courage, and one day, provided with a letter of introduction from Taine, found myself on the third floor of a house in Rue de Vannes, where Renan lived. His surroundings were exceedingly simple. Since he had been deprived of the chair of Hebrew in the "Collége de France," he was without any fixed income, and his first popular publication was the only one of his books that had been at all remunerative.

Judging from his works and portrait, I had imagined Renan to be a refined reproduction of Jules Simon, philanthropic, gentle, with his head slightly inclined to one side; I found him decided, terse, and bold in his utterances, firm in his convictions, with somewhat of the modesty of the savant, but still more of the confidence and air of superiority of the man of the world. Renan was at the time forty-seven years of age. He was sitting at his writing-table when I entered his room, a little, broad-shouldered man, with a slight stoop, and a large, heavy head; his features were coarsely moulded, his complexion poor; he had blue eyes that displayed a wondrous power of penetration, and a mouth that, even in repose, was eloquent and indicative of shrewdness. His far from beautiful yet unquestionably attractive face, with its expression of lofty understanding and excessive industry, was framed in a mass of long brown hair that over the temples gradually shaded into white. In looking at him I was reminded of one of his own sentences, "*La science est roturière.*"

I

In early youth I had been repelled by the works of Renan, who is by no means the author for youth. Moreover, his "Life of Jesus," the first of his writings that fell into my hands, is perhaps his weakest work; the trace of sentimentality, the occasional appearance of unction, that last remnant of a priestly education, all that to a young person must seem either unduly effeminate, or lacking in genuineness, prevented me from arriving at a correct estimation of his literary qualities. That first impression had later been lost; the noble collection, "Etudes d'histoire religieuse," had opened my eyes to the almost feminine delicacy of feeling that could only seem unmanly to very youthful and inexperienced minds, and I found it quite natural that he who had justly been called "the most gentle of the bold" should be unable to speak without melancholy of his exceptional position. "The worst penalty a man who has fought his way to a life of reflection is compelled to pay for the independent stand he has taken, is to see himself excluded from the great religious family to which belong the best souls on earth, and regarded by the very beings with whom he would most gladly live in spiritual harmony, as a corrupt man. One must be very sure of one's position not to be shaken when women and children clasp their hands and cry, Oh, believe as we do!"

I had, however, erred in my supposition that any reminder of this elegiac tone would ring through Renan's every-day mode of expression. The main characteristic of his conversation was a thorough intellectual freedom, the magnificent repose of a genial child of the world. The nerve and sinew of his words was an unbounded contempt for the majority and for the masses, such as I had never before encountered in any one who displayed neither misanthropy nor bitterness. The first time I saw him he led the conversation to human stupidity. He said, evidently in view of inspiring his younger fellow-laborer with tranquillity of mind for the coming storms of life. "Most men are not human beings at all, but apes"; but he said it without anger. The words of Géruzez occurred to my mind, "*L'âge mûr méprise avec tolérance.*" Traces of this calm contempt may be found in the prefaces to his works; many years later it received poetic expression in his translation of Shakespeare's "Tempest"; but in his essay on Lamennais he has plainly defined it. He says: "There is found in Lamennais quite too much anger and not sufficient contempt. The literary consequences of this fault are very serious. Anger leads to declamation, bluntness, often coarse insults; while contempt, on the contrary, almost always produces a refined and dignified style. Anger bears within itself a need of being shared. Contempt is a subtle, penetrating delight which does not require the sympathy of others. It is discreet and all-sufficient to itself."

Renan's manner of speaking has a certain upward-soaring flight, a certain sprightly and redundant grace, without which no one ever gains the praise in Paris accorded to Renan, that in social intercourse and conversation he was "*charmant.*" Of the solemnity which his style often displays there was not a trace in its oral form. There was nothing priestlike about him, and he was wholly devoid of the pathos of a martyr of free thought. It was his wont to introduce a turn in the discourse with his favorite expression, "*Diable!*" and he was so far removed from striking the bitter and elegiac tone, that his equanimity had rather a touch of Olympian cheerfulness. Whoever knew anything of the childishly odious attacks with which he was daily assailed from the orthodox ranks, and whoever, like myself, had observed in Veuillot's journalistic circles how opinions wavered betweeen whether the right punishment for his heresy was hanging or shooting, could not but feel interested to inquire of Renan if he had not suffered a great deal for his convictions. "I!" was the answer; "not the least! I hold no intercourse with Catholics; I am acquainted with only one of them; we have one in the 'Academie des Inscriptions,' and we are very good friends. The sermons preached against me I do not hear; the pamphlets written against me I do not read. What possible harm could they do me?" According to Renan's opinion, the devout Catholics of France constitute about one-fifth of the population; and he thought they were far more fanatical than the orthodox Catholics of other places, because Catholicism in Spain and Italy is viewed almost as a matter of custom, while in France it is stimulated by intelligent opposition.

I found Renan, in June, 1870, very much exhilarated by the events in Rome. "A statue should be erected to Pius IX.," said he. "He is an extraordinary man. Since Luther no one has rendered such great service to religious freedom as he. He has advanced the cause about three hundred years. Without him Catholicism might very well have remained unchanged for three hundred years, shut up in a closed room with its spider's web and its thick dust. Now we are airing the room, and every one can see for himself that it is empty, and that nothing lies concealed within it." He had entertained a fear that during the negotiations concerning the infallibility of the Pope, even at the last moment, some compromise or other would be effected, through which everything would practically remain in the former channels; but this possibility had just vanished, and it could readily be foreseen that the bishops would shun no consequence, not even the result anticipated by Renan, which was, that a dismemberment would take place within Catholicism similar to that existing in Protestantism. It has been proved that the policy of the Catholic Church was wiser than its opponents at the first moment supposed. The division that took place was neither deep nor important, and there is not the slightest prospect of a dismemberment that can in any way be compared with the nature of the sects of Protestantism. Renan, who thought chiefly of France, hoped that time might open the eyes of the French bourgeoisie, which had thrown itself completely into the arms of the Church since the February Revolution, and was watching with profound anxiety the position so inimical to civilization assumed by the papal power.

In his interesting novel "Ladislaus Bolski," Victor Cherbuliez has turned into mild ridicule certain pet theories of Renan, by putting into the mouth of the good-natured yet thoroughly unpractical mentor of the hero, Renan's doctrine concerning the delicate nature of truth, and the consequent necessity of approaching it with the utmost deliberation and caution. George Richardet believes with Renan, that everything depends on some shade of meaning; that truth is not simply white or black, but is one shade of these colors, and he is wrecked because we cannot act in shades, but must act totally or not at all. In fact, Richardet aims at an actual realization of the idea expressed by Renan in one of many passages on the subject, as follows: "We might as well attempt to hit a winged insect with a club, as to grasp the truth in a moral science with the coarse claws of syllogism. Logic cannot grasp delicate shades of meaning, yet truths that are of a moral nature depend solely and entirely upon these shades. It is, therefore, of no avail to pounce on truth with the clumsy violence of a wild boar, for fleet and nimble truth will escape the ruthless attack and all the pains taken to capture it will be in vain."

Whoever is familiar with Renan's literary activity knows how closely he adheres to this thought when he writes. How different is the fate of his beloved shades of meaning when he speaks! While Taine, whose writings are filled with such bold utterances, is ever moderate and subdued in conversation, only allowing himself to be guided by the strictest considerations of justice and fairness, Renan, when he speaks, goes to extremes, and is by no means the knight of the delicate shades of thought. In one point alone were the two men equally decided in their expressions. This was when the discourse turned on that spiritualistic philosophy of France which strove to gain strength in its tender alliance with the Church, that system of philosophy which originally won the hearts of fathers of families, by bearing on its shield dogmas and virtue, and that in the place of discoveries of new truths, promised to furnish the entire land with good morals as the fruits of its scientific research. It had at that time control of all the professorships of

France. In Sorbonne it was represented by Janet and Caro. Janet, the more refined, more elegant spirit, endeavored to understand his opponents and set them right, while Caro, a specimen of genuine mediocrity, won the applause of the audiences he addressed, by flinging out his arms and vigorously beating his broad chest, and by his appeals to the freedom of the will. To Renan, who, nevertheless, has treated of Cousin as an orator and an author in so elegant an essay, the entire eclectic philosophy was orally mere "official soup," "children's pap," "product of mediocrity, calculated for mediocrity." Indeed, so obstinate was he on this point, that he, the advocate of fine shadings, could never be persuaded that spiritualism was not absolutely false. For Taine, on the other hand, he cherished an admiration that was almost passionate, *"Taine, c'est l'homme du vrai, l'amour de la vérité même."* In spite of the strikingly apparent difference of their natures, —Taine's style has the strength of a fountain, Renan's style flows as much like a stream as does the verse of Lamartine, —Renan declared himself to be in accord with his friend on all essentials. And when one day I led the conversation to the so frequently discussed question, namely, how much justice there was in the universal tendency to bewail the intellectual decadence of France, Renan immediately referred to Taine. "Decadence, what do you mean by that?" he exclaimed. "Everything is relative. Is not Taine, for instance, of vastly more importance than Cousin and Villemain put together? There is yet much intellect in France." Several times he repeated the words, *"Il y a beaucoup d'esprit en France."*

In common with nearly all cultivated Frenchmen, Renan was a reverential admirer of George Sand. This remarkable woman had been able to extend her dominion over the younger generation of France, without being in the least untrue to her youthful ideals. An idealist like Renan, she had won through her idealism; a naturalist like Taine, through the mysterious endowments that testified of her nearness to nature; the younger Dumas, to whom we might believe the heroes and heroines of George Sand, concerning whom his dramas often make bitter criticisms, would be especially odious, was perhaps the one among the post-romantic authors who stood personally nearest to her. The enthusiasm of Dumas for George Sand was, upon the whole, only a consequence of his literary susceptibility; the enthusiasm of Renan was of deeper character. As strong as must necessarily be his hatred for Béranger, in whom he sees the personification of all that is frivolous and prosaic in the French national character, and whose narrow *"Dieu des bonnes gens"* is a thorn in the eye of the follower of Herder, the pantheistic thinker and dreamer, quite as lively must naturally be his sympathy for the authoress of "Lélia," "Spiridion," and so many other dreamily enthusiastic writings.

Notwithstanding his wide range of vision, Renan is not without national limitations in his literary sympathies. In a conversation about England, he had nothing whatever that was good to say of Dickens; he was not even inclined to be fair. "The pretentious style of Dickens," said he, "makes the same impression on me as the style of a provincial newspaper." His well-known unjust article on Feuerbach fills us with less astonishment, when we learn in how marked a degree the defects of Dickens caused him to overlook the merits. It is the same morbidly developed taste for a classic and well-tempered mode of expression which gives Renan an antipathy to the humorous peculiarities in the style of Dickens and to the passionate form of Feuerbach's style; the genial mannerism of the English seemed to him provincial; the violence of the German appeared to him to savor of a tobacco-like after-taste of the pedantry of German-student atheism.

II

In the spring of 1870 Renan was on the point of making a trip to Spitzbergen, in company with Prince Napoleon. Shortly before starting he was discussing politics with me one day. "You can become thoroughly acquainted with the Emperor," said he, "through his writings. He is a journalist on the throne, a publicist who takes pains to inquire into popular opinion. Since his whole power depends upon the latter, he has occasion to employ more art, notwithstanding his inferiority, than Bismarck, who can afford to disregard everything. Until now he has been merely physically, not intellectually, enfeebled, but he has been extremely cautious (*extrêmement cauteleux*), and he entertains a profound distrust of himself hitherto unknown to him.'' Renan's estimate of Napoleon was very similar to that expressed by Sainte-Beuve, in the well-known fragment on ''The Life of Cæsar.'' Ollivier, whom he had known for a long time, he criticised severely. ''He and the Emperor are admirably suited to each other,'' said he; ''they have the same kind of ambitious mysticism; they are, as it were, allied through their chimeras.'' As early as the year 1851 Ollivier had often said to Renan, ''As soon as I am at the helm, as soon as I become premier—''

When I, with my simple political principles, urged the necessity of obligatory education, a thought I constantly had occasion to advocate, and which was everywhere treated as an absurdity or as a long since abandoned whim, Renan was, in my estimation, so paradoxical that I could scarcely believe him to be in earnest. His arguments, however, are interesting, especially because similar ones were continually presented at that time by the most prominent men of France, although perhaps in a different form. Renan maintained, first of all, that enforced education was tyranny. ''I have myself,'' said he, ''a little child that is in feeble health. How despotic it would be to take that child from me in order to educate it!'' I replied that there would be exceptions made by the law. ''Then no one would send children to school,'' he answered. ''You do not know our French peasants. They would gain nothing from such legislation. Let them till the soil and pay their taxes, or give them a musket in their hand, and a knapsack on their back, and they are the best soldiers in the world. But what is well adapted to one race does not always suit another. France is not like Scotland or the Scandinavian countries; Puritanic and Teutonic customs cannot take root in our soil. France is not a religious country, and every attempt to make it so would prove abortive. Ours is a land that produces two things,—what is great and what is fine (*du grand et du fin*). Respectable mediocrity will never thrive here. These two words express the ideal needs of the population; as for the rest, there is but one thing they want, and that is to amuse themselves, to experience through pleasure that they are living. And finally, believe me, it is my firm conviction that elementary education is a downright evil. What is a human being that can read and write —I mean a human being that can do nothing but read and write? An animal, a stupid and conceited animal. Give human beings an education of from fifteen to twenty years' duration, if you can; otherwise, nothing. Anything less, so far from making them any wiser, only destroys their natural amiability, their instinct, their innate sound reason, and renders them positively unendurable. Is there anything worse than to be governed by a seminarist? The sole reason why we are forced to occupy ourselves with this question is because this mass of street boys (*ce tas de gamins*) gained the upper hand and wrung from us the right of universal suffrage. No, let us agree that culture is only a good in the case of highly-cultivated people, and that the half-cultivated are to be regarded as useless, arrogant apes." I spoke of decentralization, of elevating the condition of the provincial cities, Lyons, for instance. "Lyons!" he burst out, in absolute earnest, "why, it would never occur to any one to transform the metropolitan cities of the provinces into intellectual focuses, for they would at once come under the control of the bishops. No," he added with droll conviction, "in such cities nothing but absurdities will ever be accomplished."

After such utterances from the man of all others in France who fought most vigorously for a reform in the higher schools and universities, it is perhaps easier to understand why it was that the indifference of the liberals in that country went hand in hand with the zeal of the Catholic priesthood, whenever there arose a question of remedying that ignorance of the lower classes which later proved

so dangerous for the outer and inner security of the land.
Old Philarète Chasles, who was really no Chauvinist, made
himself very merry one evening in May, 1870, over my faith
in the efficacious power of compulsory education; he called
it my *Revalenta arabica,* and facetiously declared that I
hoped through it to make the human race happy through
all eternity. He asked me, too, if I did not think the peasants made sufficiently good fathers of families and good
soldiers, without the aid of the schoolmaster. The war soon
taught these men that the soldier who can read and write
has a power in his hands never before adequately appreciated. It was, indeed, remarkable to see how ideas we are
apt to ascribe wholly to the Catholic priesthood—as, for
instance, this idea of the absolute harmfulness of imperfect
knowledge—had gradually gained such authority in a land
saturated with Catholicism that, with a slight alteration
of form, they even swayed the opponents of the Catholic
faith.

Another equally interesting application of the Renan
theory, that what was good in Germany or in the North
was not necessarily suitable for France, I heard one day at
Renan's country villa in Sèvres when he himself was absent.
The conversation fell on French *convenance* marriages. A
lady, closely allied to Renan, a German-born lady, who was
thoroughly imbued with his ideas, defended the French
custom of founding marriages on an agreement between the
suitor and the parents, and of permitting the wedding to
take place after a few *obligato* visits. "This manner of
forming a matrimonial alliance," said she, "would not
exist without very good reasons. Although brought up in
France, I who am German by birth did not marry in this
way. As often as it was proposed to me to take a suitor
into consideration, I declared that I would not see him;
the mere fact that he came as a suitor sufficed to make him
odious in my eyes. I was acquainted with my husband
several years before our marriage. Who can offer any protest against the French custom, however, that has seen, as
I have in the case of so many of our friends—and she mentioned one and another—who were introduced but one week

before their wedding-day, and yet whose union proved so happy and satisfactory to both parties.

While I was viewing these words, partly as a subterfuge employed to escape passing judgment on the relations of near friends, partly as a symptom of the French characteristic desire to represent every national peculiarity, however unfortunate it may be, as an unalterable quality of the race, a gentleman who was present, one of the most unprejudiced of French authors, laid his hand on the head of his little daughter, a child of two years old, and said: "Do you think it would be right for me to give my little girl to the first man that might appear on the scene, and without appealing to us, her parents, manage to steal away her heart? Remember how great is the inexperience of a young girl, and do not forget the conditions of the actual world, nor what scoundrels there are abroad, nor what a past, what diseases, what bestial appetites a young man may have, which a father's eye may detect, but whose existence the innocent mind of a young maiden neither can nor should deem possible. The world is an enemy. Should not I with all my might defend my little daughter against this enemy? If, some day fifteen years hence, suitors for her hand announce themselves, we parents, if we are then living, will act as follows: we will discard those who cannot suitably be taken into consideration, either because of their social position, or because of moral or physical weaknesses; we will make a choice selection, and from this permit the young girl to choose as she pleases." To account for this mode of contemplation, the secluded education of young girls in convents, or in boarding-schools, should be borne in mind. Viewed in this light, even when consideration is taken of the greater ardor and sensuality of the Latin races, the conclusion arrived at is perhaps not unreasonable.

III

I was in London when the Franco-German war broke out, and being so fortunate as to have intercourse with some wholly unbiased men of great political insight, I foresaw sooner than my French acquaintances all the disasters the war must inevitably bring upon France. On my return to Paris, I found the people full of hope and confidence; indeed, there was, as is well known, a manifestation of arrogance that could not but affect every stranger unpleasantly. This arrogance, however, was by no means shared by men of science. As yet there had been no battle; but already the news of the suicide of Prévost Paradol in North America had filled with the most painful forebodings every one who knew him and was aware how thoroughly posted he was in the preparations and resources of France. The terrible event occurred immediately after an attack of fever, yet no one doubted that Paradol had laid hands on himself with a full consciousness of what he was doing, and with a plain design. That he had not merely sent in his resignation was because—so it would seem—he was altogether too proud to admit that he had in any way been in error; he was not even willing to make such an admission in an argument, and now he had been guilty of a triple error: believing in the justice of the constitutional tendency of the emperor; seeking the post of ambassador to Washington; and finally not giving up his post at once, when the odious comedy of universal suffrage in May had shown what the constitutional temper of the emperor indicated. The declaration of war, in his eyes identical with the downfall of France, caused him to prefer death to a position in which he could not consistently remain, and from which he was unable to withdraw without a humiliation far worse to him than death. This solitary pistol-shot, resounding across the ocean as the signal of many hundred thousand terrible volleys, deeply affected the friends and companions of Prévost Paradol's youth. Taine, who had been making a brief trip to Germany, where he went to collect materials for an essay on Schiller, which had been interrupted by the war, was profoundly moved by the thought of the impending crisis. "I have just come from Germany," said he, "and have conversed with so many industrious and excellent men. When I consider how much trouble it costs to bring a human child into the world, to tend it, bring it up, educate it, establish it in life; when I, furthermore, consider how many struggles and hardships this child must itself undergo in order to gain preparation for life, and then reflect that all this must now be cast into a ditch as a mass of bloody flesh, I can do nothing but mourn! With two regents of the nature of Louis Philippe, we might have succeeded in escaping the war; with two chieftains like Bismarck and Louis Napoleon, it became a necessity." He was at that time the first Frenchman whom I heard take into consideration the possibility of German superiority.

Then came a series of shocks in the first tidings of great defeats, only varied by false rumors of victory directly after the battle at Weissenburg. Dejected and sorrowful was the prevailing mood in the city in those days, when the proclamations at the street corners told of armies put to rout and lost battles; but more fearful still was the mood on that 6th of August, when the first half of the day was passed in the mad intoxication of triumph over victory, the last half in mortified despondency. How great would have been the humiliation had there been the slightest foreboding of the battle of Wörth, whose fate was at the same moment sealed! When, early in the morning, the news of great victories spread through the city, all Paris covered itself with banners; the citizens walked the streets with little flags in their hats; all the horses had little flags on their heads. I sat in front of a café, opposite the "Hôtel de Ville," gazing at the houses about the public square that were decked with hundreds of small flags, when suddenly there appeared, at the window of a house near me, a hand that hastily drew in the flag there floating in the breeze. Never shall I forget that hand, or that act. Trifling as was the occurrence, it startled me; for there was something so sorrowful about the movement of the hand; something in its appearance testifying so plainly of disappointment, that the thought immediately flashed through my mind: "The news of victory must be false!" Soon hands were seen at all the surrounding windows; the flags quickly disappeared, and in quarter of an hour the whole banner decoration seemed as though it had been blown away by the wind. "A proclamation from the government had declared that nothing at all was reported that day from the scene of war, and that the police were on the track of the promulgators of false news, in order to punish them severely. The promulgators of false news! As though the hungering imaginations and the languishing yearning of the great city were not the only guilty ones!

About a week later, on the 12th of August, I met Renan. He had returned from the far North before the appointed time. I have never seen him so deeply moved. He was desperate; this trivial word is the only appropriate one. He was beside himself with exasperation. "Never," said he, "was an unhappy people so governed by imbeciles as we are. One might have supposed that the emperor had had an attack of insanity. But the fact is, he is surrounded by the most contemptible flatterers. I know officers of high rank, who were well aware that the Prussian cannons far surpassed our much-lauded *mitrailleuses*, but who dared not tell him so, because he had taken an active part in the preparation of these machine-guns himself, had done a little drawing on the design, which is expressed in official language by the statement that he is the inventor of the *mitrailleuse*. Never was there so great a lack of brains (*si peu de tête*) in an imperial ministry; he was himself sensible of it. I am acquainted with a person to whom he said so, and yet he undertook a war with such a ministry. Was ever such folly known? Is it not heart-rending? As a people, we are vanquished for a long time to come. And to think that all that we men of science have been striving to build up for the past fifty years—sympathy between nations, mutual understanding, fruitful co-operation—is overthrown with one blow. How such a war destroys the love of truth! What lies, what calumnies, will not for the next fifty years be eagerly believed by one people of the other, and separate them from one another for immeasurable time! What a delay of European progress! We cannot raise up again in a hundred years what these people have torn down in a day."

No one could have been more grieved at the rupture between the two great neighbors than Renan, who had so long stood in France as the representative of German culture. Nor could any one have spoken with greater gratitude than he, of German thought. One of his favorite remarks was: "There is nothing that can hold so much as a German head." He seemed to have little liking for the Germans personally, but he spoke with respect of their noble intelligence. To the South German, however, in every other respect than in a capacity for the affairs of government, he ascribed a far higher endowment than to the North German, an opinion shared by the majority of cultivated Frenchmen.

In speaking of his journey, Renan said: "We were in Bergen when the first ambiguous tidings of the threatened war reached us from France. None of us could deem it possible. The prince and I looked at each other. He who possesses so rare and so keen an intellect merely said, 'It cannot be,' and gave orders to continue our journey. We sailed to Tromsöe. When we reached that place two despatches awaited the prince, one from his secretary in Paris, and another from Emile Ollivier with these words, '*Guerre inévitable!*' We held a brief council, but so irrational did the affair appear to us, since Leopold von Hohenzollern had withdrawn his candidacy; so impossible did it seem that this pretext could incite all Europe, and especially all Germany, against us; and, finally, so great was our desire to sail to Spitzbergen and see 'the great icebergs,' that we resolved to depart the next morning. We went to bed. My room was situated next to that of the prince's adjutant. Early in the morning I heard the valet awaken the adjutant with a despatch. I rose, we went on board, the ship set sail, and you may fancy my astonishment when I saw that we were taking a southward course. The prince sat in despair, staring fixedly before him. The first words he uttered were: '*Voilà leur dernière folie, il n'en feront pas d'autres.*' He was a true prophet; this will be their last folly." "I myself," added Renan, "was of the same opinion. I knew how badly we were prepared, but who could have dreamed that the crisis would come so soon! Do not say that we may yet be victorious. We will never be victorious again; we have never, under this emperor, conquered, in a definite way, any tribes whose subjugation could serve as a happy omen, when Prussia was in question. The Arabs are the poorest tacticians in the world." More than once he broke out with the words: "Was such a thing ever heard of before! Poor prince! Poor France!" He was so vehement that he exhausted himself in imprecations on all the leading men; according to his words, at this time uttered with little regard to shades of meaning, they were all weak-minded creatures, or villains. "What is this Palikao?" he cried. "A thief, a pronounced thief, to whom our best houses are closed; and does not every one know that one of his colleagues is a criminal, a murderer, who has only escaped capital punishment by flight! And in the hands of such men lies our fate!"

I saw tears in his eyes, and I bade him adieu. I have never seen him since that day. He quickly regained his composure and the control of his grief; but in that sorrowful outburst Renan was another man than when he wrote, "The savant is a spectator in the universe. He knows that the world belongs to him only as an object for study; and even if he could reform it, he would perhaps find it so curious an object that he would lose all desire to do so." It is scarcely likely that Renan was altogether in earnest when he uttered these audacious and aristocratic words; but even if he was, the emotions he experienced in the year 1870 would have inclined him to repudiate them.

It is difficult to estimate how demoralizing an influence, during the second empire, life under the dominion and pressure of the "*fait accompli*" exercised on the French savant. A tendency to quietism and fatalism, to the approval of everything that had once been accomplished, characterized beyond all else French moral science under Napoleon III. Traces of its influence could be observed everywhere in social life and in conversation. Entire freedom from enthusiasm was looked upon as almost equivalent to culture and ripe scholarship. A young foreigner had daily opportunity to marvel over the reserve and the passiveness of even the best of these people, as soon as there arose any question of a practical reform; and I remember well coming home one evening in May, 1870, very much out of humor, and writing in my note-book: "There was once another France." Once, indeed, there had been a wide-awake, enthusiastic, poetic France, keenly alive to the needs of humanity. It seems as though such a France must gradually arise from the debasement, which, even if it brought with it no other good, at least has given all aspiring souls a new impetus toward the truth.

With changeful emotions Renan has watched the development of republican France. Although the republicans almost immediately restored to him his professorship, their demeanor toward him, as well as toward the other friends of Prince Napoleon, was rather cool and reserved. Thoroughly aristocratic in his views as he is, he gave the democrats to understand in his "Caliban" how exceedingly little he esteemed them; yet in a letter written shortly afterward to a German friend, in explanation of his speech on entering the French Academy, he said: "What now, if, while your statesmen are absorbed in this thankless task of chastising and trampling under foot, the French peasant, with his rude understanding, his unvarnished politics, his labor, and his savings, should happily found an order-loving and enduring republic! Would it not be droll?" He is patriot and philosopher enough to become friendly, in the course of time, to any form of government which satisfied the majority of his fellow-countrymen, and corresponded to their intellectual standpoint.

Renan, as it is well known, is a native of Brittany, and has all the peculiarities of his race. The Bretons, in modern French literature, are distinguished by a common trait. Like Chateaubriand and Lamennais, Renan hates the commonplace, the easy-going, frivolous tone; and although a victim of doubt, he has the most ardent need of a faith and an ideal. For his narrow fatherland he cherishes a most profound attachment. In a hopeful moment he has even apostrophized his race with the words: "O simple clan of farmers and seamen, to whom, in an extinguished land, I owe the strength to preserve my soul alive!" We must not place too literal an interpretation on this outburst of feeling. No one realized more profoundly than Renan how far from being extinguished was that France of which he wrote to Strauss, that it was essential to Europe as "a lasting protest against pedantry and dogmatism." But the remark is characteristic of the at once obstinate and restless, enthusiastic and sceptical child of Brittany. If he renounce his faith in any one particular, as he here lost faith in France, it is only to adhere elsewhere with all the warmer enthusiasm to an ideal. In religion, too, he has a Brittany in which he believes.

[Renan died in 1892. His "Life of Jesus," which must be considered more as a brilliant novel than as the result of historical investigation, became the first of his seven volumes on the early period of Christianity. The other six volumes are: The Apostles (1866); St. Paul (1869); "The Antichrist" (1873); "The Evangelists and the Second Generation of Christianity" (1877); "The Christian Church" (1878); "Marcus Aurelius and the end of the World of Antiquity" (1882). As a continuation of this series we may consider his five volumes: History of the People of Israel (1887-94). Besides he wrote commentaries on Job, Ecclesiastes and the Song of Solomon, and produced books along philosophical lines. A splendid light on his personality is given in his letters to his sister Henrietta (1842-45) published in 1896.—TRANSLATOR.]

VI

GUSTAVE FLAUBERT

1881

GUSTAVE FLAUBERT was born at Rouen, in the year 1821. When, in 1880, he was snatched away by sudden death, he did not leave European literary art in the same condition in which he had found it. No artist, as such, could desire to hand down to posterity a better renown. The work of his life marks a step in the history of the novel.

He was a prose author of the first rank; for several years indeed no one stood higher than he in France. His strength as a prosaist reposed upon an artistic and literary conscientiousness, which was exalted almost to the dignity of genius. He became a great artist because he was unsparing in his efforts, both when he was making preparations to write and when he was engaged in writing; he collected the results of his observations, facts and illustrations, with the painstaking of a mere savant, while striving, with the passionate eagerness of a mere adorer of form, to fashion his materials in a plastic and harmonious manner. He became a master of modern fiction because he was sufficiently self-denying to be willing to represent real psychological events alone, and to shun all effects of poetic eloquence, all pathetic or dramatic situations which appeared beautiful or interesting at the expense of the truth. His name is synonymous with artistic earnestness and literary rigor.

He was not a savant who was at the same time a writer of fiction, or who, in the course of his life, became a writer of fiction. His literary work is based on earnest, slowly acquired preparatory studies. His books have nothing in them that is juvenile or frivolous, nothing that is smiling or versatile. These books are the results of a slowly developed and late maturity. He did not make his début until he was thirty-five years old, and, although he devoted his whole time to literature, he left behind him in his fifty-ninth year but seven works.[1]

His was a profoundly original, but by no means elementary character. His originality was dependent on the fact that two literary currents united in his temperament and there formed a new well-spring. In his youth he received simultaneously, or almost simultaneously, two impulses, which determined his intellectual career.

The first current that reached him was the romantic-descriptive tendency in literature originating with Chateaubriand, a tendency characterized by a style fraught with lyrical emotion and brilliant coloring, which charmed the French reading public for the first time in "Atala" and "Les Martyres," and which later gained a far finer and more powerful rhythm, as well as a far superior picturesque vigor, in Victor Hugo's "Les Orientales," and "Notre Dame de Paris." Like all poets, indeed like all human beings, Flaubert was inclined in youth to the lyrical, and his lyric muse, through the historic development of French poesie, became a varied-hued and melancholy homage to the religion of beauty. The second current directed into his inner being, was the tendency of Balzac's novels against the modern, their employment of what was hideous and brutal as characteristic, their passionate realistic bias, and their fidelity of observation.

While these two currents flowed at one and the same time through his inner being, and after the lapse of some time became blended together, they received a new coloring and a new name.

As a youth he had composed for the drawers of his writing-table many descriptive and pathetic lyrics, in Hugo's, Gautier's, and Byron's style; but justly feeling that his originality could not assert itself in this direction, and that, upon the whole, there was no longer room for anything

[1] The titles are: *Madame Bovary, Salammbô, L'education sentimentale, La Tentation de Saint-Antoine, Le Candidat, Trois Contes, Bouvard et Pécuchet.*

scription of the immediate past. The way nad just then been pointed out to him by the bolder, hardier Dumas, with whom, in spite of all his respect for the generation to which his father belonged, had commenced the direct and pertinent derision of the romantic ideal; this can be seen in the *rôles* of Nanjac, in "Le Demimonde" and of Montègre, in "L'ami des femmes." The answer that Montègre, bewildered by the superiority of Ryon, makes the latter, "*Vous êtes un physiologiste, monsieur,*" was in reality the sole reply that the elder generation could offer to the critic of the younger.

Augier was born in 1820, Dumas in 1824, Sarcey and Taine in 1828. The author of "Madame Bovary," who first saw the light in 1821, evidently had kindred spirits among his contemporaries. He differed from them in his secret, unshaken fidelity to the ideals of the past generation; but he united with them so unhesitatingly in their attacks on the caricatures of these ideals that, without further ceremony, he must be classed in the group of these anti-romantic writers.

And yet, through his harshness and coldness, he was much more of a reminder of Mérimée, who stood alone in the past generation; to many, indeed, he appeared but a heavier, broader Mérimée. For the first thing noticeable in him was that he was a cold blooded poet; and these two epithets, cold-blooded and poet, had previously been united in Mérimée alone.

A closer study, however, would have shown that the cold-blooded deliberation of Mérimée was quite a different character than that of Flaubert. Mérimée treated romantic material in an unromantic, dry, and meagre manner. His tone and his style corresponded, for the tone was ironical, the style lacking in imagery, and cold. With style and tone, however, the wildness of the theme and its barbaric, impassioned character were at variance.

Flaubert, on the contrary, harmonized theme and tone. With infinitely superior irony he pictured the vapid and the absurd; but with theme and tone his style was at variance. He was not, as Mérimée, rational and meagre; he was all radiant with coloring, and harmonious, and he spread the gold-wrought veil of this style over all the commonplace and sorrowful incidents he narrated. No one could read the book aloud without being astonished at the music of its prose. The style contains a thousand melodious secrets; it aims the keenest satire at human weakness, powerless yearnings and aspirations, self-deception and self-satisfaction, to an accompaniment of organ music. While the surgeon in the text, without the slightest manifestation of sympathy, is lacerating and tearing to pieces, a beauty-loving lyric poet is sobbing out a low, wailing accompaniment. If we should turn to a page in which a village apothecary utters his half scientific prattle, in which a diligence tour is depicted, or an old casket described, we would find it, viewed from a stylistic standpoint, as highly colored and enduring as a mosaic, owing to the freshness of its expressions and the solid structure of its sentences. Each clause is so carefully put together that no two words could possibly be removed without destroying the entire page. The assured refinement of the imagery, the metallic ring of the musical flow of words, the rolling breadth of the prose rhythms, invested the narrative with a marvellous power that was now picturesque, now comic.

There was evidently something singularly dual in his temperament. His character was composed of two distinct elements which were complements of each other: a burning hatred of stupidity and an unbounded love of art. This hatred, as is so often the case with hatred, felt itself irristibly attracted to its object. Stupidity in all its forms, such as folly, superstition, self-conceit, and illiberality, attracted him magnetically, and inspired him. He was compelled to depict it trait by trait; he deemed it, in and for itself, entertaining, even when others could not discover it to be interesting or comical. He made a formal collection of stupidities, absurd pleas for law-suits, and vapid illustrations; he collected a mass of wretched verse, written by physicians alone; every evidence of human stupidity, as such, had its value to him. In his works, indeed, he has done nothing else than erect monuments with a masterly hand to human limitation and blindness, to our misfortunes, so far as they depend upon our stupidities. I almost fear that the world's history was to him the history of human stupidity. His faith in the progress of the human race was exceedingly wavering. The mass, even the reading public, was to him "that everlasting blockhead which we call they (*on*)." If we wished to label this side of his character, and absolutely stamp him with one of those popular, but to him so detestable, words ending with "ist," it could not with full justice be pessimist, nor yet nihilist; imbecillist would be the word.

To this unremitting pursuit of stupidity, whose embittered character was shrouded in its purely impersonal form, corresponded, as before stated, a passionate love of literature, which to him signified beauty and harmony, which was considered by him the highest, in fact the only true, art, and which he cultivated with a yearning for perfection that first kept him long silent, then caused him at a late day to become a master, and finally rendered him early unfruitful again. When he depicted the commonplace, it caused him more distress than others; he therefore endeavored to elevate his materials through the artistic manner of his treatment, and since in his eyes the most important attribute of authorship was the plastic power, he strove beyond all else to attain perspicuity. He has said so himself, and we feel it to be true when we study him through his style.

In his very first work all the merits of this style came to light.

Read the following passage from "Madame Bovary," where Emma, yet unmarried, accompanies Bovary to the door, after his medical visit to her father:

She always went with him to the first step of the outside stairs. If his horse had not yet been brought forward they remained there. They had said adieu, they attempted no further remark; the fresh air encompassed her, played with the downy hair of her neck, or blew about her side the strings of her apron, which twisted and twirled like a little flag. Once when a thaw had set in, the water was trickling down from the bark of the trees, and the snow was melting on the roofs of the buildings. She stood on the threshold; she went back to get her parasol; she opened it. The parasol was of a changeable green and blue silk, and the sun shining through it lent a radiant and flickering lustre to her white complexion. She smiled beneath it, while the soft zephyrs played about her, and the raindrops were heard to come pattering down, one by one, on the outstretched silk of the parasol.

So insignificant a matter as this ordinary leavetaking becomes interesting through the loving care bestowed on the description, and the separation obtains individual life from the prominence given to a single day, when after all, nothing of moment transpires. The accuracy with which this commonplace situation is portrayed, transforms it into a painting of high rank, one that reproduces simultaneously the visible and the audible, the tableau and the mobile life.

Or recall the passage where Emma, after her marriage, falls in love for the first time:—

Emma grew thin, her cheeks became pale, her face lengthened. With her smoothly brushed black hair, neatly tied with a ribbon, her large eyes, her straight nose, her birdlike walk, and always silent as she was, she almost seemed to glide through existence without touching it, and to bear on her brow the indistinct impress of some sublime destiny. She was so sorrowful and so calm, and at the same time so gentle and so reserved, that in her presence people felt as though seized by some icy spell, just as a shudder is apt to run through the frame in church where the perfume of flowers is mingled with the chill of the marble.

The comparison is new, is striking and brief. We here detect the poet in the narrative.

We detect him still more clearly when he continues thus:—

The ladies of the city admired her housewifely taste, the patients her courtesy, the poor her benevolence. But she herself was full of desire, full of rage and hatred. Her dress, with its rigid folds, concealed a troubled heart, whose pangs these chaste lips of hers did not reveal. She was in love with Léon. . . . She investigated his every footstep; she searched his countenance; she invented a whole history in order to have a pretext for a visit to his room. She esteemed the apothecary's wife happy because she slept under the same roof with him; and her thoughts were continually alighting on the house, precisely as the doves of the 'Golden Lion' that were always flying there to moisten their rosy feet and their white wings in the muddy water of the eaves.

This is not a striking general comparison; it is a comparison borrowed from a positive occurrence in the village where Emma lives. So vividly does this village present itself to the mind's eye of the author.

Sometimes he condenses an entire description into one powerful poetic phrase. So it is in the passage where he introduces the old maid-servant who has been summoned to a meeting of the agricultural union in order to receive for her faithful service of fifty-four years on one farm a silver medal valued at twenty-five francs.

Katharina Niçaise Elizabeth Leroux, a little old woman who looks all shrivelled up in her poor garments, appears upon the estrade. We see her thin face with its deep wrinkles beneath her cap, and her long hands with their knotted joints, which had been coated by the dust of the barn, the grease of wool-picking, and the potash of the wash-tub, with so hard a crust that, although they had been washed in pure spring water, they still seemed dirty, and which could no longer be wholly closed, but always remained open, as though in testimony of too much toil. We see the nun-like rigidity of her expression, the animal stupidity of her wan visage, her motionless bewilderment at the unusual spectacle of banners, flourish of trumpets, and smiling gentlemen in black coats, decorated with the cross of the Legion of Honor. Then Flaubert condenses the picture into this one sentence:—

Thus stood in the presence of these well-to-do old fogies this half-century of slavery.

Trivially accurate as are the details of the description, the style of this recapitulating sentence is grand and finished. We feel plainly that for this author the art of literary composition was the highest of all arts.

Not only was literary composition his unconditional, his

sole calling, but, as may be stated without any undue exaggeration, his conception of the world was equivalent to the thought: The world exists in order that it may be described.

He once gave expression to this opinion of his in a thoroughly suggestive manner. In his introduction to the posthumous poems of Louis Bouilhet, alluding to his friendship with the author, he addresses the following words to youth:—

And since upon every occasion a moral is demanded, here follows mine:

If there be anywhere two young people who pass their Sundays in reading the poets together, who confide to each other all their efforts and their plans, all the striking similes and every pertinent word that may occur to them, and who, although otherwise indifferent to the opinion of the world, conceal this passion of theirs with virgin modesty, I would give them this advice.

Go, side by side, into the forests, repeat verses to each other, take into your souls the sap of the trees, and the everlasting might of the masterworks of creation, yield to the impression of the sublime. Should you ever progress so far that, in all the occurrences about you, as soon as they fall under your observation, you see only an illusion that is to be described, and this to so great a degree that nothing, not even your own existence seems to you to have any other purpose than to serve as an object for description, and you become firmly resolved to make whatever sacrifice the calling may demand, then come boldly forward and give books to the world.

Rarely has an author, without making a direct effort to that effect, more keenly characterized his own peculiarity. He has consecrated his life to the calling of describing illusions. I know very well that, in his estimation, everything that transpires is for the true author an image, merely a phantom to be held fast by art. We can, however, unhesitatingly invest his words with the wider significance that life, as a whole, is to be conceived as a series of dissolving phantoms, and then the sentence applies accurately to himself. Take a mental survey of his materials from the first unworldly and worldly dreams through which Emma Bovary strives to rise above the emptiness of provincial life and the insipidity of her marriage, to the hallucinations of a St. Antonius,—what else have they all been to him than illusions for description.

An illusion has the dual character that corresponds to Flaubert's temperament. The phantom, apart from its delusive attribute, is beautiful; it has coloring and perfume; it fills the mind and communicates to it an increase of life. Thus tempered, it attracted the adorer of beauty in Flaubert. But an illusion is, furthermore, hollow and empty, is often foolish and hideous, is not rarely, at the same time, comic; and thus conceived it captivated the realist in Flaubert, the man whose gaze penetrated the soul's life, and who found satisfaction in dissolving the air-castles of fancy into their simplest elements.

II

How did he become what in his first novel we learned him to be?

His father was a celebrated surgeon in Rouen, a strictly upright, and kind-hearted man, who brought up his son independently and well. That his first home was the house of a physician is felt in his books. He studied medicine himself for a little while, later took up the study of law, but even in his school-days cast himself passionately into literature; and in this enthusiasm of his he met a friend of his own age, who became a friend for life,—the poet Louis Bouilhet. Without doubt there are autobiographical elements in the description of the friendship between Frédéric and Deslauriers in his novel, "L'éducation sentimentale." Flaubert, like Frédéric, went to Paris when nineteen years old, to pursue his studies. His father purchased the villa Croisset at Rouen, which he afterward inherited; he passed his life alternately in Rouen and in Paris, a life in which there were but two external events,—a journey to the Orient, which he undertook when he was thirty years of age, and a later journey to northern Africa, which preceded the completion of "Salammbô." In Rouen he took delight in shutting himself up for months at a time, to study and to write; in Paris he chiefly sought diversion. He was in youth persevering in his labors and violent in his pleasures.

His temperament corresponded to his exterior. I only saw him in his later years, and then I had but a cursory view of him. But no one could forget this large-eyed, blue-eyed Hercules, with his rosy-hued complexion, his high, bald brow, and his long mustache, which concealed the large mouth and the vigorous jaws. He carried his head high and slightly thrown back; his abdomen protruded somewhat. He was not fond of walking; but he inclined to violent gestures; and he beat the air wildly with his arms, when hurling forth monstrous paradoxes in tones of thunder. Like all blustering giants, he was good-natured. His wrath, says one of his friends, boiled over and fell like milk.

He had, indeed, grown up at the time when the French romantic school was in its prime. He had received his first stamp from this school, and retained traces of it in his style and in his manner of abusing the *bourgeoise,* which recalled Théophile Gautier's "truculent" form of speech, as well as in his mode of dress. He was fond of wearing large, broad-brimmed hats, enormously wide pantaloons, and coats that were made to fit tight at the waist. In the summer time he went about his own dwelling in broad, white and red striped breeches, and a sort of jacket that made him resemble a Turk. There was a report among his friends that the citizens of Rouen, when preparing for Sunday excursions into the country, would promise their children to let them see M. Flaubert in his garden if they were good.

I said that some journeys were the main events of his life. Women have taken less place in it than in the lives of most men. He had, when he was twenty years old, loved them as a troubadour. At that time he had repeatedly walked several miles in order to kiss the muzzle of a Newfoundland dog that a lady he admired was in the habit of caressing. Later he accustomed himself to a more matter-of-fact mode of contemplation and practice in erotic matters. He was a friend of anecdotes and stories of the manner of Rabelais, and in his books the erotic illusion was grasped by him with quite as hardy hands as all other illusions.

Nevertheless, in this point, as in so many others in the character of Flaubert, there was an abiding duality. He, the old bachelor, the passionate tobacco-smoker, who held intimate, friendly relations with men alone, and who felt at ease in no other female society than in that of certain pretty but not over-fastidious ladies,—held the belief, apparently the result of personal experience as well as of a deeply rooted abstract conviction, that it was the natural, so to say proper, thing for man to cherish for life one grand amatory passion, which must forever remain unrequited.

Fully in accord with this, we find in a letter to a lady, dating from the last year of Flaubert's life, the playful, yet at the same time mournfully true, words: "We poor laborers of literature! Why is that denied to us which is so readily granted to commonplace people? They have a heart! We have none at all! So I repeat to you once again that I, for my part, am an uncomprehended soul, the last *grisette*, the sole survivor of the old race of troubadours."

This "uncomprehended soul," however, was not in the habit of turning to women for comprehension. He dreaded love as a danger and a burden. Friendship alone was to him a religion, and among his friends there was no one who stood so near to him as that first and enduring friend, Bouilhet.

I do not exactly know if there have been times that were especially propitious to independent minds. But this much I do know: these two young men, who stepped forth into life when the *bourgeoise* under Louis Philippe had gained the Dominion and acquired a poetic expression partly from the feeble and righteously inclined *École de bon sens*, and partly from the "Vaudevilles" of Scribe, found the period it was their destiny to live in, the worst of all times. The romantic school had outlived itself and produced its own caricature. It was the fashion everywhere to praise common sense and to deride poesy. Inspiration and passion were out of date, and consequently laughable. Everything

that was not commonplace was found tiresome. The two
youths conceived the age in which they lived to be that of
the sway of mediocrity and of the commonplace; they saw
the victorious mediocrity, like a monstrous black water-
spout, absorb all things, and whirl all things away with it.

This gave them both a fund of melancholy and deep
earnestness, an under-current of contempt for humanity, a
sensation of spiritual isolation, and through it an inclination for productions of an impersonal, objective kind.

III

As the result of such a frame of mind it was that Flaubert, in mature manhood, resolved to come forward as an
author, and wrote "Madame Bovary." There was wafted
from this book a breath of icy coldness. It seemed as
though the author at length had succeeded in drawing forth
the truth from the deep, cold well where it had been lying,
and as though it were now standing on its pedestal and
freezing, having brought with it all the cold, shuddering
horror of the abyss. A singular book, written without the
slightest degree of tenderness for its subject! Others had
depicted the simple life of the country and of the province
with melancholy, with humor, and at least with that attempt at idealizing which contemplation from afar is apt
to bring with it. He regarded it without sympathy, and
represented it as insipid and spiritless as it was. His landscapes were devoid of so-called poetry, and were painted
briefly and yet completely. In his severe, masterly style
he contented himself with reproducing the chief outlines
and coloring, but gave thus an accurate presentation of the
landscape. And he was wholly without tenderness for his
principal character, a rare phenomenon in a poet whose
principal character is a young, beautiful, and exceedingly
attractive woman, who passes her life in yearning, languishing, and passionate desire, who errs and is deceived, is
ruined, and finally perishes without properly sinking beneath the level of her surroundings. But every dream,
every hope, every delusion, every naïve and unhealthy de-

sire that floated through her brain was investigated and brought to light without agitation, indeed with an overwhelming irony. There was scarcely a phase of her existence in which she failed to appear ridiculous or morally repulsive, and not until she dies a hideous death does the suppressed irony wholly recede, and she breathes her last, not as an object of sympathy, it is true, yet not as an object of contempt.

The author seemed thoroughly cold, even in the description of the hour of her death. That this appearance was deceptive is proved by a letter from Flaubert, which may be found in Taine's work, "De l'intelligence" (I., 94), and in which he says, "When I wrote the poisoning scene of Emma Bovary, I had so strong a taste of arsenic in my mouth, I was so thoroughly poisoned myself, that for two consecutive days I could digest nothing; indeed, I found it impossible to keep a morsel of food on my stomach." How deeply the author was affected, body and soul, was concealed in the novel, owing to the supreme self-control he had exercised while engaged on the work.

Throughout the entire book there appeared not a single personage with whom the author could possibly have anything in common, or with whom he could, in ever so slight a degree, be supposed to wish to change places. His characters were all, without exception, commonplace, unlovely, vicious, or unfortunate. Nor did he attempt the slightest deviation from the standpoint taken. The young wife, for instance, dangerous though her instincts were, in her yearning for the beautiful, her aspirations after the ideal, and her persistent faith in the romance of love, possesses attributes which, if portrayed differently, or with a more sparing hand, might have rendered the character noble, even in its errors. What would not George Sand have made of her! But Flaubert is determined not to fall into the old ruts, and so he assiduously robs the so-called fascinating sins of every trace of poetry. The betrayed husband, likewise, notwithstanding his lack of skill as a physician and his awkwardness as a man, is kind-hearted, patient, upright, and truly devoted to Emma, and thus has elements which, under other circumstances, might have produced a most touching effect. Moreover he develops, at her death, qualities, such as profound attachment and self-forgetfulness, which a slight pressure from the finger of the author might have made seem significant and worthy of respect. But the creative artist refuses to give the clay this slight pressure; his love of truth compels him to keep the form within the limits that to him appear the correct ones, and so he permits Bovary to remain, from beginning to end, a good-natured, undignified, inefficient, and unattractive person.

There is in the novel but a single character with whom we are made to feel partially in sympathy, and that is the little apothecary apprentice, Justin, who adores Emma from afar. There is one situation, after her death, in which the author almost seems inclined to idealize him. When all the other mourners have left the churchyard, Justin draws near her grave, and we read:—

On the grave among the fir-trees there knelt a weeping child, whose heart was ready to burst with the sobs that shook his frame; and there he remained, in that shaded spot, groaning beneath the weight of an immeasurable anguish, which was milder than the moon, and more unfathomable than the night.

We marvel to think that these lines have Flaubert for their author. But then we read in continuation: "Suddenly the wicket gate turned on creaking hinges. It was the grave-digger Lestiboudois; he came in search of his spade, which he had forgotten a little while before. He recognized Justin, as the boy clambered over the wall, and knew at once who was the offender that had stolen his potatoes."

This passage is the only one that remained in my mind ten years after my first perusal of "Madame Bovary," and it is a most admirable passage. It is not arbitrarily ironical, *à la* Heine; irony, in this case, is simply keen penetration, the work of a versatile mind. It is quite natural that Justin should be stirred to the most profound and poetic emotions by the death of the lady whom he adored; but it is none the less natural that he should previously have stolen potatoes, and that the grave-digger should intuitively discover in the fact of his clambering over the wall of the churchyard an indication of his potato theft. But that Flaubert should have these two circumstances, these two sides of life, before his eyes at the same time, is proof of an intellectual vigor and a command of his subject which, as far as I am aware, have never before appeared in a similar form.

The artistic irony of Flaubert is here impersonal, necessary, true, and profound, in quite a different way than that of Mérimée. It is merely a stereoscopic view, by means of which reality is set forth in bold relief.

It is no wonder that at first people scarcely discovered anything else in the work than this mode of contemplation, and the fidelity to real life that was its product. If we leave out of consideration the brief period when the absurd notion was afloat that Flaubert was an immoral writer, it may safely be said that the prevailing idea concerning him was that he was what is called a realist. He copied the insignificant and the important with equal conscientiousness, but with an evident predilection for the commonplace and the morally repulsive; in fact, everything with him centred in one plan, vigorous but harsh. The admirers of the book found it a most remarkable work; the fault-finders pronounced the tendency introduced by Flaubert photographic, but not artistic. People expected, or rather dreaded, a new "Madame Bovary" from his hand.

But they waited for it in vain, for nothing further was heard from him. Years passed, and he still remained silent. Finally, after the lapse of seven years, he appeared before the public with a new novel, and the reading world proclaimed aloud its astonishment. This new book bore the reader far away from the villages of Normandy and the nineteenth century. The vanished author of "Madame Bovary" was found again amid the ruins of ancient Carthage. He represented, in "Salammbô," nothing more or less than Carthage in the days of Hamilcar; a city and a civilization of which people had scarcely any reliable knowledge,—a war between Carthage and the hireling troops of the city, which did not so much as offer general historic, or even so-called ideal interest. A Parisian novel, whose plot centred in violated marriage vows, had been looked for, and in its stead was received one whose scenes were laid amid ancient Punic culture, Tanit's worship, and Moloch adoration, sieges and battles, terrors without number or measure, the death of an entire army by starvation, and the slow martyrdom of an imprisoned Lybian chieftain.

And the strangest part of it was that all this subject-matter, about which no one knew anything, or could in the least control, this whole extinct barbaric world, was produced with a clearness and a minute accuracy that was in no respect inferior to that of "Madame Bovary." People discovered that Flaubert's methods were in no wise dependent upon the character of his materials, that they were the same in regard to this colossal, foreign subject as they had been in dealing with his former commonplace theme. He had played a prank on the public, manifesting in a striking manner how little he had been understood. Any one who had looked upon him as a realist servilely bound to the clod, could now learn how thoroughly at home Flaubert felt in tropical lands. Any one who had thought that the petty affairs of every-day life, in their ugliness and their absurdity, were the sole objects that had power to captivate him, must now discover that Flaubert in his youth had shared the enthusiasms of the men of 1830, and that he, as well as they, had been attracted by primitive passions and barbaric customs. Yet to how great a degree Flaubert actually entered into the sympathies and naïveté of the extreme romantic school, very few had the most remote idea, even after reading "Salammbô." The sun of Africa and the life of the Orient had been made hallowed to him by Byron and Victor Hugo, and his personal impressions in the Orient had only confirmed the poetic ones. The aroma of coffee gave him hallucinations of wandering caravans, and he swallowed the most horrible dishes with a sense of piety, if they but had an exotic name.

Flaubert had done his utmost to produce something that resembled ancient Carthage. He was artist enough, however, to know that the main point was not the outward truth, but the inner truth which makes probability. His descriptions were to many unconditionally convincing. A doubt concerning their conformity with a long since vanished reality, was once answered in my presence by one of the first critics in France with a simple "I am quite sure it is true." Flaubert himself came out openly and boldly against the doubters, in his defensive reply to an attack of Sainte-Beuve, with the following words:

> I believe I have produced something that resembles Carthage. But that is not the question. I don't care a straw for archæology! If the colors are not harmonious, if the details do not accord, if the morals cannot be traced to religion or the occurrences to passion, if the characters are not well sustained, if the costumes do not correspond to the customs, or the buildings to the climate, then my book is, of course, untrue. Otherwise it is true.

These words hit the nail on the head; we are impressed by them with the master's good conscience and the authority with which it invests him. His work was not, as were so many later archæological novels, a masquerade, in which modern emotions and views of life are brought forward in antique costumes. No; everything here was on a par, and had the same wild, formidable stamp. Love, stratagem, revenge, piety, strength of character, all were unmodern.

The poet's love of truth was evidently as ardent and as vehement at it had been when he had written his first novel. Now, however, in the presence of this victory over death and the past, it seemed absurd to speak of Flaubert's photographing. Therefore this new book yielded a more correct standpoint for the "realism" of its predecessor. That Flaubert could not be classed among those who were copyists of accidental truth, became clear. It was seen that his accuracy of description and information was rooted in a peculiar precision of imagination. He evidently possessed in an equally high degree the two elements that constitute the being of the artist: the gift of observation and the power of investing with form. He had the bias and the capacity for the study of nature and for historic study, the scrutinizing eye which no relation between details escaped. To speak now of photography in connection with him was impossible. For study implies activity, ardor, and an eye for the essential; while photography, on the other hand, is something passive, mechanical, and totally indifferent to the distinctions between essential and non-essential matters. And Flaubert, furthermore, had the temperament of the artist, that condition of mind which heats red-hot everything acquired by observation, marking it with its own stamp, and which reveals itself as style through the impress given. For what is style but the sensated result of the temperament, the medium by means of which an author compels the reader to see as he has seen! Style marks the difference between the artistically truthful delineation and a good photography, and style is omnipresent with Flaubert.

No sooner had he collected his observations, and made his preliminary studies for a book, than they ceased, as such, to interest him. Thenceforth the chief matter of import to him was to write this book in perfect language. And language became everything, while the carefully prepared notes dwindled into wholly subordinate affairs. That he was accurate and reliable he was in the habit of declaring to be no merit on his part, simply the justice an author owed the public; for truthfulness, in and for itself, had nothing whatever to do with art. "No," he would cry, in tones of thunder, flinging out his arms as he spoke, "the only important and enduring thing under the sun, is a well-formed sentence, a sentence with hand and foot, that harmonizes with the sentences preceding and following it, and that falls pleasantly on the ear when it is read aloud. So he wrote very little each day, at the utmost not more than two or three pages, weighed each word in order to avoid repetitions, rhymes, and crude expressions, and relentlessly pursued a repeated word, even at a distance of thirty or forty lines; indeed he could not so much as endure the recurrence of the same syllable in one sentence. Often a single letter vexed him, and he would search patiently for words in which it was not found; sometimes

he devoted considerable energy to an eager chase for an
"r" when he needed a rolling sound. He always read
aloud what he had written, singing it out in his stentorian
voice, so that the passers-by would stand still in front of
his house to listen. Many called him the advocate, and believed that he was practising a speech for court.

He suffered torments during his efforts to attain perfection. They were the pangs of childbirth which every author
knows, but his were so agonizing that he was many times
forced to spring to his feet, shriek aloud, and call himself a
blockhead, an idiot! for no sooner was one doubt overcome
than another had already arisen. At his writing-table he
sat as one magnetized, wholly absorbed in his work, and
lost in silent contemplation of his subject. Turgenief, who
was his faithful and intimate friend, and saw him very
often, declared that it was exceedingly touching to see
Flaubert, the most impatient of mortals, so patient in his
struggles with language. One day, after he had been
working uninterruptedly the whole day at a single page
of his last novel, he went out to take a meal, and when he
returned late in the evening he thought he would edify
himself by reading his page in bed; but alas! it failed to
satisfy him. He sprang excitedly out of bed,—tall man
of over fifty years of age as he was,—began to rewrite the
page, clad in no other apparel than his night-shirt, and
wrote and rewrote the whole night long, sometimes working at his writing-table, sometimes, when driven from it by
the cold, continuing his labors in bed.

How he loved and how he cursed his language! Is it
not highly characteristic that in "Madame Bovary" he
only forgets himself and speaks in his own name in a
single place, and that is the passage where, in referring to
Raoul's *blasé* indifference to Emma's declaration of affection, which proceeded from a genuine passion, however
commonplace it may have sounded, he indignantly exclaims, "As though the abundance of the soul did not at
times overflow in the most vapid similitudes, as though
any one could reproduce the exact measure of his needs,
conceptions, or sufferings, since human language is but a

cracked kettledrum, upon which we hammer out melodies
that sound as though they were played for a bear-dance,
when it is our wish to move the stars!"

Such a lament from such lips is, nevertheless, what it declares human words not to be: the exact *measure* of the
agonized striving of the great stylist for artistic perfection.

When an aspiration of that kind has once appeared in
an art, it cannot become extinct. None of the initiated
who have written after Flaubert, and who understood his
literary ideal, have been able with clear consciences to
make essentially smaller demands upon themselves than he
made upon himself. Therefore the friends, the spiritual
kindred, the disciples of Flaubert, are the most severe, the
most original stylists of our century.

Not that Flaubert himself theoretically favored originality of style. He cherished a naïve belief in one ideal,
absolutely correct style. He called this style, which he
strove earnestly to realize, wholly impersonal, because it
was nothing but an expression of his own personality,
which had not occurred to him in what he had written.

Guy de Maupassant has wittily remarked that the trite
saying, "The style is the man!" admitted of being reversed
in Flaubert's case. He was the man who was the style.
In other words, he was the personification of style. It is
no unimportant or indifferent matter that the author who
beyond all others represents the modern tendency and the
modern formula of French literature, far from being an
imitator of chance nature, or, as the reproach was usually
worded, a photographer, was, on the contrary, an artist
sans reproche.

IV

Flaubert, personally, has never made the slightest revelation to the public concerning himself. He has *maintained*
the same silence in regard to his artistic principles as in
reference to his private experiences. Under these circumstances we must examine all the paths that are open and
that might lead us into his inner being. One of the nearest and best of these that presents itself to us is a careful

study of the works of his fraternal friend and companion-in-arms, Louis Bouilhet. These two men, superficially considered, appear very unlike in their tastes and in their endowments. Flaubert was an epoch-maker in French literature; Bouilhet, a second or third rate poet. Flaubert was a novel writer; Bouilhet, a lyric and dramatic poet. But this dissimilarity does not affect the character of the friends. They were fond of each other because they were spiritually akin. Not without cogent reasons did Flaubert dedicate his first book to Bouilhet, and the latter all his best productions to Flaubert. A careful comparison shows such striking analogies between the poetry of Bouilhet and the prose works of Flaubert that it puts the eyes keenly on the alert to detect the more suppressed of the peculiarities of the greater of the two friends.

One of the most remarkable of Bouilhet's poems, "Les fossiles," opens with an ambitious picture of prehistoric scenery and animal life, followed by a portrayal, in poetic form and scientific spirit, of the development of the globe until the appearance of the first human pair, and ends with a glowing vision of the humanity of the future.

We encounter this predilection for the colossal and marvellously prodigious once more in the author of "Salammbô." In Flaubert's excavation of vanished nations and religions we detect the same proclivity for fossils displayed by Bouilhet, and finally, there is plainly revealed in Flaubert the tendency manifested by his friend, in more poems than one, to blend science and poetry in one perfect whole.

As Flaubert was absorbed in classic and Semitic literature, so Bouilhet studied Chinese, and treated Chinese themes and plots in a long series of poems. Through these investigations, and the poetic efforts that were their results, both hoped to escape from a period that was distasteful to them, and both were unconsciously following the example of Goethe. They were both, moreover, satisfying one and the same impulse to show the reader the relative nature of all life-forms, to teach him not to pride himself on the glorious progress the world had made, and to impart to him some idea of the fact that our civilization, excavates and described after the lapse of centuries, would not make a much more reasonable figure than that of far-off antiquity.

Both desired to bring forward antiquity in its historic and prehistoric purity, without any disturbing modern additions, and were deterred by no difficulties. As though it were not difficult enough in itself to depict the antediluvian world, with its singular vegetation, its formless, stupendous animals, Bouilhet has deprived himself of every expression that might recall modern ideas. He describes the pterodactyls, the ichthyosaurs and plesiosaurs, the mammoths and mastodons, without calling them by name; we only recognize them by their form, their bearing, their demeanor. In a similar way Flaubert, in his "Salammbô," has refrained from making the most remote allusion to the modern world; he seems to be wholly unacquainted with it, or to have forgotten its existence. The artistic objectivity here accords with the scientific.

And this, with both authors, is the main point. They obeyed, consciously or unconsciously, a new idea of the relation of poetry to science. They wished to contribute their share toward creating a poesy built wholly upon a scientific foundation.

The highest ambition of Bouilhet was to write a poem which should embrace the results of modern science, and be to our age what that most admirable poem of Lucretius, "De rerum natura," was to antiquity. Flaubert had apparently a similar dream. But in his case the desire was more decidedly stamped with his hatred of human stupidity. He brought it into realization negatively, and in two different forms; in his work, "La Tentation de Sainte Antoine" (The Temptation of Saint Anthony), where he allowed all the religious and moral systems of humanity to pass in review before the reader's eye, as the insane hallucinations of the hermit; and, in his last story, "Bouvard et Pécuchet," where the numerous errors and blunders of two poor blockheads gave the author a pretext for furnishing a sort of encyclopædia of all the departments of human knowledge in which they had made mistakes. In "La

Tentation de Sainte Antoine,'' he gave the tragedy of the human mind, which here reveals itself in magnificent, frantic, and wailing madness, a King Lear on the world's health. In "Bouvard et Pécuchet" he delineates caricature, naïve ignorance, and the bungling of dilettanteism in all scientific and technical provinces, as personified by two ludicrous old bachelors. The work is posthumous, and only the first part exists, even that being in an unfinished state; but highly characteristic of Flaubert was his design to supplement this first part with a second, in which the two poor old bachelors, who begin and end their career as clerks, carry out the idea of taking notes on the blunders of all the well-known writers (M. Flaubert included), and collecting them into a volume.

Both Flaubert and Bouilhet, therefore, were spurred on in their labors by the powerful impulse to preserve in their works, in one form or another, either positive or negative, the results of modern science. What Flaubert said of Bouilhet is equally applicable to both, that the fundamental thought, the innate element of his mind, was a sort of naturalism, that was a reminder of the *renaissance.* But while Bouilhet dissipated his best powers in mediocre and traditional romantic dramas, Flaubert has not paid homage to tradition in a single one of his works; on the contrary, he has always made profound scientific study the preparation for literary composition; and for this reason the relation between science and poetry is with him the nerve and sinew and the main interest of the work.

V

It almost seems as if, in our day, the time were past when the novelist would sit calmly down before a large sheet of white paper some fine day, and, without further preparation, begin the execution of his work of fiction.

Flaubert, at all events, has introduced a method which places poetic production very nearly on a scientific basis. It was his wont to pass whole weeks in the libraries, that he might gain light on some single point in his subject; and he would devote hours to a careful study of a mass of engravings, in order to acquire a thorough knowledge of the costumes or bearing of a former generation. In the course of his preparatory studies for "Salammbô," he read ninety-eight volumes of ancient and modern literature, and undertook, besides, a journey to Tunis, in view of studying the landscapes and monuments of ancient Carthage. Indeed, even in order to paint phantastic landscapes, such as those in "La Légende de St. Julien," he visited regions calculated to give him an impression similar to that of which he had dreamed.

As soon as he had sketched the plan for a book, he began to seek reliable facts for each separate chapter; each had its own individual outline, which must be gradually filled in. He read through the entire collection of the "Charivari" from the time of Louis Philippe to the latest date, in order to supply the literary Bohemian, Hussonet, in "L'éducation sentimentale," with witticisms in the style of his period. He made a study of not less than one hundred and seven works, in order to be able to write the thirty pages on agriculture in "Bouvard et Pécuchet." His excerpts for this last novel, if printed, would fill no less than five octavo volumes.

During all these preliminary studies he apparently lost sight, for a time, of his novel, and merely kept in view the desire to increase his knowledge. His fondness for accumulating information was almost as intense as that for fashioning the phychic contents of his work, or rather it gradually became so.

If we take a survey of his productions, in chronologic order, we shall find an ever plainer transfer of the centre of gravity from the poetic to the scientific element; in other words, from the human, psychologic element to historic, technical, and scientific externalities, which fill an unwarranted amount of space. Flaubert was always in danger of becoming a tedious author, and grew more and more prolix as time went on.

He was actuated by a belief—in my estimation a correct

one—that the writer of fiction in our day cannot be a mere writer for amusement, or a *maître de plaisir*. He felt that the ship of poesy, without scientific ballast, ran great risk of being capsized. It was soon proved, too, that with this ballast it sailed better, more securely, and with a prouder bearing. By degrees, however, as his development progressed, the passion for overcoming difficulties took complete possession of him; he wanted to carry the heaviest loads, the largest stones he could find, until gradually his vessel became freighted with so enormous a cargo that it grew too heavy, sank too far into the water, and was stranded. His last novel is little else than a wearisome series of abstracts from a couple of dozen different scientific discoveries and technical methods. As a work of fiction it is scarcely readable, and is only interesting psychologically as a consistent and definite expression of a remarkable personality and of an erroneous æsthetic standpoint.

The general tendency to the study of externals is not peculiar to Flaubert; it characterizes the entire group of creative minds to which he belongs. It sprang from a justifiable aversion to the rationalistic conception of man as an abstract rational being, and from the bias of our age toward determinism, which aimed at explaining the psychic life of the individual from climatic, national, psychological and physiological causes. This endeavor is found in various phases in the most noted of the contemporaries and fellow-countrymen of Flaubert; in his friend and teacher, Théophile Gautier, in Renan, in Taine, and in the Goncourt brothers. Different as these minds are, they have in common this very modern stamp, and, moreover, nearly all of them possess, also, the no less modern quality of displaying too decidedly marked traces in their artistically executed works of the labor that lies behind these and the pains with which they were created, often producing an extremely distressing impression of being over-freighted. Renan, to whom this is less applicable than to the others, not infrequently portrays matters which lie wholly beyond his framework. Gautier is, perhaps, the only one of these great artists from whose brain word and image seem to flow without constraint, and even he was rarely without the dictionary and the encyclopædia in his hand.

With Flaubert the encyclopædia gradually supplants the emotions. Gautier, as years passed, grew to be less of a poet and more of a picturesque delineator. Flaubert, with the lapse of years, became ever more and more of a savant and a collector.

If we cast a glance over his entire literary production, from its first beginning until its close, we shall find that the human element, which originally bubbled over and fructified everything, gradually ebbed, withdrew, and left behind it only the arid, stony soil of historic or scientific fact.

In "Madame Bovary" all is yet life. The descriptions are infrequent and brief. Even the description of Rouen, the birthplace of the author, which occurs in the part where Emma journeys in the diligence from Yonville to meet Léon, is given in a very few lines, and is, moreover, enlivened by the account of the dizziness that ascends to Emma from this trobbing mass of thousands of existences, as though the fumes of the passions she attributed to them had been wafted toward her. The direct description of the city, the picturesque point, gives place at once to the psychologic analysis of the impression the great city makes upon the main character of the book,—a tendency which becomes more and more rare with Flaubert. In "Salammbô," the previous study and all that is purely descriptive must necessarily assert themselves more vigorously. There are long passages of this work which would be far more likely to lead us to think we were reading a scrap of the history of an ancient warfare, or some archæologic treatise, than a novel, and which, therefore, are exceedingly tedious. Nevertheless, "Salammbô" was rich in purely human themes and delineations. Read, by way of example, the chapter that tells about how the priests resolve to propitiate Moloch through the sacrifice of the first-born son of each house; how some of them knock at the door of Hamilcar, and how he strives to rescue his little son Hannibal. The state of public sentiment here represented by Flaubert is precisely what must have existed in a Tunic city the moment such a wholesale slaughter of the innocents was commanded, and this single incident stands forth from the background of this sentiment in a manner never to be forgotten. Hamilcar rushes into his daughter's room, grasps Hannibal with one hand, and with the other a cord that is lying on the floor, binds the boy hand and foot, thrusts what still remains of the cord into his mouth for a gag, and hides him under the bed. Then he claps his hands, and calls for a slave child of eight or nine years of age, with black hair and protruding brow. There is brought to him a poor, wasted, yet at the same time bloated child, whose skin is as gray as the cloth about its loins. Hamilcar is in despair. How would it be possible to make this child pass for Hannibal? But the minutes are precious, and, in spite of his repugnance, the proud Suffet begins to wash, to rub, and to anoint the wretched slave child. He attires it in a purple robe, which he fastens at the shoulders with diamond clasps, and the little fellow laughs, delighted with all this splendor, and skips about the room with joy. Hamilcar leads the child away with him. When, with feigned anguish, he is giving it up to the priests in the court below, there appears, between the ivory pillars on the third floor, of the house, a pale, wretchedly clad, dreadful looking man, with outstretched arm. "My child!" he cries. "He is the foster-father of the boy," Hamilcar hastens to say; and, as though to make the parting brief, he pushes the priests from the door. When they are gone, he sends the slave the best that his kitchen can afford,—meat, beans, and conserves. The old man, who for a long time has not tasted a morsel of food, pounces upon the bounteous supply, and devours it amid tears. Coming home in the evening, Hamilcar finds the slave, surfeited and half-intoxicated, lying asleep on the marble floor of the great hall, through the crevices of whose dome a flood of moonlight streams. Hamilcar gazes at him, and something akin to pity stirs within his soul. With the tip of his foot he pushes a rug under the slumberer's head.

Here is the essence of human universality extracted from a specific Carthaginian situation.

"Salammbô," as already intimated, created not a little sensation, but was none the less of a disappointment to the reading world and the critics. People did not share the author's fondness for colossal and tropical themes; they did not enjoy wading through long descriptions of antique catapults, battering-rams and sieges, and they begged Flaubert to write a new "romance de passion," a love story.

Toward the close of the year 1869, he finally yielded to their solicitations by issuing his novel "L'éducation sentimentale," his most charactertistic and most profound work, which, however, met with a decided failure. From this time forth he experienced nothing but literary defeats. The public favor which had been cooled by "Salammbô," now wholly forsook him.

The new novel was a new style of book altogether. The almost untranslatable title (the approximate meaning being "The education of the heart") is not a correct one; for no one and nothing is educated throughout the work. The novel treats, to be sure, of an emotional life; but it deals rather with the gradual drilling and final extirpation of the emotion of love than with any development of the latter. It might more justly be called, "The illusion of love and its eradication." It is one of Flaubert's main efforts to distill absolute nothing in the form of pure illusion out of all the aspirations and pursuits of ordinary, everyday human life. In "Salammbô" everything revolves about a sacred veil of the goddess Tanit, known as Zaimpf. This veil is radiant and light; the city from which it is stolen goes to ruin; the mortal who wears it is invulnerable as long as he is enveloped in it; but whoever has once been shrouded in it is sure to perish. Illusion is like this veil. It is as radiant as the sun and as light as the air; it imparts the security of the somnambulist, and it consumes as surely as a Nessos robe.

I said that Flaubert believed in a passionate love which, although never gratified, was capable of enduring throughout life. Such a love he has depicted in the affection of

Frédéric for Madame Arnoux. It is utterly hopeless; utterly bashful; it is suppressed; it only finds vent in certain unwise sacrifices for the husband of Madame Arnoux, and in certain half-uttered Platonic assurances of mutual sympathy. Nor does it lead to anything beyond a promise that is withdrawn by the lady, a few attempts which fail, and finally, after the lapse of twenty years, a fruitless confession and one single embrace, from which the lover recoils in terror, as the object of his affections has, meanwhile, grown old, and, with her white hair, inspires him with repugnance.

The peculiarity of this novel, in a still more striking way than in "Madame Bovary," is that it has no hero, and is quite as devoid of claims to a heroine. In the antiquated epithet "hero" lies the entire traditional usage of old-fashioned poesy. For centuries authors had paraded a hero before the public; he was characterized by his manly strength and beauty, was grand in his virtues or his vices, and was in every respect an example to be imitated or shunned. There had at length arisen a poet who was willing to deal with a young man of the average type, and who, without expressing either disapproval or regret, showed how completely null and void was the life of such a young man, and how disappointments were showered upon him. These were neither great nor unusual disappointments; to be sure, there was nothing great or unusual in the young man's experiences,—no, they were all those petty disappointments that go to make up the sum of existence. A long chain of petty disappointments, intermingled with a few great ones, is to Flaubert the definition of human life. The charm of the book, however, does not rest chiefly on the prevailing sentiment of its pages. Its main charm to me is the graceful, chaste manner in which the pen is wielded in passages descriptive of Frédéric's great love. This profound comprehension of the young man's dreamy devotion denotes personal experience. Nowhere has Flaubert written more directly from the depths of his own soul and gained less from the five or six artificial souls which he, in common with every critically disposed and critically endowed nature, had the power to give himself.

Frédéric loves without any ulterior thought, without hope of reciprocal affection, with a feeling that is akin to gratitude, with a positive need of utter self-renunciation and complete self-sacrifice for the sake of the object of his devotion, which is all the stronger because it finds no requital. As the years pass, however, a feeling of a similar nature develops in the breast of the woman whom he loves. It is a settled thing between them that they can never belong to each other; but their tastes, their judgment, are in harmony.

Often one of them, listening to words of the other, would exclaim: 'I too!' and very soon the other in turn would also cry: 'I too!' And they dream that if Providence had so willed, their lives would have been filled with love alone, 'something as sweet, as glittering, and as sublime as the twinkling of the stars.'

The greater part of their time was passed on the veranda in the open air, while the trees, with their autumnal crowns of glory, were spread in rich masses before them, gradually sloping up to the pale horizon; or they sat in a pavilion at the end of the alley, whose sole article of furniture was a sofa covered with gray linen. Black spots defiled the mirror; the walls exhaled a mouldy odor; yet the two sat undisturbed, chatting of themselves, of others, of anything whatsoever, in a state of mutual rapture. Sometimes the sunbeams, working their way through the Venetian blinds from the ceiling to the floor, formed the strings of an enormous lyre.

This lyre, I am quite confident, was the genuine lyre of old, dating from the days of the troubadours, and the days of Flaubert's youth. At this point, it actually seems as though Flaubert had wakened it from its slumbers.

"L'éducation sentimentale" appeared just as the empire was entering upon the epoch of its last crisis. The book had but a moderate sale. The press unanimously pronounced it tedious, and, of course, immoral. The most painful thing of all to Flaubert was the long silence that followed. The work of seven years seemed lost.

The cause of this was simply that the author had labored too hard. In order to portray the Paris of the forties, he had studied old pictures and old plans of the city, had reconstructed vanished streets, and had searched through several thousand newspapers for references to public speeches, and descriptions of street life and street fights. It had been his desire to give an absolutely perfect picture of the times, and he had made it too elaborate. The historic apparatus is most wearisome in its effect. Flaubert's hatred of stupidity, as is so many other instances, had led him too far. Even in his youth it had belonged to the amusements he and Bouilhet had entered into together, to make as faithful copies as possible of official speeches, of poems written for special occasions, such as the dedication of a bell, or the burial of a monarch, of festival addresses and popular orations of every kind. Great quantities of such things were found after Bouilhet's death. In "Madame Bovary" Flaubert had entertained himself by communicating the entire speech of a *chef de bureau* at the agricultural exposition, with its feigned enthusiasm and stylistic naïveté; in this last work he furnished *in extenso* and, furthermore, in Spanish, a liberal speech delivered by a "patriot from Barcelona," in the year 1848, at an assemblage of the people in Paris. The speech is unsurpassed as an example of the phraseology of freedom and progress; but both the speech and the entire assemblage before whom it is delivered, are out of place owing to their very slight connection with the main personages of the book. The picture of the times exceeds its proper limits; here, as well as in "Salammbô," the pedestal has become too large for the figure. Flaubert must undoubtedly have felt this himself, for while he was still at work on "Salammbô" he wrote dejectedly to a friend: "The study of costumes beguiles us to forget the soul. I would gladly give the half-ream of paper I have been filling with notes for the past five months, merely to feel truly moved for three seconds by the passions of my characters." But he was unable to keep in the background his descriptions of the surroundings of his theme and the general state of public sentiment and conditions in the country and period where the scenes were laid. We feel that his studies follow ever closer and closer on the tracks of his imagination, precisely as the monster Maanegarm (the moon-swallower) in Norse mythology pursues the moon, and the poor moon is continually in danger of being devoured.

The three stories, "A Simple Heart," "The Legend of St. Julien the Hospitable," and "Herodias" are a triology of master-works: a novel of the day, a legend of the Middle Ages, and a picture of antiquity. "Herodias" gives, in the style of "Salammbô," a gloomy, vigorous portraiture of Palestine in the time of John the Baptist, from which the inquisitive and gluttonous visage of Vitellius gleams upon the reader as he gazes into the fading eyes of the decapitated head of John. "The Legend of St. Julien" is a model of a regeneration of the spirit of the Middle Ages. No monk has ever written a more genuine Christian legend than has this freethinker. Nothing can be more strictly legendary in style than the conclusion about the leprous beggar who devours Julian's last morsel of bacon and last crumb of bread, pollutes his plate and cup, and finally not content with stretching himself upon Julian's couch, demands that Julian shall warm him with his naked body. When the former prince, in the lowliness of his heart, humbles himself to do as he is asked, the leper embraces him with violence, and at the same moment the form of the leper is transfigured: the eyes become as luminous as the stars, the hair as long and glittering as the sunbeams, the breath as fragrant as roses. The roof of the hut flies off, and Julian floats upward in the blue ether, face to face with the Lord Jesus Christ, who bears him in his arms to Heaven.

In "A Simple Heart," Flaubert has, so to say, related the history of the old serving maid to whom the prize was awarded in "Madame Bovary." It is a touching narrative of an old worn-out maid-servant, who, forsaken by all, at length bestows the entire love of her heart upon a parrot. She admires this parrot beyond all else in the world; it seems to her, in her simplicity, to resemble the Holy Ghost as a dove in the altar-painting of the village church, and gradually it comes to occupy in her consciousness the place of the Holy Ghost. The bird dies and she has it stuffed. In her dying hour, she sees it in colossal size, with outspread wings, waiting to receive her and bear her upward into Paradise. This is like a profoundly melancholy parody on the conclusion of the legend. In one, as in the other, all is vision and illusion. Owing to the frailty of our nature, our capacity for being deceived, our need of consolation, and our readiness to sink into despair,—Flaubert seems to say,—one straw will serve us quite as well as another in our extremity.

These three stories met with no success whatever. In them study had made one step forward at the cost of life. They contained scarcely any conversations, scarcely any isolated remarks; they were rather tables of contents than novels. People felt that the author had begun to despise the poetic form proper. Furthermore, they contained too great a display of erudition. The reader can readily conjecture how many legends Flaubert must have read in order to reproduce their character so accurately. But no attempt is made to place the result of this erudition in perspective before the eyes of the modern reader. Not a single path is hewn in the primitive forest of the legendary world; it is a dense thicket, which wholly impedes the free course of the vision. The story seems rather adapted to the public of the thirteenth century, or to polished connoisseurs, than to ordinary modern readers.

VI

The year 1874 finally brought the work which Flaubert himself considered his *chef d'œuvre*,— a work on which he had labored for twenty years, and which furnished the sharpest definition in his mind,—a most startling work. When it was first rumored that a French novelist had written "The Temptation of St. Antonius," as least nine-tenths of the public entertained not the slightest doubt that the title was to be accepted facetiously of symbolically. Who could surmise that the work was a thoroughly serious history of the temptation of the ancient Egyptian hermit!

No novelist, indeed no poet of any kind, had ever attempted anything similar. It is true, Goethe had written "Die classische Walpurgisnacht" (The Classic Walpurgis Night); Byron in the second act of "Cain" had furnished a model for certain portions; Turgenief, in "Visions," had treated in a masterly way, a remotely related subject within a very small framework. A drama in seven parts, however, consisting of one long drawn out monologue, or, more accurately speaking, a detailed presentation of what had passed during a night of terror, through the brain of one single mortal who had become a prey to hallucinations; such a work had never before been written. And yet this work, failure though it is in some respects, displayed a quiet grandeur, in its melancholy monotony, and an absolutely modern stamp, attained by but few poetic works of French literature.

St. Antonius stands on the threshold of his hut on a mountain in Egypt. A tall cross is planted in the earth; an old twisted palm-tree bends over the edge of the precipice; the Nile forms a lake at the foot of the mountain. The sun is setting. The hermit, exhausted from a day passed in fasting, labor, and self-torture, feels his spiritual strength give way, as darkness falls upon the earth. A dreary yearning for the external world fills his heart. Now sensual, now proud, now idyllic and laughing memories allure and torment him.

First of all Antonius yearns for his childhood, for Ammonaria, a young maiden whom he once loved; he thinks of his charming pupil, Hilarion, who has forsaken him; he curses his solitary life. The migratory birds that pass over his head awaken within him the desire to fly onward as they do. He deplores his lot; he begins to lament and groan with anguish. Why had not he become a peaceful monk in a cell? Why had not he chosen the calm and useful life of a priest? He wishes that he were a grammarian or a philosopher, a toll-keeper on a bridge, a rich married merchant, or a brave, jovial soldier; his physical strength would then have had employment. He is overcome with despair at his position, bursts into tears, and seeks consolation and

edification in the Holy Scriptures. Opening at the Acts of
the Apostles, he reads the passage where Peter is permitted
to eat all animals, clean or unclean, while he, Antonius, is
tormenting himself with strict fasting. Turning to the Old
Testament at the same time, he reads how the right is given
to the Jews to kill all their enemies, to slaughter them by
the wholesale, while he is commanded to forgive his enemies; he reads of Nebuchadnezzar, and envies him his festivals; of Ezekias, and shudders with desire when he thinks
of all his precious perfumes and golden treasures; of the
beautiful Queen of Sheba, and asks himself how she could
possibly hope to lead the wise Solomon into temptation;
and it seems to him that the shadows which the two arms
of the cross cast on the earth, approach each other like two
horns. He calls upon God, and the two shadows assume
their old places once more. Vainly does he seek to humili-
ate himself; he thinks with pride of his long martyrdom;
his heart swells when he recalls the honor that has been
shown him from every quarter, for even the emperor has
written to him three times; and then he sees that his water-
jug is empty and his bread consumed. Hunger and thirst
gnaw at his vitals.

He remembers the envy and the hatred which the Church
Fathers showed toward him at the Council of Nice, and
his soul cries for revenge. He dreams of the aristocratic
women who formerly visited him so often in his wilderness,
in order to confess to him and entreat him to permit them
to remain with him, the saint. He is absorbed in these
dreams so long that they become realities to him. He sees
the fine ladies from the city approach, borne in their sedan
chairs; he extinguishes his torch in hopes of dispelling the
apparitions, and now for the first time clearly beholds the
visions in the dark canopy of the night sky, like scarlet
images on a ground of ebony, whirling past him in bewil-
dering haste.

Voices which resound from the obscurity proffer him
beautiful women, heaps of gold, and scenes of splendor.
This is the beginning of the temptation, the thirst of animal
instincts. Then he dreams that he is the confidant of the

emperor, the prime minister, with the reins of power in his hands. The emperor crowns him with his diadem. He avenges himself cruelly on his enemies among the Church Fathers, wades in their blood, and suddenly finds himself in the midst of one of Nebuchadnezzar's festivals, in a glittering palace, where the viands and drinks form mountains and streams. Anointed, and decorated with precious stones, the emperor sits upon his throne, while Antonius from afar reads upon his brow his haughty, ambitious thoughts. He penetrates him so thoroughly, that suddenly he himself becomes Nebuchadnezzar, and amidst all his revelling feels the need of becoming an animal. Flinging himself down, he creeps on the ground, bellowing like a steer, and then he scratches his hand on a stone and awakens. He lashes himself so long in punishment for this vision, that the pain becomes a rapturous delight, and suddenly the Queen of Sheba appears before him. Her hair is powdered blue; she is all radiant with gold and diamonds, and she offers herself to him with wanton coquetry. She is all women in one, and he knows that if he were to touch her shoulder with one finger a stream of liquid fire would shoot through his veins. There she stands, all fragrant with the perfume of the Orient. Her words ring upon his ear like singularly captivating music, and, seized with burning desire, he stretches forth his arms toward her. Then he controls himself and orders her from his presence. She and her whole train vanish. And now the devil assumes the form of his pupil, Hilarion, who comes to shake his faith.

The little, withered Hilarion, to his alarm, calls his attention to the fact than in fancy he has been mastered by the enjoyments which in real life he has renounced, assuring him that God is no Moloch, who forbids the enjoyment of life, and that the endeavor to understand God is worth more than all the self-torture in the world. He first points out to Antonius the contradictions between the Old and the New Testament; then the various contradictions of the New. And Hilarion grows. Then there arise in the brain of Antonius recollections of all the heresies of which he has heard and read in Alexandria and elsewhere, and has victoriously overcome: the hundreds upon hundreds of heresies of the early Christian sects; views, of which one is more monstrous than the other, are howled in his ears by the heretics themselves. They clamor about him like so many hyenas. Each one belches out its madness upon him. Hysterical women and the sweethearts of the martyrs cast themselves wailing upon the ashes of the dead. Antonius sees heretics who emasculate themselves, heretics who burn themselves. Apollonius of Tyre reveals himself to him as a miracle-worker in no respect inferior to Christ. And Hilarion continues to grow. Following in the train of the heretics come the gods of the different religions in a monstrous procession, from the most abhorrent and grotesque stone idols and wooden fetiches of ancient times, to the blood-thirsty gods of Eastern lands, and the gods of beauty of Greece. They all move swiftly past, and uttering a loud wail of lamentation, disappear with a wild leap in the great vacuum. He sees gods that fall into a swoon, others that are whirled away, others that are crushed, torn to pieces, and precipitated into a black hole; gods that are drowned or dissolved into air, and gods that are guilty of self-destruction. Among them looms up Buddha, who in everything that he narrates concerning himself bears the most startling resemblance to the Saviour. Finally Crepitus, that Roman god of digestion, and Jehovah, the Lord of Hosts, make the leap down into the abyss.

A terrible silence, a deep night ensues.

"They are all gone," says Antonius.

"I still remain," replies a voice.

And Hilarion stands before him, by far larger than before, transfigured, beautiful as an archangel, radiant as the sun, and so tall that Antonius is compelled to throw back his head in order to see him.

"Who are you?"

Hilarion replies: "My kingdom is as large as the world, and my desire knows no bounds. I am always marching forward, freeing minds and weighing worlds, without fear, without pity, without love, and without God. They call me Science."

Antonius recoils in horror. "You are, rather, the devil!"

"Do you wish to see him?" A horse's hoof shows itself, the devil takes the saint on his horns and bears him through space, through the heavens of modern science, wherein the planets are as abundant as grains of dust. And the firmament expands with the thoughts of Antonius. "Higher, higher!" he exclaims. Infinity reveals itself to his gaze. Timidly he inquires of the devil for God. The devil answers him with new queries, new doubts. "What you call form is perhaps but a delusion of your senses," he says; "what you call substance is only a conceit of your mind. Who knows if the world is not an eternal stream of facts and occurrences, the semblance the only truth, the illusion the only reality!"

"Adore me!" suddenly exclaims the devil, "and curse the mockery you have called God!" He vanishes, and Antonius awakens, lying on his back on the brink of his rock.

But his teeth are chattering, he is ill; he has no longer either bread or water in his hut, and his hallucinations begin anew. He loses himself in the swarm of fabulous animals that throng about him, the fantastic monsters of the earth. He finds himself on a strand amid the inhabitants and plants of the sea and land, and he can no longer distinguish plants and animals. The twining plants wind and curve like serpents; he confuses the vegetable and mineral world with that of mortals. The gourds look like human breasts; the Babylonian tree Dedaim, bears human heads as its fruit; pebbles seem like skulls; diamonds glitter like eyes. He experiences the pantheistic yearning to blend with universal nature, and this is his last wail:——

"I have a desire to fly, to swim, to bark, to roar, to howl. Would that I had wings, a horny plate, a shell, a beak! Would that I could coil my body like a serpent, divide myself, be in everything, be wafted around like a perfume, unfold myself like a plant, sound like a tune, shine like a light, conceal myself in all forms and penetrate every atom!"

The night is at an end. It was only a new incubus. The sun rises, and in its disk the face of Christ beams upon him. Then follows the last discreet irony of the author. Antonius makes the sign of the cross, and begins anew the prayer that was interrupted by these visions.

In this work of fiction we have Flaubert complete, with his sluggish blood, his gloomy imagination, his intrusive erudition, and his need of bringing to a level old and new illusions, ancient and modern faiths. The almost savage vehemence of his temperament reveals itself when he thrusts the god Crepitus before the God Jehovah. That he chose the legend of St. Antonius as a medium through which to free his mind, and utter some bitter truths to mankind, was because he was brought into contact by this material with antiquity and the Orient which he loved. Through it he could use the large cities and landscapes of Egypt as a background on which to lavish brilliant colors and gigantic forms. And with this theme he no longer painted the helplessness and stupidity of a society, but of a world. He depicted, quite impersonally, humanity as having waded up to its ankles until that hour of its existence, in mire and in blood, and pointed to science—which is as much shunned and dreaded as the devil—as the sole salvation.

The idea was as grand as it was new. The execution by no means attained the level of the plan. The book was crushed by the material used in its preparation. It is not a poetic work; it is partly a theogony, partly a piece of church history, and it is moulded in the form of a psychology of frenzy. There is in it an enumeration of details that is as wearisome as the ascent of an almost perpendicular mountain wall. Certain parts in it, indeed, are only thoroughly intelligible to savants, and seem almost unreadable to the general public. The great author had gradually passed into abstract erudition and abstract style. "It was a sorrowful sight," Émile Zola has pertinently remarked, "to see this powerful talent become petrified like the forms of antique mythology. Very slowly, from the feet to the girdle, from the girdle to the head, Flaubert became a marble statue."

VII

I have delayed speaking of the last vision of St. Antonius because it seems to me the most remarkable of all, and was undoubtedly the poet's own vision. After all the gods have vanished, and the journey through the heavens has come to an end, Antonius beholds, upon the opposite shore of the Nile, the Sphinx, lying on its belly, with outstretched claws. But springing, flying, howling, snorting fire through its nostrils, and beating its wings and its dragon's tail, Chimera is circling about the Sphinx. What is the Sphinx? What else than the gloomy riddle that is chained to earth, the eternal question,—brooding science! What is the Chimera? What else than the winged imagination, which speeds through space, and touches the stars with the tips of its wings.

The Sphinx (the word is of the masculine gender in French) says: "Stand still, Chimera! Do not run so fast, do not fly so high, do not howl so loud. Cease snorting thy flames into my face; thou canst not possibly melt my granite."

The Chimera replies, "I never stand still. Thou canst never grasp me, thou dread Sphinx."

The Chimera gallops through the corridor of the labyrinth, flies across the sea, and holds fast with its teeth to the sailing clouds.

The Sphinx lies motionless, tracing the alphabet in the sand with its claws, musing and calculating; and while the sea ebbs and flows, the grain waves to and fro, caravans pass by, and cities fall to decay, it keeps its firm gaze bent fixedly on the horizon.

Finally it exclaims, "O phantasy! lift me up on thy pinions, out of my deadly ennui!"

And Chimera replies, "Thou unknown one! I am enamored with thine eyes; like an inflamed hyena I circle about thee. Oh, embrace me! Fructify me!"

The Sphinx rises up; but Chimera flees in terror of being crushed beneath the stony weight. "Impossible!" says the Sphinx, and sinks into the deep sand.

I see in this scene the last confession of Flaubert, his stifled wail over the imperfection of his entire life-work, and this master-work of his life in especial. The Sphinx and the Chimera, science and poetry, desire each other in him, seek each other again and again, circle about each other with passionate yearning and ardor; but the true impregnation of poetry through science he did not accomplish.

Not that his principle was unsound or incorrect. On the contrary, the future of poetry is embodied in it; this I most truly believe, for in it was its past. The greatest poets, an Æschylus, a Dante, a Shakespeare, a Goethe, possessed all the essential knowledge of their day, and deposited it in their poetry. True, erudition and scientific culture, in and for themselves, have no poetic value. They can never in the world take the place of poetic sentiment and artistic creative power. When the poetic endowment, however, exists, the gaze is sharpened by an acquaintance with the laws of nature and the human soul and expanded by the study of history. In our day, when modern science is reconstructed in every direction, however, it is undoubtedly far more difficult than ever to span the materials of science without being overwhelmed, and Flaubert did not possess that native harmony of spirit which renders difficult things easy, and reconciles the profound antitheses of the world of ideas.

"La Tentation de St. Antoine" was disposed of in Paris with a merry boulevard jest. Few people, indeed, had the patience to enter thoroughly into the volume, and the public at large was soon ready with its judgment: the book was mortally tedious. How could the author expect that such a work would entertain the Parisians? Now "Madame Bovary" was quite another thing. Why did not Flaubert repeat himself (as all poor writers do)? Why did not he write ten new "Madame Bovarys"?

He retired to Croisset, shut himself up in solitude, deeply wounded as he was, for long months, and slowly began to work anew. He grew old. He lost by death his older friends, George Sand and Théophile Gautier; the friends of his youth and those who were his comrades in thought, Louis Bouilhet, Feydeau, Jules de Goncourt, and others.

He grew lonely. His health gave way; there came a time when he could not endure walking,—indeed, could not even bear to see others walk. He became poor. He lost his property, which from the kindness of his heart he had intrusted to his only niece, and which her husband had foolishly squandered, and during the latter years of his life he was tormented with anxieties regarding means of subsistence. Toward the last he rarely went to Paris; indeed, he did not even go into his garden. His sole exercise consisted in an occasional walk from his bed-chamber to his study, and down stairs to take his solitary meals.

He died in May, 1880, and was buried at Rouen. The funeral procession was small; only a few friends from Paris followed him to his last resting-place. From Rouen scarcely any one attended the funeral, for he was almost entirely unknown to the majority of the inhabitants, and by the minority who knew him, he was hated as an immoral and irreligious writer.

VII

FREDERICK PALUDAN-MÜLLER

1881

From Germans who were conversant with the Danish language, I have frequently heard the remark, "Paludan-Müller, not Oehlenschläger, is the greatest poet Denmark has produced in this century. How strange this has never been recognized!"

It has never been recognized because it is not the case. Intellectual superiority has here been confounded with poetic, or personal maturity preferred to the originality of genius. In Meyer's "Konversations-Lexikon" we read: "Paludan-Müller is unconditionally the most important Danish author of our century, quite as much owing to his wealth of ideas, as to the depth of his moral earnestness and the beauty of form displayed in his diction." Questionable as the justice of this assertion appears to me, it is equally unquestionable that Paludan-Müller (born Feb. 7, 1809, died Dec. 28, 1876) is far more calculated to interest the foreign reader than any other modern Danish author, and his deep, inquiring mind is especially in harmony with the German mind.

I

I need only close my eyes to see him before me as he appeared in life. I behold the cheerful smile with which he said "Good day" to a guest. I hear the roguish playfulness with which in lively conversation, almost in the style of Shakespeare's Mercutio, he clung to a merry pun. In the last years of his life a severe illness had broken his strength, and age had set its mark on his noble form. But I can see him in the freshness and healthful appearance of his robust years, as he was when I first became acquainted with him.

One August day, in 1863, I saw and spoke with him for the first time. On a pedestrian trip with a young relative of his, I came to Fredensborg, in Zealand, and with beating heart set foot on the threshold of his summer residence. Every poem he had written was familiar to me, and I experienced a sense of disquietude, mingled with rejoicing, at the thought of being so near the man whom I had so long admired in the distance. We waited a while in the rustic, modest room; I had just time to cast a glance at the unpretending household furniture, when the door of the adjoining room opened, and he whom we sought appeared, bidding us welcome in his singularly refined and impressive voice. An aristocratic face met my gaze, with features that might have been chiseled by an idealistic sculptor. The sensitive, quivering nostrils, and the deep, strong, handsome blue eyes, shaded by vigorous eyebrows, gave life to the face; a slight deafness, too, imparted to it a listening, attentive look. On his head Paludan-Müller wore a high, pointed cap, which was extremely becoming to him, and caused his noble face to resemble an old Florentine portrait. His finely shaped, sarcastic mouth was made doubly beautiful by the smile that hovered about it; his white necktie imparted a certain dignity to the poise of the head, and he looked equally distinguished and amiable.

After the first interchange of greetings the conversation fell on the relation between the beautiful in nature and in art, and, zealous idealist as he was, he maintained that everything in nature must be called beautiful, or nothing. It was a sort of echo of the Hegelian doctrine of beauty as the work of man alone.

During this talk we had strolled out into the Fredensborg castle garden. Paludan-Müller sat down on the banks of Lake Esrom, and pointing with his stick to a monstrous toad, he said, "Voltaire was right when he made his toad exclaim, '*La beau idéal c'est ma crapaude.*'"

He seemed to take a certain naïve pleasure in making use of terse sportive sentences of this kind. There might also be detected in his conversation at times, an interesting antithesis; he would now employ certain abstract and solemn phrases that have become foreign to the younger generation; would speak, for instance, of the "worshippers of beauty," and more to like effect; and again, he would amuse himself by clothing his thoughts in some extravagantly cynical expression. This changeful attitude of tone may be recognized in his humoristic poetry. In his discourse it produced a peculiar effect, much as when a swan interrupts its calm, royal flight, to thrust its tail upward in the air. This, however, was only the first impression; it was entirely effaced by a more intimate acquaintance with him. To those who knew him well, it was very evident that the ermine-like purity of his nature and his aversion to the uncleanness and flatness of the daily life of the period, which had made him a hermit, found their complement in the witty, sportively polemic tendency of his mind, in his scorn for much that was excessively admired by others, and in the keen sense of the comic which had made him the poet of satire.

II

He passed his summers in Fredensborg, and his winters in the "Ny-Adelgade" in Copenhagen, and it sometimes occurred to me that this double place of residence corresponded with the different phases of his character and his poetry. He was well adapted to his summer home. There was something in his nature that was akin to the slender, proud alleys, and the pure air and perfect order of the regularly laid out gardens. The white statues of the un-Grecian Greek gods and goddesses among the trees were reminders of his mythologic poems, and harmonized with the character of the poet who has so often surprised and portrayed Venus and Aurora at their morning toilets. With all his great and rare poetic gifts, Paludan-Müller, in his poetry, lacked naïveté; he was never, properly speaking, the poet of nature; and, therefore, a garden was much better adapted to his poetic mood than a forest. The little castle, of which the new royal family promptly took possession, was very dear to him. He was devoted to royalty, as were but few of his contemporaries; he was as loyal as

a citizen of the days of Frederick VI. He was rejoiced and
felt honored when he received an occassional visit from the
young princesses, whose amiability and simple manners
won his heart; he was put in an especially good humor one
day when the Princess Dagmar[1] sent him her portrait with
a few friendly lines. Finally, the spot suited his need of
living in retirement. He went to Fredensborg long before
the other guests from Copenhagen, and remained there
long after they had all departed; he always left the city
when the calendar promised spring, and did not return
until the last leaves had fallen. Thus he had an opportunity of enjoying profound solitude in his favorite retreat.

Any one who visited him during the winter in Copenhagen, found him in very different surroundings. His
street was in one of the worst and most notorious quarters
of the city at that time. The fact that he was not in very
affluent circumstances had evidently been the cause of his
settling in a place of the kind. It was a singular coinci-
dence that the pure and rigorous author of "Kalanus"
could never step to his door of a winter evening without
having before his eye abundant and loud testimony of
human shame and misery. Many an evening I have seen
him in the streets of this vicinity, leaning on his cane, and
looking neither to the right nor to the left, while numerous
rude and noisy couples drifted past him. I would then
remember that the author of "Kalanus" was also the author
of "Adam Homo"; and were not these the accessory figures
of "Adam Homo," the original of the beautiful Lina and
the swarthy Trina which the poet had before his eyes day
after day? Thus it was not an altogether incongruous
decree of fate that located Paludan-Müller in the midst of
the most wretched and hideous vices of Copenhagen. When
the threshold of his house was once crossed, however, the
repulsive neighborhood was wholly forgotten. The door
to the peaceful dwelling, where everything was animated
by the good genius and good humor of the poet, was
usually opened by a faithful old maid-servant who was
thoroughly devoted to her employer, and with whose favor

[1] Later, the Empress of Russia.

no guest could dispense, since, according to the playful assertion of the poet, she tyrannized over his home.

III

In conversation with Paludan-Müller, little was learned concerning his life. He never made any communications regarding it to the public, nor was it his wont to speak in private of his personal experiences. He was by no means a good narrator. He discussed every great problem with interest; but facts, as such, occupied his mind in but a trifling degree. His mode of speech was argumentative, not figurative; the poetic element manifested itself in brilliant flashes, but scarcely ever in a picturesque expression. In a critical, or even violently exciting situation, I have never seen Paludan-Müller. I do not even know whether his external life ever presented momentous critical situations. The external lives of the Danish writers of his day were as a rule empty. They were educated in one school of learning or another, passed several years at the University of Copenhagen in vain endeavors to acquire some professional science, published their first poetry, undertook an extended journey abroad, and had awarded to them some official position, or a poet's stipend. To the lot of some of them was added a long and obstinate struggle for recognition. But even this dramatic element was lacking in the life of Paludan-Müller. He took part in no intellectual campaign. True, he was for a time not estimated according to his deserts, but he was never wholly misunderstood. His life seems, therefore, to have had as few sharp angles as that of most of our modern men of talent.

He was born in 1809 at a parsonage in Fünen, became a student in 1828, passed a mediocre examination in jurisprudence in 1835, married in 1838, and during the years 1838-40 travelled through Middle and Southern Europe. In 1851 he was made a knight of the order of Danebrog, and in 1854 received a professor's title. Moreover, in his mature manhood, he was a poet and a recluse.

What he was as a youth, we must conjecture from his

works. From what I have heard, I imagine him to have been greatly fêted in social circles, the decided lion of the aristocratic houses of Fünen; it has been told to me that he possessed such humor and so decided a faculty for impromptu invention, that he would sometimes create on the spur of the moment an entire little drama, and play it entirely alone, running from one side of his improvised stage to the other, in order to reply to his own speeches. I remember, too, having heard that in his younger days he had experienced a deep heart-grief, a young girl whom he loved having been snatched from him by death. Very early, at all events, the chain of bitter experiences, without which he could not have written the first part of "Adam Homo" in his thirty-first year, subdued his original love of life, and when still young, he retired from the world, withdrawing entirely from public, almost entirely from social life, and devoting himself exclusively to his home, his art, and his theological and philosophic studies. His marriage was childless, so that even in his household life there was nothing to fix his gaze on the world without. The more completely he severed the cords that had bound him to his surroundings, the more self-controlled and contemplative he became. Through accidental remarks alone, through words that he dropped in the course of conversation, without dreaming what an impression they must make upon a young man, did I gain a clear idea of the nature of the results at which he had arrived in the course of his life-experience and knowledge of human nature. These results were not of an optimistic nature.

Never shall I forget the day when I carried to him a pamphlet, my first published work. "I thank you," said he. "It will give me great pleasure to read the book. How soon do you want it back?" "I beg of you to keep it." "You want to present the book to me. Oh, innocence! He gives his own books to people. Do you carry it to others as well? What? To your friends and near acquaintances? Well, believe me, you will not long continue such a course. This is something authors only do when they are very young." At that time such a speech excited me to very much the same opposition as the cold, cruel irony of "Adam Homo"; later I learned to understand better the freedom from illusion and the caution from which it sprang. To-day Paludan-Müller's reserve appears only natural to me.

The sharp suspicion he sometimes manifested was rather touching than insulting, for Paludan-Müller was not suspicious on his own account, but rather for the sake of those who enjoyed his favor. He always feared that the wicked world, especially dangerous womankind, would lure his favorites to destruction, and warnings on his part were never lacking. Among his precepts may be found some of those half-worldly, half-Christian admixtures of well-calculated egotism and conventional morality, which are so full of good sense, and yet are listened to so unwillingly by young people. One day in the year 1867, for instance, he exclaimed: "What is that you are saying? Some Italian ladies whom you visited frequently at Paris have invited you to stay at their house during the Exposition? You should not think of such a thing!" "And why not? I can assure you these ladies are not only thoroughly irreproachable in character, but are people of the highest culture." "That makes no difference, no difference whatever, nor did I say anything to the contrary; I only remarked that it would be wiser to have nothing to do with these Italian women. Use your time and your talents for whole relations; that is what we should do. It is wisest to sow where we can ourselves reap the harvest; a young man would do better to employ his time for the benefit of his mother, his sister, his wife, in other words, in whole relations; everything else is lost time." He said this with great earnestness, and in a peculiarly domineering way, as though he were resolved not to listen to any objections that might be offered. It made me a little angry at the time, because the innocent invitation of these foreign ladies was by no means cause sufficient for such an outburst; but when I think of it now, this mistrust only seems to me one of the spiritual conditions from which "Adam Homo" proceeded.

It was but comparatively seldom, however, that this negative side of his character came to light. I have preserved a far stronger impression of the loving and thoughtful care for others manifested by Paludan-Müller, of the princely refinement of his nature. His bearing to his wife, who was ten years older than himself, was the perfection of chivalry, and a similar chivalrous demeanor marked his intercourse with the many ladies, by no means endowed with personal attractions, who visited at his home. To the admiration and flatteries of beautiful women, he was absolutely unsusceptible. I remember one case, when an exceedingly handsome lady, who had succeeded in getting a seat next to him at a social gathering, overwhelmed him with honestly meant thanks, not unmingled with a critic's appreciation, for "Adam Homo." She utterly failed to win the favor of Paludan-Müller. What he said to me afterwards was, "She has, no doubt, in her not very long life, wrought a considerable amount of mischief." On the other hand, he treated with peculiar warmth ladies who were in humble and reduced circumstances. There was in his family an old unmarried aunt, who was well advanced in the sixties, and who, although a good-hearted, excellent person, was most unattractive in personal appearance. Paludan-Müller became the self-appointed knight of this old lady; he always paid her the choicest attention, and he who scarcely ever invited any one to dine with him always celebrated her birthday each summer with a little dinner party, and each time proposed a toast for her in the most hearty words.

IV

Frederick Paludan-Müller was the son of a refined and highly cultured Danish bishop. He inherited his father's talents for idealistic reflection. He does not belong, like Grundtvig and Ingemann, Heiberg and Poul Möller, Hauch and Christian Winther, Aarestrup and Bötdcher, to the great Oehlenschläger group. Like Henrik Hertz, he belongs to the circle of J. L. Heiberg. Unquestionably, Heiberg was the Danish master of poetic art, to whom from the outset he looked up. He was, as he once told me himself, so captivated in his youth with the personal presence and conversation of Heiberg that sometimes the latter, in order to get clear of him when they had been together until late in the night, was forced to repeat the formula: "Now listen to me once for all, Paludan-Müller; if you do not leave immediately, I shall be obliged to order a bed for you on the floor." He never referred to Heiberg's poetry but with the greatest warmth. It was attractive to him because of its lucidity, its wealth of thought, and its romantic flight. He rejoiced in its satire, the related chords met with a response within his own soul, and its speculative tendencies harmonized with his own propensity to depict what was universally valid, universally human. His judgments regarding other poets were instructive so far as they afforded an insight into the nature of his own talent. He who so highly esteemed reflection in poetry, could not sympathize with Oehlenschläger. One day when the discourse turned on Oehlenschläger, he exclaimed, with the most comical gravity, "In short, Oehlenschläger was stupid." I laughed, and asked, "Do you think that 'Axel and Valborg' amount to nothing?" He replied, "There may be much that is fine in the work, yet only in temper and sentiment; there is no thought in it." Thought, which Théophile Gautier once defined, "the final medium in which the poet takes refuge when he is devoid of both passion and coloring," was the main essential with Paludan-Müller, if not in his poetry, at least in his æsthetics. He himself always strove to represent the idea, in the Platonic sense of the word, as what was eternally typical. Therefore it was that he wrote "Amor and Psyche," "Adam Homo," and "Ahasuerus." When he failed to find this universality, this typical element, he could discover no merit in poetry. He had no patience, for instance, with Björnson's novels of peasant life. "Anything of that kind may be very well on a small scale," he said. "It is great folly, however, to devote an entire book to the inner emotions of a little poultry-yard maiden." What made this remark peculiarly individual was the fact that he offered no critical objections to the mode of treatment; he simply protested against the material as material, against the propriety of a detailed description of an uncultured inner life. A taste for naïveté was wholly lacking in him. On the other hand, he had an actual horror of the theatrical, and in his zealous antipathy he many times found it where others had not discovered it. He called Runeberg theatrical, for instance, and with critical assurance he cited one of the extremely few passages of the Finnish poet where a glimmer of the theatrical can be found. "What a theatre hero is not his Sandel," said he.

'My horse! bid them saddle my noble Bijou!'

Who else than a hero of the coulisses would speak so? And then the description of his position on the redoubt,—

> 'He proudly remained, unmoved was his mien,
> As at first he still sat in view;
> His eye it was calm, his brow was serene,
> And he shone on his noble Bijou!'

Paludan-Müller hated the theatrical because he was always on his guard against all greatness that manifested itself in æsthetic form. He found the great Alexander small, and the Indian ascetic Kalanus sublime. In his eyes, human greatness was confined to moral greatness, and moral greatness for him passed entirely into moral purity.

V

Though he started in his general æsthetic views on the career pointed out by Heiberg, he nevertheless struck ere long into his own independent course. Heiberg was only a moralist in the name of true culture and of good taste; Paludan-Müller became one in the name of stern religious discipline. In religious questions, Heiberg had espoused the cause of Hegelian speculative Christianity; Paludan-Müller became an orthodox theologian. Thus his path for not an inconsiderable distance ran parallel with that of Sören Kierkegaard. Not that he was in any way influenced by this solitary thinker. He cherished but little sympathy for him, and was repelled by his broad, unclassical form, for whose merits he had no comprehension, and whose inner harmony with the mind of the author he did not perceive. It was the general spirit of the times which produced the intellectual harmony of these two solitary chastisers of their contemporaries. Step by step, Danish literature had departed from the ideals of the period of enlightenment, which had still continued to exist in the poetic creations of Oehlenschläger, as well as in the popular scientific works of Hans Christian Oersted. Their life had been of but brief duration. The Danish churchman to whom Schleiermacher corresponded was Mynster, but there is a wide gulf between Schleiermacher's freethinking and Mynster's orthodoxy. At the beginning of the nineteenth century, a single theologian, Clausen, was the sole spokesman of rationalism; he soon, however, turned completely toward the religious reaction then beginning. Rationalism, it is true, for a short time seemed to have become metamorphosed and developed into Hegelian philosophy of religion; but this movement, too, was wholly unproductive of results. Heiberg, who was its leader, became a follower of that speculative theologian of the Hegelian right flank, Martensen, and Martensen, in his turn, became thoroughly converted to high-church dogmatism. Nothing was now lacking for the completion of this spiritual movement but to deduce from it the practical, ethical results of dogmatic faith. This was done when the race of Oehlenschlägers and Oersteds had begotten the race of Kierkegaards and Paludan-Müllers.

In Kierkegaard's "Either—Or" is found the sentence, "There are poets who, through their poetic creations, have found themselves." This remark can well be applied to Paludan-Müller. For what else has a poet done who has traversed the path from coquetry to simplicity, from the intellectual to the true, from the sportive and brilliant to the transparently clear, and from the pleasing to the great?

Paludan-Müller appeared in his early days to be the *virtuoso* among the contemporary poets of Denmark. The themes of his first works were almost completely buried beneath the trills of caprice and the delicate gradations of wit. In his "Kjærlighed ved Hoffet" (Love at Court, translated into German by E. v. Zoller, 1832), a comedy after the pattern of the times which was partly inspired by Shakespeare, partly by Gozzi, pastoral poetry and lyrical court phraseology, puns and witticisms, dreamy enthusiasm, and fool's bells, all jingled together. The fact was, the work had been enriched from the horn of plenty of a highly endowed youth, who was free from care and without any defined plan. In the poem "Danserinden" (The Dancing-Girl), whose form and rhythm remind the reader so strongly of Byron's "Beppo," or Alfred de Musset's "Namouna," the virtuosity was more unbridled and capricious; the smooth-flowing stanzas narrated, lamented, laughed, mocked, played pranks, and glided one into the other with a loquacious flexibility, recalling the manner in which one arabesque passes into another. The serious portions of the narrative do not impress the reader as having actually occurred; the satirical remarks do not seem to be meant in earnest. When, however, a command to believe in the immortality of the soul is interwoven, for instance, with a recommendation of tea, a warning against the insipid poets, and other warnings of a still more captious nature, the cause may be traced less to a frivolous state of mind than to the youthful exuberance that fills the poet from the moment he feels his favorite form of verse, the eight-line stanza, galloping and prancing beneath his efforts. "The Dancing-Girl" is a mingling of intellect and inspiration, out of which neither clear colors nor distinct forms have developed themselves. It is a musical composition that now expresses the light dance of jig, now the yearning of melancholy, as these emotions alternate in the years of puberty, with their bold hopes, their uncomprehended yearnings, their thoughtless squandering of the powers of life. "The Dancing-Girl" was followed the next year by "Amor and Psyche," a new work of artistic virtuosity, which impresses itself most harmoniously upon the reader's favor, but has no power to burn forms or images into the soul. It is a music that is at once apprehended, but almost as promptly forgotten, one continual melodious solo and chorus song of spirits, zephyrs, and nymphs, whose sole fault is that it is too perfect in artistic form, too polished and smooth. The whole long dramatic poem does not contain a single characteristic or individual peculiarity, either in diction or in the mode of treatment, and yet something characteristic, that is to say, something unusually marked or sharply defined, would have had a most pleasing effect. As astonishing as is the *technique,* it is not felt, and only where the *technique* is present can we speak of style in the true sense of the word. Not those parts which are loaded with the greatest metrical display contain the most vital strophes, bearing most distinctly the impress of the poet's genius; they are found in the following words of Sorrow, where she casts her dark veil over the sorrowing Psyche: —

> Round each mortal's cradle flying,
>   Close the mother's couch beside,
> Hordes of woes are softly sighing,
>   Gloom and care with them abide.
> Tears the tender eyes bedewing.
> Fears the budding smile subduing,
> Shrieks the infant's lips are parting,
>   While dawn's heralds onward glide.
> And when childhood's time is vanished,
>   Youth's brief joy has had its day,
> Garlands won are faded, banished,
>   Gone is love's bewitching play—
> When, alas! the dreams have perished,
> Once so fondly, proudly cherished,
> Hide e'en dead delights and pleasures
>   In the pangs of death away.

In these stanzas the melancholy that was peculiar to Paludan-Müller becomes apparent. There is here betrayed that view of death which developed into a tendency to dwell on the thought of death, and which was destined eventually to burst forth in the love of death manifested

by a Tithon, a Kalanus, or an Ahasuerus. We here detect
the interest in the law of destruction which later produced
the poem "Abels Död" (The Death of Abel), the belief that
dead happiness embraces within itself all the pangs of death
which found expression in "Tithon," and the feeling that
dissolution lurks ever on the threshold of life and of joy,
which so often breaks through the poetry of Paludan-Müller. Pay heed, for instance, to the following lines from the
poem entitled "Dance Music":—

> Lo! the sunshine, golden, gleaming,
>   Lights with smiles the azure skies!
> Yonder cloud speeds onward, beaming;
>   Like a bird, with wings, it flies.
> Hear the ringing
> Now of singing
> That is filling
> Lofty trees with music thrilling,—
>   All this glory swiftly dies.

We may call this tone shrill, yet it did not jar like a
false note in the ear of Paludan-Müller. On the contrary,
he found a certain satisfaction, a certain consolation, indeed, in keeping before his own eyes and those of others the
inexorable, the inevitable fate of all that is finite. When
the custom of circulating the photographs of celebrated
men, with a brief autograph inscription, came into vogue,
he wrote beneath a picture that represented him reading a
book, the characteristic words:—

> All earthly things, 'tis written here,
>   Go up and down by turns;
> So he who stands above to-day
>   What is before him learns.

Justice, however, has not been accorded to the drama
"Amor and Psyche," if attention be merely called to the
fact that it is the harbinger of the poet's most beautiful
and profound works. As intellectual poetry it has a connected and complete symbolism which obliges the author
to be more rigid than ever before in handling his materials,
and it is distinguished by that peculiar tinting which is so

characteristic of Paludan-Müller's mythological poems. It is not a strong tinting, now gray in gray, now light in light; yet the poem is by no means colorless. The truth is, its hue is that of the reflection of pearls, the glimmer of mother of pearl, the delicate play of prismatic shades that might have radiated from the shell in which venus emerged from the sea. The Phantasus of Paludan-Müller paints the portrait of Psyche for Amor on just such a "pearl-white" shell; and this is almost symbolic of the way in which the poet himself has executed the form of Psyche. This class of his creations, indeed, is not of an earthly nature; earth is not their true home, and even those among them who like Psyche are of earthly descent, must bid to earth a final imperative farewell.

> *Psyche* (kneeling).
> Gaia, thou hallowéd mother,
> Who gave me birth and protection.
> Thou from whose lips ever tender,
> I heard life's earliest accents,
> Take thou thy daughter's farewell!
> Nevermore shall I behold thee,
> Never again shall I wander
> Over the loved spots of memory.
>
> *   *   *   *   *
>
> Yonder, in heavenly mansions,
> Earthly sorrows will vanish.

The entire poetic endeavor of Paludan-Müller in this period was, upon the whole, one magnificent, many-shaded leave-taking of Gaia. What else, indeed, was the tendency of romance! It feared and shunned the life about it, and the era so wholly devoid of character in which its poets, to their sorrow, found themselves born. Paludan-Müller with his whole soul shared this repugnance of the romantic school for the actual surrounding of the poet, as well as its aversion to lingering, even in fancy, about this heavy, dark globe which kept up its ceaseless revolutions with the poet and all his air-castles, whether he would have it so or not. The age in which he lived was loathsome to him, and he had his own era and his own contemporaries in mind when he permitted Tithon to say of his:—

> What fruits thinkest thou this era will develop?
> An era 'tis that needs a mighty storm
> To rouse its energies from heavy slumber;
> An era full of dreams instead of efforts,
> Of petty competition, not of action bold;
> An era when each crowns himself with glory
> And sees himself in heroes of the past,
> When mortals would be loftly as immortals
> And yet have servile minds—how I abhor them!

True, this description concerns Asia Minor at the time of the Trojan War; but it is one that accords marvellously well with that given in "Adam Homo" of the reign of Christian VIII. in Denmark:—

> It was a time when mediocre mortals
> Were puffed up everywhere with boastful pride;
> *   *   *   *   *   *   *
> A time when there were those together clustered
> Who something great to pass proposed to bring,
> While they at best accomplished not a thing.

It is readily comprehensible that a poet who cast so gloomy a gaze upon his surroundings should have preferred, like Tithon, a sojourn in the "realm of the aurora" to that among his own contemporaries.

The most singular fact of all was that he was not alone in his predilection for this higher sphere. All the best brains of the period had instituted the same comparison and made the same choice; there was a poetic vein in most of them, and so it came to pass that in the realm of the aurora the poet found himself in a numerous company.

This wrought a change in the poetic tendency of Paludan-Müller. He paused suddenly in his flight from reality, wheeled about, and took the direction back to earth again. In the poem "Tithon" he paints life on the island of the morning dawn, on the coast of the sea of ether, to which the love of Aurora has uplifted Tithon. It is an existence such as that of Rinaldo in the enchanted gardens of Armida, and a veil of roseate hue is spread over all the surroundings, over the skies as well as over the beautiful women of the island. It is a life passed amid song, clinking of goblets, love, and music, and sails on the sea of ether in eternal youth, during an eternal spring. And yet this life is never spiritless and insipid, nor are its enjoyments ever commonplace; they are blissful enjoyments. It is akin to the life of which so many noble enthusiasts among the Danish contemporaries of our poet dreamed; the life that hovered before Carsten Hauch, for instance, when he sang of that "sea of the milky way, where the spirits of the redeemed, freed from care and sorrow, their eyes illumined with the brilliant light of immortality, glide onward through unknown clouds." It is that *alibi* of enjoyment that Ludwig Bödtcher and so many other similar artist natures, during the best years of their lives, sought beneath the skies of Italy; it is that never-ending spring and that eternal youth which Christian Winther and Hans Christian Andersen, and all those men of their generation who like themselves did not know how to grow old, permitted themselves to cling to and conjure up. It is a strong proof, however, of the greatness of Paludan-Müller's spirit that this life and this beauty did not long attract him. His poetic muse depicts Tithon, in the midst of his forgetfulness of earth and his revelling in enjoyment, devoured with half-unconcious yearning for his country, his people, his relations, and the entire un-ideal reality which he has forsaken. Nor is this yearning without foundation; for nothing less than Priam's ascension to the throne, the abduction of Helen, the ten-years' war of which Homer is supposed to have sung, and the complete destruction of Troy, has taken place while Tithon is revelling in the cloud-land of the morning dawn. Thus it was once upon a time, when the French Revolution was enacting from beginning to end its magnificent drama, that certain people on the coast of the Sound were singing drinking-songs and club-songs. Thus it was that Copenhagen played its private comedy during the battle of Waterloo, and Denmark rioted in beautiful verses and rejoiced in æsthetic tilting-matches while the July Revolution was in full blast.

Paludan-Müller has his Tithon compel Aurora to give him permission to return to earth, and the following words uttered by Tithon at the moment when, after long absence, he once more sets foot upon earth, indicate perhaps the most significant turning-point of the poet's own course of development:—

> O Earth, thy air is heavy! Like a burden
> It falls upon my limbs and on my bosom;
> A deadly weight, it presses on my shoulders.
> Unfriendly is thy greeting—cold and sharp,
> To meet me sendest thou thy wind inclement.
> And in thy winter garb hast clad thyself.
> Where'er I gaze, thy plains look bare and dreary;
> The leaves upon thy trees are sere and yellow;
> Thy grass is withered; decked hast thou already
> Yon hill-tops far away with wreaths of snow.
> Wilt thou alarm me? Is so stern thy visage?
> Because in utter folly I forsook thee?
> All hail to thee, O thou, my native soil!
> With this fond kiss my tears of joy I tender!
> Thou fill'st my heart e'en tho' thou'rt bare and dreary.

The territory here trodden by Paludan-Müller with Tithon is the territory of Adam Homo. At the moment when the atmosphere of earth weighs heavily on Tithon's shoulders, Paludan-Müller once more hails Gaia. He had at that time already completed the first part of "Adam Homo."

VI

"This is flesh of our flesh and blood of our blood," Paludan-Müller's contemporaries might have exclaimed when "Adam Homo" appeared. The same poet who in youth had painted nebulous images in the clouds, and who as an old man, having returned to the standpoint of his youth, wrote: "People demand flesh and blood of poetry; flesh and blood are to be found in the slaughter-houses; of the poetic art, sentiment, and soul alone should be required"—this same poet, in the meridian of his manhood, gave to his contemporaries and to posterity the truest, most lifelike poem Danish literature, up to that time, had produced,—a work whose hero, far from resembling its author's former heroes, who were simply poetically clad thoughts, was the reader's own brother, a being whose character is a cruel satire. Like Shylock's pound of flesh, the book was cut from the spot nearest the heart of the living generation, with the knife of inexorable moral law.

Almost reluctantly the poet seems to have attacked his task. As the realistic epoch was but of brief duration with him, he gives us the impression of having actually drawn close to reality merely in order to settle his account with it once for all, through his bitter derision and his scathing judgment, and then to forsake it again in the utmost haste. It seems as though he would say: "You have reproached me with having no eye for the home-life about me, you have always charged me with the foreign nature of my delineations; very well, I will make it right with you, I will single out one from your very midst and take him for my hero." About the same time Kierkegaard, who was also moved by a bitter scorn for his contemporaries, wrote in his "Stages on the Path of Life": "One step is yet to be taken, a veritable *non plus ultra*, since such a generation of pot-house politicians and life-insurers charge poesy with injustice because she does not select her heroes among its own worthy contemporaries. Surely this is doing poesy a wrong; but it would be well not to pursue her too long; otherwise she might end Aristophanes-like by seizing the first sausage-dealer that came in her way and making a hero of him." This step is actually taken in "Adam Homo." The naked reality, all that is ugly in the external world, the lack of ideality in social life, all the frailty, wretchedness, baseness, and despicable in the inner life of humanity, is laid bare without reserve, without mercy. The poet's muse, which formerly, in his "Dancing-Girl," coquettishly veiled in crêpe and gauze, had sped lightly over the polished floor in dainty slippers, has now transformed itself into a Sister of Mercy, who, at once stern and gentle, ventures out in the worst weather, well shod in stout shoes. Fearless of misery wherever it may be found, not susceptible to any contagion whatever, she passes unharmed through the filthiest and most wretched streets, or she stands in the houses of the aristocrats, undazzled by their lustre and splendor, and penetrates all hearts with her sublime, superior gaze. She calls everything by its true name, the most delicate falsehood as well as the coarsest misery.

The poem was a bit of Denmark, a bit of history,—a bit of living web cut from the great loom of time. The metaphysical mirror of the humanity that the mythical poesies had produced was here supplanted by the phychological and ethical study of a single individual. The scene was no longer laid in a court in the land of romance, nor in an air-castle in the realm of ether; the action took place in Jutland, Zealand, and Fünen, and the period being neither the eternal moment nor the fantastic "Once upon a time," embraced the years 1830-48, the golden years of the bourgeoisie in Western Europe, and those in which it founded its dominion in Northern Europe. For the first time, space and time were recognized as significant powers by Paludan-Müller.

Yet while the poet's task had thus become individualized, and had acquired defined boundary lines in time and space, it none the less aimed at universality. Adam Homo— that was meant, as the title itself indicated, to represent man in general, and the hero was no less typical than the poet's previous mythical heroes. He is in the main a mythical form; his history is the mythical biography of the Danish bourgeoisie.

There was one expression that kept continually recurring in the discourse of Paludan-Müller when he spoke of science or art, and that expression was "great tasks." In these words were comprised his claims upon himself and his fellow-laborers. He himself always sought out great tasks, because it was his firm belief that they alone develop the powers and are worthy of an effort of strength, and he was continually encouraging us, his younger fellow-laborers, to set ourselves the task of dealing with great problems, because only through the solution of such could our work win a permanent place in literature. "There is," said he, "in all literatures more than enough that is scattered to the winds like chaff; make it your task to attempt something that will endure, something that has a future before it." The surest means of attaining this end was, in his estimation, in his own art, the endeavor to represent, in the characters and destinies of the individual personalities, the type of universal humanity. Those poets, in whose efforts the casual plays a certain rôle, will not attain so high a plane, it is true, yet will often acquire, by way of compensation, a more volatile, more sportive life, a more captivating charm; for the accidental in poetic art is synonymous with the *bizarre*, the gracefully surprising, the incalculable, and yet so natural irregularity. In the choice of his plots Paludan-Müller is to a rare degree the enemy of chance. His perception of what is fundamentally human, no less than his lack of original creative genius, prevented him from ever selecting psychologically singular subjects. The race of the normal *homo sapiens*, in its entire folly, was the sole material that possessed for him a thorough power of attraction.

In "Adam Homo," the task the poet set himself was to show how a man, taken from the masses, and equipped with neither the best nor the poorest endowments, from youth up, a man as full of ideal hopes and resolutions as his betters, can squander his entire intellectual fortune, and finally end as a spiritless, narrow-minded old fogy. At the same time he wished to portray how the hero for every degree he descended in the intellectual and moral scale, was compelled, of a necessity, to climb one round higher in the social ladder.

Paludan-Müller was little inclined to throw any light on the history of his works; but when once, without any preliminary, I asked, "What part of 'Adam Homo' did you write first?" he replied, unhesitatingly, "The epitaph,"— the only lines in the poem that are printed in italics.

Here Adam Homo rests, a worthy soul and bright,
A Baron, Statesman, too, who wore the ribbon white.

Had his contemporaries possessed this elucidation, which did not surprise me in the least, they would not have fumbled about so blindly in their efforts to understand the first six cantos of the poem that appeared in 1841, and whose continuation and completion did not follow until seven years later. Even Heiberg, the foremost Danish critic of the day, after reading the first part, deemed it possible that the poet might intend to let Adam end as a happy married man, in an idyllic country parsonage. So far was the public at first removed from comprehending the wrathful pessimism and the well-considered irony from which the poetic work had proceeded. People had no idea that from the moment Paludan-Müller had put pen to paper, it had been his design to allow this representative of the Danish bourgeoisie, who began life with youthful amiability and youthful enthusiasm, gradually to give up all he had once believed in, and to betray the confidence of all those who believed in him. No one suspected that it was Adam Homo's destiny to come out as a popular man and a popular orator, only directly afterwards to alter his "ideal," and to drop the love of common people, to develop into a "polished man," to seek refuge amid courtiers and statesmen, and finally, covered with titles, and hung all over with orders, to be solemnly buried as a baron, a privy councillor, a chevalier, etc.

And if Heiberg had no conception of this, can we wonder that the public at first remained wholly without comprehension of the significance of the poem? The book met with no success, and was pronounced decidedly dull. The reading world, unaccustomed to such substantial food, and having been so often invited by Palulan-Müller to feast at the table of the gods on Olympus, found some passages offensive, others commonplace, and came to the conclusion that Paludan-Müller must this time have chosen a theme that lay quite beyond the province of his genius. And yet this so deliberately condemned "Adam Homo" was destined, when completed, not many years later, to take the rank of the most typical and most significant existing Danish work of the narrative kind.

Doctrinal æsthetics would naturally object not a little to

an epos presenting a picture which, as a whole, is so little edifying, an epos whose prevailing mood presents so imperfect an atonement, indeed, properly speaking, only a theological atonement. Even from a non-doctrinal standpoint there is also a fundamental objection to be made. The great difficulty, based on the subject itself, was that Paludan-Müller did not aim, as such an infinite number of other authors have aimed, at portraying for the reader the narrow-minded, commonplace citizen in his full glory, in order to submit him at once to sharp criticism. He on the contrary wanted to show how such strait-laced old fogies become what they are. Now most characters of the kind in poetry, as well as in real life, do not become what they are, or at least only become so to a trifling degree; they are born Philistines. In such forms the ugly element is resolved, without the slightest inharmonious echo, into the comical. The father of Adam Homo is one of these native-born Philistines, and is, therefore, thoroughly comical. But to delineate the gradual growth of the comic character is upon the whole a stumbling-block for modern poesy. Aristophanes would not attempt it; as the Greek tragedy began with the catastrophe, so Greek comedy began at once with the complete upheaval of the world. In "Adam Homo" the consequence of the hero becoming comical instead of being so from the beginning, is, in short, that at first he calls forth sympathy through his amiability, and that toward the end he arouses merriment through the ridiculousness that he manifests. But the transition itself, which consists in the gradual ruin of a well-endowed human being, is repulsively sorrowful, and yet it is the point of the whole.

Adam Homo is a weak person, whose weakness makes him faithless in love and unreliable in politics. He is not weak, however, in the same way as are so many of Goethe's principal characters, such as Weislingen, Fernando, Clavigo, or Eduard; for he is not charmingly attractive in his weakness. In common with the majority of modern authors, Goethe has often invested weakness with the charm of amiability, as in modern poetry generally it is but too frequently the secret of amiability. Nothing, however, is the object of a more scathing irony on the part of Paludan-Müller than a defence of Adam Homo, such as that of the *advocatus hominis*, in the last canto, which is based on the amiability of the hero.

Without being directly amiable, weak people may have something attractive from a humorous point of view. There is an old method, based on the nature of the case, by means of which they are most sure of pleasing. Personal amiability can invest weakness only for a time with the lustre of freedom and the form of strength, yet it is always on the point of transforming itself into something base or odious. Against this downfall, however, it can secure itself by the acceptance of an inexorable fate; for viewed in a fatalistic light it arouses only laughter and deteriorates wholly into the comical. This general application Paludan-Müller has succeeded in making with perhaps more depth, and, from a psychological standpoint, more correctness, than has ever before been employed. His Adam is a theoretician, who always has at his command a ready supply of half-conscious sophistry, and who throughout his entire life casts the responsibility of his pitiful weakness alternately upon mere chance and upon stern necessity.

If, notwithstanding all this, the total impression be not unconditionally comical, it is because of a circumstance that Mendelssohn in his "Rhapsodien" has thus keenly and justly characterized: "We cease to laugh," said he, "at persons who are dear to us, or in any way near to us, as soon as their faults or follies begin to assume an important character." Every one, however, is his own nearest neighbor, and if a continual "Thou art the man" be hurled at us, it becomes impossible for us to laugh.

In the course of the narrative, the author of "Adam Homo" is continually telling us indirectly what he utters directly in the last canto, as follows:—

> Thou, too, shalt make one day the selfsame journey,
> When thou at length with life on earth art done;
> And as the actor needs initiation,
> So thou must make beforehand preparation.

> In Homo's stead thyself thou well mightst be,
> And words that served for Homo's just confession,
> When him behind the grave's dark brink we see,
> Might rouse the thought: View all with due discretion;
> Whate'er applies to him, applies as well to me.

Even the most ludicrous matters in such a case cease to be wholly absurd, and absolute terror at thought of the possibilities that dwell within his own soul readily seizes the reader, especially the youthful reader, in considering passages which the author had meant to have a purely poetic effect. Thus, for instance, in the place where Homo has become lord chamberlain, we read:—

> There swayed his solitude a wondrous feeling;
> His soul seemed freed from every narrowing band;
> Within his heart of hearts he blessed the hand
> That dealt his wounds and gave him means of healing,
> That now so tenderly was balsam dealing,
> That helped his spirit ruin to withstand.
> A guiding Providence he saw most clearly,
> And, deeply moved, his thanks he gave sincerely.

The biting satire in this gratitude for the keys of office has almost a painful effect. The poet takes the matter too gravely to be able to excite us to laughter over his hero; he does not venture to designate him as amiable, for Adam is seriously to be condemned; he will not abandon him to comedy, for Adam—in accordance with the author's views of life as a theologian—must preserve a loop-hole for mercy.

The standpoint of Paludan-Müller is not that of humor but of ethical irony, for what distinguishes irony from humor is its lack of sympathy with its object. This standpoint is not the purely artistic one that lingers with the same loving absorption over the sick and over the well, over vice and over virtue, over what the artist hates in the actual world, and over that which is dear to him. Nor is his mode of contemplation the purely humane, which, arrayed by the love of humanity, remains mild, considerate, and harmonious, and which begets a laughter that is without bitterness. Paludan-Müller's satire is cold and scathing, and thus acquires a peculiar power of its own. Just observe how the burning scorn of the poet almost imperceptibly breaks a path for itself through an adjective or an incidental remark, as often as there is occasion to deride the hero's good impulses, which are of such brief duration.

Here are a few examples: A letter from home announces to Adam that his mother, who has long been in failing health, is lying at the point of death, and in order to be able to see her once more, he tears himself away from his affianced bride and starts on the journey to Jutland. But while still under way he learns of his mother's death that has meanwhile taken place. Deeply affected, he communicates the sorrowful tidings to his sweetheart, assuring her at the same time of his faith in the future and of his unchangeable fidelity. The letter is not hypocritical, can scarcely even be called hollow; it is merely naïve. The poet, however, who knows long before the reader how Adam is to end, can scarcely wait for the moment when the change in him takes place. A long time before Adam has merited the satirical chastisement Paludan-Müller swings the scourge of mockery above his head to an accompaniment of laughter, as follows:—

> He rose and his epistle sealed with power,
> And then he sought the post-office once more,
> Where he all franked his full confession bore,
> Thus yielding up his bosom's richest dower.

Adam goes on board the steamer to hasten home to visit his mother's newly made grave. On the vessel, however, he most unexpectedly encounters his first flame, the Countess Clara, who in order to secure the escort of Adam to her country estate, introduces him to her husband, the corpulent, dull Chamberlain Galt. In vain does Adam struggle against accepting the invitation, under the plea that his mother has just died. Clara declares it to be her positive duty to console him in his affliction. His betrothal he has either concealed or denied. He allows himself to be persuaded to postpone his journey home. Clara and he sally forth to make purchases; she wishes to buy a feather for her hat, he a weed of crêpe for his. Clara first secures her ostrich feather in her own hat:—

> Round Adam's hat she folded then the sable,
> And that it charmingly became him found;
> They entered now the carriage,—he complacently,
> And Clara, waving plume and all, triumphantly.

If we but pause to remember that this weed is the badge of mourning for his glorious, ardently loved mother, we find ourselves painfully affected by this cruel irony. "If it be true," we involuntarily exclaim, "that we are so completely children of the moment, of the passing mood, of self-deception, that our best feelings, our most earnest resolutions and our purest memories, may thus evaporate into mist, or vanish like smoke, how canst thou, O poet, make so satirical a face at the thought? Hast thou no tears for that singular and dismal mixture of human nature that renders such misery possible? The questioner must compel himself to recall the fact that this poet beyond all else is an enraged moralist, who is pursuing a combined religious and poetical tendency in his poem. Personal morality is to him everything, and he does not regard it as a link of the great whole, a special organic function of the organism of the world, comparable to that of the liver or the heart in the human body. He has eyes for it alone. Wherever he finds it, his gaze becomes obscure to all else; wherever it is lacking, he sees only its absence; and *"eo ipso profulget, quod non videtur."*

Adam may be said to live through three periods; in the first he is naïve, in the second he is wicked, in the third he is stupid. In the first and third the masterly power of the portrayal is only entertaining; in the middle period of self-delusion and of slow inner debasement and corruption, the same masterly power produces a painfully distressing effect on the tender-hearted reader, especially the lady reader. But objections of this kind cannot mar the worth of a poem if it but possess the merit of being alive, and "Adam Homo" bears within itself a life that will survive the existence of a series of human generations. The works which were mentioned in the same breath with this poem at the time of its appearance are already forgotten, and after the lapse of several hundred years people will in all probability still turn back to it as one of the classic works of Danish literature; for "Adam Homo" is not only a work of art, it is an historic record of the first rank.

Unquestionably the views of a past period have left behind them strong traces in the satire which uplifts itself above this period and judges it. But without his vigorous hold on the current theological and social views of life, the poet, on the other hand, would scarcely have been able to preserve his never-failing surety of moral judgment, which now makes the poem so clear and transparent. To him, as to his contemporaries in Denmark, Strauss is a horror and George Sand an absurdity. He is so eager to attack Strauss that he has the sponsors mention him in the very first conversation in the book, at the time of Adam's christening; although Adam, at the appearance of the poem in 1841, must have been about twenty-five years old, and "The Life of Jesus," by Strauss, only appeared in 1835. And if he wants to delineate a representative of the female type that he detests, he knows no better way than to make her a caricature of female emancipation, and let her have the portrait of George Sand hanging on her wall. We would do wrong, however, to cling to a single unwise judgment, or a limitation in any one point, where there is so much that bears witness of the keenest and most comprehensive mind. What though the metaphysical threads that wind their way through the narrative, the numerous reflections regarding the freedom of the will, chance, and necessity appear to us a trifle antiquated; they occupy upon the whole so little space that they could not prejudice the effect of the totality on any susceptible mind. And what a fulness of deep and clear impressions do not remain!

It appears to me unquestionable that this is the most masculine poetic work that has been written in the Danish language. Many other poets of modern times have been children, or blind enthusiasts, or wanton youths, or vain egotists; the author of "Adam Homo" was a man. Who would have thought that Paludan-Müller, when he once resolved to descend from the ivory tower where he had hitherto held sway, would have set foot on the pavement with so bold a tread! Other poetic works of Danish literature are characterized by grace, beauty, romantic enthusiasm, or thorough apprehension of nature; this book is true, and is thus more instructive and more profound than all the rest combined. Read it more than once, and you will be convinced of its truth.

The six last cantos of the poem appeared at an inopportune moment, in December, 1848, just as an awakening national life had engendered a host of bright hopes and beautiful illusions, in the midst of whose brilliancy this book in its remoteness from the moment seemed to signify no more than the light of a single star signifies to a ball held in the open air with an illumination of a thousand torchlights. Some nights later, however, long after the torches are burned out, the star becomes visible. Or is it possible that the present generation of cultured youth in Denmark does not yet see it? Often one cannot help asking to what use the youth of a nation puts its most excellent books. Are they really only extant that they may be handsomely bound and placed on the book-shelves for display? Were it otherwise, how could it be that so few traces of their influence are found? Or has the influence of "Adam Homo" perhaps been that it has served other sons of Adam as a sort of guide-book for the journey through life, with directions concerning the goal that is to be reached, the means which must be used, and the rocks that must be avoided, if they would attain as many of the splendors of this earthly life as the hero of the poem?

"Adam Homo," more than all else that Paludan-Müller has written, is a national poem. There is not the slightest doubt that it, like Puschkin's "Eugen Onägin," was called forth and suggested by Byron's "Don Juan"; the form of the work, the metre, the changeful mood, the quaint swaying to and fro between irony and pathos, finally certain points in Adam's amorous susceptibility when a schoolboy, and certain details of his wedding, are reminders of the celebrated English epopee; but although "Adam Homo" could never have gained its present shape had it not been for the previous existence of the Byronic poem, the Danish poetic work has such an aroma and earthly flavor of the soil which engendered it that it can claim a place among the few original epic poems of first rank which Europe has produced during the century. It is a poem that stands alone in the field of literature.

VII

Next to "Adam Homo," the most interesting work of Paludan-Müller is "Kalanus." It is the positive expression of his ideal, as "Adam Homo" is the negative. Nowhere is his intellectual tendency more akin to the native bent of his great contemporary Kierkegaard than in this work. The problem which "Kalanus" endeavors to solve is precisely the same as the one whose solution Kierkegaard attacked in his "Either—Or" (Enten—Eller), namely, that of contrasting two personalities, one of whom is the direct representative of innate genius, of the pleasure-loving, extremely energetic view of life; and the other the incarnation of ethical profundity and moral grandeur, allowing them to struggle and contend, and convincing the reader of the decisive defeat of the purely natural views of life. With Kierkegaard the two opposing modes of contemplation of life are represented by a follower of æsthetics, and a judge of the supreme court, with Paludan-Müller by celebrated names in history; no less a man than the conqueror of the world, Alexander the Great, represents in "Kalanus" the æsthetic view of life, and the opponent allotted to him is the philosopher Kalanus. The ideal situation in the presentation of an intellectual wrestling-match of this sort would be that the author should succeed in equipping the contending parties with an equal degree of excellency. The actual situation, in this case, is that with Kierkegaard the representative of æsthetics is lavishly endowed with intellectual gifts, while the endowments of the representative of ethics, on the other hand, appear somewhat wooden and weak; and that with Paludan-Müller, on the contrary, the representative of ethics is no less intellectual than inspired, a man of the purest spiritual beauty, while the great Alexander is not placed upon the pinnacle of his historic fame. Such an Alexander as that of Paludan-Müller would never have vanquished Asia. In his enthusiasm for the thinker of India, our author seems to have lost the vital impression that Alexander was a genius, not merely heroic like Achilles, but great like Cæsar. And in the same way as with Alexander, the Grecian mind, as a whole, is degraded to a lower sphere, while the great representatives of Grecian philosophy, in the period of its glory, are permitted to make occasional remarks of so insignificant a nature, and so indicative of poverty of thought, that the Indian recluse has no difficulty whatever in overcoming their arguments. Thus, to be sure, the conqueror remains the only one who is in the slightest degree a worthy opponent of the ascetic.

The plot represents the Indian hermit Kalanus as believing devoutly that he has discovered in Alexander, who has just reached India on his triumphal progress through Asia, a revelation of Brahma's eternal light. He approaches the king in humble adoration, follows him at a respectful distance in his march through the desert as far as Pasargada, where he has the good fortune to be led once more into the presence of the mighty ruler, and falling upon his bended knee, he addresses him with the titles, "God, Ruler, Prince of Wisdom, King of Power." Alexander, recognizing the rare worth of the man, with kindly purpose attaches him to his person, and permits him to participate in a festival he holds that same evening. At this celebration, which the poet has portrayed with marked success, there are present some beautiful Greek courtesans, who sing the praises of Alexander, and amid loud rejoicing ransack his jewel-casket. To his profound astonishment and infinite horror, Kalanus now discovers that the great potentate, in whom he had seen the incarnate god, is neither inclined to shun the intoxication slumbering in the dregs of the flowing goblet, nor is master of the demon that lies concealed behind the mask of female beauty. In the first moment of consternation he plunges, knife in hand, at one of the courtesans, but is soon disarmed. Like one paralyzed he stands rooted to the spot when the banquet is over, not only bitterly disabused in his faith, but crushed with contrition to think that he should have confounded Brahma with a weak and mortal man like himself. Through self-annihilation alone can he hope to atone for his sin, and return to the god. He resolves, after Indian fashion, to immolate himself on the flaming pyre.

The next day, however, when Alexander, having slept off his intoxication, learns the resolution of Kalanus, he fears that he dealt too sternly the previous evening with his foreign adorer. So he hastens to Kalanus to gladden the hermit's heart with the assurance that he still enjoys the favor of Alexander. He arrives at the moment when Kalanus, thoroughly prepared in spirit for the sacrificial fires, has just been anointed by his mother for death. The potentate makes an effort to calm the ascetic, and learns to his surprise that Kalanus has not been swayed by fear of Alexander's wrath. He implores him to cast aside his resolve, but in vain. The tyrant in Alexander is aroused; he threatens Kalanus, he commands him to live; but his menaces rebound from him who is about to die of his own free will. On the wondering at the defiance of the Indian follows in the king's heart fury, and when the quiet thinker, remaining in an unruffled state of composure, only lays stress on the unworthy attitude of permitting the mind to be transported with anger, Alexander believes that scorn has followed in the footsteps of defiance. With the exclamation "slave!" he raises his hand to smite the ascetic. The blow, however, is parried, and the bitterness of the monarch, dispelled by the calm, tender efforts at persuasion, becomes transformed into noble entreaties, magnanimous promises,—all in vain. Alexander implores Kalanus to live out of friendship for him, entreats him to share with him his throne, to accept crown and sceptre from his hand, —his words produce as little impression as his previous threats. Then follows a sublime scene: Alexander casts himself upon his knees before Kalanus, and supplicates him to live.

This scene is the most beautiful, the most dramatic, the most spiritual that Paludan-Müller ever wrote. It is the crown of his dramatic scenes. It is the sum total of his thoughts and dreams. In the moment when Paludan-Müller allows Alexander to sink upon his knees, he casts all the greatness of the world, its splendor and its honor, genius and fame as well, at the feet of moral purity. This bending of the knee outweighs the prostration of Kalanus before Alexander in the first act. But even the utmost self-abasement of the hero is in vain, and the drama ends with the ascension from the funeral pyre of the spirit of Kalanus, purified in the sacred flames, to the heaven of Brahma. With all that Kierkegaard has to offer of intellectual endeavor, wit, learning, dialectics, and moral enthusiasm, in his "Either—Or," he has achieved no such brilliant triumph for the ethical mode of viewing life as that of Paludan-Müller in this one scene.

And as we must accept the obstinate adherences of Tithon to his resolution to return to earth as a symptom of the approach of the brief-lived yet so happy tendency of Paludan-Müller to realism, so we can see in the equally obstinate adherence of Kalanus to his resolve to forsake earthly life a symptom of the poet's return to the abstract poesy of his youth. The heathen mythological element reappears in his works "Paradise" and "Ahasuerus" as biblical myths. In the works that follow "Adam Homo," to be sure, there is a far deeper psychology than in those of the author's first youth; the psychological insight gained in the years of mature manhood could not possibly be lost; but these later works no longer treat of life in its breadth and with its motley coloring. They are works that withdraw from reality, and find vent in cloister life, in the hermit ideal, in expiatory death, or in the destruction of the universe; their poetry is that of renunciation, of the annihilation of self and of the universe.

VIII

The most vigorous product of this last period is the dramatic poem "Ahasuerus," an emphatic prologue of the Last Judgment. We experience, with the cobbler of Jerusalem, the last day of the world, learn from him of the course of earthly life since Christianity redeemed humanity, are informed how beastliness followed close upon the heels of humanity until the rule of the animal nature was followed by the Antichrist, as described in the poem. It is a drama to which Joseph de Maistre might with rapture have signed his name, and its attacks on constitutionalism and tolerancy form a versified commentary on the syllabus of the Vatican. The poem denotes, in common with some of the later writings of Kierkegaard, the crisis of the reaction in Danish literature against the eighteenth century. In its monologue there are some very tedious portions; but it has some dazzlingly superb, and at the same time, exceedingly touching passages in the songs of the choruses, which express the anguish of mortals in the contemplation of the coming misfortune, and no less in the exquisite song of the angels who lull Ahasuerus into eternal repose. Yet the most individual part of the poem, a passage which displays an almost Michael-Angelo-like grandeur, is that where the trumpet tones evoke annihilation in all that is finite. Let me cite the first three stanzas:—

The Trumpet (from the clouds).
Kneel, kneel, O earth! in sack-cloth clad and ashes,
Discard the mask with boastful pride that flashes!
The angel hosts in the sky are now appearing;
    Your doom is nearing!

Down, down to dust, ye vanities resplendent,
Ye stones of nature, works of art transcendent!
Each crowned turret, and each lofty tower,
    Destroyed your power.

Down, down to dust, the cup of death there draining,
From dreams of honor, schemes of pride refraining,
Down, down, and learn the worth, all steeped in degradation,
    Of reputation.

These trumpet tones are the *résumé* of Paludan-Müller's poetry.

As an antithesis to the repentant Wandering Jew in "Ahasuerus" is given the Antichrist. Unfortunately the weakness of this form is somewhat prejudicial to the effect of the poem. This Antichrist accords thoroughly with ecclesiastical tradition; he is no Lucifer, no fallen angel; in his commonplace, feeble attitude he vividly recalls the vacillating, deceitful Antichrist of Luca Signorelli in the cathedral of Orvieto. Moreover, it can readily be comprehended that Paludan-Müller, in his adherence to the orthodox impressions of his childhood, might fancy he could not paint the devil black enough, or, more correctly speaking, flat enough. Now, in order to invest the drama with play and counter-play, and thrilling interest, the Antichrist should have been equipped with powerful and brilliant qualities, that would in themselves have explained his authority. If Alexander was placed at a disadvantage, however, still less justice was done the Antichrist, and no better fate was reserved for the Lucifer in Paludan-Müller's double drama "Paradise." This Lucifer, to be sure, is enterprising and keen-sighted; he conceives, for instance, the original idea to split the kernel from which the Tree of Knowledge is to grow; but such a Lucifer after the "Cain" of Byron is after all only an Iliad after the Iliad of Homer. The first half of "Paradise" contains the most exquisite lyric strains. In the alternating song between spirit and nature, and in the song of the angel to the morning star, may be found a cosmic poetry which, in its purity and freshness, is only surpassed by that of Shelley; but the insignificance of Lucifer combined with the unsuccessful, and by far too childish naïveté of Adam and Eve, weakens the impression of the great plan of the poem. The orthodoxy of Paludan-Müller checked the flight of his fancy in "Ahasuerus" as well as in "Paradise": *in majorem gloriam dei* Antichrist became a prattler; Lucifer a spirit of the second rank.

IX

As an artist, Paludan-Müller presents the contradiction that in his entire intellectual tendency he is a pronounced spiritualist with a marked bias for the supernatural and abstract, while in his unquestionably most important and most vital work, which would surely preserve his name from oblivion, even had he written nothing else, he proved himself a decided realist, and looked actual life in the face with a persistence that is very rare in Danish poetry. Now this contradiction in itself indicates still another, as follows:—

Only reluctantly, as a rule, did he approach earth, and yet it was extremely seldom that he engaged in spiritual poetry according to the traditional acceptation of the phrase. His Pegasus bore him quite as often to the heathen Elysium as to the Christian heaven, and even where he seems to be directly expressing the Christian ideal, he is merely touching upon it to leave it in the next breath. "Kalanus," for instance, appears at the first glance as though it should properly be called a Christian poem; for it unquestionably arouses the thought in the reader's mind that if Kalanus, instead of being the contemporary of Alexander, had been a contemporary of Christ, and if the latter, as the orthodox maintain, had called himself God, all the hopes and aspirations of the ascetic would assuredly have been fulfilled. If we regard it a little more closely, however, we shall find that the poem contains rather an Indian than a Christian enthusiasm for death. Suicide, which Christianity has always condemned, is represented as the one absolutely ideal action, and even if the flames of the funeral pyre be accepted as a purgatory, similar to that with which "Adam Homo" ends, it is, nevertheless, extremely singular that the sole dogma which seems to exercise an inspiring influence upon this Protestant poet is the dogma of purgatory that has been rejected by Protestantism, just as the sole moral type which he passionately extols is that of the hermit which Protestantism has discountenanced.

It was an honest and true remark that the brother of the

poet uttered over his coffin, when, after the attempt made by Bishop Martensen to claim Paludan-Müller as the poet of the official Protestant Church, he said that he who had never employed his poetry in the service of the Church could not, without some reservation, be called a Christian poet. With all his private orthodoxy, Paludan-Müller never wrote a single hymn. With all his poetic predilection for the Bible and Christian legends, he always turned back to the heathen myth as to the mirror of his soul. He was a Christian because he was spiritual by nature, not the reverse, and his spirituality, therefore, accorded quite as fully with the withdrawal from earth in the holy Nirvana, and with the classical enthusiasm for Venus Urania, as with the Christian enthusiasm for saints and martyrs. Under all forms, self-abnegation, penance, mortification of the flesh and blood were dear to him.

He might well, like the Greek philosopher of old, have borne the surname Peisithanatos. He belonged, like Leopardi, to that little group of spirits that may justly be called the lovers of death. When his contemporary, the great Danish erotic poet, Christian Winther, became old, he wrote a poem in which he gave expression to his love of life, and declared that when his last hour should strike, he would "place himself in Charon's boat with sullen mien and deep chagrin"; Paludan-Müller, on the contrary, wanted to cry to Charon, like that Adonis about whom he wrote his last poem, "Take me, too!" and, before the ferryman could distinguish whence the voice came, he wanted to spring into the boat.

I do not speak here of his personal faith as a man; I know that he believed in a life after death; I even remember how, when he learned that David Strauss had dedicated a book to the memory of his deceased brother, he, in his naïve orthodoxy, conceived this to be a proof that Strauss had been able to tear himself free from the idea of personal immortality. I merely wish to speak of Paludan-Müller as a thinker, as a poet; and as such he loved death, not immortality. How weary, how deadly weary of life is Tithon! With what earnestness Kalanus asks of Alexander: "O tell me, what can better be than death?" With what rapture does not Ahasuerus take refuge in his sheltered grave at the moment when all other poor mortals must arise from theirs, and with what blissful joy does not he repeat his refrain, "Away to repose, eternal!"

As an old man, Paludan-Müller wrote his lengthy novel "Ivar Lykke," which contains a beautiful testimony of his ardent patriotic love and his upright mode of thought, but which otherwise is a work of but little poetic merit. He, who for thirty years had lived the life of a recluse, could not write novels. The colossal work in three volumes is completely outbalanced by the short poem, occupying but comparatively few pages, "Adonis," which was his parting word to the reading world. The latter is a heathen apotheosis of death. Wearied of Venus and of her restless pleasures, Adonis takes refuge in the realm of Proserpine, and there reposes in a state of eternal meditation. Proserpine accosts him in the following tender words:—

> Consolation seek with me!
> None of passion's fancies learning,
> No regrets, no sighs, no yearning—
> Meditation first shall be.

And the poem ends with this solemn and beautiful stanza:—

> In the realm to death made blest,
> Lethe's waters round them closing,
> These two lovers sat reposing,
> As for everlasting rest.
> All is silent as can be,
> And the vaulted skies up yonder
> Swarm with many a starry wonder,
> While the moon sinks in the sea.

In this dreamy attitude, at the feet of the goddess of death, let us leave the noble poet.

There he sits, while his most beautiful poetic visions glide in nebulous form before his eyes. He sees the River Styx. Venus, Urania, and Endymion sail in a boat down the stream, while the crown which Venus wears casts a brilliant starry sheen over the gloomy waves and shores. He sees Amor and Psyche blissfully floating by in lofty Kassiopeia and proud Orion; he descries Adam and Alma gliding past, as closely wrapped in the purifying flames of purgatory; he beholds Alexander kneeling before Kalanus, and the slender, refined form of the Indian, with the white bandage about his brow, and singing his swan's song, ascend from the funeral pyre through the smoke and the black clouds to Brahma.

> At the feet of her, his goddess,
> Happy now he sits and dreams;
> All aglow death's kingdom seems,

while his works survive him and render his name immortal.

There was always a great deal of sky in his paintings, but his name will be most enduringly united with that part of his pictures which portrays earth and the earthly.

VIII

BJÖRNSTJERNE BJÖRNSON

1882

BEYOND his fatherland Björnstjerne Björnson is known as a great poet. To Norway he is more than a poet. Not only has he written beautiful stories, songs, and dramas for his people; he lives the daily life of this people, and holds unbroken intercourse with them. He who has it in his power to create the most refined, the most delicate poetry, does not esteem himself above the rudest tasks, those of the journalist and the popular orator, where there is a question of furthering the moral and political education of the Norwegian people, by combating an error or a lie, or by ensuring the propagation of some simple, but as yet unrecognized truth. There emanates from him a breath of life. Where his spirit now penetrates there follows a development of self-knowledge and love of truth, national faults are shaken off, a growing interest is manifested in all intellectual topics, all public affairs, and a wholesome self-confidence appears side by side with this interest. He has grasped the significance of the poet's mission in its broadest sense.

In his oration at the unveiling of the Wergeland monument, May 17, 1881, Björnson said of his great predecessor, the European poet, who ranks next to Shelley:—

You have all heard how Henrik Wergeland, during one period of his life, was in the habit of carrying his pockets full of the seeds of trees, ever and anon strewing a handful of these about him in his daily walks, and how he endeavored to persuade his associates to do the same, because no one could know what the results might be. This is so true-hearted, so touchingly poetic an instance of patriotism, that it stands on the pinnacle of the best he has written.

What is here related in a literal sense of Wergeland may be told in a higher sense of Björnson. He is the great seed-

sower of Norway. This country is a mountainous land; it
is rocky, rugged, and barren. The seed falls on stony
ground, and many a grain is blown away by the wind.
Nevertheless, Björnson perseveres unweariedly in his labors.
A large quantity of his seed has already sprouted; many
a tree planted by his hand is already in blossom, and so far
as the fruit is concerned, his efforts were never designed
for the present generation alone.

I

It is only necessary to bestow a glance upon Björnson, in
order to be convinced how admirably he is equipped by
nature for the hot strife a literary career brings with it in
most lands, and especially in the combat-loving North.
Shoulders as broad as his are not often seen, nor do we
often behold so vigorous a form, one that seems as though
created to be chiselled in granite.

There is perhaps, no labor which so completely excites
all the vital forces, exhausts the nerves, refines and ener-
vates the feelings, as that of literary production. There
has never been the slightest danger, however, that the exer-
tions of his poetic productiveness would affect his lungs, as
in the case of Schiller, or his spine, as in the case of Heine;
there has been no cause to fear that inimical articles in the
public journals would ever give him his death-blow, as they
did Halvdan, the hero of his drama "Redaktören" (The
Editor), or that he would yield, as so many modern poets
have yielded, to the temptation of resorting to pernicious
stimulants or dissipations, as antidotes for the overwrought
or depleted state of the nervous system, occasioned by
creative activity. Nothing has injured Björnson's spine,
his lungs are without blemish and know no cough, while his
shoulders were fashioned to bear, without discomposure, the
rude thrusts which the world gives, and to return them.
As for his nerves, I am convinced that he has not learned
from personal experience the significance of the word. As
an author he is never nervous, neither when he displays his
true delicacy, nor even when he evinces his most marked

sentimentality. He has nothing of the refinement that a
light degree of work, duty, or fatigue gives.

Strong as the beast of prey whose name twice occurs in
his,[1] muscular, without the slightest trace of corpulence, of
an athletic build, he looms up vigorously in my mind, with
his massive head, his firmly compressed lips, and his sharp,
penetrating gaze from behind his spectacles. His exterior
reveals the son of a preacher, his voice, play of features and
gestures betray more of the actor's talent than poets usually
possess. It would be impossible for literary hostilities to
overthrow this man, and for him there never existed that
greatest danger to authors (a danger which for a long time
menaced his great rival, Henrik Ibsen), namely: that of
having his name shrouded in silence. Even as a very young
author (as a theatrical critic and political writer), he had
entered the field of literature with such an eagerness for
combat, that a rumbling noise arose about him wherever he
appeared. Like his own Thorbjörn in "Synnöve Solbakken" he displayed in early youth the combative tendency
of the athlete, but like his Sigurd in "Sigurd's Flight,"
he fought not merely to practise his strength, but from
genuine, although often mistaken love of truth and justice.
At all events, he understood thoroughly how to attract attention.

An author may possess great and rare gifts, and yet,
through lack of harmony between his own personal endowments and the national characteristics or the degree of
development of his people, may long be prevented from
attaining a brilliant success. Many of the world's greatest
minds have suffered from this cause. Many, as Byron,
Heine, and Henrik Ibsen, have left their native land; many
more who have remained at home have felt forsaken by
their compatriots. With Björnson the case is quite different. He has never, it is true, been peacefully recognized
by the entire Norwegian people; at first, because the form
he used was too new and unfamiliar; later, because his ideas
were of too challenging a nature for the ruling, conservative, and highly orthodox circles of the land; even at the

[1] Björn signifies bear.

present time he is pursued by the press of the Norwegian
government and by the leading official society, with a fury
which is as little choice in its selection of means as is in
other countries the exasperation felt by the champions of
thrones and altars. In spite of all this, Björnstjerne
Björnson has his people behind him and about him, as perhaps no other poet, unless it be Victor Hugo. When his
name is mentioned it is equivalent to hoisting the flag of
Norway. In his noble qualities and in his faults, in his
genius and in his weak points, he as thorougly bears the
stamp of Norway as Voltaire bore that of France. His
boldness and his naïveté, his open-heartedness as a man, and
the terseness of his style as an artist, the highly wrought
and sensitive Norwegian popular sentiment, and the lively
consciousness of the one-sidedness and the intellectual needs
of his fellow-countrymen that has driven him to Scandinavianism, Pan-Germanism, and cosmopolitanism,—all this
in its peculiar combination in him is so markedly national,
that his personality may be said to offer a *résumé* of the entire people. None of his contemporaries so fully represent
this people's love of home and of freedom, its self-consciousness, rectitude, and fresh energy. Indeed, just now
he also exemplifies, on a large scale, the people's tendency
to self-criticism, not that scourging criticism which chastises with scorpions, and whose representative in Norway is
Ibsen, in Russia, Turgenief, but that sharp, bold expression
of opinion begotten of love. He never calls attention to
an evil in whose improvement and cure he does not believe,
or to a vice which he despairs of seeing outrooted. For he
has implicit faith in the good in humanity, and possesses
entire the invincible optimism of a large, genial, sanguine
nature.

According to his character, he is half chieftain of a clan,
half poet. He unites the two forms most prominent in
ancient Norway: that of the warrior, and that of the skald.
In his intellectual constitution he is partly a tribune of
the people, partly a lay preacher; in other words, he combines, in his public demeanor, the political and religious
pathos of his Norwegian contemporaries, and this was yet

more apparent after he broke loose from orthodoxy than it was before. Since his so-called apostasy, in fact, he has been a missionary and a reformer to a greater degree than ever.

He could have been the product of no other land than Norway, and far less than other authors could he thrive in any but his native soil. In the year 1880, when the rumor spread through the German press, that Björnson, weary of continual wrangling at home, was about to settle in Germany, he wrote to me, "In Norway will I live, in Norway will I lash and be lashed, in Norway will I sing and die."

To hold such intimate relations with one's fatherland is most fortunate for a person who is sympathetically comprehended by this fatherland. And this is the case with Björnson. It is a matter dependent on conditions deeply rooted in his nature. He who cherishes so profound an enthusiasm for the reserved, solitary Michael Angelo, and who feels constrained, as a matter of course, to place him above Raphael, is himself a man of a totally different temperament,—one who is never lonely, even when most alone (as he has been since 1873 on his *gard* in remote Gausdal), but who is social to the core, or more correctly speaking, a thoroughly national character. He admires Michael Angelo because he reveres and understands the element of greatness, of profound earnestness, of mighty ruggedness in the human heart and in style; but he has nothing in common with the great Florentine's melancholy sense of isolation. He was born to be the founder of a party, and was, therefore, early attracted to enthusiastic and popular party leaders, such as the Dane Grundtvig and the Norwegian Wergeland, although wholly unlike either in his plastic, creative power. He is a man who needs to feel himself the centre, or rather the focus of sympathy, and insensibly he forms a circle about him, because his own nature is the *résumé* of a social union.

II

Björnstjerne Björnson was born Dec. 8, 1832, in a valley of the Dovre Mountains at a place called Kvikne, where his father was parish priest. The natural scenery of this region is cheerless, poor, and barren; the cliffs are mostly naked; here and there fir and birch may be dotted about, but the soil is so wretched, and the weather so severe, that the peasant can only count on a harvest one year out of every five. No grain-field would thrive in the vicinity of the parsonage. In the sparsely populated valley the farmhouses lay widely separated from one another. High banks of snow covered mountain and valley in the winter, surrounding every house with a bulwark, and inviting to trips in sledges and on snow-shoes. When the little Björnstjerne was six years old, his father was removed to Nässet in Romsdal, the region of all Norway most celebrated for its beauty. Lofty and majestic in their grandeur, the mountains rise up on either side of the valley with their boldly-formed pinnacles, which, as the plain sinks lower and lower, and the fjord is approached, gradually present themselves in more and more remarkable outlines to the eye. Very few Norwegian valleys can compare in wealth of varied beauty with Romsdal; even the flat character of the valley, as well as its unusual mountain formations, invest it with a peculiar stamp. The region was fertile and comparatively well populated; the farm-houses, most of them two stories high, were neat and pretty, and the inhabitants friendly, notwithstanding their silent reserve. The difference between this and the former place of residence was striking and impressive; it taught the child to reflect and to compare, to see the old in the light of the new, the new in the light of the old; to look upon himself with the eyes of others, and to become conscious of his own character. The grandeur of the surrounding nature and the busy, eager life of the people filled with glowing pictures the susceptible soul of the vigorous and richly endowed youth. Sent to the Latin school of the little town of Molde, he organized societies among the boys, and soon became a leader among his schoolmates. He read everything in the way of history and poetry he could get into his possession, the folk-lore tales of Asbjörnsen, the folk-songs of Landstad,—both but newly collected at that time,—the old Norse sagas of the kings, popular romances and poems, especially the works of Wergeland, which he devoured with passionate eagerness. At seventeen years of age he went to Christiania, in order to prepare for the entrance examination at the university. There he devoted himself chiefly to Danish literature, entered into intimate relations of friendship with the genial, although eccentric, Aasmund Vinje, who had already won a name as a dialect poet, as well as with the historian Ernst Sars, a young man of his own age, who did not become known to fame until later, and overflowing with youthful spirits, he led a life agitated by many and varied intellectual pursuits. The Danish theatre, at that time under the most careful management, interested him and exercised the most lively influence upon him. When, in the year 1852, he returned as a student to the parental roof, and passed there a year, the life of the people was revealed to him in a new light. He lived with the people, and wrote popular songs, which were often committed to memory and sung by the peasants.

Returned to Christiania, he came before the public as a critic, especially as a dramatic critic, wrote with all the vehemence of genial youth, with all the injustice of a rising poet, and gained many enemies. In his reading at this period, he gave the preference to Danish thinkers of the epoch in literature then drawing to a close,—Heiberg, Sibbern, Kierkegaard,—and a little later he became gradually absorbed in the emotional world of Grundtvig. The latter's doctrine of a "cheerful Christianity" attracted Björnson as the antithesis of the gloomy pietism of his native land, the strong faith in the lofty endowments and mission of the Scandinavian North, which he found in Grundtvig, could not but captivate this typically northern youth who was so wholly unacquainted with Europe. Until a very few years ago traces of Grundtvig's influence could be detected in him. Even at the present time it is not wholly obliterated. In those early days he found within the boundaries of Grundtvigianism all that which later, when he had torn himself free from the magic spell of Grundtvig's sphere, he sought and found, outside of these limits,—humanity in its highest freedom and beauty. This was the result of the narrowness of his horizon. The conclusions of modern philosophy and social science had not been introduced in those days into the university of Christiania. Valuable results were accomplished in specialties, but intellectual intercourse with Europe was otherwise cut off here as well as in Denmark. In fact there was no European consciousness at the university. The priest's son from a retired village, the scholar from a small city, was not removed, even in the metropolis, from the circles of variously shaded orthodoxy. Hence the circumscribed, sometimes childish element in Björnson's first works; hence the self-sufficient naïveté, so unique of its kind, which at this period constitutes his strength as a poet.

A few trips into the neighboring countries,—first of all his participation in the expedition of the students to Upsala, in 1856, immediately thereupon a prolonged residence in Copenhagen,—brought his poetic talents to maturity. He had already begun his little drama "De Nygifte" (The Newly Married Couple), but had laid it aside with a keen sense of the inadequacy of his powers, not to resume work on it until ten years later. In brief lyric poems of the genuine folk-song character he had calmed his creative impulse without satisfying it. He now wrote the firstling of his dramatic muse, "Mellem Slagene" (Between the Battles), an earnest little play in one act, that treats of an episode from the Norwegian civil war of the early Middle Ages, and whose terse, rugged prose style, which formed the sharpest contrast to the sonorous, verbose iambics of the Danish dramas of the Oehlenschläger school, inaugurated a new form of the Northern style. The play was rejected by Heiberg, at that time director of the royal theatre at Copenhagen, was first produced on the stage in Christiania, and was not printed until some time afterward. How far Björnson and the entire later poetic literature have progressed on the path thus broken, can be best observed by witnessing to-day a theatrical performance of this little drama, which on its first appearance repelled, because of the supposed wildness of its materials and the harshness of their treatment, and which now actually seems to us quite idyllic and by far too sentimental.

Meanwhile, his mission to write novels of peasant life became even clearer to Björnson, and after publishing anonymously a few shorter stories, by way of experiment, he gave the public, in 1857, his "Synnöve Solbakken." This literary début was a victory, and the reception of the little volume in Denmark, whose verdict is usually the decisive one for the poetic creations of Norway, especially tended to make it a decided triumph. The fresh originality, the novelty of the materials, and the manner in which they were handled, does not sufficiently explain this success. It was the result of the remarkable harmony of the book, with all that was desired and demanded of a poetic work by a portion of the reading world of the day. The national liberal party of that time (the party name was first adopted in Germany at a later period) absolutely determined the literary taste; it demanded something of a primeval Northern, vigorously national, ancient Scandinavian character, and at the same time,—an element which seemed curiously at variance with this,—Christian ethics, combined with an innocent idyllic tone, a poetry which banished Titanic defiance and modern passion with equal severity from its sphere. In the eyes of the national liberal party, passion was unpoetic and melancholy was affectation; the party of intelligence, as it is modestly called and still calls itself, deemed everything European suspicious, and believed that the far North alone had preserved that moral purity and freshness which was to regenerate the decaying civilization of Europe, and as for modern ideas, in the strictest sense of the words, they simply had no existence for the blissful ignorance of this party. Björnson's stories of peasant life, without considering their great and true merits, almost seemed like the fulfilment of the party programme. The circumstances of the poet's youth, and his early reading had led him to regard peasant life in the light of the old Norse sagas; while he had gained through his familiarity with the life and thought of the peasants, on the other hand, a comprehension of the ancient sagas. His first long story, as well as many of his very short ones (as "The Father," "The Eagle's Nest," etc.), produced a revival of the old saga style, while the materials, in conformity with the wishes of the people, were popular, without being characterized by sharply pronounced realism. In Germany Teutonists alone are familiar with the Icelandic sagas; in the Scandinavian countries, these in many respects admirable and almost always interesting narratives, have not only been popular since the revival of the national sentiment, but have been surrounded by a certain halo of glory, as venerable monuments of a great past. Beyond all else their style has been held in high esteem. And this style, calm, epic in nature, always presenting a clear picture that in the antique time sprang into existence as the form suitable for the narration of discord, murder, revenge for bloodshed, arson, adventurous voyages and deeds of valor, was preserved by Björnson, or rather it was revived by him, and through its grandeur ennobled and exalted the subject-matter, the love life of young Norwegian peasant lads and lasses. The temperament of the poet was so thoroughly akin to that of the ancient story-teller, and the human race depicted by him was so completely in accord with that represented in ancient saga lore, that in spite of everything a harmonious whole was produced.

Björnson belongs to those fortunate beings who are not compelled to seek a form, because they possess one of their own. His earliest novel is a thoroughly ripe fruit. In his first venture he is classic. He is not one of those poets who throughout a long life are continually increasing the perfection of the artistic form of their works, and are unable to invest the latter with inner equilibrium until after hard struggles with refractory materials have been undergone. His career has not been like that of so many others, a mountain ascent amid clouds of mist, crowned only with a few sunny hours at the top; it has rather been an upward climbing, during which beautiful prospects have been disclosed to the eye at every stage. Indeed, his development has been of such a nature that even at the outset, with his original comparative narrowness or poverty of ideas, he grasped the highest artistic perfection of form, and eventually imparted to his works an ever richer ideal life and an ever increasing knowledge of the human heart. In thus enlarging their scope, however, he has never marred their poetic worth, but he has frequently somewhat sacrificed their plastic and classic equilibrium.

Nevertheless, it must not be thought that Björnson's first works were hailed with the unanimous applause which people now often profess to believe they received. There are many individuals to be found today in the Scandinavian countries, to whom it is satisfactory to point out some work of Björnson which they have always praised, in order that they may, with all the greater appearance of impartiality, censure his later creations. His first novels and dramas formed too strong a contrast with all that the public had been accustomed to admire to be received without opposition, and many people of literary culture who had been in hearty sympathy with the previously prevailing poesy, could not but feel their æsthetic creed to be violated by them. In Denmark, indeed, a great and rich school of poetry, whose influence had extended far into Norway, was on the eve of its decline. The sonorous pathos of Oehlenschläger still rang with its musical accents in every ear, his representations of the antiquity and early middle ages of the North seemed to men of the old school, even if outwardly less true, at least inwardly more true than the writings of Björnson; the unsurpassed elegance and grace of Henrik Hertz had enfeebled their taste for primitive simplicity, and finally people missed in the new Norwegian poetry the lofty philosophic culture which Heiberg had accustomed the public to require of the poet and to find in his works. I recollect distinctly how strange and novel "Synnöve Solbakken" and "Arne" seemed to me on their first appearance.

The opposing voices were hushed by the healthy taste for all that was genuine which has almost everywhere been preserved by the great reading-world, but the rapidity of the success was dependent on the circumstances that the ruling Scandinavian party took the new poetry under its protection and proclaimed the poet's fame abroad with a flourish of trumpets. In those days the adherents of the national liberal party of the three Scandinavian countries were favorably inclined to the peasant in literature. People loved the peasant in the abstract; the real, concrete peasant was yet unknown to them. They had granted him the right of suffrage, they had felt convinced that he would continue throughout all time to permit himself to be guided by those "who had conferred on him the gift of freedom," and they lived in hopes that he would never use this "freedom" for any other purpose than to elect and honor his city benefactors. For this reason the peasant at that time was still called by the organs of the great cities the healthy pith of the people; in him was seen the scion of the knights of antiquity; he was celebrated in song and addressed in flattering terms. Works of fiction which glorified his life with extreme delicacy, and at the same time in a new and elevated style, were sure of an enthusiastic reception in Denmark, especially when they originated in one of the sister-countries, which stood almost nearer to the heart of every true Scandinavian than his own fatherland.

The blasé citizen of Copenhagen had, moreover, the same predilection for the peasant novels of Björnson that in the past century had been cherished for pastoral romances and pastoral plays. The world had now become too critical to desire shepherdesses with red crooks, and lambs with red silk ribbons about their necks; but a substitute was found in the Norwegian lads and lasses, whose emotional life was as thoroughly refined and deep as that of a student or a young lady of the higher circles.

The peasant novel was in itself no new variety. The Jutland village and heath pictures of Steen Steensen Blicher began the series; they appeared about twenty years earlier than the first village tales of Berthold Auerbach, who, however, had been unacquainted with them, as no German translation of them had been published until toward the middle of the fourth decade of the century. It was Auerbach, who, after the way had been pointed out by Immermann in his "Oberhof," first in Germany treated the story of peasant life as an independent variety of the novel; for the first time a German poet became absorbed in the events and characters of the quiet villages. But several years before Auerbach's first attempt the great French novelist, George Sand, had achieved success in this field. She who had been born in the country, and who had passed beyond the stormy period of her life, felt an impulse to venture on pastoral poems, and she gave to France in "La mare au diable," "François le champi," etc., a little series of refined, ideally executed rural scenes.

Neither the "Village Tales of the Black Forest," nor the country stories of George Sand were known to Björnson when he made his début. He had learned nothing from Auerbach, nor had he anything in common with him. Two marked peculiarities distinguish the Norwegian peasant novels from the German. Auerbach is an epic poet; he depicts rural life in its entire breadth, he shows us the peasant in his daily occupations in the field and in the stable, enables us to observe his half-lazy, half-dignified sluggishness, his state of bondage in manners and customs, his daily routine. Björnson is neither decidedly an epic poet nor a dramatist proper; his strength lies in producing dramatic effects within epic limits; and this is the reason why everything with him is so brief and so concise. The fact is, exterior matters are related by him solely for the sake of the heart history for which they form a setting. Another distinction is the following: the rural tales of Auerbach are written from a view of life which the poet does not share with the peasant, which he does not hold in common with his hero and heroine. Auerbach did not write from the standpoint of a childlike mind and a childlike faith. He was a man of learning, and a thinker; he possessed the rich and many-sided culture of the German mind of his young days. He had been a pupil of Schelling; he had made his début with a novel about Spinoza, whose works he had translated, and whose views of life he had made his own, to proclaim them abroad as long as he lived. To be sure, he had remodelled Spinozaism to suit his own needs and sympathies,—for it is indeed, more than doubtful whether Spinoza would have especially warmed to the idea of making a hero of that finite being, that circumscribed intelligence, called the villager,—but he accepted the doctrines of Spinoza as the gospel of nature, the philosopher himself as the apostle of religion of nature, the worship of nature. Auerbach was partial to the representation of the peasant, because the latter was to him a bit of nature, and it delighted him to seek in the unsophisticated soul the germ of that life philosophy which to him seemed the only true philosophy, the one which was destined to gain a speedy triumph over all others. Let the reader observe in his classic novel "Barfüssele" (Little Barefoot) how the bold young peasant maiden, far from heeding the command to offer her left cheek to any one who might smite her on the right, passes through life with clenched fists, and neither deems herself in the slightest degree to blame, nor suffers on that account the least humiliation. The spirit pervading these books is the political passion of Germany before the March revolution, to elevate the common man to a comprehension of the political and religious ideal of the educated classes. Quite different is the relation of the narrator to his materials in Björnson's peasant tales. In all essentials the poet was grounded in the same views of life as his heroes; his writings are no effusions of a philosophic mind. A poetic and artistic genius, no superior intellect addresses the reader from these pages. Hence the remarkable unity of sentiment and tone.

The excellencies were specifically poetic; the tenderest sentiment was cast in the hardest form; the most refined, versatile observation was united with a lyric ardor which permeated the whole and burst into a freer course in numerous fugitive child, folk, and love songs. A vein of fundamental romance hovered over the narrative. The new order of novel admitted of being preluded without any disharmony by a nursery story, as in "Arne," in which plants conversed and vied with one another in their efforts. Notwithstanding the dry realism of certain of the characters, it was so idyllic that little detached stories, in which woodland sprites played a rôle, became wedded to the universally prevailing tone without causing any breach with the spirit of the general action. Björnson was a good observer and had amassed a store of little traits from which he constructed his tales. When his Arne is asked, "How do you manage when you make songs?" he replies, "I hoard up the thoughts that others are in the habit of letting go." Björnson might have given the same answer himself. And yet sagas, folk-songs, and folk-tales were the currents through whose intermingling his art-form became crystallized. He did not give it isolated grandeur, but kept himself through it in rapport with the popular mind.

"Synnöve Solbakken" was the plastic harmony within the limitation of Norwegian life, and the hero Thorbjörn was the type of the vigorous, stubborn youth, whose nature could only ripen to maturity through calming, soothing influences. "Arne," on the other hand, represented the lyric, yearning tendency of the people, that impulse of the viking blood which has been transformed into desire for travel, and the hero the type of the tender-hearted, dreamy youth who needed to be steeled in order to become a man. Much of the deepest, most elementary propensity of the Norwegian people, much of the peculiar youthful yearning of the poet himself, was committed to Arne's principal song which has become so celebrated. A sigh from the heart of the people may be heard in the following lines:—

> Shall I the journey never take
>   Over the lofty mountains?
> Must my poor thoughts on this rock-wall break?
> Must it a dread, ice-bound prison make,
>   Shutting at last in around me,
>   Till for my tomb it surround me?
> Forth will I! forth! Oh, far, far, away,
>   Over the lofty mountains!
> I will be crushed and consumed if I stay;
> Courage tow'rs up and seeks the way;
>   Let it its flight now be taking,
>   Not on this rock-wall be breaking![2]

---

[2] See Arne, pp. 167-169 (Houghton, Mifflin & Co., Boston) and The Norway Music Album, pp. 173-176 (Oliver Ditson & Co., Boston).

The yearning expressed in this poem is that which drove the sea-kings of old to the West and to the South, that which led Holberg, the great founder of the Norwegian-Danish literature, to roam over half of Europe on foot, and which at the present day is manifested in the emigration of so many Norwegian artists of all kinds.

If the two larger stories "Synnöve" and "Arne" formed such perfect complements of each other, the third story "En glad Gut" (A Happy Boy) was like a refreshing breeze bringing deliverance from the brooding melancholy that oppresses the Norwegian mind, and sweeping it away in the name of a healthy temperament. This production contained the joyous message of unsophisticated vital powers and love of life; it was like a fresh song, bubbling over with laughter and purifying the atmosphere.

III

Then followed dramas and poems. The strong personality of Björnson gradually worked its way out of the swaddling-clothes of the national mind. In "Between the Battles," "Sigurd Slembe" (Sigurd the Bad), and "Arnliot Gelline," will be found the same grand type, the hero born to be a chieftain, created to be the benefactor of his people, a being alike powerful and noble, but whose rights are withheld from him, and who is compelled, owing to the injustice under which he suffers, to cause a large amount of evil on his way to the goal, although he desires only good. Whole towns are left in flames behind Sverre, wherever he may fare. He tells of this with the bitterest anguish in "Between the Battles." "I know a chieftain," he exclaims, "who longed to be a blessing to his country, but who became its curse. He shudders with horror at his own wretched fate, and would have fled from all the hideous corpses that stare him in the face from border to border of the land; would have fled as an exile from his own hereditary kingdom, had there not been those who clung to his mantle. So he is led, as by an inexorable fate, from one bloody deed of violence to another, from conflagration to conflagration, over reeking corpses and heaps of ruins, while shrieks and wails of lamentation pursue him, and all hell is let loose about him, and people say the devil walks at his side; in truth, some say he is the devil! I know— ah! I know that while those about him are slaughtering one another like so many cattle, he has not the heart to lay his hand on a single man, lest he should intensify his own misery. And masses are sung before the battle, and masses after the battle; he strives to make atonement and to heal; he brings relief to the suffering and assuages ills; to those who ask it of him he gives peace; but there is one to whom it will be long ere he can bring peace, and that is himself." Sigurd, the hero of the trilogy "Sigurd Slembe," is despised and persecuted because he who desired only justice for himself and happiness for Norway, betrayed into the hands of his enemies by his half-brother, the feeble-minded Harold Gille, becomes the murderer of the latter. He had gone to his brother, after long renunciation and bitter inward struggles, with the best intention in the world, and the most ardent desire to come to a peaceful understanding with him, and he leaves him, having escaped from the guard to whom the murder was entrusted, "a king in the armor of revenge, with the eye of despair and a flaming sword." Arnljot, who in the innermost depths of his soul is so good, so humble, becomes an incendiary and a pillager until the day when, as the knight of Olaf, he meets his death at Stiklestad. These characters are deeply rooted in the poet's soul. He had early encountered passionate opposition, had felt himself misunderstood and hated by his opponents. With his indomitable ambition, with the vehemence that was inherent in his nature, and the tenderness that belonged to his temperament, he felt himself wondrously akin to those saga forms, and whenever he was conscious of being misunderstood and unjustly scorned by his people, he laid the burden of his longing to elevate this people, and to harmonize them with himself, and his consciousness that with all his good designs he had estranged his people from him at times, upon the characters of these old chieftains; this Sigurd, for instance, who when excited becomes a changed being, "hard as a steel-spring, bounding without a footfall o'er the floor, with flashing, evil eyes, and voice that seemed to come from a long, dark passage," but who, nevertheless, conceals within his soul a veritable horn of plenty, overflowing with magnificent plans for the public weal. Profoundly, indeed, must Björnson have suffered in his youth to be able to write Sigurd's soliloquy in the winter night, or the one toward the end of the drama, beginning with the words, "The Danes have forsaken me? Lost the battle? Thus far—and never farther?" in which mighty plans,—to assemble an army, to sail far away, to become a merchant, a crusader,—arise with giddy swiftness and are rejected, until the impression of approaching dissolution again obtrudes itself. Then the words "Thus far—and never farther," return no longer as a question, but refrain-like as an answer. Even in the midst of despair love of fatherland, which in this case is love of the enemy, thus finds utterance: "Ah, this beautiful land was not by me to be governed. Great is the wrong I have done it! How, ah! how was this possible? When absent I saw in ev'ry cloud thy mountains; I yearned for home like a child for Christmas; and yet I sought not my home,—and I gave thee wound on wound."

Great personality with Björnson is not encased in Michael-Angelo-like pride; it works its way out of the national spirit only to strive, yearningly, to return to it again. Its most ardent desire is to become united with this spirit, and profound, indeed, is the tragedy where this union is prevented.

In this point Björnson forms the sharpest contrast to the man who is his peer among contemporary Norwegian poets, Henrik Ibsen. Ibsen is solitary by nature. "In distant lands I rest lonely," he cries. These lines, which are the refrain of the well-known poem, "Langt borte" (In Distant Lands), written on the occasion of the trip of the Scandinavian students to Upsala in 1875, form the motto of his life. He penetrates the depths of the earth, like his miner.

> Make way for me, thou heavy hammer,
> To the heart's most secret chamber.

Ibsen seeks the solitary silence of night. In his poem
"Lysræd" (Afraid of Light), he declares that as a child
he was afraid of being in the dark; but that everything has
become changed, the glare of daylight now bewilders him,
the noise of life makes him weak and ready to swoon away.
Only hid beneath the shelter of night's veil of terror, his
will is armed for deeds of daring. Without the cover of
night he is helpless, and he well knows that if ever he accomplishes a great work, it will be a deed of darkness.

In the spirited and beautiful words of the poem the
author has depicted his own temperament. The nature of
Björnson, on the contrary, does not strive downward; its
aspirations rise upward and outward. His genius has open
arms.

Another contrast between the two poets may be felt in
the Northern dramas penned by both during their first
period. As a born dramatist, Ibsen has no bent, no inclination, for descriptions of nature. His principal dramatic
characters, in his youth, were personifications of an idea,
not modelled directly from nature, and in his almost exceptionally dramatic poems, exterior nature necessarily
plays but an evanescent rôle. Even where nature is introduced by him, with most thrilling effect, as in the "ice-church" in "Brand," it is rather as a symbol than as a
reality; the ice-church is the church in which he who forsakes the established churches runs great danger of meeting
his end. The freer, more expansive spirit of Björnson
dwells lingeringly on the natural surroundings of Norway
and imparts the impressions received from them to his
dramas. Let us give as an example of this the scene between
Sigurd and the Finnish maiden, one of the most beautiful
scenes that Björnson has written. When the maiden, announced by her long quavering shout of exultation, steps
upon the stage, she brings with her the entire nature of the
Northland, as her realm. The daughter of the Finnish
chieftain reveals herself as a glimpse of the radiance of
the Northern Lights; her words have the brilliant charm of
the midnight sun; her glad love of life, of the sunshine of
summer, her unreciprocated love for Sigurd, the delicate

and transitory nature of her sorrow,—all this is a fragment of the living poetry of nature. Masterly, indeed, is the description of her appearance given by Sigurd.

The Finnish Maiden.—Can you feel how beautiful it is here?
Sigurd.—Oh, yes! at times I can. When I stand before my cavern and gaze upon the eternal snow;—o'er it the tree-tops by twilight resemble weird spectres, each other approaching. Then you, on your snowshoes, come stormily down the mountains; all your dogs are around you, your troop follows after, and the size of all seems to grow three times larger. O'er your wild and blustering train, and this world of enchanting romance around it, the Northern Lights, with their brilliant colors and forms, now congregating, now spreading wide their splendor. . . .

This keen sense of nature is common to all Björnson's Norse characters of the olden time. He has imparted to them his own modern feelings. The little epic poem, "Arnljot Gelline" (consisting of fifteen brief cantos), in particular, is unsurpassed for the beauty of its descriptions of nature. The song, "During the Springtime Inundation," describing the plunge which the mountain streams, swollen by the water from the melting snow, make into the valleys below, and the anxious huddling together in the mountain caves of the terrified wild beasts, paints in indelible colors an annual episode of Norwegian nature, transplanted some eight hundred years into the past, and which is consequently rendered wilder and more forcible than at the present day. The canto "Arnljot's Yearning for the Ocean," in whose rhythm we feel the monotonous ebb and flow of the sea, is one of the most beautiful of all the poems that have ever portrayed the poetry of the sea. Byron had depicted the unruliness, the inexorableness, the fury of the ocean; Björnson paints the deep melancholy, the phlegmatic coldness, the ransoming freshness of the surging billows. Listen to the opening stanzas of the poem:—

> The sea I long for, the mighty ocean,
> That onward rolls in its calm majestic;
> With banks of billowy vapor freighted,
> To meet itself it doth ever wander.

> The sky may lower, the shore may signal,
> The sea recedes not, nor pauses ever;
> In summer nights, 'mid the storms of winter,
> Its billows murmur the self-same yearning.
> The sea I pine for, ah, yes! the ocean,
> With brow so cold tow'rd the heaven lifted.
> Behold how earth in the sea casts shadows,
> And whispering mirrors there all her sorrows!
> The sun tho' strokes it with warm, bright touches,
> Of life's delights utters words intrepid;
> Yet ever ice-cold, mournfully peaceful
> It buries sorrow and consolation.
> The full moon draws it, the tempest rouses,
> Yet vain all effort to stay its current;
> Laid waste tho' the lowland, tho' mountains crumble,
> It grandly sweeps tow'rd eternity.
> Yet all it draws must its waves close over;
> What once is sunk in the sea never rises.
> No shrieks are heard, and reveal'd no message,
> The ocean's language there's none can interpret.
> Then seek the sea, go out on the ocean,
> All ye who never can know atonement!
> To all who sorrow it brings deliv'rance,
> Yet onward carries its own enigma.
> That singular bond with Death but consider,
> It gives him all but itself—the ocean.
> Thy melancholy allures me, O ocean!
> My feeble plans how they fade and dwindle;
> I swiftly banish my anxious yearnings;
> Thy cold, cold breath brings peace to my bosom.

The music of the waves here produces the effect of a magnificent cradle song. It is one to the dreaming hero whose great hope is that he may be able to see the nails give way in the planks of his ship, as death opens the portals to the stream of ransoming waters, and himself, covered by eternal silence, rest in the depths below, while in sublime moonlight nights, when the silver sheen of the moonbeams plays on the mighty surface, "the waves his name tow'rd the strand are rolling."

IV

Twice in his life Björnson has officiated as theatre-director: 1857-59 in Bergen, 1865-67 in Christania. In the

autumn of 1857, in pursuance of an invitation from Ole
Bull, he undertook the management of the stage in the
former provincial city, which is always alive with political
and intellectual agitations, and he brought the theatre,
which had greatly run down, to a high degree of excellence,
while at the same time he passed happy days of his youth
in the society of Ole Bull. As director of the stage in
Christiania he had a successful but all too brief career.
He himself possesses so many of the qualities of a great
actor that he was well calculated to make an admirable
manager; the scenic art of his native land owes much to
him, for it was he who guided the first wavering efforts to
make a national stage.

His experiences as a stage-manager have served him in
very good stead as a play-writer; nevertheless, he has
never attained technical perfection in this capacity. His
dramas contain far more poetry than skilful manipulation.
"Sigurd," the great trilogy, is not adapted to the stage,
and, as far as I am aware, has never been performed.[3]
His vigorous and wildly passionate youthful drama,
"Hulda," gains little or nothing by being put on the
stage. Two of the plays of his first period, however, have
met with a complete stage success. "Maria Stuart in
Scotland" (1864) and De Nygifte" (The Newly Married
Couple, 1865).

"Maria Stuart" is a rich and powerful work, full of
dramatic life, almost too violently intense. All the details of the plot are admirably linked together,—Rizzio's
murder, Darnley's death, and Bothwell's elopement with
Maria; the finale alone is weak, or more correctly speaking,
the drama has no finale. It is my belief that the poet succeeded so well simply because on Scottish soil he still felt
himself encompassed by the atmosphere of Norway. These
Scots of his are of Norse origin. Bothwell says: "Since
the hour when my will struck root in events, I have seen it
grow. One day in a tempest I sought refuge with my fleet

[3] After this was written it was placed on the stage by Björnson's own son Björn Björnson, then manager of the Christiania
Theatre.—Tr.

among the Orkney Islands; the sea tossed us wildly, the clouds drifted o'er us like bits of wet sails, the billows broke with loud rumbling on the sharp and treeless shore. Ah, then I felt my kindred near at hand, the Norse Viking race that drifted in days of yore to this coast, and from which we are descended. Aye, it was a tree of rugged will, that took root in the rocks, but 'neath the shelter of this tree a people build to-day." In this Norwegian-Scottish world, the poet feels perfectly at home, and the characters, created by him without any breach with local coloring, have traits very nearly akin to the forms from the Norse Middle Ages that he was so well accustomed to portray. The most marked of the main characters are the Puritan John Knox, the gloomy yet pleasure-loving, wildly energetic Bothwell, and the weak, boyishly revengeful and unworthily humble Darnley; Bothwell a genuine Renaissance personality, Darnley almost too modern. Maria Stuart herself is not so successfully drawn; the traits of her character are too effeminately indistinct. She is conceived as a being, the mysterious foundation of whose nature is revealed in two opposite poles,—that of absolute feminine weakness, and that of absolute feminine strength. Her fate is dependent on her nature, so far as this weakness is the cause of her power over men, and this strength is useless in the affairs given her to manage in that violent age. She is, however, by virtue of Northern idealism, by virtue of the innate modesty of the poet who is a priest's son, entirely too lacking in the sensuous element, moreover, too passive to be the heroine of a drama. She is delineated less through what she says and does than through enthusiastic or deprecatory mention and the direct influence exercised by her personality. She is enveloped in a cloud of adjectives designating her character, hurled at her in masses by the other characters in the drama. "Maria Stuart" owes its origin to a period in the progress of Björnson's development, when he had a tendency, perhaps owing to Kierkegaard's influence, to describe his characters psychologically, instead of allowing their natures to unfold of themselves without any commentary. All the personages in these dramas are psychologists; they study one another, explain one another's temperaments, and experiment with one another. Even the page, William Taylor, understands and describes the spiritual condition of Darnley, as a physician understands and draws a diagnosis of a disease. Murray and Darnley paint themselves, Lethington portrays Bothwell and Murray, Maria queries about the key to Rizzio's character, Knox about that to Darnley's; indeed, the murder of Rizzio is a psychological experiment performed by Darnley on Maria, in view of winning her back through terror, as he has failed to win her through love. While all the characters thus think like psychologists, they all speak like poets, and this Shakespearean splendor of diction, so true to life because the people of the Renaissance period, being poetic throughout in their feelings, used a flowery, highly figurative language, enhances the charm with which the profound originality of the main characters invests the drama.

The little drama, "The Newly Married Couple," treats of a very simple yet universal human relation, the severing of the ties that bind a young wife to the parental home, the collision in the soul of a young woman between the inbred and familiar affection for her parents, and the yet new and feeble love for her husband,—a revolution, or rather an evolution, which is preceded by the natural conditions and the pangs of a spiritual birth. Under ordinary, normal circumstances the significance of this breach is not brought into such sharp prominence, because it is accepted as something which cannot be otherwise, and which frequently bears the stamp of a release rather than of a rupture. If, however, the relations be conceived as a trifle less normal, if the affection of the parents be uncommonly egotistical or tender, and if the love of the good and dutiful daughter for her husband be far less developed than her well-cultivated feeling of reverence for her father and mother, there arises a problem to be solved, a dramatic collision, and a struggle with an uncertain *dénouement*. It is greatly to Björnson's credit and honor that he has grasped this idea.

Its execution suffers under a twofold defect. The fact is, the tone of this drama, as well as of "Maria Stuart," is weakened, in the first place, by excessive Northern modesty, and in the second place, by the psychological caprice of the author. Necessarily the question forces itself upon the spectator: Is Laura, in the beginning of the play, Axel's wife, in the full sense of the word, or is she not? She must be his wife, for her coldness is not of a character that would explain the opposite; and yet, how can it be that she is his wife? for if she were, the difficulties would be removed, and tenderness would gradually take effect without all this noise in the presence of witnesses. A still more serious objection to the plan of the little drama is the following: How can Axel, when he has already, by a most energetic effort, torn Laura from the parental home, be weak and stupid enough to permit this home, in the form of Mathilde, to accompany Laura on her journey? Without Mathilde, everything would, of course, have been far more easily managed and have gone far more smoothly. To be sure, we are told at the end of the play that without her the husband and wife would never have truly found each other. This is, however, by no means obvious, and is not at all happy. The poetic task proper would have been to show how the young couple, without any outside aid, became truly wedded; it is a very poor expedient to have a *dea ex machina* write an anonymous novel, which startles Axel and Laura by its treatment of their position, and drives them into each other's arms. In this I see a token of the epoch in which this little drama arose. The air was filled with the Kierkegaard ideas. The method of the natural sciences (observation and essay), applied to the intercourse between one human being and another, the psychologic experiment that plays so large a rôle with Kierkegaard, and that became so expansive in "Maria Stuart," is represented in "The Newly Married Couple" by the household friend Mathilde. The manner in which love and passion are treated throughout this drama is peculiar to that period in the spiritual life of Björnson, and of Norwegian-Danish literature in general. Northern people took very little interest at that time in the tender passion for itself alone; the emotions were studied and portrayed in their relation to morality and religion. The representation of love before marriage, or outside of marriage, was looked upon as trivial or frivolous, and what was demanded of the poet was conjugal love, which Kierkegaard in his "Either—Or" had extolled as by far the higher love. The love that in "The Newly Married Couple" is pointed out as great, is described as the debt the wife owes her husband, and is held up before her eyes, from every side, as that which is chiefly required of her. It is no plant of free, wild growth; it unfolds itself in the hot-house of duty, nurtured by the tenderness of Axel, artificially forced into growth by the jealousy, unrest, and dread of loss with which Mathilde heats the hot-house. A little French folk-song says:—

> Ah! si l'amour prenait racine,
> J'en planterais dans mon jardin,
> J'en planterais, j'en semerais
> Aux quatre coins,
> J'en donnerais aux amoureux
> Qui n'en ont point.

These lines have always come into my mind whenever I have read or seen "The Newly Married Couple." Yet the fault lies, perhaps, in my partiality; I love beautiful, great Eros, but I find no satisfaction in those little, pale, erotic offshoots that hale to be wearisomely nurtured from the bottle. The public has not shared my opinion, however, for few plays have had so marked a success on the stage, or lived through so many editions in book form.

V

An enterprising Danish bookseller, some time during the sixth decade of the present century, issued a calendar, for which he solicited short vignette poems by well-known authors, each one of whom was requested to choose his own month. When the man applied to Björnson, the latter wrote:—

> Young April's praise I'll sing!
> The old in April falleth,
> The new is firmly planted;
> Its turmoil wild appalleth,—

> And yet, if peace were granted,
>   Nor will, nor deed, 'twould bring.
> Yes, April's praise I'll sing!
>   Because it stormeth, sweepeth,
> Because, with forces living,
>   It smileth, melteth, weepeth,
> Because it is life-giving,—
>   For summer's born in spring.

It would scarcely have been possible to give a better characterization of his entrance into his own first period. The beautiful novel, Fiskerjenten'' (The Fisher Maiden), 1868, which, less idealistic than the author's tales of peasant life, yet more nearly approaching his later style, conveyed in the poem introduced into it, called "The Young Viking," a remarkable presentation of the poet's own first struggles and his speedily gained mastership. Although Björnson has not written a large number of lyric poems, and is no correct versifier, he has, nevertheless, accomplished some ever-memorable and imperishable results in the domain of lyrics. His popular songs are noted for their purity and genuineness. His patriotic poems have become national songs. His few old Norse descriptions or monologues have hit that style of the ancient North which Oehlenschläger and Tegnér never attained. Read in the drama "Hulda" the little poem written in dialect, which Gunnar sings, and of which Lobedanz, the German translator, appropriately remarks, "In the Norwegian summer, which knows no nightingale, winter has a terror-inspiring influence as it appears in the song of Nils Finn, a sort of ballad that may be ranked with Goethe's "Erl-King." It is the story of a little boy who has lost his snow-shoes, and who, dragged downward by the powers of the deep, is swallowed up in the snow. This simple occurrence, however, is represented with a power of imagination that renders it immortal, especially the concluding lines, in which the two long snow-shoes are represented as being all that was left behind, are most impressive and awe-inspiring. Let me here cite the last stanzas, viz. :—

> The rock laughs with scorn, snow covers its side,
> But Nils knit his fist, and swore that it lied.

'Have a care!' was heard below.
But the avalanche yawns, the clouds break asunder,
Thought Nils Finn: 'My grave I see yonder.'
'Art ready?' was heard below.
Two shoes stood in the snow and looked around,
They saw not a thing, and heard not a sound.
'Where is Nils?' was heard below.

It is only needful to study a few lines of Björnson's patriotic poems in order to comprehend fully why it was they became national songs. Let me choose by way of example four lines of the most peculiarly Björnsonic national song, which has completely supplanted the older national songs of Norway. The lines read as follows, in the metrical translation:—

> Yes, we love with fond devotion
> Norway's mountain domes,
> Rising storm-lashed, o'er the ocean,
> With their thousand homes.[4]

Literally they read thus: "Yes, we love this country, as it rises furrowed, weather-beaten, from the ocean, with its thousand homes." It would be impossible to reproduce in a more accurate, genial way, the impression which the coast of Norway makes upon the son of the land when he approaches it from the ocean.

Among all the shorter compositions of Björnson the most eminent is the monologue "Bergliot." It is the wail of a chieftain's wife over her assassinated husband, Einar Tambarskelver, and her only son who lies slain at his side. I know of nothing in the modern reproduction of old Norse poetry that has ever made so deep an impression on me as the refrain-like recurrence of the words with which Bergliot addresses the driver of the cart on which she had had the dead body of her husband lifted: —

> Drive slowly; for thus drove Einar ever—
> Even so will home be reached soon enough.

[4] See Synnöve Solbakken, p. 16 (Houghton, Mifflin & Co., Boston), and Norway Music Album, pp. 131, 132 (Oliver Ditson & Co., Boston).

The first line represents with wonderful simplicity the calm and proud dignity of the slain chieftain, the second embraces in the fewest possible words the profound bitterness of the desolated life.

VI

This eminence was early reached by Björnson. When but thirty-one years of age he had written all the best works of his first period, and they were even then viewed by the public as a completed whole. No one could overlook his magnificent endowments; it produced rather a painful effect, however, that no development of them could be detected. His creative power for a long time remained centered in one and the same point; but his views of life did not expand; they remained childish and narrow. Sometimes he could actually be trivial. Now and then he wrote poems that almost had the tone and coloring of Northern songs of the people's school-teacher style. Too strong traces of the influence of Grundtvig could be detected in them. It is to the credit of this great man (1783-1872), the intellectual awakener of the Northern peasant classes, that he gave a vigorous impulse to the education of the people through the establishment of numerous peasants' high schools. For a leader of the people, however, the culture represented by his high schools was not adequate, and for a long time Björnson vainly endeavored to make poetic progress in the wooden shoes of the Grundtvigians. He kept himself, for the most part, at a distressing distance from the life and the ideas of his contemporaries. Or rather, if he did represent the ideas of his contemporaries, it was involuntarily; they were brought forward in the theatrical costumes of the ancient Norsemen or of the Scottish Middle Ages. In "Sigurd Slembe," Helga and Frakark discuss in the year 1127 the relation between the immortality of the individual and that of the race in phrases which remind us too strongly of the year 1862; and the same chieftains, whose minds are filled with almost modern political reflections, who use such expressions as vocation and fundamental law, and speak of establishing order on a foundation without law, etc., have the imprisoned Sigurd, from motives of revenge, broken limb by limb on the wheel; in other words, they are guilty of an action which would presuppose a far more barbarous inner life than they have otherwise displayed. People that express themselves in terms indicative of so much culture do not break their enemies on the wheel; they scourge them with their tongues.

To this lack of unity in passion and thought was added the unhappy necessity of the poet to so group and combine his principal dramatic forms that the mantle of the orthodox church faith should be draped about them at the moment when the curtain falls. In "Maria Stuart" the form of John Knox is not subject to the dramatic irony that governs the other personages. Björnson does not reserve to himself a poetic supremacy over him: for Knox is destined to step forth from the theatrical framework at the conclusion of the play, with the pathos of the poet on his lips, and, as the representative of the people, receive the political inheritance of Maria. The vigorous combats in "Sigurd," as well as the passionate emotions in "Maria Stuart," find their outlet in a hymn. The action in both dramas is brought to so fine a point that in one it flows into the crusader's song of the pious Danish poet Ingemann, in the other into the mystic hymn of the Puritans. Gradually it began to appear as though the once so rich vein of the poet was well nigh drained. His later stories ("The Railroad and the Churchyard" and "A Problem of Life") bore no comparison to his earlier ones, and the drama "Sigurd Jorsalfar" (Sigurd the Crusader) could be compared quite as little to the older Norse dramas of the poet. The last cantos of "Arnljot Gelline," which were written several years later than the rest, are decidedly inferior to those composed in the first glow of inspiration. Evidently no new ideas germinated in Björnson's mind. People began to ask if the history of this author was to be that of so many Danish authors who had grown mute in the prime of their manhood because their genius lacked the capacity to shed its chrysalis. Björnson had apparently exhausted his original intellectual capital. The public wondered if he could acquire new wealth, as the others had been unable to do.

These years are indelibly stamped on my memory. The mind of youth experienced somewhat of a pang in comparing the literary condition of the greater part of Europe with that of the North. There was a sense of being shut out from the cultured life of Europe. In Denmark, the elder generation, through its repugnance to everything German, had interrupted the intellectual intercourse with Germany; the channel through which European civilized thought had hitherto been received was obstructed; at the same time, French culture was shunned as frivolous, and English culture was but rarely comprehended, as the English language was excluded from the course of studies in the schools of learning. In Denmark people looked to Norway as the land of literary revival; in Norway all eyes were turned to Denmark as the land of older civilization, and people scarcely noticed the lull in Danish culture. Now while intellectual life faded and drooped, as a plant becomes blighted in a damp place, the cultivated classes of both countries believed themselves to be the salt of Europe. People did not know that the foreign nations they had dreamed of rejuvenating through their idealism, their Grundtvigianism, their faith, had taken a great start in advance of them especially in literary culture. In the leading social circles of the Scandinavian countries, people spoke of David Strauss and Feuerbach, as the most narrow-minded circles of Germany had spoken of them in the period from 1840 to 1850; Stuart Mill, Darwin, and Herbert Spencer were scarcely known by name, and there was not the slightest conception of the development of English poetry from Shelley to Swinburne. Modern French literature was condemned without any conception of the significance of the fact that the drama and the romance in France had long since forsaken historical and legendary material, and had grasped subjects from the immediate present, the only ones a poet can observe with his own eyes and study.

People scarcely dared raise for themselves so much as a corner of the curtain that concealed the contemporary world from their gaze.

VII

Immediately after this, in the years 1871-72, there began in Denmark a modern literary movement out of which arose during the succeeding ten years a new poetic and critical school. The intellectual life thus awakened in Denmark was quickly transplanted to Norway, and soon the poetic creations of Björnson revealed the fact, as he has himself expressed it, that after his fortieth year new and rich streams had welled up in the innermost depths of his being. Suddenly it became apparent that his productiveness had soared upward into a new state of activity. The modern world lay open before his eyes. He had gained, as he once wrote to me "eyes that saw and ears that heard." The ideas of the century had, unconsciously to himself, worked their way into his receptive spirit and secretly fructified it. During these years he had read, with ravenous eagerness, books in all languages and of every variety, works on the natural sciences, critical, philosophical, and historical works, romances, foreign periodicals, and newspapers by the quantities. A profound impression was made upon him by the calm grandeur and the sublime free thought of Stuart Mill; Darwin's powerful hypotheses widened his intellectual horizon; the philological critique of a Steinthal, or a Max Müller, taught him to review religions, the literary critique of a Taine taught him to view literatures with new eyes. The young Danish school contributed not a little, as he has himself publicly declared, toward tearing him away from old things. The significance of the eighteenth, the problems of the nineteenth century unfolded before him. In a charming private letter once written to me by him concerning the circumstances that had acted as determining influences on his youth, and more especially regarding the great change he had undergone, he expressed himself as follows:—

With such antecedents I could not but become the prey of

Grundtvig. Yet nothing in the world can bribe me, although I can but too easily be led astray. Therefore I was released from these circles the day my eyes were first opened to see. My worst enemy may possess the truth; I am stupid and strong; but the moment I see the truth, if only through an accident, it attracts me irresistibly. Tell me, is not such a nature very easy to understand? Should not you think it would be especially natural for the Norsemen to understand it? I am a Norseman. I am human. Of late I might subscribe myself: man. For it seems to me that this word at present calls up new ideas with us.

VIII

The first extensive work with which Björnson made his appearance before the public, after a silence of several years, was the drama "En Fallit" (The Bankrupt), that met with such unwonted success in Germany as well as at home. It was a leap into modern life. The poetic hand which had wielded the battle-swords of the Sigurds did not esteem itself too good to count the cash of Tjælde or to sum up his debts. Björnson was the first Scandinavian poet who entered with serious earnestness into the tragic-comedy of money, and the victory that crowned his effort was a brilliant one. Simultaneously with "The Bankrupt" he issued the play called "Redaktören" (The Editor), a scathing satire on the condition of the press in Norway. Then followed in rapid succession the great dramatic poem "Kongen" (The King), the novels "Magnhild" and "Captain Mansana," the dramas "Det ny System" (The New System), and "Leonarda," new poems, republican essays, etc., and a profound and delicately written story, entitled "Stöv" (Dust).

In conservative circles of Norway there has been a strenuous effort to undervalue Björnson's poetic works in this new phase, by calling them tendency poetry. This word "tendency" is the bugbear by means of which attempts have too long been made to banish from the Danish-Norweigian poetry all ideas of the modern world. By so doing the conviction is fostered naïvely enough, that Björnson's older poetic works, which are so highly extolled, are without any tendency, because they have the opposite tendency from the later ones; the fact is, people had become as thoroughly accustomed to that earlier tendency as to the atmosphere of a room they never left. The obligato pagan and especially Viking conversions, so common throughout the Northern literature of this century, have never been regarded in the light of tendency efforts; even the conversion in "Arnljot Gelline" was not considered so because the tendency was one that pleased. So what was now frowned upon was not the idea of a tendency in itself, but the new tendency, that is to say, the spirit and the ideas of the nineteenth century. These ideas, however, are to poetry precisely what the circulation of the blood is to the human body. What must be demanded in the true interest of poetry is merely, that the veins which people like to see with a blue glimmer beneath the skin, should not stand out in bold relief, swollen and black, as in the case of a sick person, or one who is excited to anger. Very rarely, indeed, does Björnson's tendency take such a form as, for instance, in the hemorrhage, of which the young politician in "The Editor" dies, solely that the mark of Cain may be stamped upon the brow of the main personage of the drama; or in the vision in the drama, "The King," which terrifies and kills the daughter of the political martyr on the way to her marriage with the young king. No one, however, who looks farther than failures in details can be obtuse enough not to detect the fountain of new and individual poesy which streams through all of Björnson's works of the second period, or second youth, as it might be called. An ardent love of truth has imprinted its seal on these books; a manly firmness of character proclaims itself in them. What a wealth of new thoughts in all provinces of state and society, marriage and home! What an energetic demand for veracity toward one's self and toward others! Finally, what benignity, what sympathy with people of opposite lines of thought, who are dealt with sparingly, even idealized, as the bishop in "Leonarda," or the king in the drama of the same name, while all attacks are aimed at institutions as such. This is perhaps nowhere more sharply felt than in "The King," the leading thought of which is the simple, and in itself by no means new idea, that constitutional monarchy is a mere transitional form leading to the republic, but whose originality consists in viewing the problem from the inner ranks, by taking the person of the king as the starting point of attack on the institution. This the author does by showing how the nature of this institution must harm the king as an individual, how it must blight his soul, at the same time portraying the character with a sympathy, an intense warmth, that makes him the hero of the drama in the proper sense of the word.

The opponents of Björnson's new departure now maintain that, as long as he kept outside of the circle of burning questions and living ideas, he was great and good as a poet, but declare that he has retrograded since he embarked on the sea of modern problems and thought; that, at all events, he no longer produces artistically finished works. Similar judgments have been pronounced all over Europe whenever a poet who, in his youth, had won the public favor by neutral, inoffensive productions, showed his contemporaries that he studied and knew them. There are numberless readers who place Byron's youthful poem "Childe Harold" above the powerful, yet seldom pleasing realistic poetry of "Don Juan." In Russia and elsewhere, there may be found a refined public that prefers the first simple narratives of Turgenief, the "Memoirs of a Sportsman," to the great romances "Fathers and Sons" and "Virgin Soil"; there are in Germany many people who are overwhelmed with regret because Paul Heyse forsook for a time his peculiar form of love story to write his "Children of the World." It is true that Björnson, in his second period has not yet attained the lucidity and harmony of style that characterized his first efforts; but it is neither just nor wise to declare for this reason that he has retrograded. A new, rich, and seething group of ideas finds its form slowly, sometimes fermenting and bubbling over its limits; strong feelings and thoughts have a certain fire, a certain vibration, that renders them less capable of appearing in a pleasing form than the idyl with its poverty of thought.

In spite of all this, how much that is admirable from a

technical point of view Björnson has accomplished of late years! The exposé in "The Bankrupt" is one of the best the literature of any land can produce, and the diction in "The Editor," especially in the first act, is the most excellent that Björnson has attained. These two dramas, with which he first entered the career opened by Henrik Ibsen with his drama "De Unges Forbund" (The Young Men's Union), follow close in the footsteps of the latter's vigorously built and witty play. "The Young Men's Union" actually contains the germ of both "The Bankrupt" and "The Editor." There the bankruptcy was that of the light-minded Erik Brattsberg; feeble outlines of "The Editor" may be found in Steensgaard's relation to Aslaksen's newspaper and the article against the chamberlain that was to have been printed first, and so did not get printed at all. The public has usually viewed "The Young Men's Union" and "The Editor" as contrasts, that is, as contradictory presentations of different political situations. This is simply because in the first play a dishonorable representative of the progressive party is derided, and in the second a still bolder, more deceitful representative of the conservative party. Viewed from a purely poetic standpoint, however, these two plays are very nearly akin. Björnson's editor is Steinhoff grown older (as years creep on he becomes highly conservative), a Steensgaard, in whom the softer, more pliant elements, through disappointments, defeats, and wild attacks of contempt of himself and others, have been ossified, and in whom, therefore, coarse recklessness alone remains.

In "The Bankrupt" the demands of truth in the humble walks of life are urged. The poet holds up, within the plain, commonplace life of the people, the ideal of truth as a simple matter of rectitude. His poetic eye, however, sees that rectitude is not so simple as it appears. Nothing is so reprehensible for the merchant as to risk the money of others, and yet, to a certain degree, it is impossible for him to avoid it. The moral problem revolves about the delicate boundary lines between where it is allowable and where not allowable to risk it. "The Editor" demands truth in the higher domains, where it is a bounden duty to keep it in sight, and yet dangerous to carry it into execution. While in the mercantile world there is danger of disappointing and ruining others through self deception, in the journalistic world the temptation is to keep silence concerning the truth, or to deny it. And this, too, cannot be altogether avoided; for it is out of the question for the politician to acknowledge everything he knows. It might be esteemed a defect in Björnson's "Editor" that the representative of journalism does not fully represent the dialectics of his class, the inevitable collisions to which those connected with the daily press are subjected. On the other hand, his opponent and victim, Halvdan, is too passive and long-suffering to prove of thorough interest to the reader. Björnson expressly attacks in this play the ideal of composure which the hard necessities of our day have led us to hold up as a model; he protests, in the name of the child within our souls, against the doctrine that we must harden our hearts, and there is some justice in his protest. But the fact is, we now-a-days only cherish a qualified sympathy with those public personages who can never succumb to persecutions of the press. The Christian ideal of the suffering martyr has, in this case, lost its power over the reading world and theatregoers; there is a demand for a man from whom all the combined written and spoken attacks of his opponents will glance off, leaving him unharmed,—a man whom no idle words, not even a storm of idle words can shake. It is not for me to decide whether such a mode of contemplation is natural, but it certainly has much to recommend it.

"The Editor" may perhaps be most correctly comprehended as a great allegory. The elder brother, Halvdan, who succumbs in the political and literary strife, is Wergeland, who, after a life passed in enthusiastic struggles for freedom, galled by the agitations caused by his own attacks and the persecution of his opponents, lay so long stretched on a couch of sickness,—a far greater and more poetic form shortly before death than during the long feuds of his life. In the younger brother, Harald, to whom falls the inheritance of Halvdan, I cannot but think that Björnson wished to symbolize his own political endeavors, together with the misunderstandings to which they have been exposed, and the opponents they have found. Hakon, the eldest brother, who became a farmer, and his wife, who plays a rôle without appearing on the stage, represent the Norwegian people. The unusual vigor of the play, however, is dependent on the fact that, in addition to the great breadth of its horizon, it is individual and characteristic to a degree that has never been surpassed by Björnson.

"The King" deals with political questions, as "The Bankrupt" and "The Editor" with social ones. Here the problem is psychological. The poet himself fights with the king of the drama his inner fight, and lets his attempts to reconcile the requirements of his nature with those of his position strand. Is the problem satisfactorily solved? Is not the unhappy result in too high a degree caused by the king's wretched past and his weak character? The worth of the play does not depend on the answer, but on the depths to which it penetrates, on the fresh charm which hovers about its love scenes, and on the rich, sparkling wit of its dialogues. In "Magnhild" and "Leonarda," a new modern problem is dealt with that had germed in the poet's own soul,—the relation between morality as a virtue and as an institution, as a law of the heart, and as a law of society. The doctrine proclaimed in "Magnhild" is imparted in the modest form of a question: Are there not immoral marriages, which it is our highest duty to dissolve?

"Magnhild" is a work that, in its search for reality, denotes a turning-point in Björnson's novel-writing. In its characterizations it displays a delicacy and a power the author had not previously attained. The public had scarcely credited him with the ability to portray figures like the young musician Tande, the beautiful Mrs. Bang and her husband. And Magnhild's relation to this group is quite as exquisitely delineated and as correctly conceived. Nevertheless, it is very apparent that the author is moving in a sphere which is still somewhat an unfamiliar one to him, that of social high life. It is a curious fact, too, that Tande's cowardly denial of the woman he loves, at the moment when she is scorned by the mob, has the poet's sympathy on the ground of morality.

The novel suffers from a double defect. In the first place there is a decided lack of clearness in the characterization of one of the main personages, Skarlie. He is meant to impress the reader as a sort of monster, and yet the reader feels continually obliged to sympathize with him in his relations with his reserved, ideal wife. In the most guarded manner conceivable, it is indicated that Skarlie is a highly depraved person, and yet this monster of sensuality, in his dealings with his own wife, of whom he has gained possession by a not particularly sharp intrigue, displays a moonshine-like ideal of a Platonic relation between husband and wife, in the Ingemann style, and is content with the modest satisfaction of clothing and feeding her. The second deficiency strikes deeper into the philosophy of the novel. There is a good deal of old mysticism in the handling of the doctrine concerning the "destiny" of men and women, about which the story revolves, and (as is always the case with both Björnson and Ibsen) the mysticism is strangely interwoven with rationalism. Björnson seems to wish to have it firmly established as the sum of the story that there is another way to happiness and beneficent activity for woman than a relation to the man whom she loves, but the idea is not clearly expressed.

"Leonarda," although not conspicuous for its dramatic merits, belongs to the most thoroughly and richly poetic of the author's works. Outside of the Scandinavian North, a drama of this kind cannot be fully appreciated; perhaps the powerful, intellectual influence it has exercised can scarcely be comprehended. When placed upon the boards in Christiania it made its marked sensation, because it rang like a word of deliverance into Norwegian affairs. The message of "Leonarda" is that of moral and religious tolerance, from which the author himself, in his early days, was so far removed. In this drama, with wonderful display of intellectual superiority, Björnson brought forward a whole series of generations of Norwegian society, showing the faults and virtues of each generation, and allowing the

great-grandmother, who, as the grandmother in George
Sand's drama, "L'autre," represents the culture of the
eighteenth century, so meanly estimated during the long
period of Northern reaction, to utter the solemn amen of
the play. Her concluding words read as follows:—

"The time of deep emotions has, indeed, come back
again."

With "Leonarda," however, not only the time of deep
emotions but that of hardy thoughts had returned, although
the poet, as already indicated, fought his opponents with a
benignity and forbearance, a benevolence above all partisan-
ship, that forms, perhaps, his most marked characteristic.

Henrik Ibsen is a judge, stern as one of the judges of
Israel of old; Björnson is a prophet, the delightful herald
of a better age. In the depths of his nature, Ibsen is a
great revolutionist. In his "Kjaerlighedens Komedie"
(Love's Comedy), and in "Et Dukkehjem" (A Doll's
House, known as "Nora" in Germany and England), he
applies the scourge to the marriage relation of the day; in
"Brand" to the state church; in "Samfundets Stötter"
(The Pillars of Society), to the entire civil society of his
native land. Whatever he attacks is crushed beneath the
weight of his superior and penetrating criticism. Björnson's is a conciliatory mind; he wages warfare without bitterness. His poetry sparkles with the sunshine of April,
while that of Ibsen, with its deep earnestness, seems to lurk
in dark shadows. Ibsen loves the idea,—that logical, and
psychological consistency which drives Brand out of the
church, and Nora out of the marriage relation. Ibsen's
love of ideas corresponds with Björnson's love of humanity.

IX

When still young, Björnson began to deal with politics,
and throughout his whole life he has worked in one direction. He has fought unweariedly to secure the independence of Norway in the (almost purely dynastic) union with
its larger neighbor, Sweden. For four hundred years Norway, as is well known, was a Danish and indeed a misgov-

erned Danish province, until, in the year 1814, it was united with Sweden, as a free kingdom, with a wellnigh republican constitution. Since that time the house of Bernadotte has made repeated efforts to limit the independence and curtail the constitutional rights of the sparsely populated rocky land. Beyond all else it has striven to amalgamate the land with Sweden, and externally it has so far succeeded that Norway is viewed throughout Europe, even in Germany, as a province of Sweden, a sort of "seditious Ireland." As early as 1858, when editor of "Bergensposten," Björnson fought against the amalgamation plans, and it was largely due to his efforts that those representatives of Bergen, who had voted for a closer tariff union between Sweden and Norway, were not re-elected to the Storthing. In 1859, as editor of "Aftenbladet," in Christiania, he successfully contested the right of the king to place a Swedish royal governor at the head of Norwegian affairs. In 1866-67, as editor of the "Norsk Folkeblad," Björnson was one of the most valiant opponents of the so-called "union proposition," an attempt of the government to make a closer union between the two realms that were bound together in one dynasty. Since the dispute concerning the king's veto (previously only recognized as suspensive), between King Oscar and the Storthing, Björnson has become one of the most prominent political leaders of Norway. Especially since his visit to the United States, in the year 1880, he has burst forth from the chrysalis as the greatest popular orator of Scandinavia, teeming with marvellously captivating and, at the same time, thoroughly calm eloquence. As soon as his presence at a public assemblage is an established fact, thousands of peasants stream together to hear him. After the great president of the Storthing, Johan Sverdrup, no man in Norway has so powerful an influence as an orator.

The two countries, Norway and Denmark, for so many hundred years politically united and still united through a common language and a common ancient literature,—almost more intimately united, since they became outwardly separated, than before,—have common aspirations and aims in all political questions and in all problems of civilization. The same struggle for freedom and modern enlightenment which Björnson and his comrades in thought carry on in Norway, is fought in Denmark by the younger school of authors. Norwegians and Danes labor each in their own way to till the common soil of language and literature. I believe that the result will be similar to that which Björnson has described in the little legend that is the prelude to "Arne," and virtually to his tales of peasant life in general, where juniper, oak, fir, birch, and heather resolve to clothe the naked mountain lying before them. The effort long failed; it was all plain enough; the mountain did not wish to be clad. Whenever the trees had worked their way forward a little, there appeared a brook that grew and grew, and finally threw them all down.

Then the day came when the heather could peep with one eye over the edge of the mountain. 'Oh dear, oh dear, oh dear!' said the heather, and away it went. 'Dear me! what is it the heather sees?' said the juniper, and moved on until it could peer up. 'Oh dear, oh dear!' it shrieked, and was gone. 'What is the matter with the juniper today?' said the fir, and took long strides onward in the heat of the sun. Soon it could raise itself on its toes and peep up. 'Oh dear!' Branches and needles stood on end in wonderment. It worked its way forward, came up, and was gone. 'What is it all the others see, and not I?' said the birch, and lifting well its skirts, it tripped after. It stretched its whole head up at once. 'Oh!—oh!—is not here a great forest of fir and heather, of juniper and birch, standing upon the table-land waiting for us?' said the birch; and its leaves quivered in the sunshine so that the dew trembled. They meet the work done on the other side. The trees of the mountains find the forest of the table-land.

'Aye, this is what it is to reach the goal!' said the juniper.[5]

[Since this essay was written Björnson wrote the following dramas and novels: *En Handske* (The Gauntlet); *Over Ævne* (Beyond his Power) I and II; *Geografi och Kjarlighed* (Geography and Love); *Laboremus; Paul Lange and Tora Parsberg; Paa Storhove* (At Storhove); *Daglannet* (The Dayland); *Det Flager i Byen og paa Havnen* (Flags in City and Harbor); *Paa Guds Veie* (In God's Footsteps); and *Mary*. He was busy with his pen until shortly before his death, which occurred in

[5] See Arne, pp. 12, 13 (Houghton, Mifflin & Co., Boston).

Paris, April 26, 1910, and besides the books here noted he produced a large number of poems and countless contributions to the press on politics, religion and social questions. He also frequently appeared as a public speaker. In 1903 he was awarded the Nobel prize. No matter how severely he might criticize, no matter how heavily he might lay the lash on his contemporaries, he never ceased to be the idol of the Norwegian people.—Translator's Note.]

IX

HENRIK IBSEN

1883

I

WHEN Henrik Ibsen, at thirty-six years of age, left Norway to go into that exile from which he has not yet returned, it was with a heavy and embittered heart, after a youth passed on the sunless side of life. He was born March 20, 1828, in the small Norwegian town of Skien, amid circumstances of very precarious prosperity. His parents, on their paternal as well as maternal side, belonged to families of the highest standing in the town. His father was a merchant, engaged in varied and extensive activities, and enjoying the exercise of an almost unlimited hospitality. In 1836, however, the worthy gentleman was compelled to suspend payments, and from the wreck of his fortunes nothing was saved for his family but a country estate a short distance from the town. Thither they removed, and were thus carried beyond the range of the circles to which they had previously belonged. In "Peer Gynt" Ibsen has employed the recollections of his own childhood as a sort of model for his description of life in wealthy Jon Gynt's home. As a lad, Henrik Ibsen became apprentice in a drug-store. He worked his way through countless difficulties before he was able, at the age of twenty-two, to enter on a student's career; even then he had neither inclination nor means for professional study; for a long time he had not so much as the means to secure for himself regular meals. His youth was hard and stern, his daily life a struggle; the paternal roof seems to have offered him no place of refuge.

Although conditions of this kind signify less in so poor and so democratic a country as Norway than elsewhere, and although Ibsen has lacked neither the faculty of youth, nor that of the poet, to rise superior to actual adversity through enthusiasm for ideas and an independent dream-life, still, early poverty always leaves its marks on the character. It may breed humility; it may develop opposition; it may render the nature wavering, or independent, or hard throughout life. To Ibsen's reserved, combative, and satirical temperament, which was far more gifted to occupy the curiosity of the surroundings than to win their hearts, it must have served as a challenge. It has probably imparted to him a certain insecurity regarding his social status, a certain ambition in the direction of those external distinctions that were calculated to place him on an equal footing with the class from which in youth he had been cut off, and a powerful sense of being compelled to depend on himself and his own resources alone.

A nine weeks' activity as publisher of a weekly newspaper without many subscribers was followed, 1851-57, by a period of labor as stage-manager of the small theatre in Bergen, and after the last-named year as director of the Christiania Theatre, which in 1862 went into bankruptcy. Ibsen, who, as years have gone on, has become so staid and sedate, and whose days pass with the regularity of clockwork, is said to have lived a rather irregular life as a young man, and was pursued, therefore, by that evil report which even some trifling aberration, especially when caused by the erratic tendency of genius, will call forth in a small place where all eyes keep watch on each and every one. I can well imagine Ibsen just entering on manhood, tormented by creditors, and daily executed in effigy by the followers of the coffee-party ethics of female gossips. He had written fine poems in no insignificant number, as well as a series of dramas which are now celebrated, and some of which belong to his most admired productions, but which were published in Norway in unsightly editions on wretched paper, had a sale of only a few hundred copies, and yielded the author, even on the part of his friends, but a moderately cool recognition of talent, together with the morally crushing sentence that he "lacked ideal faith and conviction." He became disgusted with Norway. In 1862, fully equipped with the weapons of polemics and satire, he had published "Kjærlighedens Komedie" (Love's Comedy), a drama which unites cutting scorn at the erotic affairs of conventional society, with deep distrust in the power of love to endure through all the vicissitudes of life, and profound doubt of its ability to preserve its ideal and ardent nature unscathed and unchanged in marriage. It could not have been unknown to the poet that society, with all the tenacity of the instinct of self-preservation, has made it a duty to have confidence in the immutability of normal love between man and woman; but he was young enough, and defiant enough, to justify relatively the most trivial conceptions of matrimony, as exemplified in the union of Guldstad and Svanhild, rather than withhold his doubts concerning the existing dogmatics of love. The book raised a howl of exasperation. People were indignant at this attack on the amatory relations of society, betrothals, marriages, etc. Instead of taking home to themselves his fierce thrusts, they began, as is quite customary in such cases, to pry into Ibsen's own private life, to investigate the circumstances of his marriage, and, as Ibsen once remarked to me, "Though the published criticisms of the comedy might have been endured, the verbal and private censure was altogether insufferable." Henrik Ibsen was condemned as a talented *mauvais sujet*. Even so superb a work as "Kongs-Emnerne" (The Pretenders), which followed in 1864, did not suffice to purify and exalt the poet's name. As far as I am aware, this drama was not actually condemned by the critics, but it was by no means estimated according to its merits, and it created no sensation whatever. I do not think twenty copies reached Denmark. At all events, it was "Brand" that first made the poet's name known beyond Norway. An essay, in which the works of Ibsen were reviewed by me in 1867, and which called attention to their rare worth, was the first presentation of his life as an author given to the public.[1] To Henrik Ibsen's private reasons

[1] Let me here take the liberty of referring the reader to this essay (Æsthetiske Studier, 234-286), as I consider it in the main correct, and will not here repeat its statements. A few individual sentences, however, I have felt compelled to reproduce.

for melancholy was added a sense of profound dissatisfaction with Norway's political attitude during the Danish-German war. When Norway and Sweden, in 1864, failed to stand by Denmark against Prussia and Austria, notwithstanding all the promises given at students' meetings, as well as by a press ostensibly devoted to Scandinavian interests, and which were understood by Ibsen to be binding, or at least considered obligatory, home became so odious to him, as the seat of shallowness, laxity, and pusillanimity, that he turned his back upon it.

Since that time he has dwelt alternately in Italy, in Dresden, in Munich, and again in Italy, in each of the German cities five or six years at a time. But a permanent abiding-place he has not had. He has led a quiet, orderly family-life, or more accurately speaking, he has, within the framework of family-life, had his real life in his work. He has had intercourse in public places with the most eminent men of foreign cities; has received into his house a multitude of Scandinavians who happened to be passing through the town where he was staying; but he has lived as in a tent, amidst hired furniture which could be returned to its owners any day his departure was fixed upon; for seventeen years he has not set foot beneath his own table, or reposed in his own bed. He has never settled anywhere in the stricter sense of the term; he has accustomed himself to feel at home in homelessness. When last I visited him he replied to my question, if nothing in the suite of rooms he occupied belonged to him, by pointing to a row of paintings on the walls; that was all he could there call his own. Even now, as a man of means, he feels no desire to own his own house and home, to say nothing of farming lands and buildings, the pride of Björnson. He is separated from his people, without any activity that binds him to an institution, or a party, or even so much as to a magazine, or to a newspaper at home or abroad—a solitary man. And in his isolation he writes:—

> My people, who to me from goblet foaming
> A wholesome, bitter draught of strength once gave,
> That roused the poet, ling'ring near his grave,

To arm himself and labor through the gloaming—
My people, who on me the exile's stave,
With sorrow's scrip and sandals swift for roaming,
Bestowed, the outfit stern for strife completing—
From distant realms I send thee home my greeting!

Many and important indeed are the greetings he has sent home; but over all his productions, both before and during his exile, there lingers one and the same prevailing mood, that of his temperament, a mood whose main characteristics are freedom from restraint and cheerless despondency. This fundamental tone, so natural to the homeless, permeates everything with which he creates the strongest impression. Recall some of his most characteristic, moreover some of his most diametrically opposed works, as for instance, the poem "Paa Vidderne" (On the Mountain Plains), in which the narrator, from the lofty mountain heights, sees the cottage of his mother surrounded by lurid flames and his mother burned alive, while he himself, wholly deprived of will-power and in a state of utter despair, stands watching the effective illumination, or "Fra Mit Husliv" (From My Household Life), in which the creations of the poet's fancy, his winged offspring, take flight as soon as he sees himself in the glass with his leaden eyes, closely-buttoned vest, and felt shoes; think of the thrilling poetry of that dismal scene where Brand wrests from his wife their dead child's clothing; call to mind the scene where Brand consigns his mother to hell, and that superbly original scene in which Peer Gynt paves the way to heaven for his mother with lies; conjure up "Liget i Lasten" (The Corpse in the Cargo), or the overwhelmingly painful impression aroused by Nora (A Doll's House),—that butterfly, which is pricked with a needle through three acts, only to be pierced at last, —and it will be felt that the prevailing atmosphere, corresponding to the landscape background of a painter, in all pathetic parts is fierce, cheerless gloom. It may rise to a pitch of tragical awe, but that is no proof that its author is simply a writer of tragedy. Schiller's tragedies, as well as those of Oehlenschläger, are gloomy only in occasional situations, and even the author of "King Lear" and of "Macbeth" has produced such harmoniously moulded creations as "The Tempest" or, "A Midsummer Night's Dream." With Ibsen, however, this tone is the fundamental one. It could not be otherwise in the case of a born idealist who, from the outset of his career, thirsted for beauty in its highest forms, as purely ideal, spiritual beauty; or, in the case of a born rigorist who, thoroughly Germanic, especially Norse, by character and temperament, influenced, moreover, by circumstances to Christian views, was inclined to esteem the life of the senses repellent or sinful, and not to admire seriously, or even to recognize other than moral beauty. In his innermost soul he was shy; that is to say, but few disappointments were required to make him withdraw into himself, even with distrust of the surrounding world in his heart. How early must he not have been wounded, repulsed, humiliated, as it were, in his original proneness to believe and to admire! His first deep impression as an intellectual being must have been, I think, an impression of the rarity—non-existence, he may have added in moments of bitterness—of moral worth, and disappointed in his quest for beauty, he found a certain relief in unveiling the sorrowful truth that lay concealed behind the glamour of appearances. The atmosphere about him reverberated with words denoting ideals and telling of eternal love, of profound seriousness, of fidelity, of decision of character, of Norse patriotic sentiment (the national sentiment of "det lille, men klippefaste Klippefolk": the little, yet cliff-like, steadfast mountain-folk); he looked about him, he searched eagerly, but found nothing in the world of reality corresponding to these words. Thus there was developed in him, through his very yearning for an ideal, a peculiar faculty for discovering everything to be spurious. It became an instinct with him to apply a crucial test to whatever seemed genuine, and to feel little if any astonishment when he proved it to be false. It became a passion with him to rap with his fingers on all that seemed like solid metal, and it gave him a sense of painful satisfaction to hear the ring of hollowness, which at the same time offended his ear and corroborated his foreboding. Whenever he came into contact with what was supposed to be great, it became both a habit and a necessity with him, to ask as in "Rimbrevet til en Svensk Dame" (Letter in Rhyme to a Swedish Lady): "Is it truly great, this greatness?" He became keenly alive to all the egotism, all the untruthfulness, inherent in imaginative life, to all the wretched bungling the phrases of freedom and progress may conceal, and gradually a stupendous ideal or moral distrust became his muse. It inspired him to ever more and more daring investigations. Nothing overawed, nothing startled him, either what appeared like idyllic happiness in domestic life, or what resembled dogmatic security in social life. The more audacious his investigations, the greater became his dauntless courage in communicating, disseminating, proclaiming the result. It came to be his chief intellectual delight to disturb the equanimity, to arouse the ire of all those whose interest it was to conceal with euphemisms existing evils. Just as it had always seemed to him that too much was said about ideals that were never realized in actual life, so too he felt, with ever increasing certainty and wrathful indignation, that people, as it were by common consent, maintained silence in regard to the deepest, most irretrievable breach with ideals, in regard to the true, unmistakable causes of horror and dismay. In polite society they were avoided as improbable, or unsuitable to be mentioned; in poetry, as appalling and gloomy; for æsthetics had once for all banished from belles-lettres all that was unduly harsh, painful, or irreconcilable. Thus it was, as nearly as can be defined, that Ibsen became the poet of haunting gloom, and thence comes his inherent tendency to justify, in sharp and bitter expressions, his attitude toward the majority.

Henrik Ibsen's personal appearance is suggestive of the qualities manifested in his poetry. In his countenance the reflection of a soul full of tenderness, even though disguised by the stern or sarcastic earnestness of the physiognomy, will occasionally make itself apparent. Ibsen is below the medium height, is heavily built, dresses with a certain style and elegance, and has altogether a very distinguished appearance. His gait is slow, his bearing dignified, his carriage worthy. His head is large, interesting, framed with a wealth of grizzled hair, which he wears pretty long. The forehead, which is the dominating feature of the face, is unusual in form, is high, almost perpendicular, broad, and at the same time well modelled, and bears the impress of greatness and marked intellectual vigor. The mouth, when in repose, is so tightly compressed that there is scarcely any trace of lips; its closeness and firmness betray the fact that Ibsen is a man of few words. In truth, it is his wont, when in the society of a large number of people, to remain as taciturn as though he were the mute, and at times almost crabbed guardian of the sanctuary of his mind. He can talk when in the society of one person alone, or in a very small circle, but even then he is far from communicative. A Frenchman, whom I once took in Rome to see Runeberg's bust of the poet, said, "The expression is more *spirituelle* than poetic." It is very apparent to the observer that Ibsen is a satiric poet, a brooding thinker, but not a visionary. His most exquisite poems, however, such as "Borte" (Absent) and some others, indicate plainly that at some time in the battle of life a lyric Pegasus has been slain under him.

I am familiar with two expressions in his face. The first is the one in which his smile,—his kind, delicate smile, penetrates and animates the mask of his countenance, in which all that is cordial and heartfelt, all that lies deepest in his soul, rises uppermost. Ibsen has a certain tendency to embarrassment, as is apt to be the case with melancholy, serious natures. He has, however, a most charming smile, and through smile, look, and pressure of the hand, he expresses much which he neither could, nor would, clothe in words. And he has a habit, when engaged in conversation, of smiling playfully, with a twinkle of good-natured raillery, as he tosses off some brief, not-at-all-good-natured remark, in which the lovable side of his character is plainly manifested. The smile softens the sharpness of the outburst.

But I am also familiar with another expression in his

countenance, one in which impatience, anger, righteous indignation, cutting scorn, impart to it a look of almost cruel austerity, forcibly reminding the observer of the words in his beautiful old poem Terje Vigen:—

> Yet, sometimes, in stormy weather, a kind
> Of madness would kindle his eye;—
> And few there were then who could courage find
> To come Terje Vigen nigh.

This is the expression his poetic soul has most frequently assumed before the world.

Ibsen is by nature a polemic, and his first poetic outburst (Catiline) was at the same time his first declaration of war. From the moment he arrived at years of maturity—which, by the way, was not very early—he has never actually doubted that he, the individual, on one scale, and on the other what is called society—in Ibsen's eyes the embodiment of those who shun the truth, and who are ever on the alert to conceal evils with empty phrases—would balance evenly. He is in the habit of asserting, among many whimsical paradoxes, that in every age there is a certain sum of intelligence for distribution; in the event of some individuals being especially well equipped,—as, for instance, Goethe and Schiller in their day in Germany,—their contemporaries will be all the more stupid in proportion. Ibsen, I may safely assert, is inclined to believe that he has received his endowments at a time when there were very few with whom to divide the sum.

He has, therefore, no consciousness of being the child of a people, a part of the whole, the leader of a group, a member of society; he feels himself exclusively a gifted individual, and the sole object in which he believes, and for which he cherishes respect is personality. In this emancipation from all natural relations, in this exaltation of the *ego* as an intellectual force, there is a lively reminder of that period in Northern history, in which Ibsen received his culture. Above all else, the influence of Kierkegaard[2] is

[2] Let me here call the reader's attention to my work, Sören Kierkegaard, Copenhagen; German edition, Leipsic, 1879.

apparent. Ibsen's isolation, however, has a totally different stamp, upon whose moulding Björnson's quite opposite personality has had no trifling influence. It is always of vast significance to an individual to be historically so situated that destiny places at its side a contrasting companion-piece. Not infrequently it is a misfortune for a noted man to see his name continually coupled with another, it may be for glorification, it may be for censure, but always by way of comparison. The compulsory twin relation that cannot be shaken off may irritate and harm. In the case of Ibsen, it has, perhaps, aided in forcing the peculiarities of his nature to their utmost extremities; in other words, it has intensified his fervor and reserve. No one who, like Ibsen, believes in the rights and capabilities of the emancipated individual, no one who, as early in life as he, has placed himself on a war footing with his surroundings, holds a very flattering opinion of the masses. There evidently developed within him, on the very threshold of manhood, a contempt for his fellow-creatures. It was not because he had from the first an exaggerated opinion of his own talents, or his own worth. His is a brooding, doubting, questioning nature. He says himself:—

"My calling is to question, not to answer," and minds like his have no tendency to conceit. It may be noted, too, how long he was in finding the right language and form with which to clothe his thought; how crude his first effort "Catiline" was; how strong the evidence displayed in his unpublished drama "Kjæmpehöjen" (The Barrow), of the influence of Oehlenschläger, especially of "Landet fundet og forsvundet" (The land that was found, and that disappeared); how constantly the reader is reminded, even to the very metre, in the drama "Gildet paa Solhaug" (The Feast at Solhaug) of a totally dissimilar genius Henrik Hertz, especially of the latter's drama, "Svend Dyring's House," and how, in his "Hærmændene paa Helgeland" (The Vikings), he availed himself of the effective features of saga literature on a large scale before he presumed to take satisfaction in his own resources, and his own markedly individual style.[3] At the outset of his career he belonged rather to those natures that enter upon life with profound reverence, prepared to recognize the superiority of others, until adversity gives them a consciousness of their own power. From the moment the discovery is made, however, such natures become, as a rule, far more rigid and stubborn than those that were originally self-complacent. They accustom themselves to weigh those whose superiority formerly they would have accepted as a matter of course, with the eye as on an invisible scale, and cast them aside the moment they fall below the standard weight.

Ibsen finds the average mortal petty, egotistic, worthless. His mode of apprehension is not the purely scientific one of the observer; it is that of the moralist; and in his quality of moralist he dwells far more on the wickedness of humanity, than on its blindness and lack of discretion. To Flaubert mankind is wicked because it is stupid; to Ibsen, on the contrary, it is stupid because it is wicked. Recall, for instance, the case of Thorvald Helmer. Throughout the entire drama in which he plays so sorrowful a rôle, he views his wife with eyes of utter stupidity,—the hopeless stupidity of a blockhead. In the place where Nora bids Dr. Rank the last farewell, where thoughts of suicide are brought face to face with thoughts of death, and the doctor's reply is couched in terms of sympathizing tenderness, Helmer stands, drunk and lascivious, his arms outstretched. Yet he is thus stupid solely on account of his self-righteous egotism.

And simply wrong-doers Ibsen finds mankind, not vicious by nature. On a previous occasion I quoted an aphorism from Kierkegaard's "Enten—Eller" (Either—Or), which seems peculiarly well adapted to be a motto for Ibsen: "Let others lament that the times are evil: I lament that they are paltry and contemptible, for they are utterly without passion. The thoughts of mankind are as thin and

[3] In the preface to the second edition of Gildet paa Solhaug, issued in 1883, after the work had been out of print some twenty-seven years, Ibsen offered a protest against this suggestion of the influence of Henrik Hertz.

as feeble as lace-women. The thoughts of their hearts are too insignificant to be sinful." What else does Brand say when he bewails the God of his generation and holds up in contrast his own God, his own ideal, as follows:—

> And like the race, its God is hoary,
> His silv'ry hair its pride and glory.
> But this thy God cannot be mine,
> For mine is storm, while wind is thine.
> * * * * * *
> And mine like Hercules is young,
> No aged sire as thou hast sung.

What else says the "Knappestöber" (The Buttonmoulder)? He answers Peer Gynt about as Mephistopheles in Heiberg's "En Sjæl efter Döden" (A Soul After Death), replied to the "soul." Peer Gynt is not destined to be plunged into the brimstone pit; he is merely to be returned to the casting-ladle, that he may be moulded over again. He was no sinner, for, as the text declares, "der skal Kraft og Alvor til en Synd" (it requires power and earnestness to commit a sin), he belonged to the mediocre classes, and therefore, he "must be cast into the waste-box to be moulded over again."

According to Ibsen's conception, Peer Gynt is the typical expression of the national vices of the Norwegian people. It is very evident the poet was inspired with less horror than contempt by these vices.

This view of the matter explains even those of Ibsen's youthful works, in which his characteristics as an author are yet undeveloped. Margit, in "The Feast at Solhaug," for instance, cannot help reminding the reader of the Ragnhild of Hertz. Yet the figure is moulded of quite different metal from that of Hertz; it is harder, less pliable, more tenacious. A woman of to-day, whose heart was filled with despairing love, would feel more akin to Ragnhild than to Margit; for Margit stands as a token to such a woman that she, the reader, is the child of an enfeebled age, devoid of either the courage or the consequence of passion, lost in half-measures. And wherefore does Ibsen, in his "Vikings," reach back to the wild tragedy, the magnificent horror, of the "Volsunga Saga"? In order that he may present this picture of the past to the contemplation of the present, in order to awe, in order to reproach the generation of to-day, by showing it the grandeur of its forefathers,—that passionate intensity which once unbridled, rushed madly onward toward its goal, looking neither to the right nor to the left, regardless of all minor considerations; that pride and strength which is chary of words, which silently acts, silently suffers, silently dies; those wills of iron; those hearts of gold; those deeds which a thousand years have not buried in oblivion. Aye, behold yourselves in the mirror!

Take this combative pathos in its first outburst,—it is his "Catiline" conceived with the entire sympathy of an enthusiastic university student. Catiline despises and hates the Roman social life, in which violence and selfishness hold sway; where men become rulers through intrigue and strategy; and he, the single individual, rebels against society. Take this combative pathos in one of Ibsen's later works, in the most admirable of his dramas, "Et Dukkehjem" (A Doll's House), where it rings with a subdued, but none the less penetrating tone from female lips. Where Nora, the singing-bird, the squirrel, the child, finally collects herself and says, "I must try to find out which is right: society, or myself"; where this frail creature dares place herself on one side and all society on the other, we feel plainly that she is a true daughter of Ibsen. Take, finally, the pathos, so filled with thirst for battle, in a later work, "Gjengangere" (Ghosts), in Mrs. Alving's words concerning the teachings of modern official society, as follows: "I only intended to meddle with a single knot, but when that was untied, everything fell to pieces. And then I became aware that I was handling machine sewing." In these words, remote though the poet may be from the heroine of the play, may be heard a sigh of relief, that for once, if only indirectly, utterance has been given to the utmost that could be said.

With Catiline and with Mrs. Alving,—Ibsen's first male

and last prominent female creation,—there is the same sense of isolation as in the intermediate characters, Falk, Brand, and Nora, and the same despairing beating of the head against a stone wall. In his drama "En Folkefiende" (Enemy of the People), the entire plot revolves about the one idea of how much strength there lies in isolation, and the play ends with the didactically expressed paradox, —"The fact is, you see, the strongest man in the world is he who stands absolutely alone."

The current name in modern Europe for this mode of regarding the world and humanity is pessimism. There are, however, many kinds and degrees of pessimism. It may be, as with Schopenhauer and von Hartmann, a grave conviction that life itself is an evil, that the sum of joys is overwhelmingly insignificant in comparison with the sum of griefs and torments a human life contains; it may content itself by proving the worthlessness of life's highest good, showing how melancholy is youth, how joyless labor, how empty pleasure is in itself, and how repetition dulls our satisfaction in it. By virtue of this insight, it may either recommend self-denial as did Schopenhauer, or labor for the advancement of civilization as does Hartmann, yet with the unwavering conviction that every advance in civilization bears with it increasing unhappiness for the human race. Such pessimism is not that of Ibsen. He too finds the world base, but the question whether life is a good does not occupy him. His entire mode of contemplation is moral.

The pessimistic philosopher is prone to linger on the illusory nature of love; he demonstrates how small an amount of happiness it affords; how it rests mainly on a delusion, as its true goal is not the happiness of the individual, but the greatest possible perfection of the coming generation. To Ibsen, the comedy of love does not consist in the unavoidable erotic illusion,—this alone is in his eyes uplifted above the province of comedy and has his full sympathy,—but in the deterioration of character, the abandonment of life ideals, that is the result of conventional engagements and marriages, even though based originally on love. That the young theologian, with his preparation for a missionary's career, should be transformed on his betrothal into an instructor in a young ladies' seminary, is an occasion for satire to Ibsen, is the true comedy of love in his eyes. In a single instance, and then but as though illumined by a passing flash of light, has he risen far above his usual moral conception of the erotic sphere, without, therefore, renouncing the satirical standpoint, and that is in the poem "Forviklinger" (Entanglements), the wittiest, as well as the most profound of all Ibsen's poems.

The pessimistic philosopher is prone to dwell on the thought that happiness is as unattainable for the individual as for the masses. He lays great stress on the fact than enjoyment slips through our fingers, that all our heart's desires are attained too late, and that when we have them within our grasp they are far from producing the effect upon us our craving for them had deluded us into anticipating. In such an utterance as the well-known remark of Goethe that in seventy-five years he had not enjoyed four weeks of actual pleasure, but had ever been compelled to roll a stone which must continually be raised and started afresh, he sees the decisive proof of the impossibility of happiness. For what the favorite of gods and men, Goethe, failed to obtain, is not likely to be gained by any ordinary mortal. This is not so with Ibsen. Sceptical as he may otherwise be, he by no means doubts the possibility of happiness. Even Mrs. Alving, hard-pressed as she was by circumstances, believes that under other conditions she might have been happy; aye, is truly of the opinion that even her wretched husband might have been prosperous. And Ibsen apparently shares her opinion. Her words about the "half great city," which has no joy to offer, only pleasures; no life vocation, only an office; no actual work, only business affairs, are spoken from his own heart. Life itself does not seem an evil to him. Existence itself is not joyless. Nay, some one is to blame, or rather many are guilty when a life is shorn of joy; and he points to the dreary, conventional society in Norway, rude in its pleasures, bigoted in its conceptions of duty, as the sole object of censure.

To the pessimistic philosopher, optimism is a sort of materialism. In the fact that optimism is preached at every corner, he sees the cause of the social question threatening to become a firebrand to the whole world. According to his conception, the most important thing is to teach the masses they need expect nothing from the future; the pessimistic recognition of universal suffering alone can explain to them the fruitlessness of their efforts. This mode of contemplation is never found in Ibsen. Where he touches the social question, as in "Samfundets Stötter" (The Pillars of Society), and elsewhere, the evil designated is always of a moral nature. Every injury sustained is dependent on a wrong committed. It is the entire stratum of society that is rotten, whole rows of pillars of society that are decaying and hollow. The stifling air of a small community is bad; in large communities there is room for "great deeds." A breath from the outside world, that is to say, a breath of the spirit of truth and freedom, can purify the atmosphere.

Thus it is that when Ibsen finds the world bad he feels no compassion for mankind, only indignation at it. His pessimism is not of a metaphysical but of a moral nature; it has its roots in a conviction of the possibility of the realization of the ideal; it is, in a word, an indignation-pessimism. And his lack of sympathy with many sufferings is dependent on his firm belief in the educating power of suffering. These petty, narrow human beings can only become large through suffering. These small, wretched communities can only become healthy through struggles, defeats, castigations. He who has himself felt how mightily a human being may be equipped by adversity, he who has himself drained the health-giving, tonic draught of bitterness, believes in the use of pain, of adversity, and of oppression. This is perhaps most plainly visible in his "Kejser og Galilæer" (Emperor and Galilean). His conception of Julian is that of a man who, through his persecution of his Christian subjects, becomes the actual framer of the Christianity of his time; that is to say, its rescuscitator from the dead. Julian's universal historical significance for Ibsen is this: by transforming Christianity from a court and state religion to a persecuted and oppressed belief, he restored to it its original spiritual character and its primitive martyrdom. Challenged by the Christians, Julian punishes with severity; but the result of his persecutions is one he himself has little anticipated. The old comrades of his student days, that Gregor who lacked courage for any decisive act, but who had "his little circle, his kinsfolk to protect," and who had neither power nor ability to effect more, and that Basilios who "sought for worldy wisdom in his country estate,"—both rise up, strengthened by persecution, like lions, against him.

II

That an author does not wholly reveal himself in his works is a self-evident fact. In some instances his personal traits give a pretty different impression than his writings. This, however, is by no means the case with Henrik Ibsen, and that he does not hold the views referred to as a mere matter of display, or for the benefit of his books, I am able to show, after an acquaintance of sixteen years' standing, by sundry trifling incidents.

Let me call attention to certain of his unpremeditated oral utterances, illustrating the poet's intellectual life, in the form of a jest, a paradox, or a figure,—but which I do not claim to be absolutely correct, although they have been preserved in a faithful remembrance,—and to certain written remarks, communicated with Ibsen's consent. Thus some of the main outlines of a pen-and-ink sketch of this author may be attempted in a more faithful and life-like manner than from his books alone.

In 1870, when France lay maimed and bleeding at the feet of Germany, Ibsen, whose sympathies were at that time chiefly on the side of France, was far from sharing the dejection universally experienced in the Scandinavian countries on account of the sorrowful fact. While all other friends of France were exhausting themselves in outbursts of sympathy, Ibsen wrote, Dec. 20, 1870: —

. . . Moreover, historic events are claiming a large share of my thoughts. The old illusory France is all slashed to pieces;

and when the modern matter-of-fact Prussia shall also be cut into fragments, we shall have made a leap into the midst of a growing epoch. Oh! how ideas will then come tumbling about our heads. Verily, it is high time they should do so. All we have had to live upon up to the present date are crumbs from the revolutionary table of the past century, and even this fare has been masticated over and over again. These ideas of the past require new substance, new interpretation. Freedom, equality, and fraternity are no longer the same things they were in the days of the guillotine of blessed memory. This is what the politicians will not understand, and therefore it is I hate them. These people demand only special revolutions, revolutions in the outside world, in the sphere of politics. But all this is sheer nonsense. What is really needed is a revolting of the human spirit. . . .

No one can fail to discern in this letter the historic optimism I have indicated in Ibsen. Gloomy though his views may seem, he has the highest hopes, the greatest confidence in the new life that will be called into being through misfortune. Aye, still more; only so long as the misfortunes and calamities which accompany the entrance of ideas into the world hold the senses awake, does he esteem the ideas of actual worth. Even the sound of the guillotine's fall, far from terrifying him, rings harmoniously into his optimistic and revolutionary contemplation of the world. Not freedom as a dead condition, but freedom as a struggle, an endeavor, seems to him of value. Lessing said that if God should offer him truth with his right and truth-seeking with his left hand, he for one would grasp God's left hand. Ibsen would undoubtedly subscribe to the proposition if for "truth" could be substituted the word "freedom." If he despises politicians, it is because, according to his opinion, they conceive and treat freedom as something external and soulless.

From Ibsen's optimistic, and, so to speak, pedagogic conception of suffering, may in a large measure be explained his zeal to have Norway stand by Denmark in the Schleswig controversy. As a matter of course, he took for his starting-point, as did other Scandinavians, the kinship of the two countries, promises given, Denmark's right; but it was his optimism that led him to view the use of such aid as subordinate. To the outburst, "You would have had many a beating," he once replied, "To be sure, many a one; but what harm would that have done? We should have been brought into the movement, should have belonged to Europe. Anything in preference to remaining outside."

At another time—in 1874, I believe—Ibsen was praising Russia in a high strain. "A magnificent land," said he, smiling. "The oppression there is truly brilliant."

"How so?"

"Why, think of all the glorious love of freedom it engenders. Russia is one of the few countries on earth where men still love freedom, and offer sacrifices to it. That is the reason why the land stands so high in poetry and in art. Think of the Russians having a poet like Turgenief! And there are Turgeniefs among their painters, also. We do not know them, but I saw their paintings as Vienna."

"If all these good things are the result of oppression," said I, "we may well bestow our praises on it. But how is it with knout? Are you enthusiastic about that, too? Suppose you were a Russian, would you have your little boy (and I pointed to his then half-grown son) receive stripes from the knout?" Ibsen was silent for a moment, while his countenance wore an impenetrable look. Then he replied, laughing, "No, he should not receive stripes, he should inflict them." This humorous sally is Ibsen through and through. He himself is all the time inflicting the knout on his contemporaries in his dramas. It is to be hoped that the eventual infliction of stripes in Russia, by way of change, might be bestowed on the oppressors.

It need be no matter of surprise that with such views, Henrik Ibsen was anything but enthusiastic when Rome was taken possession of by the Italian troops. In moody despondency, he wrote:—

And so Rome has been taken from us human beings, and given to the politicians! Where shall we now seek refuge? Rome was the sole spot in Europe that was consecrated to freedom, the sole spot that enjoyed true freedom,—that is to say, freedom from political tyranny. . . . And then all the beautiful yearning for freedom,—that, too, is gone now. Ah, I may well say the one thing I love in freedom is the struggle for its attainment. Its possession does not greatly concern me.

There is, it seems to me, something dual in this standpoint concerning politics. It is partly a reminiscence of ancient romance, that antipathy to utilitarianism, which is common to the romantic schools of all lands, partly something personal and characteristic,—faith in the power of the individual and inclination for radical dilemmas. The man who in "Brand" formulated the motto "All or nothing" could never in the world lend a willing ear to the practical politician's watchword, "A little step forward each day." I should really like to know if Ibsen's warm predilection for Russia did not originate in the fact that there is no parliament in that country. From the depths of his nature Ibsen abhors parliaments. He believes in the individual, in the single great personality. A single individual, according to him, can accomplish everything, and only a single individual. Such a body as a parliament is in his eyes an assemblage of speakers and dilettanti, which naturally does not prevent him from cherishing esteem for individual members of parliaments as such.

It is, therefore, a continual source of amusement to Ibsen when he reads in a newspaper: "And then a committee was appointed," or, "After this a club was formed." He sees a symptom of the enervation of modern times in the fact that as soon as any one has a plan, or a matter of business of any kind, his first thought is to have a committee appointed or a club formed for its benefit. Recall the scornful peals of laughter that resound through "De Unges Forbund" (The Young Men's Union).

I believe that Ibsen, in the inner recesses of his soul, forces his individualism to an excess, of which but a faint impression can be gained from his works. He goes even farther in this particular than Sören Kierkegaard, of whom in other respects he strongly reminds us. Ibsen is, for example, a decided opponent of the modern, straitlaced state idea. Not in the sense that would lead him to favor small states and narrow communities. No one can cherish a greater horror than he of the tyranny they exercise, and of the petty tendencies they lead in their train. Few have been more zealous than he in urging that the Scandinavian kingdoms should follow the example of Italy and Germany, and unite in one political whole. His most significant historic drama, "Kongs-Emnerne," (The Pretenders) deals exclusively with the justification of the idea of a similar union. Ibsen goes so far in this respect, that he seems to me to overlook the dangers to the manifoldness and variety of intellectual life this endeavor for political unity conceals within itself. Italy has never stood higher in an artistic sense (and generally) than in the days when Siena and Florence represented two worlds, and Germany never stood higher intellectually (and generally) than when Königsberg (Kant) and Weimar (Schiller-Goethe) were centres. Yet in spite of his enthusiasm for unity, Ibsen's poetic brain dreams of a time when state power will afford a far greater measure of individual and communal freedom than at present, when the state, as it now is, will no longer exist. Although Ibsen reads little, and does not orient himself in the period in which he lives by means of books, it often seems to me as if he stood in a sort of secret correspondence with the fermenting, germinating ideas of the times. Once of late have I received a decided impression that thoughts which were in their outburst historic, but which were not yet recognized as such by others, occupied, and at the same time tortured him. Immediately after the close of the Franco-German war at a time when all minds were occupied with it, and when the thought of such a thing as the commune in Paris had scarcely risen up in a single Northern brain, Ibsen presented to me as political ideals, conditions and ideas whose nature did not seem to me quite clear, but which were unquestionably akin to those that were proclaimed precisely one month later, in an extremely distorted form, by the Parisian commune. In reference to our diversity of opinions regarding freedom and politics, Ibsen wrote to me, Feb. 17, 1871:—

... The struggle for freedom is to be sure nothing but the perpetual living appropriation of the idea of freedom. He who possesses freedom otherwise than as something for which he is

striving, has a dead, soulless possession; for the idea of freedom
bears that within itself which causes it to broaden and expand
under appropriation, and if any one, during the struggle for
its attainment, pauses and cries, Now, I have it,—he proves
thereby that he has lost it. Yet it is just this dead stand-still
in a certain grade of freedom that is characteristic of the body
politic, and it is this that I have had occasion to censure. To be
sure, there may be some advantage in the possession of the
right of the ballot and a voice in regard to taxation, etc., but
whom does it profit? The citizen, not the individual. There
is, however, no rational necessity whatever for the individual to
become a citizen. On the contrary. The state is the curse of
the individual. How is the strength of the state of Prussia
purchased? By the absorption of the individual into the
political and geographic idea. The waiter makes the best
soldier. The opposite case may be exemplified by the Jews, the
nobility of the human race. How have they maintained their
individuality in isolation, in poetry, notwithstanding all the
brutality of the outside world? Through the fact that they
have had no state burdens on their shoulders. Had they remained in Palestine, they would have gone to ruin in their
construction long ago, as all other peoples have done. The
state must be abolished. In a revolution that would bring about
so desirable a consummation, I should gladly take part. Undermine the idea of the commonwealth, set up spontaneity and
spiritual kinship as the sole determining points in a union, and
there will be attained the beginning of a freedom that is of
some value. Changes in the form of government are nothing
else than different degrees of trifling, a little more, or a little
less—absurd folly. The state has its root in time; it will attain
its summit in time. Greater things than it will fall. All
existing forms of religion will pass away. Neither moral conceptions, nor art forms have an eternity before them. To how
much, after all, is it our duty to hold fast? Who will vouch
for me that two and two do not make five on Jupiter?

Henrik Ibsen was certainly not aware of the ingenuous,
yet paradoxical attempt of the anonymous author "A Barrister," to prove exactly how two and two might be considered to make five on Jupiter; nor was it likely that he was
aware how vigorously Stuart Mill, and all other adherents
of radical empiricism, would applaud the last-cited lines;
the natural bent of his intellectual powers, however, has led
him to universal scepticism, which, in his case, is so marvellously united with vigorous, practical faith. In as early

a work as his "Brand," he put into his hero's mouth the words:—

> No dogma and no church shall ever
> Exalted be through my endeavor;
> They both have seen their natal day,
> 'Twould, therefore, but in reason be
> That both their final hour should see.
> For all that's made must pass away;
> It gathers moths, is gnawed by worms,
> And must, obeying laws and norms,
> Give place to other unborn forms.

The passage cited from his letter affords an energetic commentary on these words, and may readily be communicated as a proof of the presentiments of the hidden occurrences of the age, that were the natural outgrowths of Ibsen's genius, without the least danger of lowering the poet in the eyes of an honored public, since even Prince Bismarck has publicly recognized the "grain of sound reason" that was the kernel of the bewildered efforts of the commune. On May 18, 1871, Ibsen wrote:—

Is it not impudent of the commune in Paris to go and destroy my admirable state theory, or rather no state theory? The idea is now ruined for a long time to come, and I cannot even set it forth in verse with any propriety. But it bears within itself a healthy core, that I see very plainly, and some day it will be practised without any caricature. . . .

It is in his maintenance of the sovereignty of the individual, that Ibsen came to take a polemic stand in regard to the state idea as well as to the idea of society. I am not sure that I fully comprehend him on this point; his mode of thought is foreign to me. I can understand why there are those, as for instance, Lorenz von Stein, and after him Gneist, who recognize in the history of modern times a continual struggle between the state and society and who, proceeding from a new, energetic comprehension of the state idea, can turn in a polemic way against society; but I do not thoroughly understand the double front presented by Ibsen, nor am I quite sure that he is himself conscious that there is any double front in question.

But his anxiety, lest the sting of personality be dulled and its choicest treasures laid waste, extends still further. He firmly believes that the individual must stand alone, must be absolutely free, if all the fruitful possibilities of its nature are to be developed, and so his eyes are open to all the hindrances to individual growth that every association, even friendship, even marriage, bears within itself. I well remember his answer to a letter written by me in one of those melancholy moods to which youth so readily gives expression, and in which I declared, with a little sigh, as it were, that I had few or no friends. Ibsen wrote, March 6, 1870, as follows: —

. . . You say you have no friends at home. So I have long thought. Any one who like yourself stands in close relation to his life-work, cannot reasonably expect to retain his friends. Friends are an expensive luxury, and he who invests his capital in a calling and a mission in this life has no means left wherewith to maintain friends. The cost of keeping friends does not consist in what we do for them, but in what we leave undone out of regard for them. Thereby many intellectual germs are stunted in their growth. I have experienced this myself, and that is the reason why I can look back on a number of years, during which I failed to succeed in becoming myself . . .

Is not Ibsen's absolute need of independence and sense of isolation felt in the words "the cost of keeping friends"; and is there not in the words cited, the chief explanation of Ibsen's comparatively late outburst of originality. His career, as I have asserted before, was apparently begun without any high degree of self-confidence.

As friendship under certain circumstances may be a hindrance to the independence of the individual, so too may marriage. Therefore it is that Nora refuses to consider her duties toward her husband and children as her most sacred duties; for a far more sacred duty she believes she owes herself. Therefore it is that to Helmer's "You are before all else a wife and mother"; she replies: —

"I am before all else a human being,—or, at all events, I shall endeavor to become one."

Ibsen shares with Kierkegaard the conviction that in

every single human being there slumbers the soul of a warrior, an invincible power; but he cherishes it in another form than Kierkegaard, for whom the worth of the individual is something supernatural, while with Ibsen, we rest on human grounds. He believes that the individuality of the human being is to be preserved for its own sake, not for the sake of higher powers; and since beyond all else the individual should remain free and whole, all concessions made to the world represent to Ibsen the foul fiend, the evil principle.

Here we touch upon the fundamental thought in "Brand." It is embodied in the passage where Brand speaks of all those scattered fragments of the soul,—those torsos of the spirit, those heads, those hands, from which one day a noble whole shall proceed: a hero, in whom the Lord shall recognize man, His greatest work, His Adam. young and strong.

Thus, "all or nothing" becomes Brand's apparently inhuman motto. Therefore the "spirit of compromise," even in the hours of his death, is nothing to Brand but a fair temptress who demands a little finger, in order to gain possession of the whole hand; and, therefore, the spirit of compromise returns in 'Peer Gynt" as the mighty "Böjgen," the incarnation of all that is cowardly and pliable in human nature, all that readily bends and curves.

> Defend thyself!
>
>   Böjgen is not mad!
> Strike!
>   Böjgen never strikes!
>   Fight! Thou shalt!
> The mighty Böjgen wins without e'er fighting!
> * * * * * * *
> The mighty Böjgen wins all things through gentleness.

To extricate the race from "Böjgen's" stifling embrace, to capture the spirit of compromise, force it into a casket and hurl it into the deepest part of the sea,—this is the goal at which Ibsen, as a poet, has aimed. This extrication of the individual from compromise, and from the mighty "Böjgen," is the revolution that is his own.

I once asked Henrik Ibsen, "Is there among all the Danish poets a single one about whom, in your present stage of development (1871), you concern yourself in the least." After leaving me for some time to vain conjectures, he replied: "Once upon a time there was an old man in Seeland who stood behind his plough in a peasant's smock, and who had viewed mankind and the world with angry eyes. I rather like him." Is it not a significant fact that Bredahl is the Danish writer who of all others is nearest Ibsen's heart? Bredahl, too, was an indignation pessimist, —no deep-seeing psychologist, it is true, but a thinker in whose pathos may be found, as it were, the thunder which precedes Ibsen's lightning. Bredahl sees only the exterior tyranny and hypocrisy, while Ibsen searches these out in the hidden recesses of the heart. His standpoint is that of Ibsen's revolutionary orator,—

He looks after the inundations for the world's meadows.

His great successor goes more thoroughly to work,—

He takes delight in placing torpedoes under the ark.

If, then, I have designated Ibsen as a revolutionary nature, I need scarcely defend myself from the charge of having declared his to be one of those natures that are enthusiastic for violent exterior convulsions. Far from it! Indeed, quite the contrary! For, isolated as he is and feels himself to be, reluctantly opposed to all parties, simply as parties, stately, polished, reserved, "awaiting the approach of time in a spotless wedding garment," he is, so far as exteriors are concerned, strictly conservative, although his conservatism is of a peculiar nature; that is, it proceeds from radicalism, because he expects nothing from special reforms. In the depths of his soul he is a decided revolutionist, but the revolution he raves about and labors for is the purely spiritual one I have pictured. The reader will not have overlooked the concluding words of the letter of December, 1870, "What is really needed is a revolting of the human spirit." I have never been able to forget these words; for they contain, in a measure, Ibsen's entire poetic programme—an admirable programme for a poet.

I should, however, fail to be true to myself if I said that Ibsen's view of life seemed to me to possess more than a powerful element of truth. It is a view of life by virtue of which one may think and produce poetic creations, but not act, which, indeed, strictly considered, cannot even be put into plain language in the world, as it is, because it is calculated to instigate others to action, which in this instance means—capital offence. Whoever, through a yearning for great, decisive, sweeping overthrows, is led to look indifferently or contemptuously on the slow, insignificant changes of the natural course of development; on the tardy, gradual, petty improvements, the compromises, with which the practical worker must be content, because through them alone he can hope to attain the partial realization of his ideal; on the associations without which it is impossible for any one who is not in a position of brutal command to transmit a single thought into the reality of life,—such a man must relinquish all hopes of raising a finger in practical life. Like Sören Kierkegaard, like Brand, he can do nothing but point helplessly at the yawning gulf that separates existing reality from the ideal. To attempt to act himself or induce others to act in harmony with the desired goal, would simply mean to lead his followers headlong over the brink of that dizzy abyss which parts what exists from what is desired, and to expose himself to immediate arrest. Indeed, even the poet can only express so ideal a view of life indirectly, insinuatingly, ambiguously, in the drama; only through thoroughly responsible personages, and thus with a certain reservation, so far as the author himself is concerned. Only the rudest kind of opponents could possibly have taken the hideous jest about the torpedoes beneath the ark for literal, bloodthirsty earnest. This mode of contemplating life involves and necessitates, therefore, a dualism between the theoretic and the practical, between the individual and the citizen, between spiritual freedom and that practical freedom which has the form of an obligation, a dualism that in actual life can only be carried out by a dramatic poet who lives in exile, who is not obliged to have the slightest dealings with state, society, politics, groups of human beings, parties, or reforms.

Therefore the ideal of intellectual reserve that has its origin in this mode of contemplating life seems not to me the highest. To be sure, a distinguished author provides best for his outward dignity when he is never found in a skirmish or amid an excited throng. It is unquestionably aristocratic to hold one's self aloof from the vulgar crowd, never to mingle in the turmoil of the day, never to write a newspaper article. Yet to my taste it savors of a still higher aristocracy to act as did the ligitimist generals who reported themselves as simple soldiers in Condé's army, and who, notwithstanding their general's epaulettes, did not disdain to fight now and then on foot and in the first rank. Not one whit of true inner dignity is sacrificed by such a course.

III

The psychological analysis has now reached a point from which we can view this poetic mind in the light of the literary consciousness and endeavors of its contemporaries. I say expressly contemporaries, not people; for Ibsen is as strongly marked a European character as Björnson, notwithstanding his cosmopolitan culture, is national. A poet's attitude in regard to the consciousness of his contemporaries is indicative of his relation to the ideas and forms of his age. Every period has its own peculiar ideas, which in art appear in the shape of themes and ideals.

Ideas are not begotten by poets. They emerge from the labors of thinkers and inquirers; they come forward as large, genial presentiments of the laws and relations of realities; they develop and take form amid scientific investigations, amid historic or philosophic inquiries; they grow, become purified and strengthened through struggles for and against their truth, until, like the angels of the Bible, they become powers, thrones, kingdoms, and reign over the epoch.

Poets do not beget ideas; it is neither their vocation nor

their business to do so. Genuine poets, however, become overwhelmed with ideas while these are still growing and struggling, and take their stand in the great conflict of the age at the side of these ideas. They are transported by them, nor can they do otherwise; they comprehend, and yet have never learned. Mediocre poets, those who possess no poetic quality unless it may be a transmitted or an acquired routine, have no ear for the hollow rumbling of ideas as they penetrate the subterranean passages of the earth, no ear for their pinion-beats in the air. In the preface to his "Neue Gedichte," Heine states that while engaged in writing these poems it seemed to him as though he could hear the flutter of a bird's wings above his head. "When I related this to my friends, the young Berlin poets," he continues, "they exchanged significant glances, and unanimously assured me that nothing of the kind had ever come within their experience." This whizzing sound, which the Berlin poets had never heard, was nothing in the world but the pinion-beat of those ideas.

Wholly without ideas, however, it is impossible for a poet to create. Even bad poets have at their command ideas, viz., those of the past; and these ideas that were invested by the masters of an earlier period with distinctly marked poetic expressions are reproduced by them in a feeble, ineffective way. The ideas of the age, as a rule, appear to them thoroughly "unpoetic." To evolve poetry from these ideas seems to them utterly impossible. But the poet who in his youth (in "The Pretenders") wrote the memorable sentence, "For you it is impossible; all you can do is to repeat the old story; but for me it is as easy as it is for the falcon to cleave the skies," could never have been permanently alarmed by the thoughts of his day. He has invested many new ideas with flesh and blood, and in thus incarnating them has aided in their dissemination; he has, moreover, given breadth and depth to many contemporary ideas by watering them from the well-springs of his own emotional nature. How profoundly he has felt the necessity of a vital relation to the germinating ideas about him may be conjectured from the superb lament of the balls of yarn, withered leaves, and broken straws, to Peer Gynt:—

> Thoughts are we,
>   Thou shouldst have thought us.
>   * * * * * *
> We'd soar aloft
>   As songs consoling.
> Yet here as balls
>   Of yarn we're rolling
> We are a watchword,
>   Thou shouldst have proclaimed us;
> See how indiff'rence
>   Hath seized and shamed us.
> We are duties,
>   Thou hast neglected us.
> Doubts and hesitations
>   Have maimed and dejected us.

Words of reproach these are by which me may well fancy that the poet has been incited to action in periods of laxity, but which it is impossible to conceive of in the form of a Peer Gynt self-accusation. How in the world could poor Peer have given himself a watchword? How could he reproach himself with not having proclaimed it?

Let us now see what topics and ideals are especially uppermost in the consciousness of the age. They may be divided, it seems to me, into the following groups:—

First, such ideals and topics as stand in direct relation to religion; that is to say, the reverential relation of men to ideas which in their eyes are powers,—to some outward, to some inward powers—especially those ideals and topics that have a bearing on the conflict between individuals who deem these powers outward and those who deem them inward realities.

Second, those topics and ideals that revolve about distinctions between two ages, past and future, ancient and modern, old and new, especially regarding distinctions and conflicts between two generations.

Next, those that have a bearing on the grades of society and their struggle for existence, on class distinctions,—especially those between rich and poor,—social influence, and social dependence.

Finally, a whole group of topics and ideals that revolve about distinctions between the two sexes, about the mutual erotic and social relation of man and woman, especially about woman's economical, moral, and spiritual emancipation.

Religious topics and problems are dealt with in our day in the most diverse ways, although always in the modern spirit. Allow some of the principal instances to pass in review before your mind. The greatest of the elder generation of poets in France, Victor Hugo, notwithstanding his passionate tendency to free thought, displays the remnants of a vague deism, colored with pantheism. Traces of the influence of the past century may readily be detected in him: religion is glorified at the cost of religions; love which unites is extolled in opposition to faith which parts and destroys. Most of the prominent authors of the present generation, as for instance Flaubert, represent religion with scientific coldness, but always from the dark side. To him, and to his spiritual kindred, the object of religion is a hallucination, in which one believes. The greatest English poet of our day, Swinburne, is a passionate heathen with a rich poetic vein, and he conceives Christianity to be a denial of nature, the enemy with whom he must do combat. In Italy, the greatest poet of the land, Leopardi, became absorbed in a sort of sublime metaphysical pessimism, which found vent in stoic resignation. Carducci, the foremost of Italy's living poetic thinkers, is quite as modern and even more polemic than he. In Germany, the most prominent poets, as Gottfried Keller, Paul Heyse, Fr. Spielhagen, have displayed in their works a soul-felt atheistic humanitarianism.

In the North the conditions were totally different. The Danish poets of the past generation had almost invariably paid homage to orthodoxy; the only philosophically inclined one among them, J. L. Heiberg, who had begun by protesting as a free thinker, ended by making at least apparent concessions to the teachings of the clergy; and the attempt in Denmark to undermine the authority of the church, namely, Kierkegaard's violent attack on the state church, had not been aimed at the truth of the dogmas taught, but exclusively at their professors, especially in cases where the lives of the priests failed to correspond with their teachings. This attitude of Kierkegaard has been a decisive one for Danish-Norwegian polite literature, down to the present day. Modern poetry in Denmark and Norway has rarely, if ever, touched the objective side of the question, the essence of religion, but almost exclusively its subjective side; hence the extraordinary wealth of priestly forms in this literature, both before and after its authors were emancipated from orthodoxy. The priests in Björnson's and in Magdalene Thoresen's peasant stories denote the standpoint before emancipation, the priests in Björnson's Schandorph's, Kielland's, Ibsen's, Gjellerup's latest works the standpoint after emancipation.

Ibsen follows the clue given by Kierkegaard. Like all men of his generation in the North, who have grown up in the period of romance, his early relations to religion lack clearness. Moreover, there was in his nature a dual tendency, which must necessarily expose him to inner tumults: a native propensity to mysticism and an equally inbred inclination to sharp, dry common sense. Few poets who are capable of such almost convulsive flights of fancy as he, are able to linger as calmly as he can amid the prose of life. "Brand" and "Samfundets Stötter" (The Pillars of Society) differ as widely in main essentials as though written by different authors. The character of the first-named work is that of pure, unqualified mysticism, the other revolves about simple, unadulterated prose. Here boundless exultation; there good, wholesome, social morality.

No one who is familiar with the mental characteristics of the Norsemen can doubt that "Brand," which laid the foundation for Ibsen's poetic fame, excited universal attention merely because it was regarded as a sort of poetic sermon, a homily, a devotional work. It was not the real merits of the book that made it seem imposing to the public and caused the sale of so many editions; no, people streamed into the bookstores to purchase "Brand" precisely as people pour into church when a new and severely zealous priest appears. In a correspondence that Ibsen carried on with me regarding this book, he expressly stated that Brand's ministerial career was the purely exterior, incidental side of the question. In a letter, dated June 26, 1869, he writes:—

"Brand has been misunderstood, so far, at least, as my intention was concerned. The misconception is unquestionably rooted in the fact that Brand is a priest, and that the problem of the work is placed in the realm of religion. It would have been just as possible for me to apply the same syllogism to a sculptor, or a politician, as to a priest. I could just as well have given vent to the mood that impelled me to literary production, had I, instead of Brand, for instance, dealt with Galileo (with the trifling alteration in the latter's history, that he must, as a matter of course, remain firm and not concede that the earth stood still.) Indeed, who knows, had I been born a hundred years later, I might with equal relish have treated yourself and your struggle with Rasmus Nielsen's philosophy of compromise. Taken as a whole, there is much more objectivity in Brand than has hitherto been discovered, and of this, as a poet, I am proud."

Although it is my wont carefully to withhold everything of a personal nature from these quotations, I have here permitted myself to retain a playful allusion to the literary warfare of those days, because it proves how little the mere idea of priesthood concerned Ibsen. A further proof of this is afforded by an expression in one of the letters I received from Ibsen during the time when I was brooding over the introduction to my book "Hovedströmninger i det 19de. Aarhundredes Litteratur" (The main currents of the Literature of the 19th Century). It reads as follows:—

It seems to me you have reached the same crisis which I had attained in the days when I was about to write Brand, and I am convinced that you, too, will know how to find the healing drug that can expel disease from your body. In energetic production lies an admirable cure.

As the reader will see for himself, the emphasis in "Brand" is placed, according to the poet's own construction, upon the power of self-sacrifice and strength of character, not upon any special religious dogma. Now although Ibsen is, of course, the best, the only competent judge of his own design in the work, he nevertheless underrates, in my estimation, the weight of the unconscious power by which he was impelled to choose the precise materials he has chosen and no others. And this unconscious power, as I believe, was Ibsen's Norse-romantic tendency to mysticism. Yet even if "Brand" should be understood exactly in accordance with Ibsen's own interpretation of the character, the resemblance to religious phenomena in Northern religious life is equally obvious. It might look to the Danes as though Ibsen had Kierkegaard especially *in mente;* for he, too, laid the entire stress on personal sincerity. This would be due to our unfamiliarity with Ibsen's Norwegian models. Independent priests of Norway, Lammers, for instance, have had a larger share in the formation of the character of "Brand" than any direct influence from Denmark. Lammers, however, was himself led to the stand he took by the Kierkegaard agitation.

In "Kejser og Galilæer" (Emporor and Galilean), the influence of the Kierkegaard standpoint, although still strong, is on the wane. True, the passion for martyrdom is here set up as a measure for truth, and the psychological principle of the work is that no doctrine has intrinsic worth that is incapable of inspiring a spirit of martyrdom; but with this there is united a determinism that is half-mystic, half-moulded in the modern spirit; moreover, a Schopenhauer-like faith in the unconscious and irresistible worldwill; finally, a modern prophecy that Christianity, as well as paganism, will one day be resolved into a third kingdom which will be an amalgamation of the two. It is characteristic of Ibsen's intellectual *habitus* that in both of his attempts at dealing with religious themes everything that savors of conflict and endeavor is infinitely more prominent and successful than portions touching on reconciliation and harmony. "The Third Kingdom" in his "Emperor and Galilean," stands quite as obscurely in the background as that *Deus caritatis* at the conclusion of "Brand."

Themes that revolve about the relations between two successive ages or generations, or simply about the relations between different stages of life, which in Russia, Germany, Denmark, and Norway have been treated in so many different ways, have also occupied Ibsen, during his first period in "Kongs Emnerne" (The Pretenders), during the transition to his second period in "De Unges Forbund" (The Young Men's Union). Both these dramas are remarkable works, but the strength of neither lies in historic insight or historic impartiality.

"The Pretenders" is not really an historic drama; it displays no design on the part of its author to produce, through a series of pictures of the past, a portrayal of human nature as it appears under certain conditions at a defined period. The poet did not proceed from an historic standpoint; he simply used the historic as a pretext. The background of the play is mediæval, the foreground modern, for Skule Jarl is a modern figure. An historic construction would have led to the presentation of Skule as a full-blooded aristocrat, and Bishop Nicolas as a fanatical, yet thoroughly devoted and conscientious clergyman. Skule's conflict with Haakon denotes historically the last unsuccessful attempt of the aristocracy to limit the power of the king; and the bishop's conflict indicates that hatred, which was so well justified from a priestly point of view, against the enemy of the church and usurper Sverre and his race. Instead, Ibsen has transformed Nicholas into a monster, who symbolizes bigotry, envy, and dissension in Norway through long ages, and Skule into an ambitious person who, while striving to attain the highest goal, is at the same time tormented with a wretched doubt of his right and ability to reach it. Haakon and Skule are contrasted as representatives of two epochs,—the age of dissension and the age of union. But, as the poet's interest in the psychological is so much greater than his sense of the historic element, this contrast is thrust into the background by the contrast between the individual characters and their relation to ideas. Haakon represents "the king's thought," which he himself first conceived, and is wholly submerged in this relation. Skule represents no ancient historic idea, but simply lack of self-confidence. He steals Haakon's "king's thought" in order to procure for himself through it a right to the throne. He does not succeed. The skald declares to him that he cannot live for the life-work of another, and he himself recognizes the truth of this. The skald's thought is not expressed with any too great lucidity; for why could not a man live for the ideas of another, if he has himself endeavored to appreciate and transform them into his own flesh and blood, without stealing them, and causing them to pass for his own discovery? The theft, not the fact of living for the ideas of others, would make a person unhappy; and this it is which causes the unhappiness of Skule. The fact is, however, that Ibsen, with the whole intensity of his nature, interests himself more in the struggle that is taking place in the soul of the individual than in any struggle between historic powers. What attracted him to Skule, and made the latter the main personage of the play, was the "interesting" element in the character of Skule,—his complex nature, his struggling soul, which even when in the wrong eclipsed that of the simple-hearted Haakon with his certainty of coming victory. It is the despairing power in the great Nureddin which, in spite of his craving for the lamp, in spite of the theft of the lamp, is doomed to ruin. It is the representation of a soul whose aspiration is greater than its ability to rise; and this same representation it is that is varied in Bishop Nicholas, whose gigantic powers are wrecked in partly physical, partly spiritual, but wholly powerless yearning and craving. It is the relation between the ability and the desire, between the will and the possibility, in the soul of the individual, this relation which is already indicated in Catiline and in Gunnar in "The Vikings," which is brought forward anew in the relation of Skule to Haakon's thoughts. Skule stands in the same relation to the "king's thought" as Julian to Christianity. Filled with a foreboding of the greatness of the power he is combating, he holds an irreconcilably distorted relation to the great, victorious idea. The psychological interest completely routs the historic.

The relation between two succeeding generations is again represented in "The Young Men's Union," a drama which furnishes in an extremely witty manner a parody on the efforts of the younger generation, without at the same time offering any justification for these efforts. This work cannot be compared with such works as Turgenief's "Fathers and Sons," or "Virgin Soil," which unite relentless severity against the elder generation with their stern judgments on the younger, and at the same time extend to both thorough sympathy and comprehension. Ibsen's pessimism has repelled his sympathy. The sole honorable representative of the younger generation in the play last mentioned is Dr. Fjeldbo, a man of a thoroughly passive nature. That he is a physician is scarcely a matter of pure accident. The skilful physician plays, on the whole, a striking rôle in modern poetry; he is evidently the hero of the day. The cause of this is, doubtless, that he can be used as the incarnation of the ideals of the age, those strictly modern ideals, which are in respect to theory science, with its relationship to the true and the false, in respect to practice humanity, with its relationship to happiness and suffering, the opposing psychologic and social forces that claim the attention of the age.

In the dramas of Schiller, as well as in those of modern Germany, the struggle for political and spiritual freedom plays a prominent rôle. Class distinctions, too, are a favorite theme in various German dramas of an earlier period, even though it had not then become customary for poetry to deal with what is called at the present time the social problem. A glimmer of the latter appeared much earlier in the French drama, from the days of Beaumarchais to those of Victor Hugo, as this question had become a burning one in public discussion in France far earlier than elsewhere. In the polite literature of our day, the social question has gradually banished the political from its high seat. Modern poetry, in many lands, is inspired by sympathy with the poor and lowly; it reminds those who are well placed in life of their duties. The question is not one of those that have chiefly occupied Ibsen, and yet he has touched upon it. When he wrote "Catiline," he was too undeveloped to comprehend the social problem aright; but many years later, in "Samfundets Stötter" (The Pillars of Society), he aimed a blow at the leading circles of his fatherland. The play is wholly without a socialistic tendency, as is well known, yet so profound is its pessimism that those who are unfamiliar with Norwegian affairs, especially with the attitude of the poet to his public and to the various parties of his native land, might take it for granted that there was a tendency of the kind in the work. When it was played in Berlin, many spectators (and, it may safely be asserted, not those who were by any means lacking in judgment) yielded to the error that it was written by a socialist. I was myself obliged to assure many people that its author was, on the contrary, the favorite poet (at that time) of the conservative party in Norway. In "The Pillars of Society," which has the effect of a supplement to "The Young Men's Union," the two sides of the question are as little apparent as in the last-named comedy. Ibsen proceeds here, as everywhere else, from a one-sided point of view.

The relation between man and woman is one of those that has most intensely absorbed Ibsen, and in regard to which he has cherished the most original and the most modern sentiments.

In his first youthful works this relation is treated somewhat in the traditional way. He attacks in his "Gildet paa Solhaug" (Feast at Solhaug) the same theme Björnson has chosen for his "Halte Hulda" (Lame Hulda); that is, the position of a young man between the woman a little older than himself whom he has loved in his youth, and the young girl whom he longs with his whole heart to make his bride,—a theme both human and universal, yet one that has frequently been varied. He next represents, in his "Catiline" and in his "Fru Inger til Österaat" (Lady Inger) the same rather forced yet stirring motive, how a man who had led a licentious life in his youth is punished through his love for a young girl who at the same time loves, abhors, and curses him, because he had betrayed her sister and sent her to her grave.

In his "Kjærlighedens Komedie" (Love's Comedy),

Ibsen for the first time takes up the erotic condition of his fatherland for his theme. He had apparently received no trifling stimulus from contemporary Norwegian literature. While Björnson during his first period was influenced by popular tradition and popular poetry, Ibsen was incited to action in his early days by the most advanced thinkers of the time. There is something in the inspiration of "Love's Comedy" that may be traced back to Camilla Collet's "Amtmandens Dötre" (The Magistrate's Daughters). The latter daring book at that time occupied every Norwegian mind; and it contained the same witty, though rather less well planned attack on betrothals and marriages that in Ibsen's drama is conducted by a firm, manly hand. So far as similes and figures are concerned, the influence of Camilla Collet is very perceptible. Ibsen's celebrated "tea-comparison" is derived from her. In "The Magistrate's Daughters" we read of love, as follows:—

Guard, O mankind, this our life's first bloom. . . . Heed its growth and its fruit. . . . Do not lightly disturb its tender, budding leaf, in the belief that the coarse blossoms that come later are good enough. . . . No; they are not good enough. There is as great a difference between the two kinds, as there is between the tea we ordinary mortals must be content with, and that which the emperor of the Celestial Kingdom drinks, and which is the only genuine tea; it is gathered first, and is so delicate and tender that it must be plucked with gloves, after the gleaners have washed twenty-four times.

Henrik Ibsen writes:—

> Ah, ladies, in your hearts, you one and all
> A special small Celestial Empire hold,
> Where many precious budding germs unfold
> Behind your maidenhood's crumbling Chinese wall.

And the passage ends thus:—

> Behold, to us a second growth there fares
> That with the first like hemp with silk compares;
> And stalks and rubbish 'midst the leaves we see;
> This is the blackened tea—
>   It fills the market.

Ibsen has simply given further development to the simile and invested it with the solid mould of verse.

It is a well-known fact, that there is nothing clear in "Love's Comedy" except its mockery. The play presents a satire on marriage which imparts to the reader as little sympathy for the defenders of the conventional standard, as for its assailers, and from which it is impossible to detect whether in the poet's opinion it is better to maintain the present practices of society or to overthrow them. The only thing that is certain is his misanthropic view of the bethrothals and marriages that have come under his observation. I remember a conversation with Ibsen in reference to this drama, which revolved about the ideal of love among betrothed couples in general. I said, "There are blighted potatoes and there are sound potatoes." Ibsen replied, "I very much fear I have never seen any of those potatoes that were sound."

Nevertheless, there runs through Ibsen's works a continually increasing faith in woman, and tendency to glorify woman. At times this appears in a rather revolting, dogmatic way, as when Solveig, in "Peer Gynt," after the traditional styles of Goethe's "Faust" and Paludan Müller's "Adam Homo," through her faithful love, saves the soul of her lover,—in this instance an altogether too unworthy being; but this faith in woman, with which Ibsen evidently desires to counterbalance his contempt for man, is ever present, and has been productive of a series of true and beautiful female characterizations, such as Margrete in "The Pretenders," who is represented by a few delicate strokes in imperishable beauty; or Selma in "The Young Men's Union," who may be regarded as the first draught of Nora. When this figure was new, I remarked in a review that the drama did not afford sufficient play for it, that an entire new drama should be written expressly for it. This was done in "Et Dukkehjem" (A Doll's House).

As far as I can judge, the idea of woman's emancipation, in the modern acceptation of the phrase, was far from being familiar and dear to Henrik Ibsen at the outset of his career. On the contrary, he did not originally possess a large amount of sympathy for woman. There are authors who have a peculiar affinity for women, who have, indeed, a decided feminine element in their own natures. Ibsen does not belong to this class. I am quite confident he takes far more pleasure in conversation with men than with women, and he has certainly passed much less time in the society of women than is the wont of poets. Moreover, the attempt of modern literature to prove the justice of a change in woman's social status, was at first far from finding an enthusiastic admirer in him. Mill's book on the woman question was, if I mistake not, actually repulsive to him in the early days of its appearance, and Mill, as a writer, inspired him with no sympathy whatever. Indeed, to Ibsen, with his marked individuality, Mill's statement, or rather confession, that he owed much in his writings, indeed the best they contained, to his wife, seemed absurdly ludicrous. "Only fancy," he said, smiling, "what it would be to read Hegel or Krause with the idea that it was quite uncertain whether we were following the thoughts of Mr. or of Mrs. Hegel, of Mr. or of Mrs. Krause!"

It does not seem to me that this aversion on the part of Ibsen was wholly without a connection with the poet's sentiments in regard to the woman question. I am rather inclined to think there was in his mind an opposition to the latter during its early stages, partly owing to the influences of his education, partly owing to a natural irritation at the caricature forms of female emancipation, but an opposition whose destiny it was to give place to passionate adherence. It is Ibsen's reason that has wrought the change in his emotional nature. Like a true poet, he is capable of becoming, with his whole soul, the organ of an idea which once had left him cold, the moment he feels this idea to be one of those battle-thoughts of the period that are fraught with rich meaning for the future. And when we read those words, that fall like sword-strokes, in the last scene of "A Doll's House," Helmer's—

There is no one who yields up his honor for those whom he loves.

and Nora's—

'Tis what hundreds and thousands of women have done,

words in which a more hideous abyss yawns between the husband and wife that sit opposite each other at table than the nether world ever opened in the old dramas of romance, we feel, indeed, that Ibsen has not merely filled his soul with the thoughts of the age; he has fashioned them on a grander scale than any one else, he has ground them until they are sharper than in the hands of others, so that with his consummate art he can make them penetrate even the most hardened hearts. This drama produced a powerful, although alarming effect. For centuries society, through its priests and poets, had conceived a marriage, founded in love and undisturbed by the influence of a third person, as a sure haven of bliss, and had celebrated it as such in song. Now it was discovered that this haven was full of rocks and shoals. It actually seemed as though Ibsen had extinguished all the beacon lights.

"Gjengangere" (Ghosts) followed. Here, again as in "A Doll's House," a marriage was analyzed, the opposite of the one in the last-named drama. The grandeur and exquisite delicacy of "A Doll's House" consisted chiefly in the fact that Ibsen had conceded so much to the husband. For what had he not conceded to this man! He is a thoroughly honorable, conscientiously upright man, an excellent provider for his family, a man who is properly jealous of his independence in his dealings with strangers and subordinates, a strict and loving father, a good-hearted, highly cultivated man,—and yet! Yet this man's wife was a victim, and his marriage a whited sepulchre.

The man into whose marriage we gain deep insight in "Ghosts" is a person of a totally opposite character; he is a coarse-natured drunkard, is recklessly dissolute, yet is endowed with so many of those qualities licentious men often have at their command with which to win hearts, and knows how to make himself so agreeable, that it is possible for his wife to screen his life and save appearances. By remaining with him, by giving herself to him, she not only sacrifices her own welfare and happiness, she also becomes the mother of a being whose life is wrecked from birth, a son who is overtaken by deadly impotence, despair, insanity, and idiocy, as he crosses the threshold of manhood,—and yet! Yet that portion of the community which is represented by Pastor Manders deems her sacrifice of herself and her son her simple duty, and her attempted revolt at her hideous fate a crime.

This is the pathos of the play, and this same pathos it was that terrified the great Philistine world more than "A Doll's House" had done. This time it seemed as though the stars had been extinguished by Ibsen. "Not the faintest ray of light appears."

The relation between man and woman in "Ghosts" is placed in a totally new light, inasmuch as it is measured by responsibility to the child. The drama treats, in a poetic form, the thought of heredity, represents, on the basis of that determinism which is the latest word of modern science on the question, the dependence of the child's destiny on the parents, and gives this fact a background of a nature calculated to arouse profound thought and feeling by indicating the more universal fact to which the title points; namely, the hereditary transmission of emotions (and through these of dogmas) whose essential conditions are extinct, and have given place to others at variance with these emotions.

In close relation to Ibsen's psychological development there is associated a principal interest in this grasp or choice of themes, inasmuch as we here for the first time see the great dramatist break the circle it has been the wont of his disposition to cast about the single individual. In a letter of the year 1871, Ibsen wrote me the following words, which are indicative of much in his character:—

To tell the truth, I have never had a very great fancy for solidarity. I have, indeed, only taken it into my cargo as a matter of traditional dogmatism. If we only had the courage to leave it entirely out of consideration, we might possibly become rid of the ballast that weighs most heavily on personality. . . .

Now, ten years later his eyes are opened to the significance of solidarity; he has become thoroughly convinced that "courage" is of no avail in the attempt to cast it overboard, and that we are all from our birth consolidated with persons and things in a way we ourselves cannot control. Evidently, as years pass on, Ibsen enters into a more and more intimate relation with the fundamental ideas of the age.

Thus we see him, who at first, with almost all the now living older writers of the day, stood waist-deep in the romantic period, gradually work his way out of it, and become more and more modern, until finally he grows to be the most modern of modern writers. In my estimation, this is his imperishable glory, and will invest his works with enduring life. For the modern is not the ephemeral; it is the vital flame itself, the life-spark, the ideal soul of an age.

The ill feeling aroused by "Ghosts" in many circles, and the coarse criticism aimed at the drama, could have no power to repress Ibsen's literary productivity, but at first it had a very depressing effect on him. He wrote of it:—

> When I think how sluggish and dull and stupid affairs are in Norway, when I observe how superficial, how shallow, the entire mode of contemplation proves itself to be, a profound melancholy takes possession of me, and I feel inclined to put an immediate end to my literary activity. There is no demand at home for poetic works proper; people have all that is required in the "Storthing" organ and in the Lutheran weekly journal, and, besides, they have the party newspapers. I have not the least talent either for citizenship or for orthodoxy, and that for which I feel no talent I avoid. To me, freedom is the highest and first life requisite. At home, however, people do not concern themselves much about freedom; they care only for special liberties, for some more, for some less, according to party standpoint. Most painfully am I moved by this crude state of affairs, this vulgarism in our public discussions. Under the very laudable endeavor to transform our people into a democratic community, quite a long stretch of the road is being traversed that leads to plebeian conditions. The intellectual aristocracy seems to be on the decline at home. . . .

The storm aroused by "Apparitions" could exercise no other influence on Ibsen than one that strengthened him in his conviction of the stupidity of the majority. He wrote to me about this, Jan. 3, 1882, as follows:—

"Björnson says, 'The majority is always right,' and for a practical politician this is the proper thing to say. I, on the contrary, must necessarily say, The minority is always right. As a matter of course, I do not refer to that minority of people who are in a state of stagnation, and who are left in the lurch by the great intermediate party, with us called liberals; but I mean that minority which is the advance guard in the forward march toward a goal the majority is not yet in a condition to attain."[4]

A good omen for the future works of Ibsen is the fact that, in the same ratio that he becomes modern, his greatness as a literary artist increases. The ideas of the new era have not assumed the forms of symbols or of types with him, but of individuals. In his younger years, he had a proclivity for great symbolic ideals,—Brand, Peer Gynt, etc.; but singularly enough, the more his store of thoughts increased, the clearer they became and the more artistic his presentation of them. His mastery of technicalities, of late years, has increased from work to work. In "A Doll's House," he surpassed the *technique* of the most celebrated French dramatists; and in "Ghosts" notwithstanding certain unsatisfactory points), he displayed a dramatic firmness, simplicity, and delicacy, which recalls the antique tragedy in the hands of Sophocles (especially King Œdipus).

This continual progress is a matter dependent on Ibsen's artistic earnestness, his conscientious industry. He labors very slowly, writes and re-writes his works, until they appear in a neat-looking manuscript without a single correction, each page as smooth and as firm as a marble plate, on which the tooth of time can leave no impression. This never-ceasing ascent in perfection depends, too, even more closely on the fact that Ibsen is solely and entirely a poet, and has never wished to be anything but a poet. True, it may give the impression of coldness and undue reserve,

[4] In these words lie the germ of the later production, "En Folkefiende" (An Enemy of the People).

when an author can be led by no outward recurrence whatever to mingle his voice in the universal debate; when nothing that occurs can irritate or inspire him to an outburst. The only newspaper articles Ibsen has written during the past five years are probably a few that bore on his rights in reference to his publishers, or his griefs in regard to the plunderings of his foreign translators,—therefore, on his personal and private interests; but it should not be forgotten that this reserve of his has permitted him to hold the mastery in his art unwaveringly before his eyes as a fixed idea, an ideal of which he never loses sight; and this mastery he has attained. A sharper contrast can scarcely be imagined than that which is presented by this poet, who remains alone in the South, shut off on every side from the surrounding world, free from all distraction, shaping and fashioning his artistic master-works; and his brother-poet in the North, who with full, perhaps too full hands, pours into the press his great and small articles on political, social, and religious questions, who is never afraid to let his name appear anywhere, who, paying no heed to the ordinary laws of prudence which prescribe that one should allow one's absence to be felt occasionally and one's presence to be desired, writes poems, makes public speeches, causes agitations, travels from one public gathering to another, and is most at his ease on the speaker's platform, with a thousand friends and a hundred enemies about him, holding them breathless with his daring and consummate art.

Henrik Ibsen bears no likeness to any other living poet, and is influenced by none. As minds that bear a somewhat distant relationship to him, may, perhaps with some justice, be mentioned the late German poets, Otto Ludwig and Friedrich Hebbel, both of whom, however, are far less modern in their tendencies than he. In the severity of his satire, too, there may be said to be a reminder of Dumas and Sardou. With Björnson, whose name almost insensibly falls from the pen when it busies itself with Ibsen, he has, notwithstanding all dissimilarities of nature, those things in common which naturally follow in the track of compatriots and contemporaries whose development has proceeded side by side, and who have been roused to emulation in the treatment of the same themes. That Ibsen had written "De Unges Forbund" (The Young Men's Union), gave Björnson an impulse to write dramas on civil conditions. when Björnson had written "En Fallit" (The Bankrupt), Ibsen was impelled to vary the subject in "Samfundets Stötter" (The Pillars of Society). Björnson was obliged, as he has informed me, to strike out a passage in the manuscript of his "Stöv" (Dust), because it appeared almost word for word in Henrik Ibsen's "Gjengangere" (Ghosts), which was issued before the story was printed. The fact is, the two poets have traversed an almost parallel path of development. Henrik Ibsen succeeded rather earlier than Björnson in working his way out of the old historic, legendary, and fantastic materials; for in the freer position he held, torn loose from home and standing amid the breakers of contemporary ideas, he had less to hold him back from following the call of his age, less naïveté, less reverence. But the difference in time between the transition of the two poets from the period when their materials were viewed from the standpoint of romance, to that where the realistic point of view predominated, was confined to a few years, and is lost sight of entirely, when we consider the remarkable uniformity of the stages of their poetic career. Björnson and Ibsen may be compared in this respect, as it seems to me, to the two old Norse kings, Sigurd and Eystein, in the famous dialogue furnished by the saga, and of which Björnson has availed himself in his "Sigurd Jorsalfar" (Sigurd the Crusader). The one has remained at home and there civilized his fatherland; the other has torn himself away from home, has journeyed far and wide, and in his bold, adventurous courses has won honor for his fatherland. Each has his admirers, each his martial suite, who elevates the one at the expense of the other. Still, they are brothers, even though for a season they were hostile brothers, and it is simple justice that the kingdom—as it is done in the drama of Björnson—should peacefully be divided between them.

[Ibsen died May 23, 1906, in Christania, Norway. Since the above essay was written he published *Vilanden* (The Wild Duck) in 1884; *Rosmersholm* in 1886; *Fruen fra Havet* (The Lady from the Sea) in 1888; *Hedda Gabler* in 1890; *Bygmester Solness* (Master Builder) in 1892; *Lille Eyolf* (Little Eyolf) in 1894; *Ole Gabriel Borkman* in 1896; and *Naar vi döde vaagner* (When We Dead Awake) in 1899. At a festival in his honor on the 70th anniversary of his birthday, he announced, that he was going to write his memoirs, but this was never done. All the works mentioned in this paragraph are dramas.— Translator's Note.]

X

ALGERNON CHARLES SWINBURNE

1909

I

In Algernon Charles Swinburne, who died April 7, 1909, the English-speaking world, one of the largest groups on earth, lost its greatest lyric poet; in fact, the greatest lyric poet that ever wrote the English tongue, when skill and virtuosity are considered.

It seems unbelievable to me that the generation that has had Swinburne in its midst, and in whose time this greatest lyrist of an age appeared, could bear witness to his passing without a word of appreciation, even though that ear be cold which should have heard the word of gratitude.

I had never believed it possible that one could put such music into words, charge the words with tones, as it were, as Algernon Charles Swinburne did from the very beginning in his first published songs; least of all had I believed it possible in the English tongue. I had not yet come to hear Shelley and Keats when I heard Swinburne's first verse—since we learn of our contemporaries before we do of those of earlier time—but had I known all of Swinburne's predecessors and their works, all the sweet and rare wealth of earlier English poetry, the overwhelming mastership, the wonderful virtuosity, which lie in Swinburne's handling of verse, could not have affected me less. It casts its spell upon me yet, now that I am familiar with the finest verse written before his day, that of his nearest predecessor and teacher, Dante Gabriel Rossetti, and others. Shelley has created as exquisite melodies as Swinburne, if simpler, but in the latter's verse it is as if a full orchestra were heard. He should have been dazed on account of all the harmony he has created. A fine example of his skill may be found in his dedication poem to Joseph Mazzini, which introduces the volume, "Songs Before Sunrise." As an expression of ardent, youthful feeling and manly seriousness, it is one of the most beautiful Swinburne has written, as technically it is also one of the most perfect. It is an outburst of his soul's heroic aspirations and burning nobility; and it is—like the collection of poems of which it is the prelude—an outpouring of life, transcendant, ecstatic life. Of the seven strophes in which the poem is written, each has its particular character, although the form throughout is harmonious. There is a rich interchange in form. The first, a dactylic, sounding strophe, is divided in the middle; the second, iambic, is divided before the last (sixth) line; the third, anapestic, is not divided at all; the fourth has its pause after the third line's first word; the fifth is also divided in the middle. In the sixth, with strong anapestic feeling, Swinburne in this form of rhyme has produced the impression of a tempest of feeling, which rises to ecstasy, and in the closing strophe, which also begins as a dactyl, this ecstasy is changed into suffering, into pathos.

The closing lines follow:—

> Be it witness till one more strong,
> Till a loftier lyre, till a rarer
> Lute praise her than I,
> Be it witness before you, my song,
> That I know her, the world's banner-bearer,
> Who shall cry the republican cry.
> Yea, even she, as at first,
> Yea, she alone, and none other,
> Shall cast down, shall build up, shall bring home,
> Slake earth's hunger and thirst,
> Lighten and lead as a mother;
> First name of the world's names, Rome.

Or, on the other hand, we can turn in "Poems and Ballads" to the poem "In Memory of Barry Cornwall," which begins—"In the garden of death where the singers

Algernon Charles Swinburne

whose names are deathless,—one with another make music unheard of men." There is scarcely a more pathetic and heart-taking and melodious dirge than this. Swinburne must have himself felt at the time that he had created a little masterpiece as he sent a revised copy of it to Denmark, where he scarcely ever sent anything. He knew a critic there would recognize the beauty of this *marche funebre*, in which is heard the steady beat of the funeral drum and simultaneously the pipings, as it were, of birds rejoicing, in life. His grief over Barry Cornwall turns into blessings on his life and gratitude for his sweet and radiant songs.

One is constrained to linger at the beginning of this collection with the little pearl, "A Match," which has so often been imitated, or with the great matchless and stately song, "Dolores," so rich in a wild and sorrowful defiance. It seems scarcely believable to me that more essential and more metrical verse than this could be produced. That it is as perfect in its coloring as it is overpowering in its melody is the merest praise that can be given it; since its emotional and intellectual wealth ranks with its musical excellence.

The poem is entirely too long, as Swinburne's poems in general are; he, like Victor Hugo, has rare faculty for expression, but seldom enough compactness in composition. He had himself such powers of sustained endeavor that his readers might tire long before he concluded. But what a symphony this poem "Dolores"!

Those who were youthful contemporaries of Swinburne's felt their hearts beat in harmony with his, not so much when the erotic nature of his character is given expression, as when scope is given to his enthusiasm for nature and freedom, when text and music become one.

He was born in London, April 5, 1837, the eldest son of Admiral Charles Henry Swinburne, whose father was sixth in a baronetcy. His mother, Lady Jane Henrietta, was a daughter of the Third Earl of Ashburnham. On his mother's, as on his father's, side he was of distinguished and noble lineage. The Swinburne line, probably of Danish origin (Sveinbjorn) lived on the old family estate Capheaton, near the Scottish border, in the wildest and most picturesque portion of Northumberland, and which achieved distinction in the border wars under Edward III.

In his childhood Algernon spent his summers in Northumberland and his winters on the Isle of Wight, so he was early familiar with the sea. A love of the sea was thus with him an inheritance.

His mother was strongly orthodox, in this respect being quite unlike her son, although a close bond of affection existed between them. In his childhood she was not a little concerned and depressed at his bent of thought and his predilection for all sorts of reading. She exacted a promise from him that he would not read Byron until he was twenty-one, which promise he kept. However, in Walter Savage Landor, whom he met in Florence in 1862—the blind, old, exiled poet whom England had forgotten—he found a far more dangerous influence.

The nearest neighbor of the family at Capheaton was Sir Walter Trevelyan, at whose home the painter William Bell Scott came in 1853 to do some fresco work. He saw a boy with a fine and striking head riding by on his pony and called him in that he might be used as a model. The Trevelyan family, which was more accomplished and prominent than the Swinburne family, early became a second home to the young poet.

At the age of sixteen Algernon was admitted to Eton. As he had already spent some time in France, and was familiar with Racine and Hugo, he was not at ease in school where his fellows chided him because of his red hair. He did not participate in their games and sports, usually went about with an older friend, chiefly Jowett, later the translator of Plato, an unusual man, who became his true friend and of whom Swinburne has preserved a charming picture in "Studies in Prose and Poetry."

When Algernon would not write in the manner and style to suit his instructors he brought about unpleasant relations with them, as with his fellow students and complained of what he termed the tyranny of the school. He was then taken out of school and for a time had as head teacher William Stubbs, later bishop of Oxford. It is scarcely necessary to show how unlike were teacher and pupil. When Algernon's first period of instruction was over, he was sent to the University of Oxford, where he proved so deficient in mathematics that he remained for several years as a member of the lowest classes without taking any grades, and finally quit school altogether. Only once did he receive a reward for good scholarship, in French and Italian.

Swinburne's most intimate friend at Oxford was John Nichol, later professor of English literature at Glasgow. He met also here for the first time William Morris, who had then just issued the little book "The Defense of Guenevere," in which the spirit of the Middle Ages is so well expressed, and Edward Burne-Jones, the gifted painter to whom the first edition of "Poems and Ballads" was later dedicated. Through them he became acquainted with Dante Gabriel Rossetti, who had come to Oxford to paint. With all the ardor of youthful enthusiasm, he became attached to this masterful man and thus fell under pre-Raphaelite influence.

While his own art had already matured in the form of high virtuosity and mannerisms, he was none the less appreciative of this influence. Its significance to him lay in his reverence for the past which was later to lead him to write in archaic forms, for example, "The Ballad of Life," "The Ballad of Death," etc., after the manner of the old Italian canzonettes, and his dramas in the Elizabethan style. He was unwilling to ignore historical values and idealize the ancient and medieval periods, as did Tennyson. It wakened in him a deep love for the primitive in nature, for the sea, the sun, for children, in contradistinction to that which has become familiar and hackneyed. Finally the pre-Raphaelite influence showed itself early in his fondness for allegorical representations. Throughout all of this period, life and death, love and fear, appear in his verse as personages, which, however, instill in the reader the interest the poet felt.

Swinburne amused himself at Oxford by shocking his

professors and school comrades with his opinions in connection with the assassination of the tyrant Orsinis. Such opinions might be justifiable enough if agreement could be reached as to the proper retribution for tyrants. However when Lincoln is classed among them, judgment must be reserved.

Although Swinburne was not a model student, he distinguished himself by his progress in the ancient languages, to their teaching of which English universities have always pointed with pride. In minor degree, he also mastered some of the modern tongues. He knew Greek, Latin, French and Italian thoroughly. He wrote excellent Greek, Latin and French verses, and in French wrote as well in the sixteenth century style as the nineteenth. Only in the German tongue was he unable to acquire proficiency.

The struggle for Italian independence and national unity was the great event which most influenced his early years. His revolutionary bias was largely formed by this struggle, as Shelley's had been by the French revolution. The stars in his youthful heavens took the form of a republican pleiad. They were Mazzini, whose personality fascinated him; Landor, whom he visited in Italy and to whom he brought the homage of young England; Hugo, who was his ideal of a poet; and Garibaldi, his ideal of a hero.

His capacity for memorizing poetry was remarkable. An American author who met him while a young man at Lord Houghton's house has related how Swinburne first sat silent for some time, then entered into the conversation when Sophocles and Shakespeare were mentioned and astonished all with his conversation and his ability to recite verse by the hour.

He resembled Elizabeth Barrett in his enthusiasm for Italian independence, but was unlike her in his resentment at the participation in that movement of the unpopular Louis Napoleon. In this prejudice he was influenced by Victor Hugo, whose opinions he made his own, although he was not in the least influenced by Hugo's style. His friendship with Landor is also indicated in the fact that while his first essay on Byron was warm and enthusiastic, he later had only words of scorn for him. In his caustic essay on Walt Whitman he further sought to disparage him by likening him to that formless poet, while in connection with the Byron centenary he chose only to point out Byron's defects as a dramatic versifier. Landor, was, as is well known, a close friend of Southey, Byron's bitter enemy, and shared his antipathies.

For some time Swinburne, D. G. Rossetti and George Meredith lived together in the same house in Cheyne Walk, and for some years thereafter Swinburne and Rossetti were the leaders of a little circle of artists and poets. Swinburne's admiration for Rossetti's poetry, which, however, is so unlike his own, lived with him through life and is expressed in the great laudatory essay on him, in 1870. When Robert Buchanan, in 1872, wrote a sharp attack on Rossetti (and also on Swinburne) in an article entitled, "The Fleshy School of Poetry"—it is hard to think of Rossetti as fleshy—Swinburne replied with a smashing article in a pamphlet, "Under the Microscope."

In his youth Swinburne was for a time addicted to drink, and only by bringing himself under strong discipline was he able to work himself out of this demoralizing tendency. Sir Walter Trevelyan and more particularly his rare wife Pauline, to whom Rossetti and Meredith often conducted Swinburne, exercised no little influence upon him to get him to abandon his aimless life and to take on more healthful habits. Swinburne's life became more and more one of study and good associations, all in the direction of improving his art. He scarcely had time to live for anything else but his art. His existence was for music, for metrical oratorios and symphonies, odes, hymns and songs.

In his last thirty years he lived in obscurity in The Pines, Putney Hill, with his closest friend Theodore Watts (now Watts-Duntan), who supervised his funeral on the Isle of Wight. The authorities did not see fit to give the infidel a burial place in Westminster Abbey. He mingled little with people, read, rode and took long walks. He had few friends. He was frequently seen along the coast of England alone or with a friend on horseback, or on foot;

and in the summer swimming in the ocean. To the end
he was fond of riding and swimming.

II

In any critical study of Swinburne's poetry, it is necessary to make clear wherein lies its chief worth and significance. This consists in its metrical forms. In a degree Swinburne is as much a great composer as poet. He has widened the scope of melodious expression to an extent unbelievable before his time. The English tongue, with its wealth of consonants, whose sounds do not admit of hard-and-fast rules, and therefore do not form the happiest material for verse, became under his hands the most pliable and resounding of all tongues, at least of those whose forms of fine expression were most fixed. Wherever one places a finger upon his verse the words sing beneath it. Were it not that the scheme of his compositions is usually so unyielding, their lyrical development might suggest the dramatic music of Richard Wagner. The artistic advance which marked Swinburne's advent created a new epoch.

If I were to name a distinguished English poet, who would seem to me stood in sharpest contrast to Swinburne, I believe I would name Robert Burns. In spite of Swinburne's capacity for reanimation, he had not the inherent genius for folk song, or the form of lyric sprung from folk song. Poems like "Here's to thy Health," "My Bonnie Lass," or "Neabody," or like the beautiful "Farewell to Nancy," lie far beyond Swinburne's reach. His verse is art in the highest sense of the term.

Yet even between Swinburne's poetry and that of his closest friends and teachers the difference is great. It would be difficult to find anything farther removed from a hymn or song of Swinburne's than Dante Gabriel Rossetti's "Three Shadows." The artlessness in this almost juvenile, eight-line, unrhyming stanza; the simplicity and lightness—three likenesses, and no more—all this is foreign to Swinburne's taste and style. Of course, it is polished enough—"I saw thine eyes in the shadow of thine hair; I saw thine heart in the shadow of thy glance; I saw thy love in the shadow of thy heart—" it is art in all simplicity. Yet it is a form of verse which stumbles; almost babbles. Swinburne's is always steady and sure, with blow on sounding blow. The former is marked by obscurity and distant perspectives. Swinburne's is as clear as it is resounding. Nothing of its inward essence is unexpressed. Its author is a romanticist without being a mystic, a romanticist of the classic type. The lyric is glowing, compelling and inspiring, but impersonal; it gives no hint as to his private feelings, except that which he treasures and seeks to attain.

Swinburne has given to English verse a strong metallic sound and a light celestial orchestral attribute which only Milton before him had attained. In his new forms of rhyme, their variety and sounding quality, he rejuvenated it. By making the rhyming of letters the basis of his art of expression, he gave a structure to the pale form of verse. He employed the anapestic and dactylic forms with equal ease, where others before him had employed chiefly the iambic and trochaic, and he used the anapestic closing line in a manner scarcely attempted before his time, but which Drachmann has used with equal originality and effect in the Danish. Rhymes consisting of two words had hitherto been used in English chiefly for comic effects; while Swinburne gives them a natural and justifiable use, as in his "Dolores," with the rhymes upon the name of "floor is," "core is," "adore is."

He employed the anapestic and dactylic forms with numerous one-syllable and two-syllable words. Although Coleridge had attempted without success to revive the ancient hexameter, in English, Swinburne created a new six-measure verse of another cast, with richer tones and with a well-marked rhyme in the middle as well as at the end of the line. Take these lines, for example:

Where beyond the extreme sea-wall and between the remote
    sea gates
Waste water washes and tall ships founder, and deep death
    waits.

The alliteration of the words, "waste water washes," depicts well the sea, while the tramp of horses' hoofs is heard in the following lines:

Sudden and steady the music as eight hoofs trample, and thunder
Rings in the ear of the low blind winds of the night as we pass

Never in any land has there been such a master in word-music, such unerring mastership in construction.

Outside of Danish literature such has not been known. There was a time in the eighties when the young lyrists of Denmark still echoed the meters of Heine's "Buch der Lieder." At the time I observed now and then, although privately, that England now had a singer who had proved by his own art that it was impossible any longer to imitate Heinrich Heine.

After Swinburne's death an anonymous writer in *The Spectator* sought to show that Swinburne had no mastery of the music of words, but only of verse forms. He was not born, said this writer, with the instinct for melody so distinctive of Shakespeare, and in lesser degree of Wordsworth, Coleridge, and Tennyson. Even if Swinburne's artistic productions could not always meet the test of respectability which they did, it would be unworthy, almost ridiculous, to deny to him the native gift of melodious expression. If anyone has had a finer ear—as this anonymous one intimates,—it cannot be denied that he had the native gift of beautiful expression. Now and then one has a fine ear for verse without the gift to give it such expression as he would, yet when no doubt can be raised as to the gift it may be regarded as instinctive.

This reviewer would give credit to Swinburne's metrical faculty only in certain forms of writing which had not before been attempted in English verse, and he succeeded in pointing out some meters in old English poetry, which present, as it were, feeble models of some that Swinburne developed into great perfection. It is, therefore, of interest to make comparisons.

Thus in Dryden occurs the following stanza:

>The Passion you pretended
>   Was only to obtain;
>But when the charm is ended
>   The charmer you disdain,
>Your love by ours we measure
>Till we have lost our treasure,
>For dying is a pleasure
>   When living is a pain.

It is like a leap from this to Swinburne's "A Match":

>If love were what the rose is,
>   And I were like the leaf,
>Our lives would grow together
>In sad or singing weather,
>Blown fields or flowerful closes,
>   Green pleasures or grey grief;
>If love were what the rose is,
>And I were like the leaf.

The mere rhythmical swing of these lines is peculiarly Swinburne's, not to mention the abounding beauty of the whole stanza. A like comparison may be made with a poem by Walter Savage Landor, which has been cited by some critics as having been a model for a simple iambic stanza of Swinburne's. Landor's verse follows:

>If you no longer love me
>   To friendship why pretend?
>Unworthy was the lover,
>   Unworthy be the friend.
>I know there is another
>Of late preferred to me.
>Recover'd is your freedom
>   And I myself am free.

Swinburne's verse, in "Rococo," follows:

>Take hands and part with laughter;
>   Touch lips and part with tears;
>Once more and no more after,
>   Whatever comes with years.
>We twain shall not remeasure
>   The ways that left us twain;
>Nor crush the lees of pleasure
>   From sanguine grapes of pain.

Far as it is from Swinburne's intent to reveal here his virtuosity, it is yet apparent that the even verse form of Landor's with its absence of ringing quality becomes under Swinburne's hand weighty and rich. It would show a poor appreciation of poetry to discuss a certain form of verse as being the secret of its charm; the difficulties which Swinburne with sportive ease has overcome are recalled again and again in every new stanza which he builds or rebuilds.

III

Swinburne was a nature poet before he was anything else. No English writer has written of boyhood as he has. He is familiar with English landscapes as with the Provençal and the Italian and he pictures unerringly the beauties of nature at its full, as well as its loneliness and desolation. He is never a descriptive poet. He presents the landscape in large lines, in its breadth, and imbues it with the spirits once its own or which should be its own. There is always something large and free in his portrayal of nature. Take as an example of his art, "A Forsaken Garden." The first stanza reads:

> In a coign of the cliff between lowland and highland,
>   At the sea-down's edge between windward and lee,
> Walled round with rocks as an inland island,
>   The ghost of a garden fronts the sea.
> A girdle of brushwood and thorn encloses
>   The steep square slope of the blossomless bed,
> Where the weeds that grew green from the graves of its roses
>   Now lie dead.

One must needs search far to find a landscape delineation more charged with sentiment. Pictures of the lovers who have lived there come and go; both are dead, their love is a thing of the past, like the garden's roses that have disappeared. Not a pulsation of the life that once flourished there. Only the earth, the rocks and the thorns which have sprung up in the forsaken ground remain and lie open to the sun and rain along the sea and flanked by cliffs that cast a shadow over all. Then comes in the tide over terraces, meadows, fields and rocks, until death itself lies dead like a god which has slain itself upon its own altar.

Greatly enjoyable, too, are the landscape poems, "Four Songs in Four Seasons," "Winter in Northumberland," "Spring in Auvergne," "Summer in Tuscany," and "Autumn in Cornwall." There is sharp contrast between the voice of winter in the first poem, the hearty call of the north wind, and the rose-hued symphony of the second poem. Thus the first one begins:

> O stout north-easter
> Sea-king, land-waster,
> For all thine haste, or
> Thy stormy skill,
> Yet hast thou never
> For all endeavor
> Strength to dissever
> Or strength to spill.

Against this may be set the soft melody of the second:

> Rose-red lilies that bloom on the banner;
> Rose-checked gardens that revel in spring;
> Rose-mouthed acacias that laugh as they climb,
> Like plumes for a queen's hand fashioned to fan her
> With wind more soft than a wild dove's wing,
> What do they sing in the spring of their time?

Swinburne is not the nature painter who sees and hears closely, or whose work breathes the perfume of garden and heather. All his being is thrilled and stirred to music by light and sound, by flashes of color, sunlight and lightning, the tumult of the storm, the roar of the sea, the dance of the waves, the dash and fumes of the foam.

He responds to the elemental senses in which he is one with nature in its wild originality. He worships the sun and its deity as were he a devout believer in Apollo, but he loves also the darkness of night and the dread stillness of the woods. A goodly portion of his verse in various forms glorifies the solar deity. Thus the famous song, "The Last Oracle," in "Poems and Ballads," ends as follows:

> For thy kingdom is passed not away,
>   Nor thy power from the place thereof hurled;
> Out of heaven they shall cast not the day,
>   They shall cast not out song from the world.
> By the song and the light they give
> We know thy works that they live;
>   With the gift thou hast given us of speech
> We praise, we adore, we beseech,
> We arise at thy bidding and follow,
>   We cry to thee, answer, appear,
> O father of all of us, Paian, Apollo,
>   Destroyer and healer, hear!

As a nature poet, however, Swinburne is above all a singer of ocean. To realize this we must read, "On the Cliffs," "A Swimmer's Dream," and specially in "Tristram of Lyonesse," the portion in which Tristram swims in the gray dawn before the battle in which he receives his fatal wound. It is at the close of the next to the last song, "The Last Pilgrimage." When the first pale light of dawn wakens Tristram, he hears the call of the waves. The east wind has taken the waters in its broad wings, dashed them against one another, and sends a hearty blast from the heart of the morning toward the land. Then Tristram springs up eager as a youth who hears the roar of the winds and the break of the waves, and joy fills his limbs with strength. He feels the sweep and swell of the sea, and hears the song of the breaking day, with prelude of harp and horn. He casts off his garments and as he stands there naked with eager feet and beautiful form he resembles Achilles, son of the sea-god. Then springs he into the sea and with loving arms clasps the waters to his breast and feels upon his lips the sharp fresh kiss of the waves. All the life within him, and all the life of the sea, seems to strive upward toward the sun. With wonderful fervor is Tristram's translation depicted, and the gleaming sea cradle of the doomed young demi-god.

Swinburne always felt himself refreshed and rejuvenated

when he turned back to nature, to the primitive awe at the sun and gladness in the sea. The appeal to him in nature lies in her greatness and strength, the energy of life, and he has sought to unite all the voices of the sea in his song.

With him the sea is nature's symbol of freedom, and nature's symbol of England as well, his own country, whose greatness and glory he voiced with increasing splendor as the years went by. To his poetic sense the ancient Greeks and the modern Englishmen were children of the sea and the champions of freedom. Again and again he recalls the stand of Athens against the fleet of Xerxes, and England's contest with the great Armada, and sees in England's heroes of the sea descendants of the ancient Greeks. Thus in the ode "Athens," in the poem, "Tristram of Lyonesse," he says:

Sons of Athens born in spirit and truth are all born free men,
Most of all, we, nurtured where the north wind holds his reign:
Children all we sea-folk of the Salaminian seamen;
Sons of them that beat back Persia, they that beat back Spain.

Those for whom Shakespeare wrote were as if sons of those whom Aeschylus glorified. Of Britannia he says:

She that hears not what man's rage but only what the seawind saith,
She that turned Spain's ships to cloud-wrack at the blasting of her breath
By her strength of strong-souled children and of strong winds done to death.

Finally it may be said that the sea is the reflection of Swinburne's own genius. In one of his finest and most personal poems, "Thalassius," he has pictured his own personality under a name borrowed from the Greek word for the sea. Thalassius is the child of the sun and the sea. He is reared by a foster father who teaches him that he who loves life too much deserves to die as a dog; while he who loves life less than he hates wrong and those who commit it shall never be forgotten. And this foster father holds that there is one thing greater than God, which is freedom, so that one should hate all who hold free-born people in bodily or spiritual bondage. In the end the sun god blesses his son Thalassius, who is as a fugitive upon earth, with a soul as sleepless as the wind or water or fire, and which has loved nothing higher than his father, the sun, and his mother, the sea.

In order to feed the human intellect with visions truer than truth, he brings the sacrifice of all earthly joy; but in repayment the sun-god makes his song the voice of all the winds and the soul of the sea to live in his soul.

> Child of my sunlight and the sea, from birth
> A fosterling and fugitive on earth,
> Sleepless of soul as wind or wave or fire,
> A manchild with an ungrown God's desire;
> Because thou hast loved nought mortal more than me,
> Thy father and thy mother-hearted sea;
> Because thou hast set thine heart to sing, and sold
> Life and life's love for song, God's living gold,
> Because thou hast given thy flower and fire of youth
> To feed men's hearts with visions, truer than truth,
>
> Have therefore in thine heart and in thy mouth
> The sound of song that mingles north and south,
> The song of all the winds that sing of me,
> And in thy soul the sense of all the sea.

IV

When we recall the anger of the virtuous critics over the first edition of "Poems and Ballads," and the attacks Swinburne had to endure, we are surprised to find how little really erotic verse he wrote, the attacks having been due probably rather to his "Notes on Poems and Ballads and on the Reviews of Them." Nevertheless parts of his early writings were decidedly erotic. Behind these verses lay a conviction that in the cultivation of the beautiful, of freedom and honorable sacrifice, we were far behind classic antiquity, and an undoubted determination to oppose not only religious but moral heresey. They were in part a protest against the public taste of the time for the Tennysonian idyl and in part an imitation of Beaudelaire's tendency toward the erotic and unhealthy. In such poems as "Anactoria," "Hermaphroditus," "Fragoletta," "Satia te Sanguine," there was more passion than love, a tendency to go to the limit of normal bounds, or beyond them, to permit passion to lead "into pain and disaster." The great and stately poem, "Dolores," is in this spirit dedicated to "Our Lady of Pain."

This poem and the great "Hymn to Proserpina," with many other antique forms of Swinburne's verse was what *Die Goetter Griechenlands* had been before his time, a pagan's anguished protest against a new mythology that had supplanted the old in its departure from nature and its denial of it.

Living at that time in London and long afterwards—I met and talked with him in 1896—was the exiled German revolutionist, Karl Blind. In his house Swinburne, soon after the publication of "Poems and Ballads," met for the first time Giuseppe Mazzini, who exacted from him a promise not to write any more erotic verse, but to dedicate his muse to the cause of liberty.

English poets had been revolutionists before him. First and foremost came Milton, whom he resembled in his profound learning, his deep classical culture, which with him (foe of the Bible) as with Milton is charged with scriptural allusions. Such poems as "A Litany," "A Lamentation" and "Aholibah," find their prototypes in Isaiah and Ezekiel. Coleridge was for a brief time consumed with revolutionary enthusiasm, Byron, Landor, and above all, Swinburne's great predecessor, Shelley, were real revolutionists. Swinburne had also written political verses in the same spirit as these men before he fell under the influence of Mazzini. Now, however,—following "A Song for Italy," which does not take high rank in his work,—there appeared "Songs Before Sunrise," a notable production.

This book, which is inspired by a heroic spirit, is calculated to move humanity to feel deeply, to undertake greatly, and to act nobly. In England the period before the Franco-Prussian war was one of compromise. With the reign of Napoleon III drawing toward a close, it was to

Europe a time of torpor and indecision. Upon this spirit of lethargy Swinburne's poems burst like a thunderstorm.

His passion for Italy was as ardent as that of the most devoted native, and he saw in the republic the only form of government worth while, as if he were living under an absolute monarchy instead of the harmless, more ornamental one of England.

He was never the political echo of another. For a long period revolution was his only gospel. As an admirer of Kossuth he opposed the imperial designs of Russia, and joined in the more humane spirit of western Europe in denouncing Russian persecution of the Jews.

When Russia declared war on Turkey he wrote his "Notes of an English Republican on the Muscovite Crusade" (1876) and expressed therein his unrestrained contempt for Russia's English friends, Gladstone and Parnell. In this he stood with Turkey. When he later published his "Ode on the Insurrection of Candia," he was against Turkey. After the assassination of Alexander II he published his hymn, "Russia," appealing for the murder of tyrants, which barred him from the poet-laureateship on the death of Tennyson.

In his later years his revolutionary sentiments gave way to enthusiasm for British imperialism and he attacked the Boers with implacable fury.

In all his youth and sturdy manhood, however, he was invariably on the side of justice and righteousness. He gave no ground; his nature was of the intense character which adored or hated, obdurate and decisive. He was as great a master in eulogy as in denunciation. His hates like his affections formed a torrent which overwhelmed and destroyed; his revolutionary rhetoric, in copiousness, power and brilliancy, may well be placed beside that of Victor Hugo's whose defects it also possessed.

Like Hugo, he is always clear and strong in praise or condemnation, and in his passion his note is single-toned although varied as an orchestra in its expression.

If he showed Hugo's unreasonable hatred for the representatives of causes he abhorred, such as Napoleon III or

Nicholas II, he had in compensation, therefore, a capacity for appreciation and praise of ancient and contemporary heroes which is unique. He has revealed an unusual loftiness of spirit in his tributes to other poets. Not only has he exalted the dead poets like Marlowe and Shakespeare and their Elizabethan contemporaries, but just as warmly has he sung of his own contemporaries, not only the older ones like Hugo and Rossetti whom he idealized, but of the younger ones who were his fellows and whom he honored with his friendship. Nearly all his prose articles are marked with such tributes. Likewise he has eulogized in song all his other comrades in the esthetic world, Burne-Jones, William Bell Scott, William Morris, Theodore Watts and Madox-Brown.

In his political verse he resembles closely certain of the Italian poets of the middle of the century, with their hatred of tyranny, their belief in republicanism, which was like faith in the Magi, and which made no allowances for human frailties under whatever the form of government. He has never, like Ada Negri, in her poems, "Fatalita" and "Tempeste," permitted the fight for social righteousness to be secondary to that of political freedom. He was also contemporary with the heroic age of political liberty. He paid his devotions to the mother of the Cairoli brothers as were she a Madonna, when he would show his love for the martyred he knelt before their mother.

The inspiration of antiquity in his "Songs Before Sunrise," is undoubted. It was not accidental, nor was it to ingratiate himself with Mazzini that he wrote the line,

> First name of the world's names, Rome.

V

From the beginning he drank deeply at classical fountains, so that his inmost fibre is permeated with Greco-Roman culture. He was a learned man and a poet with finished philological attainments. What a chaplet of beautiful French songs, in the style of the time, in Clement

Marot's manner, has he not woven in his "Chastelard," and his "Bothwell," and what lovely poems in modern French has he not written to Hugo and of Gautier! These he sent to José Maria de Heredia, in Paris, who found little or nothing in them which he would have Swinburne change, according to a statement to me by him and his son-in-law Henri de Requier. The classics, however, were the basis of his culture. He may be called a humanist in the sixteenth century meaning of the term, as his immediate environment made less impression upon him than did the ancient Athens in which he lived in spirit. The sight of an English warship called to his mind the Battle of Salamis, and the modern battleship reminded him of the three-banked galleys of the Greeks. He thought as did Lucretius, and felt as did Julianus Apostata. In certain respects he seems more closely related to the latter than any other person. Throughout his life he hated the Christian culture with the glowing hatred of a disciple of Apollo. He not only renounced the mystical in the Christian religion, but the Christian's belief in God, so that he may more rightly be termed anti-theistic than atheistic. Even in his first ancient drama, the beautiful "Atalanta in Calydon," there is a strong denial of belief, as, for instance, in these lines:

> Who makes desire and slays desire with shame . . .
> Smites without sword, and scourges without rod . . .
> The supreme evil, God.

In Dante Gabriel Rossetti's copy of this work his sister, Christina Rossetti, pasted a piece of white paper over this last line. She could not bear to see it. It was not always, however, but only in his earliest youth, that God appeared to Swinburne as the supreme evil. He approached later to Beyle's, *"Ce qui excuse Dieu, C'est qu'il n'existe pas,"* accepted the idea of Deity psychologically and wrote:

> And death, the shadow cast by life's wide wings,
> And God, the shadow cast by the soul of man.

In his hymns to humanity, Swinburne calls upon the God

of the priests and the priests of God in the same strain as
did Elias when he turned to Baal, saying:

O God, Lord God of thy priests, rise up now and show thyself
God.
They cry out, thine elect, thine aspirants to heavenward, whose
faith is
O thou the Lord God of our tyrants, they call thee, their God,
by thy name.
By thy name that in hell-fire was written, and burned at the
point of thy sword,
Thou art smitten, thou God, thou art smitten; thy death is
upon thee, O Lord!
And the love-song of earth as thou diest resounds through the
winds of her wings . . .
Glory to Man in the highest! for Man is the master of things.

His passionate ill-will toward Christianity as the ruling
faith is given expression in his "Hymn to Proserpine," the
last song of a heathen poet after the Christian faith has
been proclaimed in Rome, with the prophecy that in time
the new religion will fall as the old has fallen:

Though before thee the throned Cytherean be fallen, and hidden
her head,
Yet thy kingdom shall pass, Galilean, thy dead shall go down
to thee dead.

In the poem "Before a Crucifix" the poet, who has
"neither tongue nor knee for prayer," uses such strong
words of contempt as "this their carrion crucified."

In the poem, "Hertha," Swinburne indicated his belief.
The name, as is well known, is erroneously taken from the
old Germanic goddess, Hertha, mentioned by Tacitus, and
in the poet's speech symbolizes the earth and through earth
symbolizes nature. It is nature itself which speaks through
the poem and, strangely enough, corresponds with what
Goethe wrote in a little prose article in his thirty-first year,
a prose article which Swinburne never saw. Nature as
the all embracing whole outside of which there is room for
nothing, whether man or God; nature, charged through
with soul, as *nativa naturans,* and *natura naturata,* in
one, active or passive, personal or impersonal, with man but

a link in nature's chain, is thus unfolded, so that the thought and its presentation run together. Nature says:

> But what thing dost thou now,
>   Looking Godward, to cry
> I am I, thou art thou,
>   I am low, thou art high.
> I am thou, whom thou seekest to find him; find thou but thyself, thou art I.

In a translation of the poem, "Hertha," in Danish, which Adolf Hansen once undertook occurs the following stanza:

> Jeg er Pilen, der rammer,
>   Og den pilramte Grund,
> Jeg er Kysset, der flammer,
>   Og den kyssede Mund,
> Den Sögte og Sögeren, Ködet og Sjaelen, alt Liv I hver Stund.[1]

The idea in Hertha is the same as that expressed by Hugo in *Le Satyre*. In the poem "Mater Triumphalis" Swinburne has set himself up as nature's bard, the minister of life, the harp in the great mother's hand, the trumpet for her lips.

> I am thine harp between thine hands, a mother!
>   All my strong cords are strained with love of thee.
> We grapple in love and wrestle as each with other
>   Wrestle the wind and the unreluctant sea.
>
> I am the trumpet at thy lips, thy clarion
>   Full of thy cry, sonorous with thy breath.
> The graves of souls born worms and creeds grown carrion
>   Thy blast of judgment fills with fires of death.

At the beginning Swinburne was intuitively negative, anti-priestly, anti-Christian. Next in importance with

[1] Literal translation:
> I am the arrow that hits its mark
> And the mark that was hit.
> I am the kiss, which flames
> And the kissed mouth,
> The sought and the seeker
> The flesh and the soul,
> All life every moment.

him was conformity to nature, his love for this great mother, his devotion to her. Finally he stressed the positive greatness and nobility of mankind, and in the poem, "The Altar of Righteousness," published some four or five years since, he has raised an altar to the ethical idea of life on which the final offering in his battle for freedom is laid.

XI

GIUSEPPE GARIBALDI

1914

I

STANDING on Janiculum Hill, which overlooks Rome, on the point where the colossal equestrian statue of Garibaldi looks out over the city, over Italy, this man's work, one is reminded of the streams of noble Italian blood which drenched this height when, from this point in 1849, Garibaldi saved Rome from the French, and stemmed the tide of reaction toward royalty.

Simultaneously rises before the imagination a vision of the man's life, a life which is like unto a great poem, a great drama, with triumphs and disasters, defeats and triumphs, without a parallel. Likewise, one is moved with gratitude and wonder to realize that such a hero has lived, not in fiction, but in a reality which transcends all fiction, and even up to our time, so late, that I, who write these lines, was contemporary with him for forty years.

All else one might expect to find in the nineteenth century, great spirits of various kinds, inventors and discoverers, scholars and poets, also brave men in great numbers —yet it is a source of wonder that a great folk-hero has lived among us, of primitive cast, simple and bold as the mythical Theseus; more human than the mythical hero, all courage, all heart and all unselfishness, yet at the same time inspired by the most advanced ideas of his time, a republican, anti-Catholic and anti-priestly, and, although a warrior, himself a champion of peace.

About the year 1859, his name had reached northern Europe; by 1861 his name was on every lip. His conquest of Sicily and Naples seemed the achievement of a demi-god. The young women of Copenhagen, as elsewhere, dressed themselves in red blouses,—*camiccia rossa,*—the Garibaldian uniform. In the parks of Copenhagen the young Savoyards, bearing their trays of plaster paris figures on their heads, entreated everyone to buy a little bust of "Galibardi," as they always called him.

When, as a young man, I set forth in the world, I met in a coach on the way to Italy, a well-speaking Italian builder, an old Garibaldian, the great event in whose life was that Garibaldi had once eaten breakfast with him at Varese. He treasured in his home, as a holy relic, a glass from which the general had drunk. In Florence I was luckily received by Francisco dall'Ongaro, who had campaigned under Garibaldi in Rome, and lived in exile as he had. In himself, this handsome man with his mild face and humane cast of mind, was a character worth knowing, but to me a glow was cast over him by the fact that he had been close to the general. My deceased friend, Vilhelm Bissen, went to Caprera to make a bust of Garibaldi, and talked with him daily when he was broken down with rheumatism and scarcely able to get about with the aid of crutches. However, later I became acquainted with the sculptor, Riccardo Ripamonti, who had known him in his vigor. In 1866, when only fourteen years old, Ripamonti presented himself before Garibaldi's free corps, and was, though with difficulty, accepted, small and frail as he was. "There was something more than human in Garibaldi's glance," said Ripamonti; "Everyone sought to win this glance, although one trembled to be reproved from his lips; but when one felt weary and worn from night marches and hardships, a look from the chieftain's eye would refresh and inspire him to battle."

Italy is now filled with statues, reliefs and busts in honor of Garibaldi. Small cities, like Taormina, which can afford no more, have a memorial tablet of him. There is not a place where he spent a day, but it has its memorial. Cities like Lodi, Cesenatico and Macerata have statues showing Garibaldi when young. Even such a little town as Intra on Lake Maggiore has its Garibaldi statue, not to mention the larger cities like Nice, Genoa, Rome and Palermo. Such a small city as Fesolo has a double statue of Garibaldi and Victor Emmanuel who are represented as meeting on horseback and extending their hands to one another.

Throughout the Italy of our day he appears to have been not only the idol of the common people, but the hero of all classes. That the only severe wound from which he ever suffered was received from an Italian bullet at Aspromonte in August, 1862, after he had directed his own men not to fire, is an astounding, if not a significant fact. It seems strange that regular Italian troops could be led to fire upon him, after all he had done for Italy. He had not, then, it would seem, gained the universal enthusiasm which came to him later. That this should be true is not strange.

As late as 1870, after Rome had been taken by the Italian army, I heard prominent young Italians of the intellectual classes, who had been brought up to admire Cavour, speak slightingly of Garibaldi as a visionary personality, whose political ideas could lead only to confusion. It may also be noted that Lord Beaconsfield in his historical romance, "Lothair" has Mirandola that is, Mazzini say during the latter's stay in London in 1867, that Garibaldi is a "poor deevell!"

Why? Because Garibaldi, with his shrewd political insight, refused to permit himself to be persuaded into proclaiming a republic, in spite of the fact that the monarchy had done him injury.

In the story the dialogue occurs in this manner: The Italian general, come to visit Mazzini, says:

"There is no doubt that Garibaldi's name is the only one that could bring together 10,000 men at any point in Italy." "Have you been to Caprera?" asked Mazzini. "I have just come from there." "What did he say?" "He would do nothing without the coöperation of the Savoyards." "He longs, no doubt, to be shot in his other foot," says Mirandola with fine sarcasm. "When will he weary of deceit?" "I found him very composed and sanguine," said the general.

It was not until the last years of his life, after he had filled his seventy years, that Garibaldi could appear anywhere in Italy or Sicily without arousing an idolatrous demonstration. But then he was no longer able to walk.

II

In the year 1817 Keats wrote the following lines quoted by Trevelyan:

> And other spirits there are standing apart
> Upon the forehead of the age to come,
> These, these will give the world another heart,
> And other pulses.

These words, written two years after Waterloo, after the monarchical reaction had been renthroned, may be said to have been prophetic to the poet's own country, of the coming of Darwin, Carlyle, Mill, Disraeli, Gladstone, Macaulay, Dickens, even to the country in which the poet died, of four men who were to make Italy again a power. Of these Trevelyan said, in substance:

"At this time a small ten-year-old boy was playing in the gardens at Nice, Giuseppe Garibaldi; at the same time a twelve-year-old boy was reading lectures in a physician's house at Genoa, Giuseppe Mazzini. At this time was living in a palace at Turin, a little seven-year-old son of nobility, Camillo Cavour. Not until three years thereafter was born the little Sardinian prince, who was to be Italy's first king, Victor Emmanuel. All were born within a comparatively few miles of each other.

Italy, at this time, was another Poland, divided among various powers; ruled by ruthless Austrians in Lombardy, Venice, Parma, and Modena; by the more cruel and rapacious Bourbon kings in Naples and Sicily; by the Pope in the papal states; while Austrian troops in white uniforms and high chacos rode up and down the highways of north and central Italy from morning till night, suppressing the activities of the people.

It was a land devoid of national feeling and with no politics except the unfortunate conspiracies of a few young men, a land in which Englishmen traveled about in coaches, proud of the victory at Waterloo, and with volumes of the *Quarterly Review* in their vehicles.

Giuseppe Garibaldi saw the light of day in 1807, at Nice, in a house beside the Strand, as the son of a plain and honest sea captain, one who sailed his own little ship and carried on trade as a merchant. He was born a subject of Napoleon, but at the age of eight passed under the house of Savoy, which then ruled Piedmont.

The common people of Nice had no patriotic feelings. Many of them were French. Many of them spoke a dialect resembling the Provençal. Hence it was that fifty years later, Nice voluntarily became a part of France.

Peppino, as his comrades called Giuseppe, was no model pupil. The freedom of the open appealed to him more than the quiet of study. The eager, adventurous little lad was tempted into all sorts of adventures, and played truant at school whenever he could borrow a gun from a fisherman and range the mountains, or could induce a fisherman to take him along in his boat. He was quick at trawling for oysters, to haul sardine catches on shore, and participated in the tun-fishing festival at Villafranca. When he had a book which interested him, he would lie for hours under the olive trees reading, and there was no power to drive him from it. Living at Nice, he became able to read French as easily at Italian. He studied Voltaire, and learned some of his poems by heart. With greater zeal, however, he read a contemporary Italian, Ugo Foscolo, whose beautiful lines he loved to repeat throughout his life. He had a beautiful voice, knew all the songs of the sailors, as well as those of the peasants, and many French songs, as well. Many years afterwards his comrades in South America learned that music and poetry exercised a great power over him. Even as a boy his fellows looked up to him, and the younger ones regarded him as their leader. He was the greatest

swimmer of them all, a real fish in water. He might have
had a better grounding in books had he applied himself
more steadily. In his memoirs in later life he complained
that he had let his opportunity pass in early youth to learn
English, in which he first acquired efficiency as a man.
This was a matter of regret with him, as he became more
and more closely attached to the English, whom he came to
know in their best light, first as seamen, and then as enthusiasts in the cause of Italy. His love for England became a sort of romantic passion, and developed in proportion with his hatred of the Catholic priesthood. England
was also the country in which he was first accorded great
renown outside of Italy, and where he was more highly
appreciated than, perhaps, in Italy itself.

Ever since 1848 the English laboring classes had been
hostile to the European reaction. In 1850, when the Austrian general, Haynou, the oppressor of Hungary, thoughtlessly visited England, the workmen in Barclay's brewery,
incensed at his barbarities toward women and men better
than himself, seized him and threw him in the great vat of
the brewery.

However, when in February, 1854, Garibaldi, as a merchant, came to Newcastle for a cargo of coal, the miners
were so cognizant of his exploits in South America and of
his deliverance of Rome, that they presented him with a
sword as a token of their esteem. In their heavy iron-soled
boots, which astonished the Italian sailors, they came on
board his ship, and their spokesman said: "This sword
has been purchased with the pennies of hundreds of workingmen, given, not only willingly, but enthusiastically, and
every penny represents a heart that beats for the cause of
freedom in Europe."

Garibaldi replied as well as he could in English, "As a
man of the people, a laborer like yourselves, I appreciate
deeply this expression of your esteem, so much more so,
because it is a witness of your solicitude for my poor, oppressed, downtrodden country. Italy will again be a nation, and its free citizenship will then come to know the
friendship shown to her exiled sons in its darkest days."

When only ten years later, 1864, Garibaldi again came to England, he was received as scarcely any foreigner before or since that time had been welcomed, and was hailed as the world-renowned deliverer of Sicily and Naples. From the Prince of Wales, the government and the aristocracy to the common people, who, to the number of 30,000 stood before the Crystal Palace, the demonstration was unanimous and hearty—the reception given by the Duke of Sutherland was the climax of distinction accorded him.

However, I am anticipating too rapidly. Garibaldi is still a child. His parents sought to keep him at home, but they could not have their way with the child, whose stubbornness was one day to astound America and Europe. He had an irresistible inclination toward a life of adventure which became a second nature to him.

From the age of fifteen to twenty-five Garibaldi rose from cabin-boy on his father's ship to sea captain, and learned such mathematics, geography, astronomy and trade requisitions as were necessary for a commander of a ship. What was to be more important, his body and spirit became hardened and strengthened to withstand privation, hunger and loss of sleep without complaint or disadvantage.

The sea which he traversed was not like the oceans of today, in which all regulations between peoples are ordered by governments. He cruised upon the Levant during the Greek war for independence, where Turks and Greeks fought with implacable fury, where pirates lay in wait in every bay and attacked vessels with axes and long knives. It was the romantic, melodramatic Mediterranean of Byron's verse that he sailed, and doing so, he came to believe in Byron's gospel, that it was better to die as a free man than to live as a slave. Three times in his expeditions he was attacked and taken prisoner by pirates, and each time he gained his freedom. With what enthusiasm has he not, in his memoirs indited a hymn to *Constanza,* his first bark, which bore him over the Mediterranean and the Black Sea, singing of its beautiful form and its feminine figurehead at the fore. His sailors were energetic young men from

San Remo, brave Ligurians, who sang ardent love songs. "Oh," said he, "If only they could have sung of our own land!" Italy was then but a hollow name to them, and to him.

Garibaldi's parents were honest and conservative people. In his childhood home he had not heard Italy spoken of as a fatherland, nor did he now. The struggles of the people of the near East, for freedom, appealed to him, but he did not think of Italy in this light. In the meantime, the influence of the French Revolution of 1830-32 had extended over western and southern Europe. Central Italy rose in revolt under the young patriot, Ciro Menotti, whom the Austrians overcame and hanged, and after whom Garibaldi named his first son. It chanced, in 1833, also, that in a harbor on the Black Sea, a young Genoese named Cuneo, told him that the Carbonari movement had come to an end with the martyrdom of hundreds of young enthusiasts, but that a young Genoese student, named Mazzini, had organized a conspiracy, "The Young Italy," which it was a duty to join. Garibaldi said that when he learned of this, he felt so fortunate that Columbus could not have been more elated on discovering America.

In reality, he had discovered his America, the land whose name was then but a geographical term; but which, through the diplomacy of Cavour and his own heroism, was, after fourteen years, again to take its place as a nation.

Now, again, appeared before his mind an image associated with terror in his youth. On one of his journeys along the Italian coast in his father's little vessel, they had gone ashore, and he had seen for the first time at the age of eighteen, the city of Rome, the Rome of the past, and never, throughout all the eventful years following, had he ever forgotten that vision. It haunted him even in the forests of South America. When he again saw Rome, he was forty-two years old, and came to confound its foes and make secure its freedom.

III

The first time that Giuseppe Garibaldi saw his name in print was when, in 1834, he read of his sentence to death. This was promulgated by the Piedmont government because of his participation in one of Mazzini's ill-fated enterprises. Mazzini entered Piedmont in February with a band of Polish, Italian, German and French troops, whom their hatred for the old forms of government held together, and Garibaldi, with naïve enthusiasm, deserted his fleet to join him. Not one officer nor one seaman would raise a hand in favor of this, so the idea was soon abandoned.

However, it was fortunate for Carlo Alberto's son that Garibaldi, disguised as a peasant, was able to escape execution. Had not this occurred, Victor Emmanuel would not have been Italy's first king.

Garibaldi then went to South America, where, during the twelve years from 1836 to 1848, as a guerilla leader for the two republics of Rio Grande de Sul and Uruguay, he underwent a thousand dangers and hardships, and earned a fame which later stood him in good stead. He began as a *condottiere* for the little republic of Rio Grande de Sul in the struggle for independence against the empire of Brazil. First, like a Viking of old, he had only a fishing boat and a few men. He soon gave up the boat for the saddle as leader of a few hundred, later several thousand, native troops, the best horsemen in the world, real centaurs, whose weapons were lances and lassos. Garibaldi soon became accomplished in the use of both and to live on horseback as they did. He survived these twelve years of almost unheard-of struggles, and privations, not only shipwreck and battle, but torture. One day, when a prisoner, his enemies hung him up by the thumbs for two hours in his cell, while the clamoring populace looked on through the open door. However, they learned nothing from him. Yet he afterward wrote, "Such tortures were indescribable."

One day in 1839, Garibaldi, following a shipwreck was case ashore in the Brazilian province of Santa Catharina, having assisted in the capture of Laguna. He was ap-

pointed to the command of a captured imperial vessel. As
he stood on the deck of his new flagship and grieved over
the loss of his closest friends in the shipwreck he saw
through his spyglass a young maiden standing alone on
the shore.

He was always very impressionable. Women form a
large chapter, in fact, a whole book in Garibaldi's life.
But this proved to be a turning point in his youth. He
fell in love through the ship's spyglass.

He ordered a boat lowered, rowed ashore, and became
one of the guests invited to drink a cup of coffee at her
father's house. She was the eighteen-year-old Anita Ribera.
She knew well who Garibaldi was. When the two looked
into one another's eyes they were irresistibly drawn toward
each other. He said in Italian (since he understood too
little Portuguese) the simple words: *Tu devi essere mia,*
—"You should be mine." Yet she understood him. His
enthusiasm was magnetic. Against her wishes, her father
had pledged her to another. A few days afterward she
went on board Garibaldi's ship and fled with him. Their
union, which was first broken by her death during the flight
from Rome ten years later, was the ideal union which should
exist between a man and a woman, since both were endowed
with high courage, nobility and greatness of character.

Together these two galloped for years over the plains of
South America and between its mountains, at the head of
the republican troops. In one battle she was taken captive
by the royal troops, and believing that Garibaldi had fallen
she obtained leave to seek for him on the battlefield, and
like another Edith Swanhild at Hastings turned the face
of every corpse upward to the light. Escaping from her
drunken guards, she disappeared in the tropic woods on
a swift horse she had obtained from a peasant, swam great
rivers and rode four days, almost without food, until she
found Garibaldi. Under such circumstances she gave birth
to her first child, which she had to carry in a cloth about
her neck while she sought to keep it warm against her
breast.

Garibaldi then lived a life like that of Robin Hood.

In the beginning of 1842, he wished to give up this strenuous life for a more peaceful one in Montevideo, the capitol of the Republic of Uruguay. The reward for his six years of service for Rio Grande do Sul was three hundred head of cattle, which was all he owned, and this he lost, so that he had to seek to earn his bread in Montevideo as a ship chandler and teacher of mathematics. After a few months had gone by, however, the government of Uruguay asked him to organize an Italian legion for the war which the Argentine Republic, under the famous tyrant Rozas (General Mansilla's Uncle) had declared. This became the legion which saved Montevideo during the sieges of 1843 and 1846.

The red blouse, which, a few years afterwards, was so famous all over Europe, became, in 1842, the uniform for the Italian legion through a curious circumstance. It was necessary to clothe the men as economically as possible, as there was little money. A merchant house in Montevideo then made a good offer, which was to sell to the government at a low price a stock of red woolen shirts, which should have been sent to Buenos Aires but which port was now closed through a blockade. They had been intended to be used in the so-called *saladeros*, the large slaughter and packing houses, since they would be warm in winter, while their color would absorb the blood connected with the work.

In 1843, a prominent merchant in Montevideo wrote to the government minister that in the house of Garibaldi, the commander of the Italian legion and the national fleet, to whom Montevideo owes its life from day to day, no lights were ever seen after sunset, as lights were not provided in the rations of the soldiers, and such rations were all that Garibaldi, himself had.

The minister thereupon, sent him five hundred francs. Garibaldi kept half this sum, and directed that the other half should be sent to a widow who had more use for the money than he. These two-hundred-fifty francs was all the money Garibaldi took from the republic. His family lived in poverty; he, himself, on the same basis as his soldiers; he could hardly be persuaded to change a worn-out blouse for a new one. All men in Montevideo were his friends, while his beautiful face and luxurious gold-brown hair made the women also admire him. One day he permitted his locks to be clipped right to the roots in order to appease Anita's jealousy.

When Garibaldi, who had followed the course of events, through exchanges of letters with the young Italians in the homeland, returned to Europe in 1848, he invited Carlo Alberto—in spite of the earlier sentence of death—to join in the war against Austria, but received a refusal.

IV

In February, 1849, when the terrible conditions in the Papal States had brought about the revolution, and the republic had been declared with Mazzini, Saffi, and Armelini as a triumvirate, Garibaldi's help was not refused. But to show Europe how regular they were, and how responsive they were to the claims of respectability, they made Garibaldi a division general under Roselli, as commander-in-chief, a man as incompetent as he was respectable, the result of which was that Garibaldi, who set many undertakings on foot and struck with lightning swiftness against the enemy's troops, was left in the lurch by the commanding general, and the defeated foes thus usually were not given pursuit. However, it was a question of life or death for the Roman Republic. King Bombas' troops advanced from the south, and General Oudinot was sent against Rome by the criminal politics of the French president.

One cannot get much idea at this time of the conditions imposed by Napoleon III for the support of the Catholics, which he sought.

Only two percent of the people in the country, and scarcely more people of the cities in the Papal States, could read. A censorship shut out all books and newspapers of any value. Every person of any attainments was suspected, and subjected to investigation. Many could not go out between sundown and sunrise. Passports could not be depended upon. So-called thinkers were driven to the bench of confession everywhere. There were spies everywhere, and the freedom-loving people made away with them without hesitation wherever they found them. The cardinals permitted suspected people to be murdered in large numbers, even of their own faith, if they found that they had lied about them in order to displace them. The head of the Inquisition, in 1841, ordered strong measures against all unbelievers, Jews and magicians who might lay things in the way of the Inquisition. Punishment for thinkers was to be chained to the wall in a dungeon or to be hanged or to be shot from behind. The dungeons of Naples were approaching these conditions.

It was under such conditions that Napoleon III later sent a grandson of one of the marshals of his great uncle to maintain order in Italy.

Upon the houses which the French Army, in its march from Civita Vecchia, passed on the way to Rome, the Italians had written a paragraph from the French Republic's constitution, which read: "France honors all foreign nationalities; its power shall never be employed against the liberties of any people." Naturally the officers were all reactionary, and cared little about the constitution of the Republic.

On April 27, Garibaldi had reached Rome. Already, on April 30, Marshall Oudinot approached the city in three columns, certain that he could break its defenses and enter. There was little opposition to expect from a few thousand poorly-armed students, artists and volunteers. The west side of Rome was commanded by the Villa Doria Pamfili with the Palace of Corsini. Upon the Corsini terrace Garibaldi stationed a force, and a well-directed artillery fire met the French army. Next, through the open space dashed a small force of a few hundred students and artists against the French, and a clash at close quarters followed. But the untried attacking force was driven back. Thereupon Garibaldi called upon eight hundred volunteers from the inner city to help, and placed himself at the head of the troops which were directed by his old officers, "The Tigers of Montevideo," and this little handful of brave men put the regular French troops to flight. Five hundred of the French fell, and three hundred and sixty-five of them were taken prisoner. Garibaldi, himself, received a bullet in his side.

Neverthless, he wished to follow up the victory, but Mazzini, who knew how many enemies the republic had, believed, in his innocence, that he could win over the French. The prisoners were first honored, "and then given their freedom, and the wounded given treatment." "The French Republic, and the Roman were like sisters," he said. De Lesseps, later the builder of the Suez Canal, came as an emissary from Oudinot, and, naïve as he, also was, he proposed in good faith, a peace treaty. This was naturally repudiated and recalled as soon as 20,000 fresh French troops had arrived at Civita Vecchia, for whom word had been sent.

When Oudinot, in order to deceive the Romans, declared that the truce did not end until June 4, Roselli believed him, and rode, on June 2, to the Garibaldians, which were holding the Villa Doria Pamfili and Corsini, and told them that they did not need to keep watch, as the Frenchmen would not come until June 4. On the the night of June 3, before daylight, Oudinot took up the two positions which commanded Rome.

In spite of his wounds, and by a series of masterly maneuvers, Garibaldi had struck the French army April 30, and also the Neapolitan army twice, at Pallaestrina and Velletri, but while confined to his bed by his injuries he received the news that Villa Corsini had been retaken. In vain he had urged the triumvirate to appoint him dictator. They feared a dictatorship and preferred to retain the incapable Roselli. Garibaldi now hastened to retake the lost position. This could be done only at great loss of life, while it could have been held at a correspondingly small loss. The terrain was in the form of an hour-glass. There was a small space through which the storming party went in a rain of bullets, yet the villa was taken again and again. Here fell the flower of the army, among them the youthful

Enrico Dandolo, of whom great things had been expected. In this desperate crisis Garibaldi's courage and resolution was strikingly shown. All day he sat upon his white horse and wearing his white cape. He refused to yield to defeat, to admit there was no hope. He called to Emilio Dandalo, Enrico's younger brother: "Summon twenty men with you and retake the villa at the point of the bayonet!" Twelve of them reached the villa, from whose windows hundreds of Frenchmen fired upon them. Six of them came back.

From this time resistance was hopeless, however stubbornly conducted. Four weeks, thereafter, the French army stormed Rome, reëstablished the old reactionary order, and remained in the captured city twenty years, or until 1870, with the exception of the period between December, 1866, to November, 1867.

Garibaldi fled, pursued like a wild animal. With his followers he escaped from his French, Neapolitan and Austrian foes and executed a march through the entire length of Italy whose like has never been known. While on this expedition he had the great sorrow to lose his wife, Anita, who died from privations near Ravenna, and whose body he had to leave behind.

On this retreat from Rome to San Marino he revealed to an astonished world a military genius of a new order.

The 4,000 men who followed him from Rome were so demoralized that they deserted by the hundreds at the beginning, later by scores a day.

Those who remained—barely 2,000 men—were poorly equipped, badly armed, and had in all only eighty rounds of ammunition per man. All of Garibaldi's best officers were killed or wounded. He could not, therefore, carry on hostilities with any large body of French or Austrians; but he went unscathed between them through Italy to the Adriatic. This was made possible by the energy and activity due to his South American training. First he did away with baggage wagons and had his burdens carried by horses and asses. He could thus leave the beaten highways and enter the Apennines. His food supply also traveled on foot in the form of cattle accompanying the army. His marches were of unregulated length, by night as well as by day, in fact, chiefly by night. Without warning, camp would be broken at sundown. Skilfully the enemy would be thrown off the track. First a false march would be made, then a course taken in another direction. False reports as to his strength were given out and fear of the red shirt disseminated. He also made extraordinary use of his cavalry. It served not only to confuse the enemy, but to act as a spy system. He knew the plans of the enemy miles away and surprised the opposition by showing his cavalry where he was never expected to go.

Needless to say, Garibaldi had no military pedantry. Throughout all his career, however, he maintained an iron discipline. Small infractions were met with minor punishments, which, however, were greatly feared. For greater ones the penalty was invariably death. Thievery, plundering and violence were punished with death on the spot. It restrained his troops to know that he could give an order to have one shot down without ever removing his cigar from his lips. In one of the wild Apennine passes near Frodo he ordered a soldier shot for the mere stealing of a chicken.

Nevertheless, he professed to be a disciple of Beccaria, who opposed the death penalty. Theoretically he was such, and in practice also in that he discountenanced political murders. He refused to join in the conspiracy for the murder of Napoleon III, when Mazzini sent his friend Sarah Nathan, mother of Rome's well known official head, to win him over to it. On the other hand, he rejoiced, in 1849, in the murder of the ambitious, but reactionary Rossi in Rome, and justified himself with a sophistry like that of Brutus, whom the world in general had set up as a hero of liberty, but whose course nevertheless cannot be defended as right.

Garibaldi was no philosopher and had not the serene faculty necessary to solve complicated problems. However, he had not only a great heart and a clear head but a rare mind. His career reminds one much of Shelley. He was a sort of Shelley of action.

While Mazzini, with all his aspirations for freedom, held to the religious beliefs of the eighteenth century, Garibaldi was entirely modern in his religious views. While Mazzini retained a reverent loyalty to the church of Rome, Garibaldi was a priest-hater and monk-hater, as everywhere revealed in his writings. Frequently he designates himself as an atheist and writes at the front of his books, *"Dio e Popolo."* In general he discourses as a pantheist of traces of God in nature, of God as the soul of the universe, and once—in a letter to the English woman, Caroline Giffard Philipson—he protests against being called an unbeliever and speaks of God as the father of all peoples. In Christianity as a system he had little faith, yet for him, as for Victor Hugo, Jesus came to free the world from slavery.

He was little concerned about the doctrine a person confessed. He looked only at peoples' acts and maintained that men showed by example, rather than by profession, what they really were. He had but one doctrine, expressed in *Avanti!* "Forward!" and his whole life was an illustration of this doctrine.

All in all, his personality had the charm of a magician. His presence inspired enthusiasm, while his voice was irresistible. When he sat upon his horse, with his gold-brown locks playing about his head, with his red shirt and his white South American poncho about his shoulders, he looked wonderfully beautiful.

After Anita's death, Garibaldi wished to visit his mother and his own motherless children at Nice, but the Piedmontese government dared not give him a guaranty of protection, since both France and Austria would demand his extradition. On his arrival at Nice he was politely arrested and requested to serve the government by leaving the country. Finally, he was permitted to remain a few hours in Nice. Thence he went to Tunis and from there to Morocco, where the Piedmontese consul at Tangier entertained him for a half year at his house and where in the enjoyment of the sea and landscape he restored his health. Then seeking another place of exile, he went to New York where he first obtained a place in a candle factory. As a workman he was obliged to bring the barrels of tallow to the vats in which the tallow was cooked. Here he suffered greatly from rheumatism, a malady resulting from his earlier privations, and which was to be one of the afflictions of his later life. When he had grown tired of making candles, he sought to engage as a sailor, but was rejected, in spite of the fact that he offered to serve without pay. Finally he was accepted, and later obtained the command of a vessel himself and cruised to Central America, along the coast of China and southern Australia, visited South America again and finally landed, as has been stated, at Newcastle, in order to bring a cargo of coal to Genoa. Not until 1854 did he return to Italy, and having inherited the property of a brother, he bought for about 6,500 crowns the northern half of the craggy little isle of Caprera, off Sardinia, which until death twenty-eight years afterwards was to be his residence.

V

When in December, 1858, Cavour asked Garibaldi to raise a corps of volunteers for the war with Austria, orders were given that 2,000 good muskets should be sent to Garibaldi's Alpine troops. He had not reckoned, however, with the jealousy of the minister of war, La Marmora. By design the muskets were sent so late that they did not reach the troops. Neither horses nor ambulance wagons were supplied, and the same was true as to baggage wagons and artillery. Even the necessary cavalry was not provided. All that Garibaldi had was fifty horsemen who had bought their own horses.

These troops, equipped with old muskets, moved upon superior numbers of Tyrolean sharpshooters, supported by artillery, and were victorious at Varese, at Como, everywhere. In spite of the King's and Cavour's express orders that all volunteers should be placed under Garibaldi, another corps was organized beside his, known as the Apennine Volunteers, under another command. The peace of Villafranca brought a speedy close to this war and to the hope of Italy's freedom through the aid of France.

At this period occurred Garibaldi's unfortunate marriage with the nineteen-year-old Marchesina Giuseppina

Raimondi, a marriage which resulted in a separation on the very day of the wedding.

A word or two relative to the influence of women upon Garibaldi may be here given. Not a word upon this point is found in Garibaldi's memoirs. His character was too high for that. But this chivalrous character which won so many men to him, even among his enemies, was particularly appealing to women. His rare physical beauty first impressed them. His figure was full and elastic. His limbs were beautiful, but, as is common with horsemen, were slightly bowed. His head was particularly noteworthy, a sort of union of the Zeus and Christ types. No artist had ever dreamt of such a type. It gave the impression of strength, sympathy and kindness. He had hardened his body in every way. He dressed simply but with taste. Previous to 1860, in his rôles as gaucho, sea captain, or member of the Italian legion, he affected white, red or green colors and a broad felt hat with a feather. Yet higher than elegance of dress he held cleanliness of person. There was no spot upon even his worn clothes, and even under the most difficult circumstances he managed to bathe himself. He cared for his hands and for his hair, the hair whose locks were to find their way all the world over, and of which he wrote naïvely to Lady Shaftsbury: "Honored Madam—My hair is growing, and as soon as it can be cut again I will send you some of it."

His manner of speech was terse and simple. He said to all "*Voi*," only to the king "*Lei*," more often "*Tu*." He listened better than he spoke, but had a direct way of interrupting a conversation. When, in 1864, Lord Palmerston artfully sought to tell him how necessary it was to let the Venetian question rest until a more favorable time, he broke in with some heat: "What is it you are trying to tell me? It is never too early for a slave to break his chains," and withdrew. Palmerston was astonished at such lack of observance of form.

When he showed himself in Naples or in Sicily, the women flocked about him and cried in their dialect: "How beautiful you are!" He received hundreds of letters from

French, German and English women. A volume could be filled with them. The Italian women who admired and loved him would pass numbering. As a rule he was too absorbed in his plans to take any notice of this adulation. His published letters show how well he held to the things in hand, although women came to his service like valkyries to a battlefield, as diplomatic representatives or in purely personal capacities. After the battle of Aspromonte, where he was wounded, the women of Russia sent him Pirogof, Russia's greatest surgeon; the French women sent Nélaton, while from England came Patridge. Marie Espérance von Schwartz (Elpis Melena) sent him the Neapolitan Prandina, who prevented the amputation of Garibaldi's foot. Many young women fought under his banner as simple soldiers, such as the young and beautiful Maria Martina, Countess of Torre, whose glowing letters reveal her pride and obedience, and other heroic fair ones like Tonina Marinelli and Alba Camozzi.

On June 1, 1859, it chanced that Garibaldi, on his way between Robarello and Varese, met a carriage containing the young Marchesina of Raimondi, who, accompanied by a priest, was to convey to Garibaldi a letter from Como and bring back his reply. He was riding with a staff officer at the head of his troops, and was smitten by the young girl's beauty as by a vision. Her father, the marquis, was one of Garibaldi's most enthusiastic admirers and was elated at the impression his daughter had made upon him. But she had already given her favor to a young man named Luigi Caroli, and only when he broke with her could she bring herself to consider a union with Garibaldi. However, she still retained her love for Caroli, and when on the nuptial night Garibaldi discovered her coldness toward him, he promptly declared that she need not fear him, but that he did not need a woman who did not love him, and left her.

Throughout the world the newspapers spread the false story that Garibaldi's young bride had betrayed him for another man. As she made no protest against this, the young man was subjected to such hatred that he did not dare to enlist under Garibaldi. Thereupon, in 1863, he joined in the Polish insurrection, participated in the first skirmish, was taken prisoner, and after being maltreated by the Cossacks, was transported to Siberia and confined in a dungeon until his death. Not until twenty-one years later, in 1880, did Garibaldi get the marriage annulled, although he never afterwards saw Giuseppina.

VI

As is well known, Garibaldi was not content to rest upon the achievements of 1859, but set himself the task, upon his own resources, to liberate Sicily and Naples. He had to oppose 40,000 regular Neapolitan troops, equipped with artillery. He decided first to undertake his enterprise with 200 volunteers, but increased this body until he had 1,089 young men. Who does not remember the words, "The One Thousand." I have owned Garibaldi's book with this title —a rare treasure—but it has been stolen from me.

Garibaldi went secretly at night in Genoa on board two freight boats, without lights, with his famous thousand young men in their own clothes, without baggage, and, it might be said, without weapons. From a privately subscribed fund, he had been promised 200 Enfield rifles from Milan. But an embarrassing situation arose when these failed to come. The expedition had to be abandoned.

In Milan there were unused 12,000 good rifles which the people had contributed to aid Garibaldi. But the governor of Milan, Marchese Massimo d'Azeglio, an altogether too conscientious official, contrary to the view of Cavour, believed it wrong to support the expedition to Sicily while still maintaining diplomatic relations with Naples, and refused therefore to deliver a single gun.

Cavour was not a countryman of Machiavelli's for nothing, yet it required no Machiavellian mind to consider all the means legitimate to a campaign against Bomba and the Naples government. The situation with reference to the papal states was as nothing to this. In 1851 all the elite of Naples, 20,000 in number, were in prison, whose plight Gladstone made known to Europe, but without producing any change in the situation.

A worse policy was not known in the darkest of the Middle Ages, nor in Russia under Nicholas II.

The courageous Massimo d' Azeglio, who had himself fought against Austria, a well-known writer and true Christian, should not have found it necessary to entertain such scruples. Farini, minister of the interior, had consigned 1,500 rifles to one La Masa—not to Garibaldi—for a movement upon Sicily. La Masa was so out of sympathy with such plans that he could not bring himself to aid the enterprise. Particularly was he averse to furnishing effective weapons to Garibaldi.

On April 24, 1860, this consignment of rifles came to Garibaldi labeled as books. There were old muskets, rusted with age, whose flint locks were out of order, and the whole stock of which had been discarded by the military authorities as obsolete.

"Old iron!" exclaimed Garibaldi when he saw them. Yet with them—or rather, with their bayonets—he redeemed the dual kingdom, although the range of these muskets was less than half of that of those of the enemy. With them he triumphed at Calatafimi and with such as remained he stormed Palermo.

Evading the Neapolitan fleet, he went by open boats to Calabria, marched through a thickly-populated hostile country, won a victory at Milazzo, and finally entered Naples as dictator.

The conquest of southern Italy was an achievement without parallel in history, accomplished through the heroism of a handful of men, not through brutality toward a weaker race, like the Spanish conquest of Mexico and Peru, but through the magic faculty of a guerilla-chieftain to sway and win all who came under the influence of his eye and voice, and to strike such terror into his enemies that they would fly, no matter how large their numbers.

Garibaldi was master of Sicily and Naples. He had now an army of 20,000 men. Only Capua and Gaeta still held out. To reduce them would require artillery. The time had now arrived when Victor Emmanuel could advance from the north with his army. When Garibaldi in October had won the bloody battle of Volturno, and the hope of the Bourbons for the reconquest of Italy was gone, a popular plebiscite was held which resulted in the election of Victor Emmanuel as Italy's first constitutional king. In order to hypnotise the people these words were painted upon the walls everywhere—*Vogliamo il regno constituzionale del re Vittorio Emanuele.* I see them before me yet.

With a few regiments Garibaldi went northward to meet the king. After having bivouaced in the broad valley between Cajanello and Vairano he saw, on the morning of October 26, 1860, the Italian army approaching him. Garibaldi and his staff dismounted and stationed themselves at a village corner while battalion after battalion filed past.

Officers and soldiers gazed upon Garibaldi, some with unfeigned admiration, others with the envy of a weary soldier or the prejudice of political conservatism. As ingrained conservatives the commanding general, Fanti, and his officers, had grave suspicions of republicanism and its promoters and their methods.

On October 8th, fourteen days before, Cavour had written to Minister Farini who maintained headquarters near the king:

In case Garibaldi's army yields allegience to the king it must be handled well. We must oppose the arrogance and pedantry of the regular army. Do not give over. Political considerations of the highest importance demand firmness on our part. Woe to us if we show ourselves ungrateful toward those who have given their blood for Italy. Europe would condemn us. A strong reaction in favor of Garibaldi would then sweep through the country. I have had a sharp struggle with Fanti over this point. He talked of the military demands. I answered that this was not Spain and that here the army had to obey.

But Cavour was in Turin, and Victor Emmanuel soon came under Fanti's influence.

When the king and his followers had come near, Garibaldi and his officers were again mounted. They were not soldiers on parade. They were garbed in the famous red woolen shirts, now spotted with blood and dust. Garibaldi, after his fashion, had a handkerchief tied about his head

and the customary cape over his shoulders. The officers of
the king in their gold-laced uniforms looked askance at them.

Garibaldi cried—"I greet Italy's first king!"

Victor Emmanuel rode towards him, extended his hand,
and said—"How are you, my dear Garibaldi?"

"Well, your majesty. And yourself?"

"Very well," replied the King.

Side by side they rode on, and members of the two staffs
likewise, the red shirts pairing with the uniforms and broad
bands of rank. Conservative and revolutionary forces
sought to blend. The conversation, however, was strained.
Cold courtesy prevailed where enthusiasm had been expected. The first information the King vouchsafed Garibaldi was that the royal army would now take over all
operations, and that Garibaldi's help would no longer be
needed. Finally he was directed to return to his army and
to take his position in march behind the last royal battalion.

Thereupon Garibaldi and his officers stationed themselves
at a side road, and the first words he spoke were to an
English woman friend, Jessie Mario White, whom he met
—"Jessie, they are sending us to the rear!" Without
a murmur, this band of heroes who had borne the heat and
burden of war for years took their places behind an army
that for a year had not known a battle.

Garibaldi received the information that on November 6,
the King would visit his camp at Caserta for a review of
his troops. The dictator of Naples would then present for
the first time his generals and younger officers and the redshirted troops would march for the first time before the
King. They were drawn up before the old bourbon castle
of Caserta, the men from Piedmont, from Tuscany, from
Emilia and Lombardy, from Calabria and Sicily, in their
strongly contrasted garbs and with their scarred and
bronzed countenances. They waited the appointed hour.
Then word was received that the King had decided not to
come. No explanation nor excuse was advanced. The King
did not even issue an order of the day thanking the men to
whom he owed his double kingdom.

A few days thereafter Garibaldi's troops were mustered out and sent home. Only a few of the higher officers went over to the regular army.

Had Garibaldi not been too proud to revenge himself, he might have received a high commission. His detractors, in their zeal, had forgotten that the King still had need of Garibaldi, such urgent need that the general could not be ignored. On the morning of November 7, 1860, the king was to make his formal entry into Naples, and it was learned that if Garibaldi would not be seated in the carriage by the King's side, a storm of disapproval would greet Victor Emmanuel and his army. It was necessary to win over the dictator the evening of the very day upon which such injustice had been visited upon him.

One of the generals, Cialdini, had shown himself markedly friendly toward Garibaldi and he was sent to win him over. It was no easy task. Garibaldi was no lamb, and he spoke bitter words of reproach against the commanding general, and no less sharp ones against Cavour, whom he unjustly believed had conspired against him. But with his deep sense of duty and his appreciation of the greater things at stake, he gave his word that he would take his place in the carriage by the King's side, the next morning.

No word was exchanged between the two as in the midst of a driving rain they made their formal entry into the city. However, the populace of Naples did not know this and in spite of the severe storm it was half-crazed with enthusiasm.

The next morning at daybreak, Garibaldi, without informing the people, boarded a small ship that lay in the harbor to return to his rocky island home at Caprera. Only three or four of his nearest officers accompanied him. He made just one short visit early in the morning before leaving and this was to the admiral of the English fleet, who had discreetly been of much aid to him in the landings made in Sicily and Naples.

Garibaldi had refused the gifts the King had proferred him. He had borrowed a few hundred francs, and took with him but a sack of grain to sow on his land at Caprera.

This was the reward the kingdom of Savoy, which had three times given its veto against an expedition to Sicily, gave to Sicily's liberator. First it had refused to permit Garibaldi to set out; then he had been forbidden to cross the straits of Messina and later to cross the Volturno river. He did all of these things and Italy was none the worse for it.

What wonder, then, that Garibaldi, who was not worldly wise, but a man of action, should after the death of Cavour lose all patience with a situation which permitted the papal states to be returned to the Pope, and Rome to the French, should, in 1862, sound the slogan—"Rome or Death." Political pressure led Victor Emmanuel to send his army against Garibaldi and to fire upon him and his young men at Aspromonte, while Garibaldi's under his orders did not fire. Garibaldi says in his memoirs—"It is against my principles to relate scandals, but so many have been revealed to me in connection with this affair that they would make even a sewer-worker to vomit."

What must Garibaldi have felt when he lay upon the ground wounded by an Italian bullet and with his son Menotti by his side wounded by another, or when in a similar situation, five years later, Garibaldi and Mentana, after having defeated the papal troops, were attacked in the rear by the troops of Napoleon III, who laid low the flower of young Italy with their rifles of improved construction! The dispatch, "*Les Chassepots ont fait merveille,*" is famous throughout Italy to this day.

I know that his viewpoint was impolitic, yet not so impolitic but that to the end he steadily refused to proclaim a republic, though himself a republican. Through Mentana, the Mazzini party induced 3,000 of his young soldiers to desert his army, with the cry, "Go home! Build barricades and proclaim a republic!" Garibaldi contended for a kingdom which inwardly hated him.

To the end of his career injustice and distrust followed him, because he was considered dangerous as a revolutionist and doubly dangerous as a visionary politician.

When he offered his services to the French Republic in

1870, the provisional government allowed his letter to remain unanswered for a month, thus losing all this valuable time. When he finally received a reply, and presented himself before Cremieux, Glais-Bezoin and Gambetta, they received him with cold courtesy and illusory compliments, which led him to think of returning to Caprera. "I understood," he wrote, "that they simply wanted to use my poor name (il mio povero nome):" and although he was not trained in the methodical warfare with which it was necessary to meet the German army, he was yet the only one in the whole campaign to capture a German standard, which, to the credit of the Germans be it said, was drawn from under a heap of bodies, and which, for this reason, he sent back. Afterwards hatred was shown him by the ungrateful French in the reactionary parliament at Bordeaux, and he was compelled to leave the hall.

The Germanic peoples are prone to ascribe to themselves the characteristics of simplicity, naïveté and straightforwardness to an equal degree with the Latin peoples. The latter, however, frequently reveal a degree of naïveté to which the Germanic peoples have never attained.

The popular hero of the Germanic mind is William Tell, who is pictured as chivalrous and bold. He has the great lack, however, of having never existed. France has her Joan of Arc, the flower of the Middle Ages, the ideal and child-like heroine whom the church burned and whom, five hundred years later, it canonized.

Italy has in Garibaldi the modern folk-hero, a real knight, not only without fear or reproach, but without self-seeking, unselfish, inspired like Joan of Arc and visionary as she, but differently equipped—having all his means and agencies in hand—lacking but a capacity for administration—and striving toward higher ideals than hers. Her ideals were faith, the church, papal aggrandizement, royal authority, and the glory of France; his were freedom of peoples, freedom of thought, civilization, the brotherhood of nations. He was as free from superstition as he was from selfishness and cowardice.

XII

NAPOLEON BONAPARTE

1915

It is now a hundred years since, with the campaign in France in 1814 and the battle of Waterloo in 1815, the Napoleonic period closed. The present war which engages the activities of three-quarters of the world and affects the destinies of the whole human race is, in the extent of territory involved, not unlike the wars of Napoleon, yet differing in high degree from them, not only in the immense masses of soldiery employed, but in the development of means of communication brought about since that time. Napoleon conducted warfare as had Alexander the Great more than two thousand years before, with infantry, with cavalry, with baggage trains upon the highways, and with ships at sea. If he desired a report for his representative at St. Petersburg, he was obliged to send his message by a courier on horseback, who returned six weeks later with the reply. His battles were fought in a day, at the most in two days. His campaigns were correspondingly short.

His whole reign was brief. He was consul a little over four years and as emperor he ruled in all ten years. Seldom has such a short period in history been so productive of activity and achievements, and so memorable.

I

The first time that Napoleon felt his plans sharply thwarted by circumstances was when he received the news of Dupont's capitulation of Baylen in 1808. From that time on, the unfailing good fortune which had borne him victoriously over all obstacles began deserting him.

Yet even as late as the beginning of October, 1812, Napoleon at Moscow stood forth as the master of the European continent. His own personal fortunes had not yet suffered a reverse. He was forty-three years old, the emperor of France and the king of Italy. He had married an emperor's daughter and had an heir to his throne. His empire stretched from the coast of Holland to the Ionic isles, from Dantzic to the southernmost tip of Italy. He reigned as absolute monarch over a hundred million people. But on the 19th of October he began the retreat from Moscow, and in 1912 the centenary of this famous retreat was celebrated throughout Russia with great festivities, as if in commemoration of a great triumph of the Russian people. However, it can scarcely be doubted that had it been Napoleon's fortune to have established a foothold in Russia it would have been a blessing to the people of that country. The Russian serfs would then have been liberated a half century before they were. The religious liberties which the czar in his fear proclaimed in 1905 would have been a reality in 1812, and without doubt the Russian people would have been led into ways of freedom and prosperity such as have since been opened to the people of France.

But the collapse of the Russian Campaign gave the final blow to Napoleon's power. Within a year and a half after he entered Moscow his domain was restricted to the isle of Elba. A year after this he was a prisoner on the rock of St. Helena. The structure of power he had built up crumbled like a house of cards.

Nevertheless, his constructive achievements within the limits of France itself have remained standing to this day, for Napoleon was not only the heir of the Revolution, but the builder of its spirit into law. He did not bring about the great movement; this must be credited to the thinkers of the eighteenth century; but he made its fruits secure. He cast the glowing ore of the Revolution into forms of law and it became hard as shining bronze and impervious to attack. When the imperial power slipped from his hands he left behind him—as did Rome of old when its world dominion was lost—his code, which in large part, survives today.

The third French republic has undertaken the difficult task of transforming this code to meet new conditions; for instance, has replaced the Concordat with the Catholic Church with a separation of church and state, a great task rather clumsily executed, and which has not yet resulted in great good, but has rather had the effect of dividing the French people into two hostile camps.

Scarcely less distinct are the traces of Napoleon's influence seen outside of France where it has made obsolete old forms of government and justice.

II

In his first scene in "Faust" Goethe has coined the word "superman." It is a scornful designation of Faust.

In his days of supreme power Napoleon appeared indeed to be a superman. In the course of the wars waged against him he came to be considered and pictured as a sort of "non-man," a being without human attributes. In the caricatures of the time, and particularly the English, he is frequently represented as the Devil himself, or with the Devil pointing toward him and saying: "This is my only-begotten son in whom I am well pleased." Grundtvig, in 1814, published an old prophecy which pictured Napoleon as "the great Anti-Christ, or the final adversary." Since that time we have come to understand the human side of him.

After his fall every good attribute was denied him. He was simply a tyrant, an unparralleled butcher, a destroyer of human life on a great scale. And this is undeniable; 1,700,000 Frenchmen and 2,000,000 of other lands fell in the wars of the empire from 1804 to 1814.

It was asserted unqualifiedly that he was thoroughly false; that he lied in his bulletins, as set forth by a famous commentator; that he appropriated to himself the honors for victories won by his generals, for Augereau's exploit at Arcole; for Desaix's victory at Marengo, in spite of the fact that in this very bulletin he speaks of Desaix almost as Achilles did of Patroclus. He was charged with taking to himself the credit for the work of his jurists, that the Code Napoleon was the work of Portalis, forgetting the fact that Napoleon had himself driven these jurists almost to the point of weariness. He was charged with having dealt in great falsehoods in writing his memoirs at St. Helena; that his whole make-up was humbug. In Alfred de Vigny's famous story "Stello" the captive emperor is alternately presented as comedian and tragedian. It was reported that he made a study of tones and attitudes under the renowned Talma, when more certainly Talma impersonates him.

Even the military talent was denied him. In Chateaubriand's pamphlet, "Buonaparte and the Bourbons" Napoleon is pictured as an incapable general, who simply permitted his troops to take the offensive, who won victories, but entirely through the valor of his soldiers, and independent of his leadership. Thus Chateaubriand says: "What was there about this foreigner by which he could so delude the people of France? His gifts for warfare? Even of this claim he has now been stripped. Without doubt he has won many great battles. But aside from that, the most obscure general is more capable than he. People have deluded themselves with the idea that he has developed and perfected the art of war, when in truth he has carried it back to its beginning." (This passage has been incorporated by Flaubert in his collection relating to notable blockheads.)

Rumor had it that Napoleon was personally a coward. Chateaubriand, for instance, in *Mémoires d'Outretombe*, pictures his anxiety during his journey through France after his abdication at Fontainebleau, when he borrowed the uniform of an Austrian colonel, a Prussian helmet and a Russian cape. He trembled and changed colors at the least stir. But the populace was then bent on tearing him to pieces. What wonder, then, that he who had often preserved the composure of a statue amid a rain of bullets should fear such a death!

In the German lampoons of the period of 1813-1814 he is uniformly designated as "coward," and every little German province, even Hessen-Darmstadt, took to itself the

credit for his overthrow. In a Darmstadt soldier-song of
the time I have found this passage:

> Napoleon, du Schustergesell'!
> Kujon, was läufest du so schnell?
> Hättest du mit Darmstadt Frieden gemacht,
> Du hättest es wahrlich weiter gebracht.

Even in France it was repeatedly asserted that in reality
he was not French at all, but Italian, an alien. His name
was Buonaparte. He lied, they declared in claiming he was
born after the conquest of Corsica (1769); that he was a
year older, hence born before the annexation of Corsica to
France, and that he had permitted the official records at
Ajaccio, containing the entry of his birth, to be falsified.

This assertion was untrue, although one may still hear
it made by intelligent men in France. I have myself investigated these records and am convinced that their falsification would have been impossible. Carelessness in the
spelling of surnames was at that time so great that "Bonaparte" is spelled differently, with and without "u," the
two times in which the name, with a few intervening lines,
occurs.

It is an article of faith in Germany that Napoleon was a
liar. Certain it is that he, who was a politician, and, like
the majority of politicians, without scruples, employed
falsehood where it served his purposes. He was, moreover,
a soldier, and as a Corsican had grown up in the belief
that stratagem in warfare was as honorable as open conflict. Yet the care which he required of his subordinates
in the use of deceit was shown in the sharp letter he sent
the Count of Rovigo after the glorious victory at Montmirail and Vauxchamps in 1814, saying:

You must have lost your head in Paris since you have permitted it to go out that we here battled one against three, when
I have proclaimed that I have 300,000 men, which the enemy
believed, and which I must now reiterate to my disgust. In
this way you destroy with a stroke of the pen all the good
results of our victory. You should understand that an empty
honor avails nothing, and that one of the first principles in war
is to exaggerate your strength. But how can this be made clear

to a poet who thinks only of flattering me and pleasing the national vanity.

Here also he lies from a sense of duty, foregoing the glory which a statement of the true facts would have brought him.

It is not necessary at this time to call attention to the violent and obstinate in Napoleon's character, his power to win men and make them the agency of his causes. Again and again his crimes were pointed out, the terrible official murder of the Duke of Enghien, which he—even before he became emperor in 1804—permitted, in order to terrify those opposing his royal ambitions; the like official murder of the book-dealer, Palm of Nuremberg in 1806, for publishing a book dealing with the downfall of Germany and the bad conduct of the French troops in Bavaria at the time; as also the execution, in 1810, of Andreas Hofer, the Tyrolean hero of liberty, over whom the weak emperor of Austria failed to extend a protecting hand.

The two last-named executions have been justified under the barbaric morals of warfare then prevailing, which also still prevail, and in even more deplorable form. The first one would appear to be unjustifiable, yet it may be noted that no less a personage than Goethe has defended it; yes, has even claimed that it required no defense. In a conversation which Goethe led at Wolzogen's table at Weimar, in October, 1808, he declared that the greatness and shrewdness of Napoleon was best revealed in the fact that he never lost sight of his goal. Other leaders indulged their sympathies or antipathies; but Napoleon never permitted himself to champion or oppose anything unless it tended to promote or retard his progress toward his goal. Whatever stood in his way was struck down. To Goethe it seemed entirely proper that Napoleon should permit a claimant to the throne like d'Enghien, or an agitator like Palm, to be shot in order that once for all examples might be made of them for terrifying the public, which everywhere disturbs the purposes of genius. And Goethe concludes (according to Falk's account): "Under trying circumstances, he contends with a corrupt century, among a corrupt people. Let us esteem him fortunate, both him and Europe, that with his mighty world projects he has not himself been corrupted."

Napoleon was considered, in 1815, by princes and peoples alike, as an absolute menace to the peace of Europe as long as he was free. Therefore, his imprisonment seemed justified, although there were few parallels then, as there are few now, for treating a captive monarch—particularly one who had surrendered of his own free will after losing a battle and abdicating his throne—as a criminal and not only holding him captive until peace had been declared but in lifelong imprisonment. The few faint parallels were those of Mary Stuart, who also relied upon an English government's magnanimity; and her husband Bothwell, who placed his faith in a Danish government's neutrality and magnanimity. We are accustomed to advise against building upon sand. Yet frequently this results in good; we have libeled the sand. It is upon magnanimity that we should never build.

III

In France, as outside of France, a great reaction set in against the July revolution, in France through Henri Beyle, through Victor Hugo (in his "Songs of Eastern Lands and Twilight Songs"); through Armand Carrel's articles; through Thiers, in his "History of the Consulate and the Empire"—unphilosophic, yet clear and greatly conceived—and finally in the songs of Beranger, among the pearls of which is *Les Souveniers du Peuple,* in which the story of the emperor is told through the lips of an old peasant woman. Here, with the eager exclamation: "And did he once speak to you, grandmother; did he speak to you?" he is presented as the beloved legendary hero, with his small three-cornered hat and his long gray coat.

Corresponding to this in Germany was Heinrich Heine's verse and prose, later Laube's and others. In the English-speaking world Napoleon did not have any admirers until late, although now he has many. Also, since he was the foe of England, he now has as many in Germany.

So great was the reaction of public sentiment in the Napoleonic revival during the reign of Louis Philippe that the government felt constrained to have Napoleon's body brought back from St. Helena by the king's own son, and his sarcophagus deposited under the dome of the Invalides.

Outside of France the deification of his memory was most strikingly exemplified by the Polish poets. To them, about 1830, Napoleon appeared as a supernatural being; an enigma which foiled all attempts at its solution. He had again awakened the natural conscience which had slumbered since the eighteenth century disasters. No mere human agencies, they felt, could overcome him, none except His Excellency General Frost and His Excellency General Hunger, in Russia. In the eyes of Mickiewicz and Krasinski, he becomes a demigod, a Messiah. His mission was to liberate the peoples; and in viewing St. Helena as a sort of second Golgatha, a ray from the passion of Christ is cast over Napooleon's captivity and death.

IV

In our own day the human side of Napoleon's make-up has been studied in an unfriendly spirit during the period of Napoleon III, when his foes sought to strike the nephew through the uncle, but in an unpartisan manner since. The "un-man" and the "super-man" have finally blended into a sort of demoniac figure whose origin makes clearer its outstanding attributes.

Napoleon was in origin a full-blooded Italian. In his early years the conquest of Corsica wakened in him a consuming hatred and bitterness toward the French. Although born a French subject, in character he was not French; he was late in learning to use the language like a native, and never learned to write French correctly, as revealed in his dictations. He had a noble Roman cast of character, of pure transparency, with no gleam of French *esprit*.

His mother was a Cornelia, no French dame of the 18th century. There was in him an antique Roman element (his head reminds one of Augustus) and a far more pronounced Italian renaissance element. His family stock was Florentine; and he had certain elements in common with the Condottiere of the 15th century, a consuming energy, and from the beginning a relative indifference toward the cause he served if thereby he mainly served himself. Like warriors of other times, he had a stubborn will, unbending resolution, the faculty to seize the occasion and form a new resolution, when an earlier was found to appear impracticable. He never lost sight of his goal and he had the conspicuous political instinct of the Italian, the instinct for advantage and the means of shifting the political viewpoint so strikingly revealed in Machiavelli, in Giulio II, and in Mazarin (Giulio Mazarini). As one reads of his political negotiations with Alexander I, one sees, as it were, Italian finesse matched against Byzantian shiftiness and cunning.

In his union of the practical with an exalted fantasy, Napoleon resembles the great figures of the Italian renaissance. French genius has a modicum of simple sound sense, clear, but devoid of fancy. It finds its most conspicuous embodiment in Montaigne (half Jewish), in La Fontaine and Molière. The most purely French genius is marked by taste and tact; it is discriminating, as in Racine or Voltaire, or verbose as in Hugo. Bonaparte is genuine, not verbal, ardent, not discriminating. Of his taste not much can be said, but of his creative fantasy a great deal, and, like Michael Angelo, he was formed on colossal and grandiose lines.

While living at Cararra, in 1505, Michael Angelo discerned a cliff which seemed to dominate the shore. A fancy he had long indulged then seized him, to transform the whole cliff into a mighty heroic countenance. This corresponds to Napoleon's plan, in 1808, to lay the foundation for world dominion by attacking England from three directions at once, by way of Suez, from central Asia and by way of the cape. To this end fleets were to be fitted out in Brest, in the Loire, in Toulon, in Spezzia, in Genoa, in Vlissingen, in Boulogne, in Dunkirk, Havre, Cherbourg, Rochefort, Bordeaux, Ferrol, Lisbon and Carthagena. The squadron from Toulon was to carry 20,000 men for the reconquest of Egypt; the fleet from Brest and the Loire was to land 18,000 men in India. The French-Russian army was to proceed directly to the Euphrates valley after dividing Turkey between France and Russia on its way. Plans for this great stroke were already under way when the revolution in Spain compelled Napoleon to postpone its execution.

With the bent in Napoleon's genius which is related to poetry and art—he not infrequently called himself an artist—he was more Italian than French. His genius has that mathematical structure which underlies Dante's "Divina Commedia," with its strong symmetrical architecture, and has also the gigantic conception so early shown in Michael Angelo, who nevertheless could picture the little David in his conflict with Goliath.

When Bonaparte, in spite of his Italian blood, had attained to soverignty over France, a new instance was given of the peculiar law by virtue of which those who have risen to high influence in a country are frequently of foreign birth.

V

Napoleon's personality cannot be understood without a consideration of the circumstances which made its development possible. There are three factors; Corsica, the French Revolution, and the French army. The powers which were to come to full fruition in him had long been accumulating in secret in the island of his birth, the unbridled energy of ancient and medieval ages, which in later times has been absent in Italian politics and government, was preserved in the lonely and wild Island of Corsica. The form which this energy took among his countrymen then was that of the blood feud, and more commonly banditry, while in Bonaparte it became ambition, desire for power. In Iceland, which furnishes a mild parallel, this heathen energy disappeared much quicker and no great man marks the newer time. In Corsica this energy became personified.

This desire for power found soil where it could strike deep roots and grow to the greatest heighths, when the French revolution, towards the end of the 18th century, had swept away all the old moorings of society and then with great enthusiasm had established a new order which was later followed by complete lawlessness. No one was any longer secure in life or property, and justice was the stock in trade of the political dilettante. One of Bonaparte's first political experiences was in the suppression of the Revolution of 1795. Under his directory France was no longer revolutionary but was revolutionized. A general disorder prevailed, with highway robbery as a marked feature. France longed for a man of power, an organizer.

A mass of prohibitory decrees and enactments were in force in 1798. Relatives of emigrants and former members of the nobility were shut out from the suffrage. The spokesmen of parliament were revolutionists voicing the temper of the government. The people in the provinces were helpless; if anyone absented himself for a fixed time from his local commune his name was placed upon the emigrant list. The press was muzzled. The owners and editors of thirty-five newspapers were deported and all newspapers were under political censorship. Religious worship was free on paper, but any priest could be deported forthwith. Freedom of assembly was likewise found only on paper, while freedom of person was, in effect, abolished, since anyone was liable to arrest at any time. The former members of the nobility who remained upon their estates were not only subjected to plunder by tax collectors, but to abuses without number. So hostile was the government to the church, that the decree that the peasants could not dance on Sunday was revoked. Naturally the instinct for freedom turned toward revolution.

On the other side, there was no longer any ruling class in society but unbounded possibilities for advancement step by step. This situation with all its teeming possibilities France offered to Napoleon and thus made possible his elevation and his historical significance.

Next to Corsica and the Revolution as factors in Napoleon's development, comes the fact that he was of military bent and a military genius. While the civil order had fallen apart and the earlier restraints of society were shattered, there was still unity in the army, still discipline, efficiency and respect. The spirit of revolution had permeated the army with its enthusiasm and with its evils, yet no one dared suggest the destruction of the army, particularly since from the first it had been victorious. The military spirit became one of the forms of the revolutionary spirit.

The motto of the Revolution had been "Liberty, Equality, Fraternity!" Liberty did not permit of equality; equality did not comprehend liberty, since equality can only be brought about by force. Of fraternity there was little, except in the army.

VI

When France, after 1799, accepted Bonaparte as a dictator, although a ten-year revolution had been waged in order to throw off the yoke of tyranny, it became apparent that of the two slogans, "liberty" and "equality," under which the revolution had been accomplished equality was considered much more precious than liberty. It is possible to criticise Bonaparte for not having made liberty secure, but he cannot be said to have destroyed it, for it was not to be found. The Jacobins had deified the word and destroyed the thing. Bonaparte held as an unassailable principle the right of everyone to rise to the highest possible place, if he were industrious and courageous. He did more than recognize equality; he honored it. He made the name dear to Frenchmen and by employing the plebiscite three times he established the revolutionary principles of the sovereignty of the people.

Even before his time the privileges of birth and wealth had been abolished, yet he extended none to the Jacobins. Napoleon protected the persecuted emigrants and their relatives, the nobility, the converts from the old order, and appointed them, as well as the republicans, to whatever positions they could fill. In this way he mollified the conservatives.

But he also made secure the new property rights for the benefit of citizen and peasant which had been wrung from them by the church and the nobility. Those who had established the Republic and survived the Revolution usually enjoyed the fruits of their works and deeds. Napoleon gave them this satisfaction. In this way he satisfied the revolutionists. The new freedom supplanting the old, which had never really been established, was now brought into being. All avenues were open for industry, the right of birth, courage, enterprise, talent, genius were free to expand.

To Europe's kaisers, kings and princesses the Revolution was naturally a thing of terror, they dreamed only of restoring the old order in France, in order that such an upheaval should not smite Europe and spread to all their lands. Napoleon secured the practises of the new time, the abolition of caste and privilege, separation of church and state, the rights of men and the new economic order against the opposition of Europe which formed one coalition after another against him.

What is more, wherever his campaign led him he took with him the spirit of the new time. He put an end to the Inquisition in Spain; he brought human rights to the Jews of Germany. He established the Code Napoleon with its liberal principles in the Rhine provinces, and in Russian Poland where despite all vicissitudes it still exists. In this manner did the man who subdued the revolution at home extend the principles of the revolution in all directions abroad.

When he had been elevated to power France expected two things of him, peace within and peace with the outside world. He did not bring about either.

He regarded a political peace with fear, yet was solicitous about preserving its form. He never condemned it, and in the end gave it approval with "L' Acte Additionel," in 1815.

Nor did he bring about peace with his neighbors. The policy of England, which again and again inflamed Europe against him, and his own strenuous temperament, precluded this. Yet he has the great distinction of having established tranquility in France. He fused the people together again who had been divided by factions, and re-established the national unity. The respect for law and order had been lost; he brought it back to the French people. He could not establish quiet at home by permitting license. Only by the exercise of strong authority could he do so. Therefore, although he directed his army to wear mourning at the death of Washington, he could not himself be a Washington. Nor could he be a Caesar, although frequently called one. He lacked the superb abandon of Caesar and revealed none of Caesar's grace and elegance. He became Napoleon, a new type, alone of his kind.

VII

With decisive energy Napoleon suppressed all opposition which sprang up against him. He unified France. He promoted equality. He made secure the fruits of the revolution's economic upheaval and extended its ideas throughout Europe.

By what faculties? By an intuition for grasping the real, the concrete, the kernel of the thing, which comes like a flash to decisive natures.

He had primarily the instinct of the artilleryman. He recognized the importance of having the greatest strength at the decisive point and at the decisive moment.

He comes as an obscure young officer to Toulon, a city then hostile to the revolution and protected against the French army by an English fleet. He sees at a glance that the high point L'Eguillette is the key to the capture of the city, as it commands the larger and smaller roadsteads of the city. He asks the authority to take it. The attempt is made by the eager lieutenant and but 300 men. It fails and the English then drag a whole park of artillery to its top. Nevertheless, he asks permission to attempt it again, and succeeds.

This achievement reveals his genius as a commander. He showed the same penetration as lawgiver, as administrator, and in his dealings with men, the ability to pierce to the heart of things. For a long time he was able to overcome all obstacles through this capacity for grasping essentials

Napoleon Bonaparte

(which first failed him when unparalleled prosperity turned his head) through the astonishing comprehension and alertness of his mind, his capacity for prompt judgment and conclusions.

As first consul he had in his offices in the Tuileries, which was a laboratory, as it were, with workshop and tools, a bookcase marked *"Etats de Situation"* (material on the military and financial situation at the time). There were found bundles of documents, account books and appointment schedules. Admirers who have sought to convey an idea of his extraordinary powers have asserted that he also carried all this material in his head. It was from these books that the spy Michel for ten years sent information to Russia, a discovery not made until 1812.

There was in Napoleon's mind, as Taine had said, three stores of supervisory intelligence. Each consisted, it might be said, of a thick mental ledger which always was kept *a jour*.

The first collection was military and included a great atlas, of a topographical character, with the dispositions of all armies and fleets and the possibilities of their transformation and employment at the time—regiments, batteries, ships of the line and frigates, clothing, supply stations and their contents, horses, wagons, weapons and food.

The next grouping related to civil and financial matters at the moment, all the routine as well as the unusual receipts and expenditures, the taxes in France, war levies on other countries, the national debt, loans and bonds, public works, and all the train of public officials, senators, deputies, ministers and judges.

The third mental collection was a great encyclopedia, as it were, containing the conditions of life and the characteristics of each of the peoples over which he ruled, or against which he was making war; every class or group and every prominent man among the thousands upon thousands that he knew, was duly entered and labeled.

In 1812 he ruled personally 70,000 square miles, the greater part of Europe, and had the whole with all its details as to conditions and administration in hand. His

unparalleled correspondence is evidence of this fact. In
the thirty-two folios of his letters published under direction
of Napoleon III, none is included the publication of which
might be regarded as impolitic.

Among the hundreds of instances revealing his grasp of
details in all things may be cited one: Following reports
of many disorders, he sent an officer to Belgium to investigate the military situation there. The officer returned and
reported. Napoleon quickly handed him back the report,
with the words: "It is short two cannon in Ostend,"
which it really was.

In 1812, he issued, while at Moscow, the regulations for
Le Théâtre Français, which, in all essential particulars,
govern today, with rules as to the duties and parts of
actors, the division of roles, under what conditions entrances shall be made, how receipts shall be divided, and
how profits shall be ordered. Only recently has this imperial authority, represented by a commission, been substituted by state authority, represented by an administrator.

He had postponed signing the decree. Yet he sat there
in Moscow, threatened by winter and the Russians, soon to
be encompassed by flames from the burning city, and had
the imperturbability and the appreciation of the artistic to
sign under such circumstances, a decree for the regulation
of theatres.

VIII

His character was not of as high an order as his genius.
The love of self which went with his genius, the greed for
power, which was his underlying weakness, led him at times
into wrong, into unwise steps.

Three periods can be recognized in his history. In the
first, his own interests and those of France fall together.
The expedition to Egypt, which resulted in the loss of the
fleet, was undertaken chiefly for his own interest, even
though France could not well spare the fleet; but it was
directed against England, and therefore justified. As the
young general, and in the beginning of the consulate, he

was a shining figure—the hope of France. The second period is that in which his own interest and those of France do not always harmonize.

The unfortunate expedition to Russia did not spring from Napoleon's weakness for power, but from the faithlessness of Alexander I, who always entertained a curious doubt as to Napoleon's attitude toward him, and his ingrained prejudice against a "usurper," of whose friendship he had recently been so proud. The interests of his dynasty, and the welfare of the French people—two highly different things, which, of course, sometimes were united—became one and the same thing in Napoleon's campaigns from 1808 to 1813. Then comes the last period, in which his interests and those of France are again one, the years 1814 and 1815, when he is simply the over-general of France.

It is when he enjoyed complete power and unfailing good fortune that the unattractive sides of his nature are revealed, the purely despotic, the desire to suppress, and the opposition to liberty.

He becomes transformed when he changes from the conqueror to the defender, from the sacrificer to the sacrificed. And in this latest period, as indeed from the beginning, he was the chieftain of his people, more particularly so at this time.

The election of 1799, for instance, was in reality not a free expression of the people, but the voice of the army. In 1814, on his return from Elba, when he again appears, defeated, exiled, empty-handed, he becomes the real idol of the people. It cannot be truthfully said that only his situation had changed; essentially he was the same. Napoleon is no exception to the rule that one's nature changes with his circumstances.

IX

Bonaparte cut a sorry figure the 18th Brumaire. His brother Lucien redeemed the situation. A *coup d'etat* is not brought about without intrigue, deceit and violence.

Yet I consider (Victor Hugo and many others to the contrary notwithstanding) that this *coup* was not in itself an outrage; the contemptible parliament of the time deserved nothing better than to be destroyed by the military, even if it had a legal standing.

Bonaparte on the 18th Brumaire could have had no other plan than that of seizing power in France, even if, as a young general in Italy,—and even more so while at St. Jean d'Acre,—he had dreamed of establishing an empire in the Orient. However, Bernard Shaw's presentation of him in "The Man of Destiny,"—in which he permits himself to be bullied by his lieutenant, have his nose tweaked by an Irish woman spy, and have his dreams of world conquest thus dissipated,—is nothing but silly caricature, in which every line is false.

Bonaparte had attained to power and it intoxicated him. He who had grown up silent and moody, foreign and disliked by his French associates, revealed a personality, an overwhelming brilliancy such as had scarcely been shown in another in like degree since ancient times. Men marvelled at him, loved him, worshipped him. His name eclipsed all other names.

It began with the army. Here was reflected that brilliancy which radiates from one who always sees correctly, acts correctly, and therefore conquers—not by chance, but by sheer force of genius.

One evening, after a great victory, his subordinate officers and members of his guard affectionately gave him, their chieftain, the designation of a subordinate, applying to him the familiar title of "The Little Corporal." He was small of stature. The title expressed a tender devotion. Yes, men were ready to die for him. Even ten years later soldiers when mortally wounded would withstand the coming of death long enough to cry, "Long live the Emperor!" Thus in the beginning of the Russian campaign the Polish cavalry, instead of seeking a fording place, rode into the river Wilya at Wilna for him to be swept away, and with their drowning cries saluted him.

Alexander Kielland's little sketch, *Keyserens Kurer*, has

reflected in masterly manner this devotion, while his bulky volume on Napoleon is worthless.

This astounding brilliancy soon captivated the French people. He was loved for his success and for his genius. He himself believed in his star and could not do otherwise. Yet he retained the admiration and loyalty of millions after this star had at length begun to sink.

X

The Greco-Roman period of antiquity was the ideal to which the men and women of the French revolution looked up. Bonaparte's officers took as their patterns the Spartans, as presented in classic tragedies, or the Romans, as they knew them from Corneille's *Horace,* or from Louis David's republican paintings in antique studies.

As the spiritual child of the revolution, he had himself the point of view of the revolutionary leader. The glass through which he saw the world from the beginning was that of the revolution. They sought to restore the manners and customs of ancient Rome; addressed one another as "Thou" and "Citizen," became heathens like the Romans, and permitted their women to dress as did the women of Rome. Madame Roland and Charlotte Corday had the make-up of Roman women, or tried to feel that they had.

Differing from them in that he sprang from real Italian stock, Napoleon yet takes a like course, assumes the title of "First Consul," an old Roman title; then that of *Imperator,* another old Roman title. His emblems are eagles, like the Roman. As did the Romans also, he permits the conquered peoples to retain their religions in peace. Furthermore, he plans for a restoration of the old Roman empire. This had been succeeded by the papal power on the one hand and the empire of Charlemagne on the other. Bonaparte takes over the papal authority in seizing Pius VII as captive. He becomes emperor in 1804, and barely two years thereafter (1806) the Holy Roman Empire of a thousand years (founded 843) may be said to have come to an end.

It seems almost childish to say that Napoleon during the hundred days was changed, became, in fact, a constitutionalist. Nevertheless, he permitted Benjamin Constant to draw up a constitution, and in 1815 abdicated the throne when the chambers requested him to do so, although a single battalion would have sufficed to scatter them. He was loyal to the constitution, when Louis XVIII, weak and vacillating as he was, dissolved the chambers soon after his accession; what is more, locked the doors, and met with no opposition.

At Waterloo Napoleon ventured his last battle. Would it have availed had he triumphed there? The future seemed to hold little of promise. His son was not even possessed of vitality. But the terrible reaction of fifteen years which swept over Europe would have been escaped if he had won. This scarcely admits of doubt.

XI

Of the purely personal side of Napoleon it is difficult to learn the truth. The sources of the time are obscured. Among sources often referred to, for instance, are the writings of two women, both of whom were once ardently attached to him, but later were bitterly hostile to him— Madame de Staël and Madame de Remusat.

Early in their relations Madame de Staël once came to Lucien Bonaparte, almost in tears, and said: "When I stand in the presence of your brother I am overcome in my desire to gain his esteem. I seek for words, weigh and turn them in order to get him to interest himself in me." She was turned away and transformed into a terribly revengeful foe.

Madame de Remusat's original memoirs were written while she was strongly under the spell of Bonaparte, but were subsequently burned. Such as we now have were written many years afterward when her sentiments had changed. Also there are Metternich's frivolous memoirs, in which Napoleon is revealed after the manner of street gossip. "He said so and so," citing some silly expression

—"but to this I replied," etc., and he (Napoleon) was soon silenced.

A certain ignorance and stupidity is revealed in Napoleon in the manner in which Metternich pressed him to the wall with his crushing answers—twenty years afterwards.

Napoleon was not lacking in simple human virtues. In school he was an industrious pupil, in the army a conscientious officer. Throughout all his life he was a good son and a good, if stern, brother.

He was inclined towards scrupulous economy, and for this reason frequently lost his temper when anyone sought to defraud him in sale or delivery. Because of this he also inspected Josephine's accounts and demanded that she should not be so extravagant as she was, that she should not contract debts, and that she should not permit accounts to be sent her in which charges double the worth of things appeared.

Under the directory the men of most influence were those who had made millions through furnishing the troops with obsolete weapons and damaged supplies. They became the great financiers of the time to whom the directory looked for loans to the state. Napoleon soon gave his attention to the strongest of these—Ouvrard, and had his wealth confiscated for fraud.

He was invariably high-minded. As emperor he stood by his old opponent Carnot, and in the noblest manner, because he recognized in him that remarkable talent, which, in spite of personal weaknesses, is the glory of Frenchmen. Again and again he pardoned breaches of his confidence, and small and large betrayals.

Most astonishing was his forbearance toward Josephine—that faithless, but elegant, Creole, that goose from a tropic isle, who not only defrauded him as wife, but betrayed him and in her corruption was on the point of dishonoring him. She had never loved him; her marriage with him was a matter of business. Before the marriage she wrote to a woman friend: "I feel lukewarm toward this matter, with such poor prospects in view."

Bonaparte was greatly loved. It has been said that he

married in order to obtain the Italian command through Josephine's earlier influence with Barras. It is true Josephine secured the command for him, but in her letters is revealed how much greater was his ambition and faith in himself than the estimates of his doubting comrades in arms. "It will be," he said, "a great piece of good fortune to the people if once I tender them my services."

Josephine wavered between her lukewarm feelings and the brilliant prospects in which Napoleon believed. "Sometimes his unshakable faith affects me so," she said, "that I am led to believe everything possible which this wonderful person would have me believe." She had not yet sensed a hint of his genius.

The first use to which she put his victories was to permit herself to be bribed by army contractors until she discovered to her astonishment and terror that neither fraud nor theft was to be permitted. Nevertheless she accepted without stint pearl necklaces, diamonds, paintings, and antiques, and with convenient deceptions declared they were presents. The wedding occurred in 1796.

Already, in 1797, she had given her preference to one M. Charles, a short, thick-set fellow. While Napoleon was in Egypt she permitted this Charles to establish a foothold at Malmaison, where he conducted himself as the master of the house.

She became greatly alarmed at Bonaparte's return; she had believed he would fall in Egypt. She drove forth to meet him, but took a wrong road so that he arrived in Paris forty-eight hours before she did. He refused to see her, but after she had remained outside of his closed door day and night, he permitted himself to be moved by her tears and entreaties, and thereafter said never a word of what had occurred.

In the same manner may be noted his relations toward Bernadotte whose treacherous nature he knew. Writing from Schonbrunn, Sept. 11, 1809, he said: "It is my purpose no longer to permit the command to rest in the hands of the Duke of Pontecorvo. He is exchanging letters with the plotters in Paris and is a man on whom I cannot rely."

And again, on Sept. 15, 1810—"To the Duke of Mollien—
Give the Duke of Pontecorvo a million from the treasury.
It shall later be settled." After he had discussed the case
with the finance minister, Napoleon took this sum from the
civil list. Bernadotte held this money until after the
Swedish Rigsdag's election in order to cut a figure as the
Crown Prince of Sweden. It would probably be difficult to
imagine a wilder farce than that by which Bernadotte, discovered and advanced by another adventurer named Mörner, by virtue of the untruth that he was loved and supported by Napoleon, finally becomes King of Sweden.

Few men have been so basely betrayed as was Napoleon.
Perhaps Caesar is a parallel.

Bernadotte not only berayed him, but sought to influence his comrades in command to desert him. After his
attempt at suicide at Fontainebleau, Napoleon said to the
Count of Vicenza: "It is not the loss of the throne that
makes me unhappy. But do you know, Coulaincourt, anything worse to bear than the betrayal of your confidence?
The depravity and ingratitude of people—how I have suffered from these in the last twenty days passes expression."

General Solignac had stolen six million francs from the
war treasury. Napoleon removed him, permitted him to
restore the sum and treated him leniently. In 1815, he was
one of the first in the chamber of deputies to demand Napoleon's abdication.

Among his generals Massena was most dishonorable.
Avariciousness was his vice. Once it became necessary for
Napoleon to compel him to return three million francs.
Yet he appointed him Duke of Rivoli and Count of Essling.

He did not do this through a need of his generals. He
pursued the same course toward his subordinate officers.
Once an adjutant of the viceroy of Italy had lost all the
emperor's dispatches while on a trip. Napoleon wrote to
his stepson: "Your adjutant has lost my dispatches.
Place him under arrest a couple of days. An adjutant
might in his distress lose his trousers on the road, but not
his sword nor his dispatches."

Bourrienne had been his fellow pupil at school in

Brienne, his private secretary during the campaigns in Italy and Egypt, and while he was first consul. He sold himself to the highest bidder, and informed Fouché of every step Bonaparte planned, for a fixed price of 25,000 francs per month. Napoleon had a suspicion of this. Not until the Coulon firm, contractors for the cavalry, had defrauded to the extent of three million francs, and it was discovered that Bourrienne was in league with the firm, did he receive his dismissal without punishment. In 1804, Napoleon again received him into his service, and made him minister to Hamburg in 1805. Here he diverted to himself an illegal income of seven or eight million francs, and began to betray Napoleon in negotiations with the bourbons at London. A few days after the emperor's fall Bourrienne wrote to Talleyrand. "Even when I was associated with the Emperor, I wished always that this remarkable prince (Louis XVIII) and his noble house might return to France." This wish he had not made known to Napoleon.

The entire world deserted him, and finally Marmont, who had heroically fought for him to the last, opened the gates of Paris in 1814 for the allied armies opposing Napoleon. In 1815, Napoleon struck his name from the roll of the army.

When word was received at St. Helena that the emperor had been betrayed by his generals, Napoleon protested that the word was too strong. "Not betrayed," said he. Fouché was always trying to show me letters, in which he declared the writers were speaking ill of me. I answered that I did not care to see the letters. When they are written to their wives and sweethearts they are tempted to say bad things of me, that I am a tyrant, etc., but this they must have permission to do; they must have an outlet. They think well of me for all that." This is one form in which greatness reveals itself.

XII

In dealing with women, Napoleon lacked good breeding, fine courtesy and charm. It is not true, however, that in his dealings with them he was uniformly rude and unchivalrous. His rough bulletins against Queen Louise of Prussia were politics, if, indeed, poor politics. He was chivalrous toward Queen Louise of Sachsen-Weimar, although little Weimar had denounced and repudiated him.

While in Warsaw, in 1807, he became smitten with the pure young Countess Walewska, born Laczinska, who was consumed with admiration for him, but would not give herself wholly to him. Thereupon the Polish nobility, with great display, in order to impress her, and in a document signed with all the first names in Poland, called to her consideration the fact that from small causes great political results often flow. "Think you," it read, "that Esther gave herself to Ahasverus out of love? The swoon into which she fell on seeing him is best proof that sensitiveness had no part in that contingency. She offered herself to save her people and won the honor of having saved them. If but we could say the same, to your glory and our good fortune!"

Napoleon won her with his pledge to do everything possible to rehabilitate her country. He had great sins upon his conscience over the Polish people, having misused and failed them. He wished greatly to please Marie Walewska, if it could be made to accord with his politics. Yet he was constantly repeating at the time that he did not wish to be the Don Quixote of Poland. In spite of this fact, we see in 1809, when he wished to have the czar give him his young sister Anna Pavlovna as wife, in order that the alliance with Russia might be strengthened, he not only promised that he would never seek to extend the duchy of Warsaw, but that he would never mention the name of Poland again. When the breach in his alliance with Alexander occurred he turned again, in 1812, to the confiding Poles.

In this respect Alexander's relations with the Poles has a noteworthy parallel. He also became attached to a beautiful Polish woman, Marie Antonovna Nariszkin, born duchess of Czetwertynska, who always offered up prayer to him to reëstablish Poland. For a long time he held out against her entreaties, even could not bear to see her name. Suddently at the outbreak of the war of 1812, Alexander issued a proclamation in which he, like the Russian overgeneral in 1914, and with the same falsity, promised the Poles rehabilitation of their ancient power under Russian sovereignty.

Napoleon's relations with Marie Walewska were, and always remained, a source of sorrow to him. Her marriage, in 1816, with one of his officers, General (Count) d'Ornano, grieved him when he learned of it at St. Helena. She died a year later.

XIII

The power of the spell exercised by Napoleon is best shown in his journey through France, after his return from Elba. He fled from Elba because he had learned that his removal to some distant, isolated island was contemplated. The name of St. Helena had already been mentioned.

Success attended his venture. He evaded the English ships, but met with disappointment soon after landing. He met with a spirit of hostility which made it necessary for him to resort on foot to the lonely road over the Alps. The first difficulty encountered was that of winning over the first troops he met, and who seemed bent upon shooting him. However, the courage, audacity and geniality he displayed won them, and likewise the next body, and the next.

Marshal Ney was pledged to make an end of Napoleon. He had expressed himself with great brutality against the Emperor at Fontainebleau, and was bound by his promise to Louis XVIII to bring Napoleon back in an iron cage. Nevertheless, he forgot his oath, so entranced did he become at Napoleon's proclamation that his eagles would soon be flying from steeple to steeple, until they arrived at the towers of Notre Dame. "So shall it be written," he said, and his spirit of opposition was dissipated.

He had only 6,000 men, as against Napoleon's 14,000, and his men were in mind devoted to the Emperor, simply waiting for the signal to cry, "Vive l'Empereur!" "I cannot hold back the sea with my hands," were his words.

When the news was received that Ney had also gone over at Besançon, ardent young Bonapartists at Paris posted up placards at the gates of Vendome reading: "Dear Brother Louis: You need not send any more troops. I have enough now.—Napoleon."

XIV

He had said: "On the 20th of March I will be in Paris." He attained his goal. At seven o'clock in the morning of that day a great throng of people streamed toward the Tuileries, eager for news, at the report that the King had fled the evening before. A tri-colored cockade borne by an officer met with a bitter reception from a group of the King's supporters, so great already was the change in sentiment.

At ten o'clock a great throng of people streamed into the palace grounds crying: "Long live the Emperor!" "Down with the Priests!" They were the workmen on the fortifications. They shook the gates of the castle and sought to tear them off but were dispersed. Not long afterwards was heard the sound of arms, of trampling of horses, near the stone bridge, and the rumbling of caissons. Sabres and bayonets gleamed in the sunshine. They were the imperial officers whom Louis had retained at half pay, whom General Excelmans was leading from St. Denis into Paris, with a squadron of cuirassiers and some artillery. Huzzahs and shouts and the blare of trumpets and pipes were heard along their way, and Excelmans entered the Tuileries; but permitted the members of the national guard to retain their places. During the remainder of the day were seen at the various entrances to the palace an officer with a tri-colored cockade side by side with a grenadier of the national guard with the white cockade and lilies.

At two o'clock the tri-colors were hoisted on the Tuileries, the municipal chamber and the Vendome. Groups of laborers went singing through the streets. The citizens were puzzled and apprehensive. They feared or suspected a new invasion of European armies, and lamented the good

King Louis, "such a brave and righteous man." Even at that hour the former members of the imperial palace's household had taken possession of the Tuileries. The crowd standing outside saw persons slipping one by one through the palace gates. The first of them in fear, as if stealing in. They were the former counselors of state, ministers, masters of chambers, directors of ceremonies, all in gala uniform, and also butlers, cooks, chamber servants in their liveries of other days.

Then there were the ladies in waiting, wives of the high officials, of generals, of financiers, and chiefs of industry, with diamond necklaces under their furs and robes of ermine, and their court gowns adorned with the imperial violets. They found one another again and felicitated one another. With child-like joy they ran through the salons, royal chambers and galleries, all the rooms they remembered so well, and where their brilliant former prospects were blasted. In the throne hall they noticed that the lilies on the carpet were simply sewed fast upon it. One of them pulled off a lily and found beneath it the imperial bee. Thereupon the women in all their finery went down upon their knees and set themselves eagerly to work. In less than half an hour's time they had transformed the carpet to its old imperial form. They looked up and saw the imperial dukes of Bassano, Gaeta, and Rovigo,—they saw Count Lavalette, Marshal Lefebvre, Generals Davout and Excelmans, Queen Hortense of Holland, Queen Julie, consort of King Joseph. Even the doorkeepers of the old days stood at their old posts. It was as if they had slept and wakened from an evil dream.

Time sped by. Fog and darkness spread over Paris, and the last idly curious ones in the grounds could see the windows in the palace lighted up. The Emperor was momentarily expected. Expectancy was giving away to anxiety. What if a bullet from some fanatical foe or some hired enemy had laid him low!

Finally at nine o'clock a distant sound of horses and wagons was heard with cries along the Seine. The tumult drew nearer, increased in volume, became unprecedented.

A postchaise swung in at a sharp trot at the palace gates, and a train of a thousand troopers of all grades of arms riding in disorder, swung their sabres and cried in a voice of thunder, "Long Live the Emperor!"

The palace grounds were soon thronged with former officers. Generals standing on the outer steps drew their swords and hurried down. The throng became so dense that the horses drew back and the postilions stopped ten steps from the conservatory entrance.

The door of the carriage was thrown open. Napoleon was pulled out of the carriage and borne from arm to arm into the hallway where other arms elevated him in the air. In this manner he was borne up the stairs. A sort of delirium seized upon his adherents. They caressed him, seized his hands and his body.

The throng bearing him soon came in contact with the other which came storming down from the story above to greet him. The two groups threatened to crush one another to death, and there were fears that the emperor would be suffocated.

Coulaincourt shouted to Lavalette, "Hold yourself, for God's sake, before him!" Lavalette stopped, turned about and braced himself against the crowd, ascending backwards up the steps, steadily one step after another before the Emperor and announcing, "It is he! It is he!"

But the Emperor seemed not to see or hear anything. He permitted himself to be carried, with his arms before him, with closed eyes and a firm smile upon his lips, as if falling asleep. Then consciousness returned to him; he knew and caressed all. Following this he went into his cabinet and locked the door behind himself. At once he sat down to a writing table and began his work of founding a new government. Gradually the tumult ceased. It became quiet. The troopers tied their horses at the gates and laid themselves down upon the ground in their coats; the palace yard resembled a bivouac in a captured city.

XV

As a rule it may be said that those who wrote of the first Napoleon fifty years ago, during the reign of Napoleon the Third (Lonfrey, Jung), were influenced by their hate of the later emperor, and sought thereby to discredit the work of the man who had brought ruin to France. While Taine has written about him without bitterness, yet with coldness, and Albert Vandal with discrimination, yet with sympathy, only few who have dealt with the subject up to the close of the last century (such as Henry Houssaye or Frederick Masson) have caught the enthusiasm which Napoleon in his great days inspired. In the meanwhile he has been the object of the ill will of the republicans. Clemenceau has always detested him. In the government schools he has been presented by teacher and text-book alike as a harmful personality, the curse of France. This can scarcely be wondered at since Napoleon seemed to hark back to an earlier period. To him military power was the highest good; to the French republicans this has always been of lesser worth. Many believed that the period of wars was past and that peace among the nations of Europe was a necessary condition to progress. Even the feeling of revenge was forgotten. Only in recent years has the hope of a decisive war been revived.

For Napoleon, as for earlier monarchs, and for the revolutionists, the centralization of all the power in the state was necessary. In the newer France democracy has been the way to political advancement. It was Napoleon, who with a view to getting the church in his power, concluded the concordat with the Pope, which in the end proved more advantageous to the Catholic church than to the French government, and which the state has only recently put to an end. But he was, it should be remembered, the chosen chieftain of his people, and could not have done as he did had he not had the people with him.

The more moderate republicans believed for a long time that they had laid bare the inward truth about him in the following superficial analysis: His advent and his rise was a great piece of good fortune to Europe, to whom he brought the ideas of the revolution, and whom he liberated from the outgrown forms of the feudal age. However, he was a great harm to France, which he exhausted, and which he deprived of all local and provincial independence. A portion of the younger generation, particularly among the ardent nationalists—with Maurice Barres as leader— are convinced that Napoleon was of real value to France, considering the word value in its higher sense. To them he appears as the most astounding example of energy the world has so far known.

To this others of the younger school may reply: "He had his share and blame for the untimely death of one and a half million Frenchmen and for the miseries the wars brought to France and Europe." Yet he did not cripple France, and never humiliated it as in later years we have seen it humiliated, in the Panama and Dreyfus cases. He radiated an enthusiasm, a heroic outlook which before the revolution had been unknown. He also inspired in France a personal deification, a delusion which brought upon it severe and bloody penalties. Yet his countrymen do not look back upon his reign with shame. There was nothing low or scandalous, or small about it. In spite of all faults it remains a bright era.

A much greater guilt than that of having played with human life in the attaining of great ends is that which dulls and represses a people so that it no longer aims at great ends. At that time the people of France looked up to their leading men; since that time they have too often been obliged to look down upon them and have had to cast about for someone or something of which to be proud.

It is a commentary on prevailing conditions that at the close of the last century it was revival of interest in Napoleon which came as a plank to a sinking national pride. Since that time the republican spirit has gained much in ground and strength until now the military ideal, due to unfortunate political conditions, has again pushed the peaceful one to the rear.

Under the stress of the terrible World War, it became a

matter of serious thought what a Napoleon was worth or would yet be worth, and the mind again dwelt with greater interest upon the great luminary of the past. It is not yet burned out.

M7T
300